Modern Polygamy in the United States

D1500614

Modern Polygamy in the United States

Historical, Cultural, and Legal Issues

EDITED BY CARDELL K. JACOBSON
WITH LARA BURTON

OXFORD
UNIVERSITY PRESS

Montante Family Library
D'Youville College

FEB 0 2 2012

OXFORD
UNIVERSITY PRESS

Oxford University Press, Inc., publishes works that further
Oxford University's objective of excellence
in research, scholarship, and education.

Oxford   New York
Auckland   Cape Town   Dar es Salaam   Hong Kong   Karachi
Kuala Lumpur   Madrid   Melbourne   Mexico City   Nairobi
New Delhi   Shanghai   Taipei   Toronto

With offices in
Argentina   Austria   Brazil   Chile   Czech Republic   France   Greece
Guatemala   Hungary   Italy   Japan   Poland   Portugal   Singapore
South Korea   Switzerland   Thailand   Turkey   Ukraine   Vietnam

Copyright © 2011 by Oxford University Press, Inc.

Published by Oxford University Press, Inc.
198 Madison Avenue, New York, New York 10016

www.oup.com

Oxford is a registered trademark of Oxford University Press

All rights reserved. No part of this publication may be reproduced,
stored in a retrieval system, or transmitted, in any form or by any means,
electronic, mechanical, photocopying, recording, or otherwise,
without the prior permission of Oxford University Press.

Library of Congress Cataloging-in-Publication Data
Modern polygamy in the United States : historical, cultural, and legal issues /
edited by Cardell K. Jacobson with Lara Burton.
     p.   cm.
ISBN 978-0-19-974637-8; 978-0-19-974638-5 (pbk.)   1. Polygamy—Religious
aspects—Fundamentalist Church of Jesus Christ of Latter-Day Saints.
2. Fundamentalist Church of Jesus Christ of Latter-Day Saints.   3. Polygamy—
United States. I. Jacobson, Cardell K., 1941–   II. Burton, Lara.
BX8680.M55M64 2010
306.84'2308828933—dc22   2009047938

1 3 5 7 9 8 6 4 2

Printed in the United States of America
on acid-free paper

BX
680
M55
I64
2011

Contents

Contributors

Janet Bennion is Professor of Anthropology at Lyndon State College and author of *Women of Principle* (Oxford University Press, 1998), *Desert Patriarchy* (University of Arizona Press, 2004), and *Evaluating the Effects of Polygamy on Women and Children* (Mellen Press, 2008).

Martha Sonntag Bradley is Dean of Honors and Professor of History at the University of Utah. She is also author of *Kidnapped from That Land: The Government Raids on the Short Creek Polygamists* (University of Utah Press, 1993).

Lara Burton is an independent scholar who has a degree in computer science and an MFA in English from Brigham Young University.

Deborah L. Cragun is a certified genetic counselor who received her BA in Biology and Psychology from the University of Utah and her MS in Medical Genetics from the University of Cincinnati. She has worked as a genetic counselor for four years and taught genetics at the University of Tampa for two years. She is currently working on a PhD in Public Health at the University of South Florida.

Ryan T. Cragun is an Assistant Professor of Sociology at the University of Tampa. Originally from Morgan, Utah, he received his BA in Psychology from the University of Utah and his MA and PhD in Sociology from the University of Cincinnati. His research interests include: the sociology of Mormonism, the growth and decline of religions, secularization, and the sociology of seculars.

Kathryn M. Daynes is Associate Professor of History and Director of the Center for Family History and Genealogy at Brigham Young University. She is the author of *More Wives Than One: Transformation of the Mormon Marriage System, 1840–1910* (University of Illinois Press, 2001), winner of the 2001 Best Book Award from both the Mormon History Association and the Utah State Historical Society.

Ken Driggs is a criminal lawyer in Atlanta specializing in death penalty defense. He has been intimately involved with the fundamentalist Mormon community since January 1988. His University of Wisconsin Master of Laws (LLM) in legal history included a thesis on the legal rights of Utah polygamous parents. He has published extensively on the subject and testified as an expert witness about the FLDS. He is a sixth-generation member of the Church of Jesus Christ of Latter-Day Saints with two generations of polygamy in his family tree.

Heber B. Hammon is a consulting associate for the Center for Teacher Effectiveness, a national education consulting firm. He is the son and grandson of polygamous leaders and has recently retired from 34 years of teaching in the polygamous communities of Hildale, Utah; Colorado City, Arizona; and Centennial Park, Arizona.

Tim B. Heaton holds a Camilla Kimball chair in the Department of Sociology at Brigham Young University. His research focuses on demographic trends in the family. His research in the United States has focused on trends in and determinants of marital dissolution. He has examined the relationship between family characteristics and children's health in Latin America. He is currently analyzing religious group differences in socioeconomic status, family characteristics, and health in developing countries. He is a co-editor of *Biodemography and Social Biology*.

Cardell K. Jacobson is a Karl G. Maeser General Education Professor and Professor of Sociology at Brigham Young University. Recent books include (edited with John P. Hoffmann and Tim B. Heaton) *Revisiting Thomas F. O'Dea's* The Mormons: *Contemporary Perspectives* (University of Utah Press, 2008) and (edited with Jeffrey C. Chin) W*ithin the Social World: Essays in Social Psychology* (Pearson/AB Longman, 2009).

William Jankowiak is Professor of Anthropology at the University of Nevada, Las Vegas. He is author of numerous scientific papers and the editor of *Intimacies: Love and Sex across Cultures* (Columbia University Press, 2008), *Romantic Passion* (Columbia University Press, 1995), and (with Dan Bradburd) *Drugs, Labor and Colonial Expansion* (University of Arizona Press, 2003). In addition, he is author of *Sex, Death, and Hierarchy in a Chinese City* (Columbia University Press, 1993).

Carrie Miles is a non-resident scholar at Baylor University and a senior research fellow at George Mason University. She is also the executive director of Empower International Ministries and an independent scholar who writes on women's issues.

Michael Nielsen is Professor of Psychology at Georgia Southern University.

Gary Shepherd and **Gordon Shepherd** are Professors of Sociology at Oakland University and the University of Arkansas, respectively. They have collaborated on various research and writing projects on the LDS Church and The Family International. Their most recent book is *Talking with the Children of God: Transformation and Change in a Radical Religious Group* (University of Illinois Press, 2010).

Linda F. Smith is Professor of Law and Clinical Program Director at the S. J. Quinney College of Law at the University of Utah.

Arland Thornton is Professor of Sociology and Research Professor at the Survey Research Center and Population Studies Center of the University of Michigan. He is author of *Reading History Sideways: The Fallacy and Enduring Impact of the Developmental Paradigm on Family Life* (University of Chicago Press, 2005).

Brooke Adams is a writer for the *Salt Lake Tribune* who is cited by most of the writers in this book. Though she does not have a chapter in the book, we give a special thanks to her for all the coverage she has provided about the FLDS and the raid in Texas.

Fundamentalist Mormon and FLDS Time Line

Compiled by Ken Driggs and Marianne Watson

July 12, 1843	Joseph Smith Jr. dictates a revelation concerning plural marriage.
1862	Morrill Anti-Bigamy Act, banned plural marriage in the United States and its territories, but was ignored by the government.
1876	The first time the *Doctrine and Covenants*, one of the four basic books of Mormon scripture, includes the Joseph Smith revelation known as section 132 about plural marriage.
1882	Edmunds Anti-Polygamy Act of 1882 declares polygamy a felony. It also revokes polygamists' rights to vote, serve on a jury, and to hold political office.
September 26–27, 1886	The fundamentalists believe the LDS Church President John Taylor received a revelation that plural marriage should continue no matter what the LDS Church might declare about doctrine on plural marriage.

1887	Edmunds-Tucker Act disincorporates the LDS Church and seizes all LDS Church properties valued over $50,000.
October 6, 1890	LDS Church President Wilford Woodruff's Manifesto ending the practice of official plural marriage is affirmed at General Conference of the Church.
January 4, 1896	Utah becomes the 45th state in the Union.
October 17, 1901	Joseph F. Smith, nephew of Joseph Smith, Jr., is ordained president of the LDS Church.
1904–1907	The Reed Smoot hearings in the United States Senate. Smoot was an LDS Apostle and a monogamist whose election was bitterly opposed by the Senate because they believed the LDS Church continued to tolerate and even encourage polygamy.
April 6, 1904	Joseph F. Smith issues the "Second Manifesto" stating that the LDS Church was no longer conducting plural marriages and that such marriages were prohibited by the Church.
October 28, 1905	Apostles John W. Taylor, a son of the third president of the LDS Church, and Mathias Cowley are forced to resign over their continued support of plural marriage.
1910	The LDS Church begins excommunications of those forming new polygamous marriages.
March 30, 1914	John W. Woolley is excommunicated from the LDS Church.
November 19, 1918	Joseph F. Smith dies and is succeeded by Heber J. Grant.
March 1929–January 1933	Lorin C. Woolley calls a "Priesthood Council" and gives its members the priesthood authority to perform plural marriages. The initial council consists of Lorin C. Woolley, Joseph Leslie Broadbent, John Y. Barlow, Joseph Musser, Charles Zitting, Dr. LeGrand Woolley, and Louis Alma Kelsch.
June 17, 1933	LDS Church President Heber J. Grant issues the lengthy "Final Manifesto" on plural marriage.

September 18, 1935	Lorin C. Woolley dies and is succeeded by Joseph Leslie Broadbent.
March 14, 1935	The Utah Legislature elevates the crime of unlawful cohabitation from a misdemeanor to a felony.
March 15, 1935	Joseph Leslie Broadbent dies and is succeeded by John Y. Barlow.
June 1935	The Priesthood Council begins publishing the monthly *Truth* magazine, edited by Joseph Musser. The Priesthood Council also agrees to colonize Short Creek as a polygamy refuge and communal living experiment.
April 14, 1941	Rulon Jeffs is excommunicated from the LDS Church.
December 14, 1941	John Y. Barlow ordains Leroy S. Johnson and Marion Hammon to the Priesthood Council.
November 9, 1942	The United Effort Plan Trust (UEP) instrument is filed in Mohave County, Arizona. The UEP involves about a dozen families and about 100 people.
March 7–8, 1944	About 50 people are arrested in a state and federal polygamy raid.
January 2, 1946	The United States Supreme Court decides *Chatwin v. United States*, 326 U.S. 455 (1946), overturning a kidnapping conviction from the 1944 raid.
November 18, 1946	The United States Supreme Court decides *Cleveland v. United States*, 329 U.S. 14 (1946), affirming Mann Act convictions from the 1944 raid.
February 9, 1948	The United States Supreme Court decides *Musser et al. v. Utah*, 333 U.S. 95 (1948), remanding a Utah conspiracy conviction from the 1944 raid.
December 29, 1949	John Y. Barlow dies in Salt Lake City at age 75, setting off a succession crisis in the Priesthood Council.
July 26, 1953	The raid on Short Creek by Arizona authorities in cooperation with Utah authorities.

January 12, 1954	Joseph W. Musser calls a new Priesthood Council, completing the split between what would become the FLDS and the Apostolic United Brethren (AUB).
March 29, 1954	Joseph W. Musser dies at 82. He is succeeded as head of the AUB by Rulon Allred.
August 16, 1955	The Utah Supreme Court decides *In re Black*, 283 P.2d 887 (Utah 1955), holding that polygamous individuals have no parental rights.
November 25, 1986	Leroy S. Johnson dies at age 98 and is succeeded by Rulon T. Jeffs.
March 26, 1991	The Utah Supreme Court decides *In the matter of W.A.T., et al.*, 808 P.2d 1083 (Utah 1991), allowing an FLDS polygamous family to adopt. This effectively reverses *In re Black*.
September 1, 1998	The Utah Supreme Court decides *Jeffs et al. v. Stubbs et al.*, 970 P.2d 1234 (1998) concerning the United Effort Plan Trust. It largely leaves the UEP intact while awarding some dissenters life estates.
Fall 2000	Most FLDS parents withdraw their children from public schools and either homeschool or enroll them in church-approved schools.
September 8, 2002	FLDS Prophet Rulon Jeffs dies at age 93.
June 26, 2003	The United States Supreme Court decides *Lawrence v. Texas*, 539 U.S. 558 (2003), decriminalizing sexual relations between consenting adults.
August 5, 2003	Warren Jeffs is ordained president and prophet of the FLDS.
August 28, 2006	Warren Jeffs, at the time a fugitive, is arrested outside Las Vegas during a routine traffic stop. He is with a plural wife and his brother.
September 14–25, 2007	Warren Jeffs trial in St. George, Utah. He is convicted of being an accomplice to rape and sentenced to two consecutive five-year to life sentences.
April 3, 2008	Texas authorities raid the Yearning for Zion Ranch outside Eldorado, Texas.

	The authorities initially identify 463 children. The figure is later reduced to 439 after the authorities find that some children were actually 18 or older. Very young children are allowed to remain with their mothers, further reducing the number of children held by the State to 401.
November 2009	Raymond Merril Jessop is found guilty and sentenced to 10 years in November of 2009 for sexual assault of a 16-year-old girl.
January 22, 2010	Michael G. Emack is sentenced to 7 years.
February, 2010	Allan E. Keate is sentenced to 33 years.
March, 2010	Merril Leroy Jessop is sentenced to 75 years in prison for the sexual assault of a 15-year-old girl to whom he was spiritually married in 2006 while at the Yearning for Zion Ranch.
April, 2010	Lehi Barlow Jeffs pleads no contest to charges of sexual assault and bigamy, charges resulting from the Texas raid. He is sentenced to two eight-year terms.
June 23, 2010	Abram Harker Jeffs is sentenced for sexual assault of a 15-year-old girl to whom he was spiritually married in 2006. He is the sixth FLDS member to be prosecuted on child sexual assault charges resulting from the Eldorado, Texas raid.
July 27, 2010	Conviction of Warren Jeffs as an accomplice for rape is overturned by the Utah State Supreme Court because of improper instructions to the jury. See: *Utah v. Jeffs*, no. 20080408 (Utah Supreme Court, July 27, 2010), Motion for Rehearing Pending. See also Dan Frosch, "Polyamist Sect Leader's Rape Convictions Are Overturned," *New York Times*, July 28, 2010, at A11.

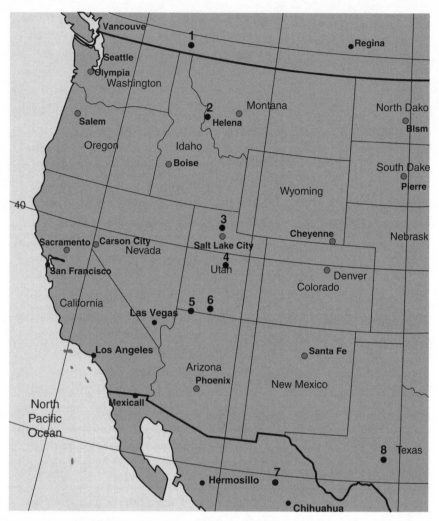

MAP 1. Major Polygamist Settlements in Western United States: 1. Bountiful, British
Columbia branch of the Fundamentalist Church of Jesus Christ of Latter-Day Saints
(FLDS) 2. Pinesdale, Montanat branch of the Apostolic United Brethren, Allred Clan
(AUB) 3. Salt Lake City and Davis County branches of the Latter-Day Church of Christ,
The Kingston Clan and the Bluffdale/Salt Lake City branch of the Apostolic United
Brethren, Allred Clan (AUB) 4. Manti, Utah branch of the True and Living Church of
Jesus Christ of Saints of the Latter-Days (Harmston)
5. Hildale, Utah/Colorado City, AZ branch of the Fundamentalist Church of Jesus
Christ of Latter-Day Saints (FLDS) 6. Big Water, Utah branch of the Alex Joseph
compound 7. Galeana, Chihuahua, Mexico branch of the Church of the First Born of
the Fullness of Times (LeBaron) 8. Yearning for Zion Ranch of the Fundamentalist
Church of Jesus Christ of Latter-Day Saints

Prologue: The Incident at Eldorado, Texas

Cardell K. Jacobson and Lara Burton

Unusual religious groups have always drawn the attention of the media and the public at large. In late March and early April of 2008, media attention turned to the Fundamentalist Church of Jesus Christ of Latter-Day Saints—the FLDS—in rural Eldorado, Texas, when over 400 children and 129 mothers were removed from their Yearning for Zion (YFZ) Ranch. The FLDS Church is a schismatic group that broke from the main Church of Jesus Christ of Latter-Day Saints (LDS) in the early part of the twentieth century. The main church has its headquarters in Salt Lake City, Utah, and disavowed polygamy in 1890. The FLDS continued to practice polygamy, and they have gradually grown. The largest FLDS group and other polygamous groups live in southern Utah, though various polygamous groups are scattered throughout the Intermountain region, including a ranch near Eldorado, Texas.

The problems for the FLDS began when a local family violence shelter in Texas received a series of telephone calls from a caller who alternately claimed to be "Sarah Jessop," and "Sarah Barlow." Sarah claimed to be a 16-year-old girl who had been forced to be the seventh wife of a middle-aged man by the name of Dale Evans Barlow. She claimed that he forced her to have sex, impregnated her, beat her, and would not let her leave the Yearning for Zion (YFZ) Ranch in Eldorado, Texas, with her baby. The family violence shelter forwarded this information to law enforcement officials and to the Department of Family and Protective Services (DFPS). DFPS realized that the caller would likely have conceived her baby when she was 15 years old, which would constitute statutory rape of a child under the age of 16.

Law enforcement officials sought and obtained a search and arrest warrant.[1] Officers were empowered to seize evidence related to marriage of any individuals under the age of 17. This included birth, prenatal, medical, and marriage records, photographs, computer drives, family Bibles, bed linens, undergarments, cameras, and cell phones. A slew of Texas state troopers, accompanied by helicopters, an armed personnel carrier, and SWAT teams armed with automatic weapons executed the search warrant. Child welfare investigators spent many hours on April 4, 5, and 6 on the ranch, investigating the facts and searching for "Sarah." By April 6, when the officers sought a second search warrant to enter the group's temple, they already knew that Dale Barlow was not at the ranch and that "Sarah" was not at the ranch.[2]

Eventually, the suspected husband was located in Arizona, but he denied knowing a "Sarah Jessop," and subsequent investigation showed that he could not have been in Texas when "Sarah" was allegedly there. The police eventually "linked the calls...to Rozita Swinton, a 33-year-old Colorado Springs, Colo., woman" who has a history of assuming different personalities and calling for help claiming abuse.[3]

With the support of a Texas District Court, the Department of Family and Protective Services removed the 129 mothers and their underage children, even nursing infants, from the YFZ Ranch.[4] Two additional children were born to the mothers while they were in the custody of the state. Only weeks later were any men arraigned and charged with crimes. The presiding judge, Barbara Walther, agreed with the DFPS's allegation that all children were in danger, and she signed warrants for their removal. Six weeks later an Appellate Court reversed Walther, holding that the DFPS had failed to present any evidence that all the children were in danger and that they had failed to establish that the need for protection was urgent and required immediate removal. The Texas Supreme Court subsequently upheld the Appellate Court and all the children but one were returned to their parents. Fifteen months later, in July 2009, ten men were awaiting trial for various crimes ranging from bigamy to sexual assault, and tampering with evidence and conducting a prohibited ceremony (plural marriage). In addition, a physician was charged with failure to report sexual abuse, and the prophet, Warren Jeffs, faced multiple charges for allegedly performing "spiritual" marriages to underage girls.

Until the raid, few people outside Utah and the immediate area of the ranch in Texas had heard of the reclusive group or their sprawling compound in the rangeland of west-central Texas. The incident brought the attention of the world to modern polygamy[5] in the United States though charges of polygamy, child abuse, and gun violence had been leveled against several other groups in the western part of the United States. Further, similar raids against the FLDS had occurred in 1953 and 1943 (see Martha Bradley's chapter 1 in this volume). For a more complete timeline of events, see Linda Smith's account of the legal issues in her chapter 12 in this book.[6]

As media attention focused on the incident, the DFPS defended its actions. Not surprisingly, the FLDS Church members defended their right to live as they would, arguing that their rights to do so were guaranteed by the freedom of religion clause of the constitution. What was surprising to many was that members of the FLDS Church, who had seemed to be living in the nineteenth century, suddenly began to use the media to frame their own stances on the issues (see the Cragun and Nielson chapter 9 in this volume for a more complete discussion of this framing). They appeared on television and developed their own web sites. These folks were not as removed from modern society as some media suggested.

The DFPS issued a series of public statements justifying the intervention. The department argued that middle-aged polygamous men at the YFZ Ranch were forcing underage girls as young as 13 into polygamous relationships.[7] The department argued that this was child abuse and statutory rape that resulted in early and frequent childbearing. DFPS also alleged that even very young girls were being abused because they were taught to enter such relationships and the boys were groomed to be perpetrators of such abuse. This, DFPS argued, justified the immediate removal of all children over the age of one year from the ranch and from their fathers and mothers.

The FLDS parents defended themselves by making public statements that they loved their children and that their children loved them and had never been abused. They asserted that marriages were both consensual and formed at appropriate ages. The FLDS members alleged that DFPS was persecuting them because of their religion, had ignored due process, violated human rights, and abused the children by separating them from their parents. The defense attorneys argued that the authorities used a hoax phone call as an excuse for staging a massively intrusive raid against them as a religious group. The FLDS also asserted that their children suffered from improper care and neglect while in the custody of DFPS and should be immediately returned to their parents.

In the end, the FLDS won the return of their children, but not without conditions. The State Supreme Court allowed the lower courts to impose restrictions. The FLDS parents had to agree to have their children's pictures taken and to be fingerprinted, to not allow women younger than 18 to marry, and to not interfere with the ongoing investigation. The DFPS retained the right to visit the homes of the children, to have access to the residence of each child for unannounced home visits, and to examine the children. The examination could include medical, psychological, or psychiatric evaluation. The parents had to provide their addresses and contact information and needed to provide seven days notice if the child's residence was to be changed. Further, all parents were required to attend parenting classes, even though many had been rearing their children for many years.

The raid and seizure of the women and children raise many public-interest as well as legal questions. The authors in this book, experts in the field of religion, examine the questions raised: What is this group, and what is it doing in the isolated rangeland in western Texas? If the men of the group were the perpetrators, why were the women and children, even infants, the ones who were seized? Why were mothers, who were not accused of anything, separated from their children?

Other questions arise about the state of Texas itself and its handling of the case. How could the state group all the cases together into one mass hearing? Rumors that lawyers and those appointed as guardians ad litem were sometimes denied access to their clients, that fathers were denied requests to visit their minor children, and that the state had ordered DNA testing of all the children raise questions about the state's ethics and the real purpose of the raid.

The average American has little knowledge of the origins of the FLDS sect, and often associates it with the Salt Lake City–headquartered Church of Jesus Christ of Latter-Day Saints (LDS)—the main church known colloquially as the "Mormons." The main LDS Church has fought to distance itself from this group and other polygamous groups. The FLDS and other polygamous groups broke with the main LDS Church early in the twentieth century. Though most modern American polygamous groups trace their origins to the main LDS Church, the LDS Church officially disavowed polygamy in 1890 and again in 1906.[8] The FLDS and several other groups formed in defiance to the main church's repudiation of polygamy. The dissidents view polygamy as central to salvation and believe that the LDS Church leaders strayed from the true teachings and became apostate. The descendant groups are located in southern Utah and northern Arizona, but others live throughout the Intermountain West from Canada in the north to Mexico in the south. Still other fundamentalist polygamists live as independent polygamists with no official affiliation with the groups. Some of these live in the greater Salt Lake City area. The FLDS group in Texas is part of one of the larger polygamist groups, though it is closely intertwined with the other groups, particularly those in southern Utah. A graphic of the relationships among the various groups is presented below.

The raid of the FLDS YFZ compound was not the first time the State of Texas had gone after fundamentalist religious groups within its borders. Fifteen years earlier, in February 1993, agents from several police agencies, including the Bureau of Alcohol, Tobacco, and Firearms (ATF) and the Federal

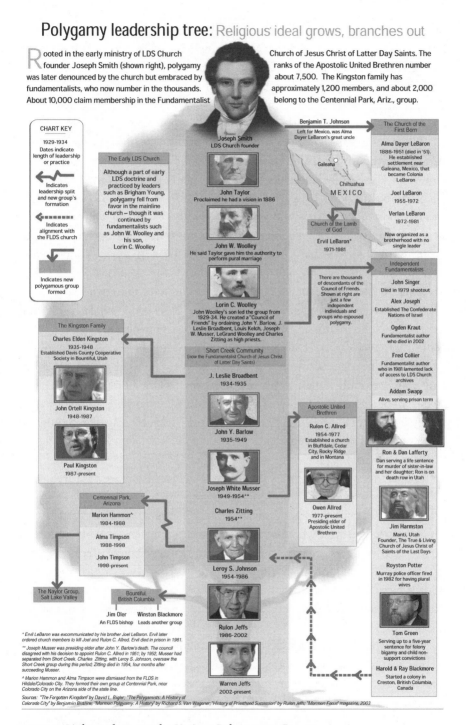

Polygamy leadership tree: Religious ideal grows, branches out

Rooted in the early ministry of LDS Church founder Joseph Smith (shown right), polygamy was later denounced by the church but embraced by fundamentalists, who now number in the thousands. About 10,000 claim membership in the Fundamentalist Church of Jesus Christ of Latter Day Saints. The ranks of the Apostolic United Brethren number about 7,500. The Kingston family has approximately 1,200 members, and about 2,000 belong to the Centennial Park, Ariz., group.

CHART KEY

1929-1934
Dates indicate length of leadership or practice

Indicates leadership split and new group's formation

Indicates alignment with the FLDS church

Indicates new polygamous group formed

The Early LDS Church
Although a part of early LDS doctrine and practiced by leaders such as Brigham Young, polygamy fell from favor in the mainline church — though it was continued by fundamentalists such as John W. Woolley and his son, Lorin C. Woolley.

Joseph Smith
LDS Church founder

John Taylor
Proclaimed he had a vision in 1886

John W. Woolley
He said Taylor gave him the authority to perform pural marriage

Lorin C. Woolley
John Woolley's son led the group from 1929-34. He created a "Council of Friends" by ordaining John Y. Barlow, J. Leslie Broadbent, Louis Kelch, Joseph W. Musser, LeGrand Woolley and Charles Zitting as high priests.

Benjamin T. Johnson
Left for Mexico, was Alma Dayer LeBaron's great uncle

Galeana

Chihuahua
MEXICO

Church of the Lamb of God

The Church of the First Born

Alma Dayer LeBaron
1886-1951 (died in '51). He established settlement near Galeana, Mexico, that became Colonia LeBaron

Joel LeBaron
1955-1972

Verlan LeBaron
1972-1981

Now organized as a brotherhood with no single leader

Ervil LeBaron*
1971-1981

Independent Fundamentalists
There are thousands of descendants of the Council of Friends. Shown at right are just a few independent individuals and groups who espoused polygamy.

John Singer
Died in 1979 shootout

Alex Joseph
Established The Confederate Nations of Israel

Ogden Kraut
Fundamentalist author who died in 2002

Fred Collier
Fundamentalist author who in 1981 lamented lack of access to LDS Church archives

Addam Swapp
Alive, serving prison term

The Kingston Family

Charles Elden Kingston
1935-1948
Established Davis County Cooperative Society in Bountiful, Utah

John Ortell Kingston
1948-1987

Paul Kingston
1987-present

Short Creek Community
(now the Fundamentalist Church of Jesus Christ of Latter Day Saints)

J. Leslie Broadbent
1934-1935

John Y. Barlow
1935-1949

Joseph White Musser
1949-1954**

Charles Zitting
1954**

Centennial Park, Arizona

Marion Hammon^
1984-1988

Alma Timpson
1988-1998

John Timpson
1998-present

The Naylor Group, Salt Lake Valley

Bountiful, British Columbia

Jim Oler   Winston Blackmore
An FLDS bishop   Leads another group

Leroy S. Johnson
1954-1986

Rulon Jeffs
1986-2002

Warren Jeffs
2002-present

Apostolic United Brethren

Rulon C. Allred
1954-1977
Established a church in Bluffdale, Cedar City, Rocky Ridge and in Montana

Owen Allred
1977-present
Presiding elder of Apostolic United Brethren

Ron & Dan Lafferty
Dan serving a life sentence for murder of sister-in-law and her daughter; Ron is on death row in Utah

Jim Harmston
Manti, Utah
Founder, The True & Living Church of Jesus Christ of Saints of the Last Days

Royston Potter
Murray police officer fired in 1982 for having plural wives

Tom Green
Serving up to a five-year sentence for felony bigamy and child non-support convictions

Harold & Ray Blackmore
Started a colony in Creston, British Columbia, Canada

* Ervil LeBaron was excommunicated by his brother Joel LeBaron. Ervil later ordered church members to kill Joel and Rulon C. Allred. Ervil died in prison in 1981.

** Joseph Musser was presiding elder after John Y. Barlow's death. The council disagreed with his decision to appoint Rulon C. Allred in 1951; by 1952, Musser was separated from Short Creek. Charles Zitting, with Leroy S. Johnson, oversaw the Short Creek group during this period; Zitting died in 1954, four months after succeeding Musser.

^ Marion Hammon and Alma Timpson were dismissed from the FLDS in Hildale/Colorado City. They formed their own group at Centennial Park, near Colorado City on the Arizona side of the state line.

Sources: "The Forgotten Kingdom" by David L. Bigler; "The Polygamists: A History of Colorado City" by Benjamin Bistline; "Mormon Polygamy: A History" by Richard S. Van Wagoner; "History of Priesthood Succession" by Rulon Jeffs; "Mormon Focus" magazine, 2003

FIGURE I. Linkages between the Various Polygamous Groups

Bureau of Investigation, raided the Mount Carmel Center of followers of David Koresh. That raid, also known as the Branch Davidian raid, resulted in the loss of several dozen lives. Unlike the FLDS seizure, the justification for the Branch Davidian raid was the possession of illegal guns and weapons materials, although charges of child abuse and polygamy also were used to justify the invasion.

Religious groups in other states and countries have been the recipients of similar attention from law enforcement and child protective services. A group known as The Family International (also formerly known as the Children of God) has been raided in several different countries. The FLDS experienced similar raids in 1935, 1943, and again 1953 in Short Creek, a community that straddled the Utah-Arizona border. The community has since been renamed as the towns of Colorado City, Arizona, and Hildale, Utah. In the 1953 raid 36 men were arrested for practicing polygamy. The raid, however, turned into a public relations nightmare and all the families were reunited within two years.

The raids on this religious group bring to light many ethical and moral issues about the treatment of "fringe" religious groups in our country. This book is about the 2008 raid in Texas, but it is also about the history of the group, its antecedent schismatic groups, and the culture of American polygamy more generally. Small secretive groups such as the FLDS arouse the suspicions of others. Accounts of their history, culture, and origins are seldom told widely. Further, little has been written about the legal issues surrounding the 2008 seizure of the children.

Few discussions give voice to the members of the FLDS themselves. The authors in this book attempt to present a balanced history, review, and comparison of these groups. They are familiar with the history and culture of the groups. Some are historians, some are social scientists, and some are lawyers. Another is a geneticist who discusses genetic testing. The authors address a variety of issues, including the history, culture, and religious practices of the groups. Additional authors examine the groups from comparative and social science perspectives. Finally, Linda Smith, a lawyer who practices and teaches child protection law, describes some of the legal issues surrounding the seizure.

The chapters in the book are grouped into three general sections. The first section includes chapters written by those who know the groups most intimately. This first section examines the historical and cultural precedents to polygamy and early marriage in the United States. Historian Martha Bradley, author of the definitive *Kidnapped from That Land: The Government Raids on the Short Creek Polygamists*, offers a unique perspective on the raid on the YFZ ranch. She compares the 2008 raid to the earlier raids on the Short Creek

Community. While the 2008 raid appears to mirror the Short Creek raid, it shows how little the various governments have learned from history. Bradley points out that the complexity and the nuances of the raids raise other issues, which should keep readers from writing off the 2008 raid as yet another repeat of history. Two chapters provide closer personal insights into the community of the FLDS. One is by Heber Hammon, whose father and grandfather were polygamists, and William Jankowiak, an anthropologist at the University of Nevada at Las Vegas. Hammon and Jankowiak provide an insider's history of the split of the FLDS community into the First and Second Wards (congregations). This split, known to very few outside the community, eventually resulted in the exodus to Eldorado and the founding of the YFZ Ranch.

The second personal chapter is written by Ken Driggs, a lawyer who practices in the Atlanta, Georgia, area, but has spent a lot of time in the community and presents his view of the FLDS people. Driggs developed a close friendship with members of the Hildale and Colorado City polygamist groups over the course of several decades. Here, he offers an intimate look inside these communities. In doing so, he dispels many of the media stereotypes of the FLDS.

Janet Bennion, who is a descendant from early nineteenth-century LDS polygamists, presents a wealth of information about the FLDS. She offers unequaled insight into the culture of the FLDS, a culture that she has observed and researched for years. Perhaps no other researcher has been more involved with these groups. She outlines the history of the FLDS Church in detail and includes histories of the various splinter groups and their leading members.

Most outsiders view the FLDS as a simple extension of the nineteenth-century practice of polygamy. Historian Kathryn Daynes, however, traces how modern polygamists have developed a culture distinct from their antecedents. Daynes, who has previously written her own book about nineteenth-century polygamy, is able to elucidate the differences between nineteenth-century LDS polygamy and that practiced by the fundamentalists today.

The authors in the second section are primarily social scientists. They examine the FLDS and other groups from several analytical perspectives. Using census data, Tim Heaton and Cardell Jacobson describe the demographics of the population in the Hildale, Utah, and Colorado City, Arizona, area. Clearly the population in this area is unusual on several characteristics: rates of childbirth, sex ratios, educational attainment, income levels, and several other descriptors.

Janet Bennion, in her second chapter in the volume, explores the alternative polygamous cultures and practices from an anthropological perspective. While the media and pop culture portray polygamy as "all about sex" and demeaning to women, both Bennion and Carrie Miles, in another chapter in this section, suggest an alternative view of polygamy. Many polygamous women find support from the other women in their families. Using a social exchange model derived from economics, Miles is able to show ways in which polygamy can be viewed as beneficial by polygamous wives. When examined from the view of social exchange, she argues that polygamy is neither sexually exploitive nor denigrating.

Sociologist Ryan Cragun and psychologist Michael Nielson analyze the social-psychological implications of news coverage of the 2008 raid. They note how subtle biases tended to shape the public's view of the FLDS communities. They trace how the media gradually changed their "framing" of the events as they became aware that less and less evidence of vile conduct from the FLDS would be forthcoming. They also explore how the FLDS community used the media to counter what the primary news outlets were distributing; the FLDS presented their own social-psychological "framing" of the raid.

Other authors provide a comparative perspective to the study of the FLDS and other polygamous groups. Two sociologists, Gary Shepherd and Gordon Shepherd, share their observations derived from extensive research into The Family International, a Christian religious organization widely maligned as a cult. They compare the experiences of the FLDS Church to the treatment of The Family International both within the United States and elsewhere. They also provide comparisons to the earlier raid on the Branch Davidians in Texas. They show how insufficient understanding of groups, stereotypes, and ignorance of movements can lead to disastrous results, as happened with the Branch Davidian compound. They conclude their chapter with suggestions that officials can use to avoid similar problems in the future.

Arland Thornton also takes a comparative approach. He provides insight into how the ideas of modernity and backwardness have been used in the United States to motivate and justify public reactions and policies toward family composition. His developmental discourse suggests that the perception of polygamy and other aspects of the FLDS community as backward and uncivilized may have played roles in the 2008 raid and in previous raids on polygamous groups.

The third and final section explores the legal and ethical issues surrounding the seizure of the FLDS children. While the media displayed images of conservatively clad FLDS women walking in and out of court, little of the actual proceedings were broadcast to the public. Law professor Linda Smith recounts and then analyzes the legal proceedings surrounding the YFZ raids—giving suggestions as to what could have happened, what should have happened, and what actually happened. In the final chapter, sociologist Ryan Cragun and geneticist Deborah Cragun focus specifically on the legal implications of the court's decision to mandate DNA testing. They describe the process of DNA testing and then explore the ethical implications of the court's decision and whether the claims of Child Protective Services were warranted.

The authors in this volume dispel many of the media myths and public misperceptions of the FLDS and other polygamous groups and present a more accurate portrait of these groups than has been available elsewhere. They explore the great variety of beliefs, culture, and practices among the individual groups and reasonably assert that polygamous groups cannot be viewed as one cohesive group; they argue that each must be considered autonomously. These authors, those most familiar with the polygamous groups, show themselves to be relatively sympathetic to the groups at the same time that they condemn abuse of any sort. They find the vast majority of the members of these groups to be delightful, even endearing people, who also abhor abuse. The information presented in the volume provides insight and understanding. As authors and editors, we hope that the information will delay if not prevent future unwarranted raids that have similar disastrous results, and we trust that the information will help outsiders to better understand the dynamics of these groups.

NOTES

1. Leslie Brooks Long, "Affidavit for Search and Arrest Warrant" in State of Texas, County of Schleicher Court, No. M-08-001 S, April 2, 2008, http://familyrights.us/news/archive/2008/flds/affidavit_leslie_brooks_long/2.html (retrieved July 30, 2009).

2. See Brooke Adams, "Defense Attorneys Try to Suppress FLDS Evidence," *Salt Lake Tribune*, Tuesday, July 14, 2009, B5.

3. Lisa Rosetta, "Woman Linked to FLDS Calls Troubled," *Salt Lake Tribune*, June 1, 2008, A1.

4. Brooke Adams reports that 439 children were removed from the ranch, but earlier reports indicated that 463 children had been removed. (See Brooke Adams, "Defense Attorneys Try to Supress FLDS Evidence," *Salt Lake Tribune*, Tuesday, July 14, 2009, B5).

5. The authors in this book generally use "polygamy" to describe the practice of plural marriage. Polygamy is a more general term used to describe several different types of plural marriage. More technically, the marriage of one man to more than one woman is called "polygyny," a term some authors also use.

6. For a fuller legal account, see her law review article about the 1953 and 2008 raids: Linda F. Smith, "Kidnapped from that Land II: A Comparison of the Two Raids to Save the Children from Polygamists," (forthcoming).

7. Tuchman, Gary, and Amanda Townsend, "A dark history repeats for religious sect." CNN.com, April 10, 2008, http://www.cnn.com/2008/CRIME/04/10/polygamist.towns/index.html

8. Polygamy continued to be practiced by a few mainstream LDS members in the early part of the twentieth century (see Hardy 1992). Any involvement and or association with the schismatic groups or practice of polygamy by members of the main LDS Church has been grounds for excommunication since the early part of the twentieth century.

Modern Polygamy in
the United States

PART I

Historical and Cultural Patterns of Polygamy in the United States: Estranged Groups

Chapter 1

A Repeat of History: A Comparison of the Short Creek and Eldorado Raids on the FLDS

Martha Sonntag Bradley

The scene was familiar: police cars bumping down rutted country roads, dust clouds crawling in their wake; an intimidating army of policemen and women, social service workers, and officers of the court scrutinizing the sacred terrain of a religious community and violating it in the process. Their intent was to save alleged victims of religious extremism and abuse. Women and children ran to hide from view, darting through the sparse vegetation of the isolated desert landscape. Elderly men, boys, and sunburned husbands and fathers stood warily at the center of the compound, anxious about what was about to transpire. For many, this scene was almost impossible to believe, a repeat of history. Once again, the government had raided a polygamist community of descendents of the Church of Jesus Christ of Latter-Day Saints (LDS), only this time it was not on the border between Utah and Arizona in the dusty town of Short Creek, but in the Eldorado, Texas, compound of the Fundamentalist Church of Jesus Christ of Latter-Day Saints (FLDS) called Yearning for Zion. This was the most recent home of some of the most faithful members of the group, under the direction of Warren Jeffs. How could this have happened again? Who was involved, and what prompted such drastic action?

For an answer in the wake of an event like the raid on the FLDS compound at Eldorado one might turn to George Santayana's familiar aphorism, "Those who cannot learn from history are doomed to repeat it." Historian Gerda Lerner would tell us instead that "what we do about history matters." The Eldorado raid seems to repeat history, but in fact it did not. In complex and nuanced ways, the stories of the two raids of the FLDS differ. In Lerner's words, "History is not a recipe book; past events are never replicated in the present in quite the same way. Historical events are infinitely variable and their interpretations are a constantly shifting process. There are no certainties to be found in the past."[1]

At first glance the 2008 raid on the Yearning for Zion compound did mirror the Short Creek raid of 1953. A deeper examination, however, reveals sharp differences: the impact of modern technologies and continuous media examination, the legal justification of charges of child abuse and underage marriages, and the shadow of the violent confrontation between the Branch Davidians and the Federal government. Despite surface resemblances, the FLDS are themselves different today because of the profound influence of their prophet Warren Jeffs.

Looking at legal, family, or religious issues can help us understand the raid on the FLDS community of Eldorado, Texas, but also critical to this effort is an examination of the group's history. Splitting off from the Church of Jesus Christ of Latter-Day Saints in the early twentieth century, the FLDS grew as a religious movement despite governmental raids in 1935, 1944, and 1953 designed to eliminate the practice of plural marriage. Each raid disrupted fundamentalist life, but each raid failed to meet this objective. Afterward, men, women, and children returned to their homes and communities fortified by a central defining myth—that God's chosen people always have been persecuted for their beliefs. After these episodic crises, the fundamentalist communities returned to a state of equilibrium and, importantly, continued to grow. During times of crisis, the fundamentalists retrenched and drew inward. In their view, the raids on the polygamous communities located the FLDS experience in a long history of religious martyrs and gave meaning to their difficult lives at the edge of mainstream society and in the context of religious community.

One FLDS member, Ada B. Timpson, tied the Short Creek raid to the group's identity, typifying the way that fundamentalists framed the raids in the search for meaning:

> These events of 1953 that we were a part of, and that we are a part of
> today, is [sic] the experience of qualifying ourselves to the point where
> we can be used in the Lord's work. It doesn't make any difference
> whether we play our major part on this side of the veil, or the other
> side. We all know people who are close to us that have gone on and

been called to do their major work, you might say, on the other side of the veil. But all of these things are a part of the same experience. And as we go through life some of these things are very sacred, and some of them touch our emotions very closely. And some of the events that took place during that time had a good deal of humor involved in it.[2]

Key to the formation of religious identity and to the establishment of boundaries that separated the FLDS from both their non-Mormon and Mormon adversaries, the narrative of the raid took on mythic dimensions as it was retold by participants and became increasingly important to group identity. The story of the raid made martyrs out of the men and women involved, proof positive of their religious devotion and commitment. Moreover, it made their lives meaningful, special, and definitely different from those they saw around them in the world beyond the boundaries of their dusty town.

The Story of the 1935, 1944, and 1953 Polygamy Raids

Prefaced dramatically by an eclipsed moon, the government of Arizona raided the polygamist community of Short Creek on July 26, 1953, at 4:00 A.M. This sleepy village in the isolated area north of the Grand Canyon, nestled into the base of the Vermillion Cliffs, was the home of a group of men, women, and children who had been denounced and excommunicated by the Church of Jesus Christ of Latter-Day Saints.[3] Plural marriage was first introduced by Prophet Joseph Smith in the mid-nineteenth century and was practiced by a minority of the Latter-Day Saints. The Manifesto of 1890 issued by Prophet and President Wilford Woodruff ended the official practice of plural marriage. It would be another twenty years before the church excommunicated polygamists. The ancestors of the FLDS believed this was an accommodation to the federal government, rather than revealed instruction from God, and they continued to marry into polygamous relationships, forming religious communities of like-minded individuals. Still identifying themselves as the direct progeny of Joseph Smith, these fundamentalist Mormons claimed priesthood authority to practice a plurality of wives, participating in a communal organization of property and intentionally separating from mainstream culture to practice their religious beliefs in the privacy afforded by the Utah-Arizona desert. They were loyal to their religious prophet because they believed he spoke with God. They lived an isolated life, contrary to contemporary mainstream society, because they believed God wanted them to do so. Their prophet, Leroy Johnson, taught them that Joseph Smith's teachings were just as binding upon the people today as they were in the days of the Prophet Joseph. We have heard from time to time how men have tried to tell us that these revelations were all right in the days of the Prophet Joseph and Brigham Young and those men, but today we are living in a new age, and they do not fit our condition, so they are not for us today.[4]

In short, the FLDS lived the principles of the nineteenth-century church.

There are multiple distinctive practices that have contributed over time to the group's unique identity, including communalism, though outsiders focus primarily on the FLDS practice of a plurality of wives. These practices and beliefs include particular interpretations of the meaning of gender difference, a racist consciousness and exclusionary practice, and intentional isolation and separation from mainstream society. Most noticeably, members believe that God commands them to live the doctrine of a plurality of wives, and that they have legitimate priesthood authority to do so.[5] Some members caught up in the 1953 Short Creek raid were originally members of the Church of Jesus Christ of Latter-Day Saints, but had been excommunicated because of their polygamous marriages. In contrast, in 2008 the majority of members were descendants of earlier fundamentalists. This formed their worldview and was their principal frame of reference.[6]

In the early 1950s the practice of plural marriage drew Short Creek to the attention of the governments of both Arizona and Utah, and prompted Arizona to action. Then governor of Arizona, Howard Pyle, proudly announced the Short Creek raid on KTAR radio at 9:00 A.M., July 26, 1953, saying:

> Before dawn today the State of Arizona began and now has substantially concluded a momentous police action against insurrection within its own borders. Arizona has mobilized and used its total police power to protect the lives and future of 263 children. They are the product and the victims of the foulest conspiracy you could possibly imagine. More than 1,500 peace officers moved into Short Creek.... They arrested almost the entire population of a community dedicated to the production of white slaves who are without hope of escaping this degrading slavery from the moment of their birth.[7]

This wasn't the first time that the government had raided the fundamentalist Mormons. Earlier raids in 1935 and in 1944 resulted in prison terms and a disruption of community life. In each case, the government perceived the practice of polygamy as a real threat to the moral fiber of the American people. As would be true for the 2008 raid on the FLDS compound at Eldorado, Texas, the government felt justified to crusade for the protection of women and children impacted by polygamy by raiding the entire community and disrupting this unique way of life (see chapter 12 in this volume for a discussion of the legal issues in the Texas raid).

When first raided, Short Creek was nothing more than a dusty outpost. Arizona's Mohave County Attorney E. Elmo Bollinger surprised the fundamentalists living in the fledgling community of Short Creek on August 16, 1935, with arrest warrants for six of the most well-known citizens: John Y. Barlow, Mary Roe Barlow, Price W. Johnson, Helen Hull Johnson, I. Carling Spencer, and Sylvia Allred Spencer.[8] The warrants charged the defendants with cohabitation, a charge that implied co-residence and sexual intercourse, rather than polygamy. The birth certificates of four children of the three defendants who did not have legally binding marriages would be used in evidence to support the charge.[9] Bollinger demonstrated clearly what might happen to those who failed to obey the law and discontinue their practice of plural marriage. Understandably, the media narrowed in on the story that had all the lurid detail of a good soap opera. The *Mohave County Miner* noted:

> The columns of publicity that have gone the rounds of the press from the Atlantic to the Pacific coasts and north and south from Canada to the Mexican border about the alleged polygamous modes of living in Mohave county's northern strip is [sic] unique in that it [sic] has brought to the attention of the people of the nation a section of the country that heretofore has been practically unknown to the public because of its isolated situation. Some of the comments have been in particularly good syndicate form and appeal to the morbid and the curious.[10]

The preliminary hearing held on October 11, 1935, was a media event. Los Angeles attorney Victor C. Hayek represented the remaining defendants, as all but the cases of Price Johnson, Carling Spencer, and Sylvia Spencer had been dismissed.[11] Reporters from national newspapers filled the small schoolhouse; the Paramount News filmed the entire proceedings with a movie camera. When Justice J. M. Lauritzen, County Attorney Bollinger, and the three defendants entered the room, cameras flashed as if a movie star had descended upon Short Creek. The scene resembled the US Supreme Court, rather than a tiny town in an isolated corner of the American West, as if "some sensational case was about to be tried. Those in charge of affairs were certainly putting on a big show."[12] The court found Price Johnson and Carling Spencer guilty of "open and notorious cohabitation" and handed them sentences that varied from 18 to 24 months in the Florence, Arizona, penitentiary.[13] After a delay in her case so she could deliver her fourth son, Sylvia Spencer received a suspended sentence.[14] When questioned in the aftermath of the trials about the likelihood of future prosecution of the polygamists, Arizona government officials were reluctant to commit.

> The matter is being treated warily; under the law the colony as a unit may not be punished, although individuals may be enjoined from violating the law. The trials of Spencer and Johnson proved costly, and there is distinct agitation against bringing others to trials.[15]

In the end, the 1935 raid did not eliminate plural marriage, but it did alert the fundamentalists to the potential for prosecution and punishment for their felonious practices. Less than a decade later, the issue would come to a head once again.

The second raid on Short Creek occurred in 1944. Once again, the press interpreted the events for its mainstream audiences. The press dubbed this raid against the fundamentalist Mormons the "Boyden Raid" after U.S. Attorney John S. Boyden, the mastermind of the raid in collaboration with Utah State Attorney General Brigham E. Roberts, who was the grandson of B. H. Roberts, a well-known LDS church leader and historian. Fueled by the goal of eradicating polygamy once and for all, the two men directed the forces of the executive branch of Utah state government, FBI agents, U.S. federal marshals, deputy sheriffs, Salt Lake City police, and supporting officials in Washington County, Utah, and Maricopa County, Arizona, to serve arrest warrants for "unlawful cohabitation" to men and women living in polygamous communities throughout the region.[16] It is complicated to deconstruct the motivations that inspired this raid. Many of the men and women involved had deep roots in the practice of plurality or ancestors who had lived in polygamous families. Once the LDS church drew a line separating those who continued the practice in violation of changed church policy and those who did not, it branded the fundamentalists as apostates. In significant ways, the practice of polygamy flaunted a disregard for ecclesiastical and civil law. The 1944 raid responded to both.

At 6:00 A.M., March 7, 1944, the shocking noise of pounding on their front doors roused polygamous families in Salt Lake County, Short Creek, and other places in Arizona, Utah, and Idaho. Policemen pushed their way into homes to serve the warrants for 66 persons, taking men and women away from their children and placing them in jail. As would be true in future raids, those seized in the raid became martyrs who were commended by their peers for their righteous devotion to a true principle. Before the raid, group leader John Y. Barlow told the *Deseret News* that "his followers would go to jail or lay down their lives in defense of their beliefs, including plural marriage."[17] In the end, they would have no choice.

By design, Rulon Allred was at his home on Lincoln Street in Salt Lake City that night because he and the other polygamists had anticipated trouble. Like most of the other men, he slept that night with his first wife. "I was in the right place; and I learned later that everyone else had had that experience, the man was found in bed with his first wife, his legal wife." An officer walked into his room, shined a flashlight on his face, and asked, "Are you Rulon Allred?" Policemen rummaged through their belongings and moved throughout the house. Allred described the aftermath:

> So we went down to the county jail—nasty place. In the course of the morning, after having been docked in the county jail, we were taken over to the Federal Building on 4th South and Main Street to be arraigned before the U.S. magistrate. The charges were conspiracy to put into the United States mail lewd and lascivious matter, like the Truth Magazine. Our charges on the state level were conspiracy to teach the practice of plural marriage and unlawful cohabitation.[18]

Later the fundamentalist Mormon publication *Truth* eulogized what it called the "Honor Roll of 1945." The men who were arrested that night included Oswald Brainich, Joseph W. Musser, Louis A. Kelsch, Dr. Rulon C. Allred, Albert E. Barlow, Ianthus W. Barlow, John Y. Barlow, Edmund F. Barlow, David B. Darger, Charles F. Zitting, J. Lyman Jessop, Heber K. Cleveland, Arnold Boss, Alma A. Timpson, Morris Q. Kunz, and Follis Gardner Petty.[19] The state arrested 12 women, including the twin sister wives of Rulon Allred, Mabel and Melba Finlayson, in Salt Lake City; Mattie Jessop, the plural wife of John Y. Barlow; and Gwen Balmforth and the 16-year-old future plural wife of Leroy Johnson, who were living in a tent home in Short Creek.[20] As would be true in each of the raids on the fundamentalist Mormons, the charges included a range of accusations rather than polygamy itself: Mann Act and Lindbergh Act violations, both federal crimes; conspiracy to commit "acts injurious to public morals" and cohabitation, state accusations.[21] Twenty individuals were accused of federal offenses. Eventually 46 fundamentalists went through the extensive judicial process. In the end, federal and state government spent more than $500,000 to prosecute the polygamy cases and 15 fundamentalists served prison sentences in the state penitentiary.[22] Their sentences ranged from six months to more than two and a half years.

The perceived "plight" of the "victims" of polygamy inspired the third and by far the most dramatic and socially devastating raid on the fundamentalists who had gathered at Short Creek on the Utah-Arizona border, launched under the direction of Arizona governor Howard Pyle, who saw in Short Creek "insurrection within its [Arizona's] own borders." He believed it was his and the state of Arizona's obligation to "protect the lives and future of 263 children...the product and the victims of the foulest conspiracy...a community dedicated to the production of white slaves...degrading slavery." Pyle dramatically pitched a picture of depravity and despair:

> Here is a community—many of the women, sadly right along with the men—unalterably dedicated to the wicked theory that every maturing girl child should be forced into the bondage of multiple wifehood with men of all ages for the sole purpose of producing more children to be reared to become mere chattels of this totally lawless enterprise.
>
> As the highest authority in Arizona, on whom is laid the constitutional injunction to "take care that the laws be faithfully executed," I have taken the ultimate responsibility for setting into motion the actions that will end this insurrection.[23]

In the two years of preparation for the raid, Pyle organized a coalition of governmental offices both in Arizona and Utah that planned for every possible exigency and considered a wide range of ramifications or consequences of the raid.[24] Although Utah authorities did not join with him officially, they cooperated in both the planning and execution of the raid. Pyle was also strategic in communicating with LDS church authorities, insuring that they knew about his plans and the information he had gathered about the fundamentalists in southern Utah and northern Arizona. Always the politician, he was conscious of the number of Latter-Day Saints who lived in Arizona and the potential political implications and religious overtones of the raid. In careful deliberations they analyzed all the difficult questions that the raid might raise, possible human rights violations, and constitutional guarantees, as well as the emotional stress involved.[25] They hoped to be prepared for any issues that might arise. Arizona hired the Burns Detective Agency out of Los Angeles in April 1951 to investigate conditions at Short Creek. Pyle described the clever plan the agency implemented in the effort to gather information to be used against the group in court:

> Pretending to be a movie company looking for locations and extras, they packed movie equipment into the town and photographed every adult and child in the community. The polygamists, uneasy but courteous, posed for their pictures, meanwhile cautioning their children to stay nearby.

Pyle loved the cleverness of the Burns Agency's approach, but he was disgusted by what they found.[26] Looking back on the raid in 1984, Pyle said, "When they brought the facts back, photographic and otherwise, we realized that the judge was right, we had a problem." He mentioned tax fraud, misuse of state electrical power, but most important that the polygamists were living in "absolutely filthy conditions, some in old abandoned cars, in unfinished shacks, and generally in subhuman conditions."[27] By the spring of 1952, they had gathered enough information to convict most of the adults in town. Judge Jessee Faulkner would later claim that the idea for the raid had originated with him. "Now in my opinion," he would say, "there are just two remedies, two ways of stopping polygamy: one is to go right down the line and prosecute and convict and sentence every man and woman guilty; and the other is to take the children of these bogus marriages and turn them over to a proper department for placement in juvenile homes or for adoption."[28] Regardless of where the idea began, by June, Arizona had prepared 122 warrants for the arrest of 36 men and 86 women.[29]

The families of Short Creek gathered for a party on July 24, the traditional Pioneer Day holiday in Utah and among the Latter-Day Saints. They held bag races and a watermelon toss, ate an ample picnic prepared by the women in town, and Joseph Jessop passed out candy to all the children. Marie Darger was eight years old at the time, and remembered Leroy Johnson telling them that "there was going to be trouble coming soon and the children might be taken away from their parents," and that she "felt so afraid inside, of being taken away" from her parents.[30] During an anniversary memorial of the event held decades later, Evelyn F. Jessop related that while traveling in Salt Lake City, Charles Zitting received news about the impending raid. Evelyn was eight months pregnant at the time of the raid. Zitting sent Lyman Jessop to Short Creek to tell them that:

> there was to be a raid on the twenty-fifth from the State of Arizona; that a lot of policemen, newspapermen, etc. would be [t]here. They were going to take our children away from us, put the men in jail, and scatter the women. It was very frightening to think of.[31]

Knowing that something was going to happen soon, the women and children of Short Creek struggled in the summer heat to settle down and sleep later that night. The town's men stood together in the area around the schoolhouse at the center of town. Lookouts perched high above the red butte looming to the side of the town spotted the caravan of government vehicles flowing out of the Kaibab Forest like a lava stream. High on a rocky knoll, David Broadbent, two of John Y. Barlow's sons—Joseph and Dan—sat tense and anxious about what would happen next, gazing into the night apprehensively. As planned, they lit a stick of dynamite and sent it up and over the town, alerting those below that the raid had begun, and to be ready.

After the first blast went off, some of the men and women dressed silently and left their sleeping children in the care of sister wives or older children to go the schoolhouse to gather for prayer. According to Evelyn Jessop they sang "We Thank Thee, O God, for a Prophet." Joseph S. Jessop offered the prayer, dedicating the group into the hands of the Lord. Leroy Johnson and others spoke briefly. Evelyn continued:

> We went back outside on the little lawn, and over the short-wave radio we could hear some of the policemen talking to each other. They have been told they were moving into a wicked, vicious situation. Each man had a map, and every home was numbered. Their destination time was 1:30 A.M. and it had passed.[32]

The men and women who drove into Short Creek at 4:00 A.M. with lights flashing and sirens wailing may have felt righteous indignation justifying their mission. Minutes before they finally arrived, they saw the people of Short Creek in the distance—men, women, and children—standing behind the picket fence that encircled the schoolhouse. As planned, the FLDS had gathered an hour earlier, dressed and well groomed, to sing while they waited. Order and quiet unease marked the moment, rather than chaos or the suggestion of violence. In contrast to their Pioneer Day party two days earlier, the music was intermittently broken by nervous gasps, tears, and whispers moving through the crowd like waves upon water.[33] The line of cars traveled slowly like a funeral parade, their sirens on low, according to Fred Jessop. "It wasn't a high siren, just a dull moan, and the red lights on, and they got right in front of the schoolhouse."[34]

When Sheriff Porter climbed out of his police car, the first to enter town, he was greeted by the group's religious leader, Leroy Johnson. Porter, whose voice was magnified by a loud speaker system, said "Stay where you are; you are under arrest!"[35] Johnson told Porter that they had run for the last time and would stand and shed their blood if need be. Jessop remembered that the cars were

> parked there [as] thick as hops, and officers came in there, uniformed officers with their hardware on, and they stood there, ready to draw at the slightest provocation. Back by the fence were other officers with machine guns and other weapons trained on this people.[36]

But no violence ensued. In total, the court had 122 warrants for 36 men and 86 women. Thirty-nine warrants were for Utah residents still living in Utah, many of whom had chosen to leave the area and hide in other parts of the state rather than face arrest.[37] As had been true in the two earlier raids, polygamy was not included in the charges against members of the group. Instead, rape, statutory rape, carnal knowledge, polygamous living, cohabitation, bigamy, adultery, and misappropriation of school funds were the offenses listed in the warrants. Supporting information alleged that group members had "encouraged, advised, counseled and induced their minor, female children under eighteen years of age to actively participate in said unlawful conduct."[38] It was clear that for Arizona officials the intent was to "rescue 263 children from virtual bondage under the communal United Effort Plan." The United Effort Plan (UEP) was the formal, legal corporation that held title to community and individual property of members of the group, the symbolic and actual expression of the group consciousness of this religious organization. Assistant Attorney General Paul LaPrade asserted this when he said to the *Mohave County Miner,* "The principle [sic] objective is to rescue these children from a life-time of immoral practices without their ever having had an opportunity to learn of or observe the outside world and its concepts of decent living."[39]

The sheriffs spread through town, stopping at each home to document the family's women and children, to interview them, photograph them in front of the home, and assess their situation.[40] "In came two men," Evelyn Jessop remembered,

> They quickly searched through our little one-room chamber, although they did not have a search warrant. My three children were playing like they were asleep in the bunk beds, not daring to hardly breathe. After going through all my dresser drawers and personal things, they took some of my religious books and some photo pictures. One of these was a picture of my father with his four daughters, two on each side of him. One of the men asked me if this was my husband and four wives.[41]

Marie Darger was still in bed when someone shouted, "Open the door in the name of the law!" Afraid that the police might shoot her, she ducked her head under the covers and listened as her mother and older sisters, Lorine and Rosemary, talked with the men at the door. They looked in their drawers and closets, periodically taking a break for a smoke. Marie remembered that they would go behind the outbuilding where she had a rabbit, and she "worried that their smoke would kill it."[42]

The government set up tents near the schoolhouse, where they took pictures and fingerprinted all the adults. They set up a kitchen in one of the tents, where they prepared and served meals for the people in town. They housed the men temporarily in the kitchen area of the schoolhouse before they took them to Kingman, Arizona. They also took the nine women who did not have children. Women were allowed to accompany their children, who were made wards of the court through a series of hearings held on the second and third days before the juvenile court judge, Lorna Lockwood, in the schoolhouse. As a teenage girl, Ada B.Timpson had to appear before Lockwood.

> They had the idea that all the girls over twelve years old were auto-
> matically married! This is what they concluded and so they had a
> doctor come in and they were going to give us—of course, some of
> the girls, not being married, don't quite understand what was going
> on because I didn't! But they were going to give us a physical exami-
> nation to see if we were married women.[43]

They asked Ada if she wanted to stay in this community, and then they "started asking very intimate questions about married life that I didn't ever understand, the words much less what they meant![44]

In 1953, Ada B. Timpson was 14 and unmarried, as was her friend Ina Black Barlow. She reported,"We were at home when the sirens came in from the Berry Knoll and from the west side. We had an upstairs window....We could see both ways. We watched them come in with their sirens and red lights flashing, and it was a real terrifying experience!"[45] Early the next morning Ada and a few of the others who lived with her tried to hide out in the fields near their home, taking with them "a number three tub, a blanket, pillow, a little bit of food, some water," and a two-year-old boy. They hid under the "old cot-tonwoods," nearby. An officer came to their home, looking for members of the family and he saw Ada hiding behind a sagebrush.

> I started out, dodging from bush to bush, and I was scared bad!...He
> came over and told me to stand up. So I stood up! He asked me if I
> was down there, my name, and he was very kind and very decent and
> respectable. Naturally, he could hear that baby crying at the top of his
> lungs and I just stood there and looked. I don't recall saying yes or
> no. Anyhow he sent me up to Dan Jessop's place and he said a lady
> was there to help me.[46] One day one of the matrons complained that
> she didn't think the polygamists appreciated being rescued from a
> "terrible fate." Aunt Fawn told her the reason she didn't appreciate it
> was because she didn't feel like she'd been rescued.[47]

The state allowed 22 young men between 15 and 20 years old to stay behind. In Evelyn F. Jessop's account, "They divided the homes between them, and each one went to his assigned homes and tried to straighten up what was there to be done: fed the livestock, took bread out of ovens, washing out of washers," and so forth.[48] Alvin S. Barlow was 15 in 1953, in the eighth grade. He remembered five decades later, "We organized together and went from home to home, took the washing out of the washers, washed the dishes up, took care of the animals, and each one of us, had certain homes assigned to us."[49] "It wasn't fun at all to be there alone," Ben Bistline recalled of the time, when he was 17 years old. "I missed my mom, of course, but life just went on. We had cows to milk. We had to get up at 4 o'clock in the morning."[50] In Evelyn Jessop's opinion, "It was a mass kidnapping of the women and children by the State of Arizona! Some of the families hadn't even had a trial of any kind!"[51]

Friday morning, the women were told they had ten minutes to prepare for a bus trip to Phoenix and to bring clothes for a three-day trip. Marie Darger's mother was canning banana squash. She related that they

> knelt down by the bed and we prayed that Heavenly Father wouldn't
> let them take us away. We went down to the school and sat around
> ALL DAY! They had five Greyhound Buses come in about 5:00 P.M.
> to carry us away. Our mothers asked that we be on the same bus
> together (our whole family). It was raining, and the road to Fredonia
> was very bad. I kept praying that the bus would get stuck so we could
> WALK BACK HOME! But Heavenly Father had other plans, so we
> went on.[52]

The majority of women and children traveled to Phoenix in buses. Ada B. Timpson remembered that they "gathered at the school building. We had been waiting there for hours and hours. It was raining, just poured down. The buses were having a hard time coming through the mud."[53] Ada would be a ward of the state for two years.

As an unmarried girl, Permilia J. Jessop missed the initial roundup of women and children, but two days later was taken into custody. The first day, Permilia left her home and went to where they were detaining her father, who was sitting in the cool provided by a bower made out of branches and simple pieces of wood. He told her to put her "hat on and start to walk up the road and we'll see what happens." Almost immediately, the officers of the state stopped her and jeeps came from two directions and cut her off. They brought her to the schoolhouse, measured and weighed her, and asked her who she was. Later that day Sheriff Porter took Permilia and her father to Fredonia, where they boarded a small airplane and flew to Kingman. At Kingman the sheriff took her to a nearby army base where they had a building prepared for some of the women and children. She said much later,

They had the jail full of men and they had to put the women somewhere, so they fixed up this old Army barracks that was a psychiatric ward, so there were heavy bars on the windows—heavy screen that was fastened on pretty good and locks on the doors— little cubby holes, separate places for people to sleep. And they had these little army cots to sleep on. That was the first day, and the next day, I got up, had breakfast, had prayer. We went down in one of the rooms down lower, kneeled down and had our prayer.[54]

Life in captivity was a clash in cultures; the FLDS were exposed to a very different life. Even though most of the foster families were LDS, the contrast between their lifestyles was profound and sometimes uncomfortable. According to Permilia Jessop:

The meals we had there were quite a lot different from what the men were experiencing, because they had some excellent cook from one of the restaurants bring our meals to us, and they were delicious meals. I think what they were trying to was [sic] wean us away from what we knew was right, by giving us this good food.... The first day they were there, the day before Permilia arrived the women had fasted. The Sheriff saw only a "hunger strike," but Grandma Balmforth really told him straight. She said, "Have you ever been so heavy in your heart that you couldn't eat? Have you ever had to have the help of the Lord to get you through an experience?" And she went on to tell him why our religion told us to fast and pray for deliverance if we needed it. Well, he backed down. He left the place fairly humble that night. [55]

Regardless of their situation, the fundamentalist women and children had no choice in the matter and were overwhelmed by the lack of control over their lives.

It's not very easy to live in a place where you know that you're locked in. One of those days, one of the matrons told me to take the garbage out to the garbage dump that was just around the corner of the house, and she unlocked the door for me and stood there and watched me while I took the garbage out and dumped it. When I got to the top step of the outside, I stopped and took a couple of deep breaths and she was really upset about that. She got me in that house real quick. But it was sure good to breathe good fresh air that didn't have to come through those bars.[56]

Evelyn F. Jessop stayed with her children at the home of Mr. and Mrs. William Rogers in Mesa, Arizona, after leaving Short Creek. Rogers took Evelyn out back of their suburban home and showed her a small shed where they would be living. Evelyn began to cry and Mrs. Rogers said, "Well, when you break the laws of the land, you have to be punished, don't you?" The room was six by eight feet with two single beds to be used by four individuals. Even so, Evelyn remembered her host mother's kindness. She indicated that not long after they arrived,

> the Welfare department told us to go to the J.C. Penney Company
> and pick out enough underclothes, shoes, material, etc. for the chil-
> dren, and charge it to the Welfare Department. . . . I remember getting
> two pair of shoes for each of the children—one for Sunday and one
> pair for everyday. They allowed us enough material for three dresses
> apiece and a few things for my expected one. They told me to send
> home and have Edson send my baby layette down along with our
> bedding and more clothes."[57]

Those in charge assigned Ada B. Timpson to the Schmid Haven of Rest at the south end of Phoenix. "We had to be right in there with the senile old people—crazy people—you name it," she remembered. "The condition that we went into was so much worse than what we came out. It was hard to understand how the papers could publish and how the people could think that we were in such dire circumstances when our own homes were so much better than what they put us in."[58] Many families lived in the Escabedo Apartments in Mesa, a nondescript multiple-family unit with enough available space for a number of polygamous women and their children to live.[59] In the weeks after they arrived in Mesa, the women walked the streets trying to find their friends and relatives. They met on Saturday mornings at the city park and once the state held a party for them at Pioneer Park.

Many, like Vera Black, thought that the Raid of 1953 was their central defining story, a narrative that distinguished the group and gave them signifi-cant religious identity. She later remembered, "This is a most faith promoting experience I had, . . . It is never to be forgotten. Little do we realize what an extra blessed people we are."[60] Rather than a tragedy, Black interpreted this part of her life story as a test of her faith. "I take no credit for the part our family was so privileged to be chosen to see just how we would stand such a test. I give the Lord every bit of the credit for such a wonderful schooling He put us through. I am proud to be numbered among true and outstanding saints."[61]

Like many other fundamentalist families, Vera Black lived on the Utah side of Short Creek in 1953. The community was divided informally between Ari-zona and Utah by geography rather than design. On a topographical map the line defining state boundaries would have been clear and distinct, but from the air or on the ground, the two parts of Short Creek would have been impossible to detect. Black remembered the raid from her vantage point on the Utah side of town. "I heard police cars coming in and a big blast letting town people know they were coming. I was on the Utah side by a big cherry orchard." Although it was not entirely clear what they were supposed to do, Vera and her family knew they didn't want to be arrested by the government. "We were told to stay there and not to cross the creek, and also to put blinds up so no one could see a light, so we did." They made herculean efforts to avoid detection.

> Then one day some boys came to our home to let us know that the
> buses had come and taken the women and children away and we
> were to be prepared to leave at midnight. They were planning to
> vacate the town so the officers would not take any more of us. So we
> were to be prepared to go that night. At midnight a knock came on
> the door. It was Truman. I think. So we took a little blanket and put
> on their coats and we followed him, walking through the alfalfa field.
> It was raining gently, all was wet.[62]

After walking some distance, careful to be quiet and joined by others along the way, Vera and the others eventually got to the main road out of town.

> A boy was there with an old car (no top on), taking people out to the
> Gap to be picked up and taken somewhere out of town. He loaded as
> many as he could cram in. One boy driving, one standing on back,
> no lights on. Off we flew. If they spied car lights they drove behind
> a bush or tree and stopped until all was clear, then went on until we
> got to the Gap.... We thanked the Lord for preserving our lives. We
> walked into the brush and lay down to rest on the damp ground. By
> this time it was getting day break. All of a sudden we heard planes
> overhead looking for us. By this time they discovered the town was
> vacant so they were out to catch us. We tried to hide but no use; all
> around us were police, some women. So they closed in on us and
> really were pushy, anyway one woman was real tough and gruff. [63]

After a discussion the officers let them return to their homes.

According to the *Phoenix Gazette*, "There were as many newsmen, cameramen, radio and television crews on hand—by prearrangement—as were present for the somewhat more historic truce signing conference going on in Korea at about the same time."[64] Editorials in local newspapers questioned the raid and its drama after the fact:

> The newsreels and the slick magazines will be full of the mock hero-
> ics and histrionics of Arizona's fearless governor and lesserly of the

stern devotion to law enforcement of its attorney general. But it is our guess that Arizonians themselves will be full of disgust that their highest officials deliberately made themselves principals in a fiasco.[65]

News reports varied. The *Deseret News* praised Pyle's move in glowing terms.

Law abiding citizens of Utah and Arizona owe a debt of gratitude to Arizona's Governor Howard Pyle and to his police officers who, Sunday, raided the polygamous settlement at Short Creek and rounded up its leaders for trial.... Again, we commend the Gov. for his forthright efforts. We have full confidence that the rights of the innocent will be protected, the accused will be given a fair trial, and we hope the unfortunate activities at Short Creek will be cleaned up once and for all.[66]

Letters to the editor similarly ranged in opinion. Some supported Pyle's position. Others focused on constitutional questions such as freedom of religion and privacy, the expense or scope of the raid, and importantly, what would happen next to the women and children. One concerned citizen, M. E. Lindsay, expressed confusion over the governor's decision to break families apart in the name of family values:

That the welfare board in Phoenix will decide which children in Short Creek a mother is to be permitted to keep and which will be put in foster homes is a violation of personal liberties that makes everything pale in comparison. These women have shown spunk and will power in every action of defiance; and in pictures, the young girls are neatly dressed with carefully braided hair, which belies the implications that these women are spineless "slaves" and victims. They are raising their families under severe economic and pioneering conditions, but they seem quite capable of raising their own children and want to do so.[67]

The *Los Angeles Times* and the *Arizona Republic* both featured front-page stories about the raid but condemned the way it exemplified totalitarianism in the isolated landscape of northern Arizona. Condemning the "misuse of public funds," the *Arizona Republic* also described it as a "cloak and dagger raid, typical of Hollywood's worst product."[68] Arizona's Young Democrats organization also attacked Pyle for the raid, characterizing it as "odious and un-American." Accusing Pyle of unconsciously seeking notoriety that would lead to a national political campaign, they portrayed the raid as "circus-like" and a self-serving use of Pyle's political position. They said:

This criticism is not based on the fact that allegedly unlawful practices were brought to a halt but rather on the method and expenses
used to achieve the above end. It is not necessarily a prerequisite for
the successful enforcement of law that the governor of a state call a
press conference of national magazines, papers and newsreels a week
prior to the raid made merely for the purpose of insuring the governor nation-wide publicity for his own benefit.[69]

Comparison of the Short Creek and Eldorado Raids

In the fifty years from 1953 and 2008, Mormon fundamentalism evolved
to become a distinctive religious culture that persisted despite considerable
opposition, including efforts by both the federal and state governments to
eliminate it. Its members had been penalized and ostracized. In the same
years, a significant dissenter community formed outside of fundamentalism
to fight for those most vulnerable in the FLDS culture and those who choose
to leave. At times during these years, legal persecution threatened the internal politics of the group. Changes in leadership placed significant pressures
on traditional fundamentalist culture. Both types of pressure have caused the
group to retrench and to become more isolated and suspicious of interaction
with the world outside. As had been true in Utah in the 1880s and the period
known as the "underground," the criminalization of the practice of polygamy
pushed the community beyond public view, and the group became more suspicious of interactions with outsiders and more isolated and secretive in its
distinctive lifestyle.

The most striking parallel between the Short Creek and Eldorado raids
was the justification for raiding an entire community to address the allegation
of a single crime. Rather than deal with the polygamists as individuals with
individual civil rights, the men and women of both communities were lumped
into a single whole with a group personality, shared history, and common set
of behaviors. Belying the guarantee provided by the Constitution for individual
civil rights, these groups received a different, extralegal treatment ostensibly
justified by their unique religious beliefs and practices.

Both raids were stimulated in part by allegations of child abuse, particularly underage marriages. Governor Pyle gathered information about alleged
marriages through the Burns Detective Agency and the filming that they
conducted under the guise of collecting images for future Hollywood films.
The story wasn't entirely outrageous in the area of southern Utah that was

often the backdrop for Hollywood Westerns; it was, nevertheless, a deception designed to trap the polygamists. The Eldorado raid centered on stories brought to government officials by apostates who had left the group for a wide range of their own personal reasons. Empowered by the successful series of child abuse cases that escalated public attention to the group in the past five years, particularly the infamous case of the group's prophet Warren Jeffs, dissenters created a pipeline for stories of the group's secretive way of life.[70]

Media attention had a significant impact on public opinion about the practice of plurality. The *Deseret News* conducted a poll in August 1998 that indicated that 92 percent of the citizens of Utah "believed the state should be more aggressive in investigating child abuse, sex abuse, marriages of minors and welfare fraud within polygamous communities."[71]

The media played a significant although different role in the FLDS raids. Responding to the titillating story of multiple wives in Short Creek, national and local newspapers wrote about the 1953 raid for months afterward. But because of the explosion of mass media with cable network and internet news, and blogs, in 2008 the public was bombarded with photographs, interpretations, and scandalous headlines. Rather than making room for individual interpretation, this media barrage framed a particular understanding of this event that played out in front of television cameras. Several themes ran through the accounts regardless of the medium, the approach, or the seriousness of the interpretations.

British sociologist James A. Beckford argues that the media focuses on groups like the FLDS and New Religious Movements when they are engaged in conflict, finding them newsworthy because they are "deviant, threatening, or simply weird."[72] While this is understandable, it highlights endemic problems with the sound bite treatment of the story of religious belief and practice. For many, short and pithy stories about the FLDS are the only information the public will ever receive about the life of this religious culture and will emphasize the scandalous and outrageous elements of the lifestyle of the group over the mundane. As Beckford writes concerning New Religious Movements (NRMS):

> Knowing that the public has a very poor opinion of NRMS, largely
> as a result of stereotyping in the mass media, police officers do
> not take much of a risk if they take high-handed action against
> these unpopular movements. Journalists function as the principal
> gatekeepers of public opinion especially on matters with which the
> person-in-the-street is not normally familiar.[73]

Trends in litigation and reporting reflect cultural norms and attitudes towards the FLDS that are worth tracking.

Preoccupation with Appearances

Often the members of religious organizations, like the fundamentalist Mormons, distinguish themselves from outsiders through unusual dress. Bolstering identity as a peculiar people, costume becomes a physical line marking the difference between insiders and those outside the faith. In the 1930s and 1940s, the fundamentalists wore typical clothing of the times. Pictures taken during the 1944 raid, for instance, portray attractively coifed women, flanking their polygamous husbands, and dressed in modest but stylish dresses cut in the lines popular in the day. Gradually, during the next decade, this changed and women started wearing clothing that their grandmothers might have worn. These were handmade dresses that covered the sacred temple garments they wore beneath and that ran to their wrists and ankles. Modesty, simplicity, and a rejection of contemporary standards expressed a group consciousness, boundary making, and a type of social control.

In the 1950s, the media described the FLDS as a rural people with a simple lifestyle, a descriptive approach that fell short of connecting the distinctive dress to a more general lack of agency or cultish behavior. Women wore the equivalent of pioneer dresses and the men plain work clothes. By 2008, this peculiar style of dress had seemed to become more aberrant or weird to mainstream audiences. Some reporters used it to prove that the members of the sect were brainwashed and isolated from the world outside. In short, the pastel dresses and up-do bangs so characteristic of FLDS women at Eldorado seemed to indicate a sort of backwardness or sameness dangerous to individual agency. "I'm quite taken by their appearance," one reporter wrote,

> First, it's clear that they are all closely inter-related. There are the
> last names, of course: predominantly Jessop, Jeffs, Steed, and
> Allred. When you consider that Merrill Jessop alone had over sixty
> children with his first seven wives, it's not that surprising. And they
> all have the same jaw line! That's some strong bloodline. Much has
> already been said about the women's clothes, restricted as they are
> to pastel colored frocks that cover every inch of body, arms, and legs
> (which are enclosed in long underwear under the dresses, even in
> this 100 degree heat). And those amazing pompadours, which lift
> these mostly petite ladies a good four inches higher! Even with the
> complicated and heavily sprayed hair-do's (I imagine it must require

help to put those long heavy tresses into place), the women still look like young girls.[74]

In photos of Warren Jeffs with 12- and 13-year-old wives, "The smiling, fresh-faced pre-teens—dressed in 'Little House on the Prairie'-style garb typical of Jeffs' cult—are also depicted hugging him and being cradled in his arms as if he were walking them across the threshold."[75] Perhaps these images were the most scandalous that came out of the community during the 2000s, raising legitimate questions about underage marriage and prophetic entitlement and provoking the most ire. Another frequent motif was the inordinate amount of control that Warren Jeffs exerted over his followers as church president. It is clear that Warren Jeffs pushed the lines of propriety within the context of the FLDS community and demonstrated a sense of extraordinary entitlement that wrapped around his role as prophet and patriarch of his own family kingdom. Jeffs' leadership created profound pressures on the group and led to its destabilization, and as important, to an increasingly extreme interpretation of church law and behavior. Without doubt, one of the most significant differences between the Short Creek community and the FLDS who lived in Eldorado was the leadership of Warren Jeffs, an individual who inspires a widely varied set of responses. Carolyn Jessop, in *Escape,* a poignant memoir that depicts her departure from the polygamous community at Colorado City, says of Jeffs:

> Warren Jeffs had our community in a chokehold. I noticed that people's faces now seemed devoid of expression. It was as if they were afraid even to look like they might be thinking. The life seemed drained from their faces. They acted as if emotions had been outlawed. People were determined to "keep sweet" even if it killed them. There was no arguing or questioning. But by "keeping sweet" we lost all our power.[76]

According to attorney and historian Ken Driggs, "When Jeffs gained power, he appeared to prefer seclusion to involvement. Jeffs seemed to think outsiders hate him, were always going to persecute him and are corrupt."[77] The human dimension of spiritual leadership, in this case, led to abuses of ecclesiastical power and influence. In this view, Jeffs was first of all a man, and like all men, prophets or not, he was subject to human emotion, including pride or greed and sexual behavior beyond accepted norms, and he sometimes let this get in the way of moral leadership. However, religious historian Timothy Miller sees little difference between the sexual behavior of the leader and regular members in groups like this one, which he would call a New Religious Movement. "You see the same situation—someone with authority and a lot of trust has the same weaknesses and desires as anyone else. These people are human. I think that is the bottom line."[78]

Lifestyle

When groups of fundamentalist Mormons first separated from the mainstream LDS church in the 1920s and gathered in enclaves in the Salt Lake Valley or in isolated locations throughout the state, it would have been difficult to distinguish them from the Latter-Day Saints. Raised in LDS culture, the members of these groups would have worn clothing similar to that of their neighbors, sang the same religious hymns and performed the same religious rituals, and read the same body of scripture. In the eight decades that followed, fundamentalist culture became distinct and increasingly foreign to Latter-Day Saints and non-LDS alike. The FLDS turned inward, creating and maintaining meaningful boundaries between themselves and outsiders in terms of life practice, belief, and space. This was accomplished in part as a matter of survival—polygamy was illegal in most states in the American West—but also as a way of maintaining the integrity of their religious lifestyle. Through the process, the FLDS became in a way more eccentric, reverting to pioneer dress and nineteenth-century gender roles. Coded behavior, such as "staying sweet," became a means of social control, evidence of righteous attitudes, and distinguished them from outsiders.[79] The FLDS world was a strictly patriarchal one in which everyone knew their place in the social and religious order and deferred to those with more authority or status.

Between the 1950s and 2000, American culture more generally passed through the women's movement, student demonstrations, and the civil rights movement. FLDS culture formed a critique of modern culture and referenced, in an almost nostalgic way, a simpler and more religiously oriented world of the past. The FLDS believed that their contemporaries in the world outside had lost their way and were doomed to unhappiness and sin.

When the media analyzed behavior at Eldorado from afar, they often focused on the contrast between the FLDS lifestyle and that of the world outside, particularly the roles of men and women. Many interpreted the way FLDS men and women followed the guidance of group's leaders as restrictive of basic civil liberties, and lacking of room for individuality or choice. Such generalizations were based on limited information or appearances. "None of them drink, smoke, or do drugs. They rise at 4:30 each morning and the men go out to do hard physical labor—construction work or farming," one reporter noted in a description that could be true of farm families everywhere. He adds:

> They rarely work outside the community. The women sew,
> garden, cook, keep house, and tend the dozens of children in each

polygamous family unit. Many of the women look so thin as to be almost malnourished, possibly a result of birthing and trying to feed their many, many offspring.[80]

Another commented on the photos coming out of Texas that depicted the lifestyle of the FLDS at the Eldorado complex, "The shots are an apparent effort to show how deeply creepy life is among Jeffs' followers, for whom multiple wives and marriage to teenagers is allegedly part of their faith."[81] These images were suggestive of religious extremism rather than rural realities for some outsider observers, who found the nineteenth-century dress and gender roles disturbing, rather than indicative of sincerely held belief. Others questioned the alarmist reporting, as in this example: "How about all those kids with a history of broken bones that were reported?" "What about the claim that there were found 31 underage teens who are or have been pregnant?" Even though the TCPS (Texas Child Protective Services) redacted the numbers, the media reported the original unredacted repeatedly. "The reporters assume that the sensationalist allegations made by the likes of disaffected ex-members who have books to sell . . . were the facts, and they have worked from that skewed perspective. Cutting through the myths, though, and getting at the actual facts, one finds a dramatically different perspective."[82] Many reports and editorial comments similarly expressed outrage at the peculiar lifestyle, including the style of dress, the extreme isolation, homeschooling, marriage of underage girls, and authoritarian culture.

Gender

Much of the impetus for both the 1953 and 2008 raids came from particular understandings about gender—the meaning of the difference between men and women—and marriage practices based on those understandings. FLDS culture was structured along patriarchal lines, a way of ordering relationships between men and women, parents and children and within the FLDS community in general. Although patriarchy persists in many modern religions and in society at large, for some observers, this extreme example created patterns destructive of a woman's agency, sense of self-respect, and ability to protect herself against potentially abusive relationships. As Deborah King, in the Huffington Post, noted about the FLDS,

> But there is a darker side to the eternal wholesomeness. Neither men nor women speak much above a whisper. The judge asks if they understand the required words: If you are not willing or able

to provide your child a safe environment, your parental rights can
be restricted or terminated. The eventual answer from the terrified
parents is a low "Yes, ma'am." The judges are always asking them
to speak up, but how can they? If they are obedient to the tenets of
their beliefs, as in any totalitarian society, they don't retain much
sense of self. All the women speak in "sweet" little girls voices. In
the "outside" world, that's usually a sign of a woman who has been
abused. And if we consider the line these women have to toe to be in
"perfect obedience" to their husbands—in order to earn a place in the
celestial kingdom of the afterlife—it's no wonder they don't grow up
to be strong-minded independent women who can fully inhabit their
womanly selves.[83]

Both the 1953 raid and the 2008 raid created significant trauma and disruption in the lives of the women and children involved. Because of the extreme
isolation of their communities, they were unaccustomed to talking with outsiders, let alone the press. Moreover, because of the series of legal proceedings, they were very conscious that what they said might be used in legal
proceedings that impacted their custody of their children. It is difficult to
judge how these women might have acted in more normal circumstances or
what their manner of speaking implies about the role that women play in the
FLDS world.

It is true that abuse occurs in some families in the fundamentalist world
and that limitations are placed on the lives of female members of the community. As I have argued elsewhere, the culture of fundamentalism feels the
pressure and responds to the stress of a range of sources, including: "the power
structure of patriarchy, the intervention of governmental agencies in the private lives of polygamous families, the abuse of prophetic leadership on the part
of the leaders of the various groups, and, finally human frailty."[84] As a result,
understanding the position of women and the particular strictures on female
lives is an incredibly complex proposition.

Mormon fundamentalist culture has always been patriarchal—inheriting
its theological and social organization from its nineteenth-century roots in the
Church of Jesus Christ of Latter-Day Saints, which was also deeply patriarchal.
In the fundamentalist family, multiple wives and children revolve around a
single family patriarch, a family organization that, in this belief system, has
significance not only on the earth but also in heaven. Male priesthood renders
men enormously powerful and influential in the FLDS world; indeed, plurality
has meaning only in the context of the concept of family kingdoms, celestial
life, and the quality of one's life both on the earth and in the hereafter. Plurality

contributes to the group's stability and identity by separating members from the world outside, providing a boundary that is meaningful and absolute. In part because of the intense family-based organization, but also because of the patriarchal nature of this organization, men have inordinate power over the lives of the women and children in the group. As was true in the nineteenth century, women are taught to be submissive, obedient, and deferential to their male counterparts, who lead the family units. This same structural element that contributes to group stability ironically creates situations that provide opportunities for abuse. It is true that patriarchy and polygamous culture alone do not produce human rights violations or spousal or child abuse. They do, however, as I have argued in *Nova Religio,* "support systemic conditions that limit a woman's ability to make her own choices. These might include leaving an abusive situation, or challenging decisions or behaviors of the patriarch in a fundamentalist family."[85]

While it is easy for reporters to describe the women of the FLDS culture as sheep—a homogeneous crowd of brainwashed girls—it is important to consider how complex and nuanced this culture is. In every way, Mormon fundamentalist culture is structured along the lines of gender, with men holding greater power than women in terms of access to material and symbolic resources. This might be expressed through priesthood, the distribution or sharing of resources such as food or other material goods or access to education or training, or in the worst scenario through spousal or child abuse. It is patriarchy rather than plurality that creates conditions that harbor this abuse and obscure its view from outsiders. Patriarchal systems ask women to be legally and morally bound to their husbands. The systems create specific and restrictive male and female family roles and, even more important, separate the private life of the plural family from the public domain of the community. Women are not taught to stand up to men but to support men's "righteous" leadership. A subtle but significant difference, this deferential practice leaves FLDS women ill equipped for the eventuality of abuse. When underage marriage occurs, it augments these factors further. It restricts the choices young women have in shaping their life course, and it reflects the fundamentalist Mormon gendered understanding of the purpose of one's life and the role that women play—only as mothers can they taste the power men feel through priesthood, of creation, of the righteous transmission of religious belief and a meaningful role in the creation of religious community. The disparate lives of men and women are sanctioned by scripture and church doctrine and belief that is embedded in life practices that distinguish the group from its nineteenth-century antecedents and from those outside the faith.

Sexual Behavior

The titillating sexual element in FLDS polygamy invites media and public attention without doubt. Like other fringe religious sects, the FLDS way of life for
many outsiders is primarily about sex. "What is it with sects and sex?" writes
Kimberly Winston of the *Religion News Service:*

> The Texas probe into allegations of child abuse at a polygamous
> compound started with an anonymous phone call about underage girls
> having sex with adult men. Reports circulated of rumpled bed linens
> inside the sect's glistening temple. Its imprisoned leader, Warren Jeffs,
> reportedly has dozens of wives and would grant and deny wives to
> his male followers depending on their perceived worthiness. Without
> multiple wives, he taught, they could never achieve salvation.[86]

More important than the details of relationships between men and women in
the group is the kind of sexual power that the leaders do hold over their followers. According to religious historian Catherine Weissenger:

> Every group has its own dynamics and diversity. A leader can use
> sexual activity to diminish ties between followers and direct their
> affections and emotions. But the thing to remember is that no one
> has that charisma unless the people behind him or her believe that
> he or she has it.[87]

Because followers believe their group leader speaks with God, his sexual behavior or relationships seem to be imbued with a special sacred holiness or sanctity. Among the FLDS, the authority of church leaders—or in the more recent
past, Warren Jeffs—to arrange or dissolve marriages lent a sacred or religious
sanctity to relationships he condoned.

In part a way of ordering relationships and partly a method for solidifying
power in the person of the church president, the FLDS practice the "Law of
Placement," through which, according to former FLDS member Elissa Wall,
"all marriages are decided by the prophet and based on a revelation that he
receives from God."[88] This lends religious sanction to the proposed union and
links it to salvation. Again according to Wall, "everything the prophet proclaims
is said to be the word of God, and thus if he directs a union, it is akin to God
commanding the union."[89]

As principal of the FLDS school, the Alta Academy, Warren Jeffs often
reminded his students of his favorite motto, "Perfect obedience produces
perfect faith, which produces perfect people."[90] Unquestioning loyalty and

obedience to Warren Jeffs as church prophet and president were evidence of one's righteousness and assurance of a position in heaven.

Name Calling, or What to Call the Group?

In reporting both raids, the media struggled to find the correct language to describe the group. Because of the power of language to connote certain meanings, this proved to be incredibly important. Framing the religious experience and lifestyle of the FLDS with certain assumptions and a sense of history, words like "church," "sect," and "cult" elicited judgments not necessarily consonant with the reality of the fundamentalist Mormon world. As reporter Trish Choate comments, "Where some see questionable motives, others see a quest for holiness and a drive to remain faithful to Mormon Church founder Joseph Smith Jr."[91]

Whether "church," "sect," or "cult" is the appropriate term to use in describing the FLDS, the quick study required for the evening news is not a sufficient basis for enduring judgment call. Three examples of the use of the word "cult" in the context of the polygamy raids demonstrate the dangers of trying to understand the FLDS through this overly simplistic label, which does not necessarily capture the unique features of this group or its religious raison d'être. First, the *Arizona Republic* argued that: "The dramatic raid on a Texas polygamist compound just slammed up against the reality of how hard it is to deal with this cult."[92] Cult here presumes a relationship between members and leaders as potentially dangerous when personal agency is limited. In another example, "Arizona knows that rushing in doesn't work unless the victims are willing to testify. In a cult, brainwashed victims don't even understand that being 'given' as a child in 'spiritual marriage' to a man with multiple wives is a crime."[93] In this way of thinking, a raid is justified because members are unable to act for themselves in their own defense. And in a final example, "As Texas is finding out, dealing with a mind-controlling cult takes more than just a desire for dramatic action."[94]

Warren Jeffs has been characterized as a cult leader who put his own interest before all others. *New York Post* reporter Todd Venezia sized up Jeffs and categorically blocked off any more finely distinguished understanding of his role as leader of a religious tradition. "Crazy polygamy cult leader Warren Jeffs likes to think of himself as a prophet—but new photos prove that he's really a pervert."[95] Moreover, the group's history and deep connection to nineteenth-century Mormonism link it to a broader and more complex religious tradition than simply the expression of Jeffs' unusual leadership and agenda.

It is too easy, after characterizing the FLDS as a cult, to justify this extraordinary reaction on the part of outsiders because of the presumption of limited agency, charismatic but perhaps unorthodox leadership, and the precarious position of women and children. But a deeper and more sustained study is necessary to analyze and consider the ramifications of such a label before the deep religious character of this group is dismissed in this way.

Reporters have proven ingenious in finding new angles to write about, including the restricted gene pool,[96] racism,[97] underage marriages, and the possibility for violence. Yet another issue was distinguishing the difference between the FLDS and the Church of Jesus Christ of Latter-Day Saints and the tangled history of the two.

Interpreting the Meaning of the Raid

For insiders and outsiders, the Eldorado raid was hauntingly familiar, a repeat of history. For the FLDS it was the materialization of their worst fears; for outside observers, the exercise of state power. The way the state justified and conceptualized the raid of Eldorado mirrored the Short Creek raid. Rather than learning from the failed raid of five decades earlier, Texas reacted to the FLDS community in the same way that Howard Pyle responded to Short Creek. In the recent past, Arizona chose a different response:

> This is a lesson Arizona learned five decades ago when our state
> raided the polygamous cult that straddles the Arizona-Utah line. It is
> a lesson that has informed our state's most recent approach to cult
> leader Warren Jeffs' nightmare community. Arizona understands the
> importance of building a case before going in like gangbusters.[98]

The attorneys general of both Arizona and Utah would take instead "a slow and deliberate path," an implication that the Texas raid would fail to lead to a beneficial result. The *Arizona Republic* recommended a different approach, one informed by history like that used in the case against Warren Jeffs:

> It led to the conviction of Warren Jeffs as an accomplice to child rape
> in Utah and his upcoming trial in Arizona. It took a toll on his finan-
> cial support in Arizona. It resulted in changes in the law enforcement
> in Colorado City, Arizona where calling the cops used to mean getting
> an officer who was loyal to the cult first and law enforcement second.[99]

Conjuring up the memory of 1953, the *Arizona Republic* urged caution and care in the legal proceedings that inevitably would follow in the wake of the Eldorado raid. "We hope Texas takes another lesson from Arizona: After Arizona raided the polygamist community 50 years ago, the failure to make charges stick left law enforcement reluctant to try anything else until just the past few years."[100] Remembering the complicated web of relationships that tied the FLDS together, the paper recommended that as this case unfolded, the FLDS should be treated legally as individuals.

> Now they've got a problem. Not the reunion of kids with their parents—investigators will still have access to interview the children one by one, which is how it should have been done in the first place. But in the absence of open, desperate complaints from Yearning for Zion's women, how will they prove anything against the ranch, if indeed laws were broken?[101]

As had been true in 1953, many interpreted the raid as a test of civil rights. This approach focused on the ability of the constitution to protect religious liberty or individual rights.

> They're people you probably don't know and couldn't be expected to understand. You might even despise their way of life and system of belief. But they're American citizens with all the rights guaranteed the rest of us, and that's why today dozens of women and children associated with the Fundamentalist Church of Jesus Christ of Latter-Day Saints are no longer enduring what one social worker described as conditions experienced by 'prisoners of war.' . . . As isolated as they might be, they're still protected under the law. . . . When a system designed to help children and families—even families we don't understand—does more harm than good, it's time to change the system."[102]

The Short Creek raid aroused comparisons to fascism or the face of Hitler in reference to what was perceived as a totalitarian regime, but in reporting the Eldorado raid, critics evoked images of the war in Iraq, a more recent cultural phenomenon. The *Los Angeles Times* made this explicit comparison in its June 2, 2008, edition:

> Strange how much the Texas raid of a polygamist ranch resembles the U.S. invasion of Iraq. Just as American leaders seemed certain that Iraqis would gratefully embrace us for deposing Saddam Hussein, the Texas authorities seemed to expect dozens of newly freed girls to come forward complaining that they had been forced into sex and detained against their wills. In the weeks after the raid,

the Texas officials seemed to launch their own search for weapons of
mass destruction—or in this case, mass molestation of young girls—
that were never found. Instead they'd trumpet whatever else they
could find—oh, here's an underage mother. Except, as it turned out,
many of those weren't underage. Even if they had been, teen mothers
hold little shock value for society these days.[103]

Ideally, historians and sociologists equipped to evaluate the story of the FLDS
in reflective and objective ways will move beyond the initial reporting of the
conflicts that occur with such groups and build an interpretive case with a
broad range of primary materials. Unarguably, the media colors the way in
which outsiders understand the religious lives of members of this community
as well as state interventions and the possibilities for their continued existence.
Media treatment is part of the story and impacts the public's ability to make
sense of the narrative of the group.

Those most affected by the raids search for meaning in their personal
narratives. Louis Barlow's attitude toward the 1953 raid typified the FLDS point
of view.

We've been accused of committing sin, violating moral laws under
the name and guise of religion. I want to remind you of the basic
freedom we have. It is the freedom of life, liberty and the pursuit
of happiness. And if any community were to do the things that
Governor Pyle accused our community of doing and called it religion,
yes, of course, it should be wiped out, smashed and done away with.
Accusations of a white slave factory, accusations of young women
being forced into marriage against their will, accusations of misappropriation of funds, accusations of tax evasion, accusations of any
kind and every kind—those accusations are FALSE as they can be!
And it is our only hope that the American people will see these
things and come to our rescue.... But in the meantime, our women
and children have been KIDNAPPED![104]

For the FLDS, plurality is a test of their righteousness and is grounded
in religious belief. Similarly, they frame their understanding of the two raids
with a religious lens. Louis Barlow commented during an interview with KSUB
Radio in August 1953 in the aftermath of the Short Creek raid, "You people may
look on this incident in Short Creek with indifference and mere curiosity, but
to us it is an attack upon everything we have lived for, fought for, prayed for,
and some of us have died for."[105] After the 1953 raid, Louis Barlow did not know
where his wives and children were, "All I know is that my house is empty. My

kids' cribs are empty."[106] At once a personal tragedy and a religious test, the raid created personal and corporate myths, stories that forged unity of purpose, shared history, and a renewed dedication to the building of what they considered the kingdom of God in preparation for the second coming of Christ.

Leroy Johnson blamed the raids on the "unfaithfulness" of the people:

> I bring it down to our day. We had a raid in 1934, in 1944, and ten
> years later we had another raid, simply because the people could
> not learn by the experience of others that God meant what He said
> when He said, 'Keep My Commandments. My word is sharper than
> a two-edged sword to the cutting asunder of both marrow and joint.'
> In 1944, after that raid, fifteen men were sentenced to the federal
> prison. They had one or two women that testified against these men
> and sent them to prison. I want you to pay attention! In 1953, there
> were a great many more men arrested and their families taken away
> from them. Women and children were carried away by the enemy,
> and the governor of the state made a public announcement that he
> would take the children away from the parents and adopt them out,
> he would put the women in detention homes and put the men in the
> prisons, and after three years, they would destroy the records and
> their identity would be forgotten. But do you know what happened?
> They were so sure that the women they were taking away would be
> so pleased to receive a little freedom that they would be glad to testify
> against their husbands. Had they been able to get one woman at that
> time to testify against her husband, it would have been too bad for
> the men because they would have gone to prison. They worked hard
> for it, but they couldn't get it.[107]

Louis Barlow described Sunday, July 26, as:

> a terrible day of this invasion, this Raid, this abuse that came upon our
> fair community! After the invasion and the fear that was put into the
> lives of every mother and child in that community, followed mock trails,
> Juvenile hearings and imprisonment! They desecrated the day! The
> places where we held Sunday School and meetings were made prisons
> the men were put in there and held by sheriffs all the way around—not
> allowed to talk to their families, treated just as if it was a movement of
> Adolph Hitler or some movement like that out of the last war![108]

In the words of Alvin Barlow:

> We are a part of a very real, a very live, a very wonderful thing. And
> there are no people in the history of the Gospel that have been

exempt from it. Sometimes our experiences in our youth don't quite bring it into focus. We see it in the written story; we hear it told from those that were there, and it takes on a certain atmosphere of historical importance, but the very time that we are living, right now, is as critical a day as ever there was.[109]

In 1953 the FLDS portrayed the raid as the battle between good and evil, that if they had faith they could prevail. The measure of the good or ill that befell them was always related to faithfulness. In the same way, in the 2000s the FLDS portrayed the world outside as the beast, as the enemy and the force of evil, designed by the devil to put these righteous people down. It has been true in each raid that a shared enemy has been a powerful binding influence over the relationships of group members.

When the stress is on from the outside it tends to drive the people together. But in peace time people are more inclined to be nettled and offended by the little things that each other do, and thereby they draw apart instead of together. And this is the great test that I think we are in today.[110]

For Fred Jessop this was the fight of good against evil, a "moral fight," a "fight of integrity," a "fight against influences that are calculated to destroy and disunite this people in other words, to get us to alienate ourselves from that chosen source of revelation and blessings on earth."[111]

Conclusion

In an ideal world we would learn what history has to teach us, but it is more often the case that we do not. This characterizes the story of the confrontation of state governments with the polygamous communities of the FLDS in the 1953 raid on Short Creek and the 2008 raid on Eldorado, Texas, and the resulting media coverage. There are no easy answers about how to protect the individual rights of members of religious communities that choose to separate from mainstream society and live distinctive lives according to their spiritual beliefs. Haunting failures that end up with damaged lives instead of enlightened rebuilding remind us of the dire consequences of misunderstanding and injudicious action. The impact of Eldorado and Short Creek may be more nuanced and complex than the inferno that burned the Mt. Carmel complex to the ground, but the damage will spread through time and space in unpredictable but painfully destructive ways in the future.

NOTES

1. George Santayana, Gerda Lerner, "Wisdom Quotes," 1, http://8/28/2008. http://www.wisdomquotes.com/002322.html

2. Ada Timpson, "1953 Raid on Short Creek," http://www.fldstruth.org/ sysmenu.php?MParent=HISTORY&MIndex=33&SParentID=10; May 30, 2008, 3. Until the recent past, firsthand accounts of the raid have been circulated privately among the fundamentalist Mormons but have not been readily available to outsiders. Martha Sonntag Bradley's book, *Kidnapped from That Land: The Government Raids on the Short Creek Polygamists* (Salt Lake City: University of Utah Press, 1993), is based in part on oral interviews with members of the group who were either involved in the raid or who associate with the group. When some in the group organized to celebrate the history of the raid of 1953, they recorded the remarks or essays composed by certain participants in the raid, already invaluable firsthand accounts that resonate with the record and give voice to the intensely personal experience had by these individuals. Because original interviews are part of the narrative of *Kidnapped from That Land,* I have chosen to use this new source material whenever possible in this chapter.

3. The story is depicted extensively in Martha Sonntag Bradley, *Kidnapped from That Land: The Government Raids on the Short Creek Polygamists* (Salt Lake City: University of Utah Press, 1993); Brian C. Hales, *Modern Polygamy and Mormon Fundamentalism: The Generations after the Manifesto* (Salt Lake City: Greg Kofford Books, 2006); and Benjamin G. Bistline, *The Polygamists: A History of Colorado City, Arizona* (Colorado City, AZ: Benjamin G. Bistline, 2004).

4. Leroy Johnson, 7 vols., *Sermons of Leroy S. Johnson* (Hildale, Utah: Twin Cities Courier, 1983–1984), 4: 1635.

5. The FLDS believe that God gave Joseph Smith the keys to perform sacred marriages and that these keys had eternal significance. Moreover, that after his death that authority transferred from Brigham Young to John Taylor. Before John Taylor's death, according to the FLDS history, Taylor authorized a group of men to continue to perform plural marriages in secret, forming a priesthood council in 1886 in Centerville, Utah.

6. Martha Sonntag Bradley, "Response Patriarchy, Intervention, and Prophetic Leadership Challenges in the Culture of Mormon Fundamentalism," *Nova Religio* 10, no. 1 (2006): 32.

7. *Arizona Republic,* July 27, 1953.

8. Bradley, *Kidnapped from That Land,* 54.

9. Isaac Carling Spencer tells about his involvement in the 1935 raid in a memoir edited by Elaine Bistline, August 7, 1975, posted on http://www.fldstruth.org/ sysmenu.php?MParent=HISTORY&MIndex=33&SParentID=10; May 30, 2008.

10. *Mohave County Miner,* September 6, 1935.

11. Bradley, *Kidnapped from That Land,* 54.

12. Elizabeth Lauritzen, "Hidden Flowers: The Life, Letters, and Poetry of Jacob Marinus Lauritzen and His Wife Annie Pratt Gardner," typescript, Genealogical Library, The Church of Jesus Christ of Latter-Day Saints, Salt Lake City, 105.

13. Bradley, *Kidnapped from That Land,* 61; Bistline, 27–28.

14. The men ended up serving twelve months in the penitentiary when they were released because of good behavior. They returned home on November 8, 1936. Bradley, *Kidnapped from That Land*, 62; Bistline, 32.

15. "Multiple Wives," *Literary Digest* (August 1, 1936): 5.

16. *Deseret News*, March 7, 1944.

17. Ibid.

18. Rulon T. Jeffs, "1944 Raid" http://www.fldstruth.org/sysmenu. php?MParent=HISTORY&MIndex=105; Accessed May 30, 2008.

19. "The Honor Roll of 1945," *Truth* 11 (June 1945): 27.

20. Bradley, *Kidnapped from That Land*, 68–69; Bistline, 58.

21. Congress enacted the Mann Act through its power to regulate interstate commerce in a creative attempt to curb prostitution and immorality more generally. In this case, the Mann Act was invoked to restrict the movement of plural wives over state lines. The Lindbergh Act again addressed the issue of the movement of plural wives over state lines but in this case, it made it a crime to kidnap.

22. "The Last Chapter of the 1944 Church Crusade Is Now Written," *Truth* 16 (March 1950): 187.

23. Radio address, July 26, 1953, KTAR Radio, Phoenix, Arizona.

24. J. Bracken Lee, oral interview with Martha S. Bradley, October 3, 1991, Salt Lake City, Utah.

25. Bradley, *Kidnapped from That Land*, 123.

26. Howard Pyle, oral interview with Martha S. Bradley, March 14, 1984, Phoenix, Arizona.

27. Ibid.

28. Faulkner's testimony was given before the U.S. Senate Committee to Investigate Juvenile Delinquency held Thursday, April 28, 1955. U.S. Senate Committee of Judiciary, 19.

29. Bradley, *Kidnapped from That Land*, 126.

30. Marie J. Darger, "1953 Raid on Short Creek," fldstruth.org/sysmenu. php?MParent=HISTORY&MIndex=138; June 18, 2008.

31. Evelyn F. Jessop, "1953 Raid on Short Creek," http:fldstruth.org/sysmenu. php?MParent=HISTORY&MIndex=138; June 18, 2008, 1.

32. Ibid., 1.

33. Bradley, *Kidnapped from That Land*, 130.

34. Ibid., 1.

35. Ibid.

36. Ibid.

37. *Salt Lake Tribune*, July 29, 1953.

38. Superior Court of Arizona, Mohave County, Arrest Warrants, July 26, 1953, Kingman County Courthouse. Photocopy in the possession of the author.

39. *Mohave County Miner*, July 30, 1953.

40. Group interview, with Martha S. Bradley, November 5, 1988, Colorado City Hall, Colorado City, Arizona.

41. Evelyn F. Jessop, 1–2.

42. Marie J. Darger, 1.

43. Ada Timpson, "1953 Raid on Short Creek," http://www.fldstruth.org/sysmenu.php?MParent=HISTORY&MIndex=33&SParentID=10; May 30, 2008.

44. Ibid.

45. Ibid.

46. Ibid.

47. Ibid.

48. Evelyn F. Jessop, 2.

49. Alvin S. Barlow, "1953 Raid on Short Creek," fldstruth.org/sysmenu.php?MParent=HISTORY&MIndex=138; June 18, 2008, 5.

50. Jaimee Rose, *The Arizona Republic,* August 16, 2008, http://www.azcentral.com/arizonapublic/arizonaliving articles/2008/08/16/20080816shortcreek0816.html, 4.

51. Evelyn F. Jessop, 2.

52. Marie J. Darger, 1.

53. Ada Timpson, 2.

54. Permilia J. Jessop, "1953 Raid on Short Creek," http://www.fldstruth.org/sysmenu.php?MParent=HISTORY&MIndex=33&SParentID=10; May 30, 2008.

55. Ibid.

56. Ibid.

57. Evelyn F. Jessop, 3.

58. Ibid.

59. Hilda Dutson, "1953 Raid on Short Creek," http://www.fldstruth.org/sysmenu.php?MParent=HISTORY&MIndex=33&SParentID=10; May 30, 2008, 3.

60. Vera J. Black, "1953 Raid on Short Creek," http://www.fldstruth.org/sysmenu.php?MParent=HISTORY&MIndex=36&SParentID=10; May 30, 2008.

61. Ibid.

62. Ibid.

63. Ibid.

64. "What Others Say, Short Creek 'Insurrection,'" *The Phoenix Gazette,* clipping posted on http://www.fldstruth.org/sysmenu.php?MParent=HISTORY&MIndex=33&SParentID=10; May 30, 2008, 17.

65. Ibid.

66. *Deseret News,* July 27, 1853.

67. *Arizona Daily Star,* August 6, 1953.

68. *Arizona Republic,* July 27, 1953.

69. *Arizona Republic,* August 30, 1953.

70. During the late 1990s significant and public cases of child abuse came before the court, stimulating the end of the laissez-faire policy of the Utah Attorney General's office and the development of a new concerted and focused attempt to prosecute violations of law among the polygamist sects.

71. Lucinda Dillon, "Majority in Utah Want Polygamists to Be Prosecuted," *Deseret News,* May 18, 2000.

72. James A. Beckford, "The Mass Media and New Religious Movements," in *New Religious Movements Challenge and Response,* Bryan Wilson and Jamie Cresswell, eds. (New York: Routledge, 1999), 115.

73. Ibid., 110.

74. Deborah King, "Keeping Sweet" in San Angelo, Texas, *Huffington Post*, May 28, 2008.

75. Todd Venezia, "'Shudder' Bug Cult Creep's Photos," *New York Post*, May 28, 2008.

76. Carolyn Jessop with Laura Palmer, *Escape* (New York: Broadway Books, 2000).

77. Ken Driggs, quoted by Trish Choate, "Yearning for Zion," *Standard-Times Washington Bureau*, May 25, 2008, original in *Journal of Church and State*.

78. Timothy Miller, quoted by Kimberly Winston, "Why Does Sex Play Such a Large Role for Fringe Religious Sects?" *Religious News Service*, June 27, 2008. http://www.religionnewsblog.com/21709/why-does-sex-play-such-a-large-role-for-fringe-religious-sects; July 17, 2008.

79. Elissa Wall with Lisa Pulitzer, *Stolen Innocence: My Story of Growing up in a Polygamous Sect, Becoming a Teenaged Bride, and Breaking Free of Warren Jeffs* (New York: William Morrow, 2008), 17.

80. Deborah King, "Keeping Sweet" in San Angelo, Texas, *Huffington Post*, May 28, 2008.

81. Todd Venezia, "'Shudder' Bug Cult Creep's Photos," *New York Post*, May 28, 2008.

82. Post by "Naiah," on http://truthwillprevail.com, June 21, 2008.

83. Deborah King, "Keeping Sweet" in San Angelo, Texas, *Huffington Post*, May 28, 2008.

84. Martha Sonntag Bradley, "Response Patriarchy, Intervention, and Prophetic Leadership Challenges in the Culture of Mormon Fundamentalism," *Nova Religio* 10, no. 1 (2006): 32.

85. Ibid., 33.

86. Kimberly Winston, "Why Does Sex Play Such a Large Role for Fringe Religious Sects?" *Religion News Service*, http://www.kansaascity.com/238/story/681989.html, June 27, 2008.

87. Catherine Weissenger, quoted by Kimberly Winston, "Why Does Sex Play Such a Large Role for Fringe Religious Sects?" *Religion News Service*, http://www.kansaascity.com/238/story/681989.html, June 27, 2008.

88. Wall, 12.

89. Ibid., 17.

90. Stephen Sinclair, *When Men Become Gods: Mormon Polygamist Warren Jeffs, His Cult of Fear, and the Women Who Fought Back* (New York: St. Martin's Press, 2008), 29.

91. Trish Choate, "Yearning for Zion," *Standard-Times Washington Bureau*, May 25, 2008.

92. N.a., "Slow and Deliberate," *Arizona Republic*, May 28, 2008.

93. Ibid.

94. Ibid.

95. Todd Venezia, "'Shudder' Bug Cult Creep's Photos, *New York Post*, May 28, 2008.

96. Dan Childs, "Polygamists Avoiding InBreeding Problems?" ABC News Medical Unit, http://abcnews.go.com/print?id=4698181, April 22, 2008.

97. The Southern Poverty Law Center placed the FLDS on its hate group list in 2005 for their racist beliefs. See "Racist FLDS Cult Surfaces in New Location," http://www.splcenter.org/blog/2008/05/14/racist-flds-cult-surfaces-in-new-location, May 14, 2008.

98. N.a., "Slow and Deliberate," *Arizona Republic*, May 28, 2008.

99. Ibid.

100. Ibid.

101. Trish Choate, "Yearning for Zion," *Standard-Times Washington Bureau*, May 25, 2008.

102. John L. Smith, "Affidavits Paint a Disturbing Picture of Texas Child Protective Services," *Las Vegas Review-Journal*, June 3, 2008.

103. N.a., "Polygamy Ain't What It Used to Be," *LA Times*, June 2, 2008.

104. Louis Barlow, interviewed by KSUB Radio, August 1953, fldstruth.org/sysmenu.php?MParent=HISTORY&MIndex=138; 6/18/2008, 2.

105. Ibid., 3.

106. Ibid., 4.

107. Leroy Johnson, "Sermons of President Leroy S. Johnson," Vol. 3: p. 969, http://www.fldstruth.org/sysmenu.php?MParent=HISTORY&MIndex=33&SParentID=10; May 30, 2008.

108. Louis Barlow, interviewed by KSUB Radio, August 1953,

109. Alvin Barlow, 3.

110. Fred Jessop, 2.

111. Ibid. 2

Chapter 2

One Vision: The Making, Unmaking, and Remaking of a Fundamentalist Polygamous Community

Heber B. Hammon and William Jankowiak

It was a tense gathering that Sunday at the meeting house, the North Auditorium of the local public school. The religious leaders of the community, Parley Harker, Virgil Jessop, Fred M. Jessop, and Alma Adelbert Timpson, had taken their seats as they had always done, sitting on the stage of the auditorium above the church membership. There were issues that had been going on for several years. President "Del" Timpson, counselor to President Leroy S. Johnson, conducted the meeting. "Uncle" Fred Jessop led in a hymn, the audience there was prayer, and "Uncle" Newell Steed led another hymn sung by the choir. Several men from the audience were called on to preach. Then Brother Timpson began his own sermon for the day. When he admonished the community to "stay away from (then ailing) President Johnson with your ungodly presence or you will be cursed," Dan Barlow, mayor of Colorado City and son and grandson of two of the founding fathers, shouted, "That's a lie." No one moved at first; some thinking Del Timpson, who was almost completely deaf, had not heard him. Then Truman Barlow, Dan's brother, stood up and began putting on his coat, but everyone else sat riveted on the edge of their seats. No one doubted something historical was happening. Outbursts like this had only happened twice before in meetings. Then the bishop, "Uncle" Fred Jessop, 72-year-old son of revered "Grandpa" Joseph Jessop and unofficial leader of the fundamentalist community, stood up. He glared at President Timpson on the stand, looked out over the audience, and gave his suit vest a quick tug as if giving a signal. More than 85 percent of the audience rose en masse and stood staring at Del Timpson. Stunned, Brother Timpson quietly but firmly said, "Dismiss yourselves at home," and began to walk off the stage. Quietly the audience filed out the exits of the meetinghouse. In mere minutes, it was empty. So began the ending of more than 40 years of consensus over what constituted the moral and political foundation of a Mormon fundamentalist polity. The year was 1981, in the late fall, and the walkout (the day they rose up against Brother Timpson, as it is referred to) represented the beginning of what would become a total fission in the oldest and largest polygamous community in North America.[1] Those who that day sided with Fred Jessop became known as the First Ward, and those who sided with Del Timpson were called the Second Ward.

The long-term repercussions resulted in the community separating into two autonomous, often openly hostile, communities—economically, politically, and socially independent of one another. The "Split" marked the formal ending of the founders' desire to create what the Puritans long ago tried to achieve: "building the City of God on earth." Now splintered into two rival sects, each would not only face the outside world alone, but would also compete with the other for legitimacy.

In this chapter, we explore the making, unmaking, and remaking of an intentional community whose social organization shifts over a 50-year period from an ad hoc cluster of struggling homesteaders to the formation of a religiously inspired communal order to the current situation of two separate communities that coexist, albeit uneasily, in close geographic proximity.

Specifically, we examine the external factors (i.e., state policies and economic opportunities) and the internal factors (i.e., religious doctrine, family and other political alliances, and local history) that shaped the perspectives, motivations, and expectations of an individual's place within a hierarchical, religiously inspired, social order. In examining the reasons for the formation, separation, and reformation of the conflicting communities, we illustrate some of the problems inherent in the fundamentalist social organization. We discuss how different families, as individuals and members of a larger collective, responded to the daily challenges inherent in trying to balance spiritual requirements with family obligations, as well as with often unvoiced personal desires. In the end, we probe the meaning of contemporary Mormon fundamentalism religion as it is practiced in two different American communities.

Fundamentalism: An Overview

Fundamentalist movements draw on a variety of organizational forms and come with different polity traditions that range from withdrawing (world rejecting) to accommodating (or world embracing). Many fundamentalist movements prefer to establish intentional communities, that is, a gathering of individuals who choose to live together with a common goal based on forms of relatedness other than blood ties. Intentional communities place a high priority on developing feelings of belonging based in fellowship and mutual support. Because fundamentalist worldviews tend to be totalizing life orientations, individuals find comfort and expression in embracing a particular view of the "Truth." In their Christian form, fundamentalists tend to be pre-millennialists, who hold that it is impossible to achieve anything lasting before the Second Coming of the Savior. Christian fundamentalist thought stresses the certainty of God's existence, the infallibility of the sacred religious texts (for example, for Mormons, the Book of Mormon and the Bible, although Mormons add the caveat: as long as it is translated correctly) and other revelations of divine will, and the necessity of personal salvation through living according to theological principles. Embracing these principles enables the membership to distinguish between good and evil, the elect and the damned, and thereby draw boundaries between insiders and outsiders. In effect, adherence to core principles enables people to recognize "us" and "them."

Christian fundamentalists vary widely in their specific denominational traditions. Spirituality or religious idealism is "the most common inspiration for launching a new community,"[2] and it serves as a basis for a bold vision for the creation of a new social and economic order. Implicit within this social transformation vision is a related conviction that individuals can change and thus improve themselves, their children, and their environment.[3]

The early American religious communities, Lyman Sargent[4] points out, "were authoritarian, patriarchal, and hierarchical." Many communal societies "resist social change, particularly regarding gender relations, preferring instead to remain retreats from the world."[5] Economically, the religiously inspired communities also practice some form of collective ownership. Political power, however, is derived from religious charisma that gives rise to various "cults of personality." Significantly, most members are devoted and want to understand and live according to the tenets of their esoteric theology, which often emphasizes spiritual fulfillment over material well-being. Because most religious communitarians believe that the Second Coming is near, they may experiment with different forms of interaction.[6] Whatever a fundamentalist community's attitude toward interacting with mainstream society is, each community is faced with the perennial dilemma: how much to render unto God, unto Caesar, unto one's family (nuclear and extended), and how much unto one's own self.

The dual commitment to things of earth and things of heaven is manifest in the way in which a community forms its social organization. To create a socially healthy community, wise leadership is required. To meet this need, many intentional communities set up a mentoring or apprenticeship system to foster and develop new leaders who will continue to advance the vision of the community based in righteous spirituality, self-sufficiency, and a concern for social justice. When leadership is perceived to be arbitrary, capricious, or to lack legitimacy, people may move away from the founders' initial idealism. Fundamentalist communities usually agree on the importance of transcending individual greed, dishonesty, egoism, and thus, factionalism. In spite of commitment to higher community goals, individual disagreements arise out of efforts to balance, juggle, and rearrange psychological needs with community grounded ethical principles.

Concepts of Religious Authority

To gain an understanding of the fundamentalist Mormon community structure, one must understand the claim to divine authority asserted by the fundamentalist religious leaders. A saying among them is, "Priesthood is paramount." Priesthood is defined as divine authority given to man to act for and in behalf of God. Fundamentalists claim that John the Baptist bestowed divine authority on Joseph Smith and Oliver Cowdery in May 1829.[7] A short time later, the apostles Peter, James, and John conferred the higher, or Melchizedek, priesthood on them. This authority was that given to the biblical apostles by Jesus Christ, the highest authority ever given to men on earth, and it included the authority or keys to organize a church.[8] These fundamentalist apostles together constitute a quorum called the Priesthood Council.[9] The fundamentalists claim that because the Priesthood Council is higher in authority than the Church, it can function independently.[10] This distinction from the mainline LDS Church is important. Another important distinction was that this order of apostles, discussed below, differed from and was higher in authority than the Council of Twelve Apostles in the Church.[11] The fundamentalists argue that Joseph Smith added new apostles to the Priesthood Council just before his assassination.

The Priesthood Council is also referred to as the Council of Friends. The official title or office of these apostles is an "apostle of Jesus Christ." This order of apostles differs from the Twelve Apostles, a high calling but wholly related to the Church rather than the priesthood. They are often called "high priest apostles" to accentuate this difference. This council governs the fundamentalist community. They are equal in authority but ranked by seniority. Any one of them can be called to direct the affairs of the people under the immediate supervision of the most senior apostle. Hence they are all called "president."[12] The presiding apostle is referred to as the "president of the high priesthood," although this is not an ordained office.[13] He presides by virtue of his seniority according to ordination. He may or may not call upon other apostles to assist him in his administration. The president has the authority to call upon whomever he needs to give him assistance or to form whatever organizations, including but not limited to, an organized church.[14]

According to the fundamentalists, John Taylor, the third president of the Church of Jesus Christ of Latter-Day Saints (LDS), was a ranking member of the Priesthood Council, as was Wilford Woodruff. By 1886, Taylor and Woodruff were the only apostles of this order still living. According to a statement by Lorin C. Woolley, in September of that year Taylor received a revelation directing the continuation of the principle of plural marriage and was also directed to ordain new members to the Priesthood Council.[15] After the 1890 Manifesto, the president of the Priesthood Council, Wilford Woodruff, made assurances to the federal government that the LDS Church would discontinue the practice of polygamy. Because of this, the fundamentalists believe that Woodruff relinquished his Priesthood Council presidency to John W. Woolley, the next senior apostle, while remaining the president of the LDS Church and also a member of the Priesthood Council.

The official LDS church excommunicated Woolley in 1914. Fundamentalists claim that Woolley still held the authority of the High Priesthood as the senior apostle and that the LDS church, in effect, removed itself from Priesthood Council direction.[16] John W. Woolley administered the Priesthood Council, which included approving plural marriages, from 1891 until his death in 1928. By that year, all of the apostles called and ordained at the September 1886 meeting had died except Lorin C. Woolley. Lorin Woolley ordained new apostles to the Priesthood Council, including J. Leslie Broadbent, John Y. Barlow, Joseph W. Musser, and Charles F. Zitting. These men went on to preside over the fundamentalist movement and, except for Broadbent, the Short Creek community.

The fundamentalist response to changes in the mainstream LDS Church began as early as 1886 when Church authorities first began to consider abandoning the practice of "plural or celestial marriage," or in common parlance, polygamy.[17] The mainstream LDS Church's current position evolved over many decades to a straightforward stance: polygamy in this life is not required for salvation. Reaction to the new policy was mixed. Many celebrated the shift; however, many others found the revision unacceptable.[18] This smaller group, opposing these new policies, came in time to be called "fundamentalists" because they adhere to the fundamental doctrines and tenets established by Joseph Smith, Jr. For them, scriptural orthodoxy remains a basis of spiritual authority, and thus they continue to consider plural marriage to be essential for salvation. At the same time, they claim that anyone opposing the principle does not represent a legitimate authority. The Manifesto of 1890 and other statements by the mainstream LDS Church promised to end Mormon polygamy. But the practice continued under the direction of John W. Woolley. This historical period is called "the underground movement"; it lasted from 1891 to 1935.[19]

Polygamists living in isolated areas spread across the American West, Canada, and Mexico.[20] Social, economic, and political organization among the polygamists slowly decentralized and came to simulate the mainstream communities in which they lived. One of these isolated areas was Short Creek in southern Utah and northern Arizona, known as the Arizona Strip. Short Creek's isolation, rather than its convenient straddling of the state lines, made its location ideal for the building of a fundamentalist intentional community.[21]

Persecution of Fundamentalists

The fundamentalist Mormons' on-and-off debate with American as well as LDS mainstream culture has been shaped by the reality that their lifestyle is often the target of government prosecution. For most of its 70-year existence, the community has repeatedly encountered social and economic discrimination and political persecution. From 1882 forward, federal and state governments sought to disenfranchise and imprison Mormons who practiced plural marriage. As a result, polygamists went into hiding, fleeing into remote areas of Utah, Idaho, Colorado, Nevada, or Arizona, and even into Mexico and Canada. By 1897, hundreds of Mormon polygamists had been convicted and imprisoned.[22] Partly in response to the persecution from mainstream America, leaders of the polygamous movement, particularly J. Leslie Broadbent and Joseph W. Musser, began to preach that the official Church of Jesus Christ of Latter-Day Saints had forfeited its right to be the "true" representative of the Mormon religion because of its abandonment of polygamy and excommunication of the apostles.[23] According to the fundamentalists, this resulted in the LDS Church actively joining the persecution of these people.

Although there were many isolated polygamists living throughout Utah and the West, government officials were most ferocious in prosecuting those who lived in organized religious communities or were attached to some sort of religious organization, however nebulous. Beginning in 1935 and continuing to

1953, Short Creek (now Colorado City, Arizona, and Hildale, Utah) was the site of several government raids (see chapter 1). An unintended consequence of these raids was to strengthen the practitioners' conviction and dedication to maintain their lifestyle. Outside pressures had, in effect, reenergized members' faith and desire to create a more perfect community of believers.[24]

Mormon Fundamentalist Communities

Mormon intellectual roots go back to a long and cherished American utopian or millennial tradition. It is a tradition that embraces the idea that humans can create a better community through self-improvement and personal dedication to specific values and behaviors. For fundamentalist Mormons, the core values involve not only forming polygamous families, but also creating a community of believers who desire to live in a perfect community on earth. In fundamentalist Mormon doctrine, this is called the "Principle of the Gathering."[25] In this way, harmonious fellowship with one's neighbors is deemed as important as creating a harmonious, plural family.

Political Organization

Politically, fundamentalist Mormon communities exhibit a closed political system with the ecclesiastical leaders also being the de facto political leaders of the community. When voting for political candidates from outside the community, the religious leaders endorse candidates who they feel will be most sympathetic to their goals. This is then communicated to the membership, and the candidates receive the vast majority of the community's vote in the general election. In local elections such as for school board members, there is often only one candidate, who thus receives a unanimous vote from the community. In some communities, there may be two candidates who are supported equally by the religious leaders on the local level. Mayors and other community members may or may not be religious leaders, depending on how high a profile the leaders wish to take. Unincorporated communities have a "presiding elder" who conducts civic affairs under the direction of the ecclesiastical leaders. In other words, various political leaders are appointed by the presiding authorities and sustained by the voice of the community.

Mormon fundamentalist groups use different avenues to groom new generations of ecclesiastical and civic leaders. Teaching assignments assure a scriptural knowledge of the religious vision for new leaders. Civic assignments give experience useful to organizing and administering important social and economic aspects of a society or community. Invariably, the people called are those qualified by good standing among the community and are supportive of the ecclesiastical leaders. The appointment of men and women to positions of civic responsibility may be changed from time to time as a person may be reassigned to other duties or responsibilities. The fundamentalists recognize the temporary nature of these appointments.

The calling of an apostle, the highest authority recognized among the group members, happens rarely. A member of the Priesthood Council of apostles holds office for life and may succeed to the presidency of the group as his seniority changes. Men called as apostles typically are men of political, social, and economic importance among the group, or they may possess special talents needed by the group. There is no limitation as to office or number as with other priesthood offices such as the Quorum of the Twelve Apostles. The calling is to be done by revelation to the senior apostle, who holds the key or authority to call and ordain other apostles. Collectively, these men are called "the Brethren" and are considered to possess a wealth of wisdom and advice such that the community gives their expressions serious consideration. These policies ensure a pool of experienced leaders to conduct the economic, social, and political affairs of the group or community.

Resolving Disputes

Disputes among members are often settled by either the religious leaders or delegated arbitrators. In early Mormon times, these were called "Bishop's Courts" and had the effect of law, though technically they had no real legal jurisdiction. Cases are handled on the principle of "what is the right thing to do" rather than "who is right and who is wrong." The traditional adversarial system is studiously avoided as leading to disharmony. Admission of evidence does not follow legal precedent and it is not unknown for the judge/ arbiter to report, "Now brethren, President _____ would like us to get this problem settled."

Maintaining Order

Order within fundamentalist communities is usually maintained informally. Each family is expected to police itself. If people act injudiciously, they may be called before the leaders to account for their indiscretions. Fines or confinement are avoided in favor of reconciliation and restitution. For crimes, the county, state, or federal law enforcement officials have jurisdiction to investigate and serve warrants. These cases are handled outside of the community by local courts. Before the 1984 Split, expulsion from the community for wrongdoing was rare. After the 1984 Split, the First Ward has ostracized members through disfellowship and has asked them to leave the community.

Economic Organization

Economically, the fundamentalist community encourages a managed capitalist system. Productivity and being actively engaged in a good cause are the driving principles. The economy of many fundamentalist communities centers on a single industry such as construction, farming, or manufacturing. The ownership of companies may be communal or individual, or a combination of the two. However, the benefits of the company must be community wide if communal funds are to capitalize it. In many communities, income from enterprises goes to a central fund from which individual families receive according to their needs. Idle time and slothfulness are condemned from the pulpit and can result in families not receiving anything if they have not contributed in some way. Even the young and aged are encouraged to contribute economically to the family or community.

The United Order

Early in mainstream LDS history, Joseph Smith, Jr., introduced the principle of the United Order to the Mormon people. Many of Short Creek's families had a long history with that economic ideal as instituted by Brigham Young and other Mormon leaders in the colonization of the West. As an intentional fundamentalist community, residents considered this principle to be as essential to their religion as plural marriage.

The property consecrated, voluntarily deeded, to the Church was used to establish "stewardships" that emphasized the productive use of resources for the betterment of both the LDS Church and its members. Members were charged with the responsibility to manage this property productively and to generate an income from it for both themselves and the Church in the form of tithes. Any excess income over and above what was necessary for their "just wants and needs" was to be returned to the Church. The formal organization of groups of families in a community was called the United Order. There were many United Orders, not just one. Collectively, they followed the tradition of early Christian socialism. The United Effort Plan was not an actual United Order. Marion Hammon, a ranking leader on the Priesthood Council, prefers to call the formal organization "living the United Order."

The Making of Short Creek: Different Visions of Community

Three concepts of community were extant among the fundamentalists in 1935. The first, promoted by John Y. Barlow, involved the creation of an intentional community and the gathering of the fundamentalist people. The second concept, voiced by some on the Priesthood Council and echoed by some of the adherents, was that the Priesthood Council should concern itself with administering spiritual affairs only and had no authority to gather the people, receive tithing, own property, or conduct business. The community was the body of true believers and practitioners of the "principle." The third concept reflected the traditional idea of community: a group of families living in proximity in a civil organization.

An Intentional Community

The township of Short Creek was settled in 1914.[26] There were several homesteaders, none polygamous, living in the area. In the mid-1920s, Leroy, Price, and Elmer Johnson and Isaac Carling became associated with the leaders of the "underground" polygamous movement. One of the leaders, John Y. Barlow, was invited to live there on land donated by one of the homesteaders. When he became president of the Priesthood Council, he suggested establishing an intentional polygamous community at Short Creek and gathering the members of the "Group" together. The highest ideal of the priesthood, Barlow preached, is the creation of a theocratic community that combines together the political, social, economic, and spiritual spheres of daily life.

A Group of True Believers

Other apostles on the Priesthood Council opposed this idea because they felt this would increase persecution by state and federal governments. Their concept of community derived from a general group of true believers and practitioners of polygamy. This faction of the movement held that the Priesthood Council had no authority to act in any way other than a spiritual way and to perform marriages. Barlow's proposal soon became policy, however, and polygamous leaders on the Priesthood Council each took up the labor, even though not all resided, in Short Creek.[27] The decision to create an intentional community represented a major shift in policy and focus for polygamists. It also established a precedent for later decision-making. Those opposed to this decision disassociated themselves from the group.

A Traditional Community

The third idea of community came about by the relocation of the Barlow and Jessop families to Short Creek around 1935. These families were interrelated by marriage with each other and with the Johnson family already living at Short Creek. Promoted primarily by the sons of these founding fathers, it advocated organizing the community along patriarchal lines of authority and to the advantage of these "elite" families.

Early Efforts in Short Creek

In these early years, Short Creek was sustained through the labors and funds of fundamentalist members living in other places, especially Salt Lake City. There were few adult men living at the settlement, and economic opportunities were extremely limited during the depression of the 1930s. Most worked cutting timber for Whiting Brothers' sawmill in Fredonia, Arizona. Some worked for Elmer Johnson, one of the early homesteaders, at his lumber and shingle mill, one of the few steady sources of income for the community. The summer months often brought temporary employment through federally funded fencing projects for the Bureau of Land Management throughout Utah, Nevada, and Arizona. During the Depression, the Civilian Conservation Corps (CCC) also worked on various town projects, including the bridge across the Short Creek Wash.[28]

Work projects provided a small but sufficient income for the community to sustain itself. In time, its success made it a refuge for other polygamists living in Idaho, northern Utah, and other places throughout the West. Many individuals who joined gave both small and large donations of money, and in some cases, like the Johnsons, the deed to their land.[29]

The early efforts in fundamentalist Short Creek illustrated some problems with a United Order effort. How was the property to be held, and how was it to be protected in case the donor died? How were resources to be divided? The Priesthood Council, which directed much of the religious efforts of the underground polygamist movement, was an unofficial organization.[30] The Council had no legal way of holding property or of receiving official donations of money such as tithing. Policy up to 1935 had been to have members pay tithing to the official LDS Church and for them to hold other property in the name of whoever either lived there or worked the land. Hence the Johnsons, who had donated land for President Barlow to build a home, simply retained the title to that property. That would not work for others of the movement who might move to Short Creek and help establish the community. Some sort of formal organization would be needed.

In 1942, the Priesthood Council tried to revitalize the Short Creek community. The first effort at formal organization was the United Trust. This arrangement did not work out very well, and the organization was dissolved and trust property returned to the trustors. However, some residents thought that the transfer of their property to the United Trust constituted a consecration to the Lord and refused to take back their property when offered. The deeds to their property were kept in a safe in Salt Lake City.[31]

The second attempt proved to be more successful. The United Effort Plan (UEP), a trust, transformed the Short Creek community into a fully intentional community.[32] Although the town itself was not incorporated by Arizona law, the UEP made governing by the religious organization feasible. The community, to be sure, remained isolated, relatively impoverished, and organized around an ascetic ethos that stressed personal sacrifice and dedication to the common good. The UEP functioned only as a property holding or business entity, not a religious trust.[33] It was not only the management arm of the community's material resources, but also a "fund of power" for individuals in charge.

Management by the UEP helped prevent the community from dividing earlier than it eventually did. Residents assumed (until recent court decisions) that the land belonged to the Priesthood Council. The houses and other improvements they constructed with their personal funds, but usually with communal labor, could not be sold. This made leaving the community difficult, even if a resident was no longer affiliated with "the Work."

The communal property of the Trust eventually, reportedly, reached $100 million in value. This provided a lot of power to Priesthood Council leaders. Based more on their religious rank than on their own material wealth, their control of the use of this property helped establish the community in important economic and social ways. In this way, Short Creek/Colorado City social organization resembled more a monastic social organization than it did a typical small town organized around individual economic standing. From an anthropological perspective, the community resembled, in some ways, a Polynesian chiefdom, whereby the social organization is based on an individual's rank within the ecclesiastical hierarchy based in "the control of collective property rights, within a religious inspired cosmology."[34]

However, the community was never a classic chiefdom in that a family's rank followed a father's social standing within the community, which could change quickly by death or disassociation. The ownership of property within the community remained fixed (with the UEP) and subject to the disposal of the UEP board (the Priesthood Council) or their designee.

The Short Creek Revival

In spite of the Priesthood Council's best efforts to assert the importance of retaining a collective spirit of cooperation, Short Creek of the 1940s was a fragmented settlement in religious, social, and economic terms. In this milieu, households were inclined to go their own way. The social structure centered on being connected in some way or other to one or more of the presiding brethren.[35]

Finally, in 1958, the Priesthood Council decided to abandon their efforts to establish an intentional community at Short Creek[36] and move their colony to Sanpete County, Utah. Two ranking members, Leroy S. Johnson and J. Marion Hammon, had already established households there. The decision was made at a solemn council meeting. Hammon suggested, "Brother Johnson, take the decision up with the Lord and report back to us tomorrow." The next day, President Johnson stated that, "The Lord has decided to give the community one last chance." And, he said, turning to Marion Hammon, "He wants you to go take charge."

The 1953 raid on Short Creek and the 1958 decision to stay in the area rejuvenated the community's religious spirit. The arrest of fathers and the removal of mothers with their children strengthened individual determination to create a better community in which to practice the "Principle" (plural marriage). To this end, and with the guidance of the Priesthood Council, the people wherever they lived—in Salt Lake, Short Creek, Idaho, or Canada—rededicated themselves to building a community.

In 1960, the community built a high school, named Colorado City Academy. The children made adobes; the men went out into the mountains to cut and mill lumber; women fed the workers and put on community dinners and social events to raise the funds for concrete; and a crew of men went up into the hills and quarried rock for the foundations. The Academy was the impetus that revitalized Colorado City.

A water system, built by the community, carried running water from springs in the canyons to homes in the valley. The community dug wells to provide water to other homes. They purchased agricultural enterprises in outlying areas. They also developed acreage in the community into a community garden. The UEP encouraged a modern dairy to move to the community from Cache County, Utah.[37]

At first, the community rejected money offered to them by various government agencies. Leaders preached against taking welfare and instructed the people to "take care of their own." They reorganized the bishop's storehouse to provide for the needy. The community purchased and stored wheat against "hard times." Various farms and ranches grew potatoes, harvested by the Academy students (spud harvest), and stored them to feed the community. Leaders stressed, "All government money has strings attached. We don't want their money. We don't want them telling us what to teach in our schools. We don't want them telling us how to live." This "bootstrap" approach gave the whole membership purpose, regardless of where they lived. The Salt Lake members largely funded these improvements.

Eventually, the community became too big. The Farmers Home Administration provided funds to build a water treatment and culinary water and sewage system. The Colorado City Unified School District received education funds from Arizona and Utah. The Small Business Administration funded a variety of business enterprises.

The 1960s brought social changes as well. Men who had previously denied they were a child's father (claiming to be an uncle) now openly lived in the same house with all their wives and children. The terms "uncle" or "aunt" were used to distinguish a person of importance. Mothers and children who had lived under assumed names like Nelson, Markham, or Hanson now acknowledged they were Hammons or Timpsons or Jessops. Sermons used terms like "sister wife" and stressed unity and harmony in families.

Dress, which had followed the fashions of the day, changed to a conservative style that would label the community's people in outlying towns. During the 1950s, the community had remained relatively poor. There were few cars, and people took turns borrowing the ones available. Cash income was short, and wives prepared dinners from raw materials and seldom from processed food. A number of families lived in large tents while building their homes. There were no television sets in the community. Telephones became available only in the mid-1960s. Electric power did not come until late 1960. Homes with running water were few. Homes used outhouses instead of toilets. Some women even spread their laundry on barbed wire fences to dry.[38] At one time, only one washing machine existed in the community, and that ran on a gasoline engine. Families took turns using it.

The limited resources of the 1950s fostered a value of hard work and personal sacrifices, the staples of a fundamentalist Christian community. People talked about their humble existence and the importance of sacrifice. In highlighting the value of sacrifice, the community recognized specific individuals as paragons of virtue. Such a person was "Aunt Susie" Barlow, the wife of President John Y. Barlow. She, along with many others, was constantly referred to as the ideal model of sacrificial endurance. The people considered Aunt Susie to be an earthly angel. Whenever there was conflict within a family, the husband would point out what Aunt Susie might have done.

The time period from 1959 to 1978 became a time of consensus, shared vision, and ardent commitment. The community's strength of commitment is evident in a 44-year-old man recalling with fondness in his voice that "in those days, any priesthood council member could have anything he wanted; we would have given him anything."

The commitment to a shared ideal legitimatized assigning community youths to specialize in various career paths that would improve the community's well-being. For example, Claude Cawley, an engineering graduate, was called to teach math and to be the principal of the Academy. Cyril Bradshaw, a chemist working for the government, was called to teach science at the Academy. John Timpson, a graduate in nuclear physics, also taught math at the Academy. Other talented youth, men and women, were assigned to study dentistry, medicine, nursing, education, or business to serve the needs of "the Work."

During the 1960s and 1970s, the community would also become part of the regional and national society. During the Vietnam War era, many individuals served in the armed forces, even though they could have escaped to Canada. Priesthood leaders counseled: "This is our country. We will defend it." The armed forces drafted every eligible man from the area, although this was not true of other non-FLDS in the area. Contrary to general public opinion, youths from the community have served in every national conflict from World War I to the present.

By the 1970s, the expansion of southern Utah's economy provided lucrative opportunities for work, especially in the construction trades. The new source of income further increased people's standard of living. One 59-year-old man wryly commented: "We went from being so poor we didn't know we were poor to being a respectable middle-class community." This resulted in most homes having one or more new cars or trucks. Moreover, a large number of families now prepared dinners using processed goods instead of making everything from scratch.

Competing Visions within the Community

In every culture there are competing models about how to do something. Short Creek was no different. From its inception, the settlement had competing visions over how best to create and sustain community spirit. The dueling visions were grounded in different philosophies that stressed different values. For those who came to be called the First Ward, collective sharing, commonality, familial loyalty, and allegiance to the prophet were important values. For those who came to be called the Second Ward, individual choice, personal responsibility, personal merit, and loyalty to the Priesthood Council as well as the president were the important values.

Issues of Leadership

In 1942, John Y. Barlow felt inspired to add new apostles to the Priesthood Council. Leroy S. Johnson and J. Marion Hammon were called in the same revelation and were ordained two weeks apart. When the Council next met, Johnson and Hammon were attending their first meeting as new apostles.[39] Their lives would be forever entwined. Marion was an evangelistic, fire and brimstone preacher who took problems head on. Leroy was very spiritual, had numerous faith-promoting experiences, and was a quiet, very patient type of manager. They made an effective team, with the older man, Leroy, the senior member.

In 1942, when Marion Hammon was called to direct priesthood efforts in Short Creek, he initially misunderstood the duality of vision in the Short Creek community. He assumed that all the residents had accepted the authority of the Priesthood Council and were working to implement its vision. He took their reluctance to obey priesthood directions as "backsliding" and gave them severe reprimands both publicly and privately.[40] He questioned the "most favored" status of some of the young Barlow sons, and they deeply resented him. "Better is as better does" was his motto regarding their actions.

The priesthood, Hammon said, wanted men to "roll up their sleeves" and get involved. He found a wealth of hard-working, willing men in the Jessops. With a tendency to be a bit stubborn, they could take on any job and "if not exactly do it right, at least get it done." Richard S. Jessop ("Uncle Rich") was one of those men and a respected member of the Priesthood Council. He, his sons, and a nephew, Edson P. Jessop, contributed tremendously to the effort to build the community. They could operate and repair just about any type of machinery, especially old machinery. They would work long hours under extreme hardship and be counted on to stay and get the work done, with or without recompense or even recognition. Physically, the Jessops built Short Creek.[41] The Jessops recognized and enjoyed affiliation as the elite families of Short Creek, but they also recognized and contributed to the religious effort. Thus, they, almost more than anyone else, perpetuated the duality of visions.

Hammon relied heavily on them to get the physical work done. He believed in and rewarded individual merit. In addition, other newcomers had the skills he needed to build a true community, and he used them. He saw no difference between newcomer and old-timer. He often stated: "There are those who do and those who don't." He hated disorder and slovenly ways of living. He was given to almost violent outbursts of temper. He expected people to "respond and then some." "Wake up and Live" was posted on the bulletin board of the meeting hall. He had no use for anyone who would accept a poor lot in life and make no effort to improve it. He did not particularly disdain poverty, but he hated "poor ways." He was the man for the job in Short Creek, and the Priest-hood Council, including President Barlow, supported him. But to the Barlow sons and some of the Jessops, he was just "that runny-nosed kid from Idaho." Ben Bistline, a resident historian, says, "There wouldn't have been a Colorado City without Marion Hammon."[42]

John Y. Barlow had far-reaching responsibilities as leader of the funda-mentalist movement, and he was often away from Short Creek. In his absence, Grandpa Joseph Jessop directed the social activities of the community and later the storehouse for the needy and the maternity clinic until his death in 1953. Thereafter, his son Fred M. Jessop performed these duties. Fred was the "go to" guy when people needed something, and he eventually controlled almost every economic opportunity within the community. Individuals needed Fred Jessop's approval for most community jobs.

Fred Jessop believed in and fostered a vision centered on the Jessop clan and those associated with them, "us folks." The Barlow sons were included in that clan through their mother Mattie. Fred Jessop's connections to President Barlow and, later, President Leroy Johnson facilitated his efforts to move into positions of de facto leadership. By the 1980s, Fred Jessop was undeniably the most powerful person in the community.[43] His position toward the theological principles of the movement was pragmatic: use them when it helps; overlook them when it doesn't.

In contrast, the Priesthood Council members who lived in Short Creek—Leroy Johnson, Marion Hammon, Richard Jessop, Carl Holm, and Alma Adelbert Timpson—urged that theological principles should govern all policy decisions. All were highly critical of the tendency to promote clan/personal loy-alty over Priesthood principles. Johnson said, "I hope there are no Johnsonites, Hammonites, or Musserites here. We should all be Godites."[44]

Fred M. Jessop preferred to foster an alternative vision that favored collec-tive, but clan-related, unity over individual achievement and personal recogni-tion. In this, President Leroy S. Johnson publicly concurred but differed in that he saw this as community- rather than clan-related. This vision was manifested in "old-timers'" reactions to a range of activities, from building and construc-tion techniques to how theatrical productions were cast and produced to how athletic events were played.

The "newcomers" to the community generally were devoted to the Priest-hood movement first and the Short Creek–Colorado City effort second. As a group, they were more educated and more active in business enterprises. Almost all were high school educated; many were college educated. Many had filled important offices in the LDS Church, such as gospel doctrine teachers, ward clerks, or even stake presidencies (an intermediate administrative unit in the organizational hierarchy of LDS, sometimes said to be similar to a Catholic diocese). They differed also in being more integrated into the regional and world economies and society. They dressed in more contemporary fashions and thus could also be distinguished from the local "us folks." They accepted authority less well, and they were more intellectual. Once convinced, however, they aggressively defended their positions. They were much less apprehensive, therefore, about interacting with Gentiles or non-believers. For example, Marion Hammon entertained Arizona senator Barry Goldwater in his home. The "newcomers" recognized and valued meritocracy, education, and experience over communal efforts and kindred ties.

The dueling visions were also manifested in striking differences in public decorum. The First Ward, local "us folk," embraced the notion that the best persona was one that resisted emotional displays, even of grief. The leaders of this faction of the community strove to be even-tempered in all interactions. In part, this was a reaction to Marion Hammon's temper and Del Timpson's fiery oratory, which they resented but could do little about. It was also a statement, very Mormon in origin, about accepting the Will of God without murmuring or complaining. Families were encouraged to stress harmony and self-restraint in their daily activities, a demeanor they labeled "keeping sweet."

The Second Ward valued the expression of honest opinions. They quoted Joseph Smith as saying, "Just because a man errors [sic] in doctrine doesn't make him a bad man." Toleration of others' feelings and opinions was critical for getting along as a community, to be sure. This faction continued to stress an orthodoxy based on core Mormon values, but they felt that the way to obtain that was through teaching and converting. Voicing one's opinion, with or without emotional emphasis, was acceptable if one could support it with scriptural evidence. The alignment of doctrine and policy with scriptural support and historical precedent was of paramount importance given the fundamentalist position and the comparison to the LDS Church.

Governmental Welfare

Another point of division had to do with welfare and care of the needy. Second Ward residents condemned those who took from but did not repay the community's general storehouse. This position of personal responsibility also carried over to negative positions toward individuals' readily "going on welfare." Further, none supported the ethos of "ripping off the government"—a policy that Fred Jessop seemed to support—as it went against the values of Christian charity and self-sufficiency.

Many of the Priesthood Council had experienced deprivation during the Depression. None of them had accepted the "public dole." Leroy Johnson had traveled as far as Texas to find work. Marion Hammon had taken a series of menial jobs to provide for his young family. All had worked for subsistence wages. Universally, the apostles deplored welfare as damaging to a person's character and no way of life for a "Saint." To the extent possible, "Saints" should look out for their own and help those in need. Accepting "welfare" was strongly discouraged. Everyone who could was expected to work for their living. The idea of "welfare mothers" was repugnant to them.

One way to fund necessary improvements and thus avoid government money was to have young men just out of high school and not yet married serve "work missions." These missions lasted from two to three years, sometimes longer. Most missionaries lived either in Edson Jessop's home or Marion Hammon's home. They came from as far away as Canada; a few were the sons of the Salt Lake members. Many did the physical work of building the community; others were sent to work at various places such as Whiting Brothers Sawmill to earn much-needed money to finance community improvements.[45] The camaraderie among them contributed in no small way to the unity of the community. Although important to improvement of the community, the program came to be seen as a threat to the vision of the community's patriarchy-based families. These residents felt that Hammon was using the men for his own ends, and thus support waned.

Another contention centered on organizing and administering the community government. Marion Hammon utilized the talents of Mary Woolley, garnered from her experiences as mayor of Ogden. She helped him organize a "planning board." The members were the movers and shakers of the community, almost all young men.[46] Older men, including the Jessops, resented Woolley's presence on the board ("petticoat government," they called it). The planning board eventually turned into the Colorado City Improvement Association, a legal corporation. During the 1960s and 1970s, the board organized and implemented the improvements of the community, though its decisions were subject to approval by the Priesthood Council. When members gathered for workdays, the planning board gave them the assignments for needed improvements.

Toward the end of President Johnson's life, everyone could see that Marion Hammon would change economic policies in Colorado City. He would not allow "free lunches as before. Everything must be repaid. No one could expect a free ride." Hammon and Del Timpson stressed individual economic accountability. In contrast, Fred Jessop and Louis Barlow, advocates of collective sharing and local, familial, bonds, were suggesting obtaining funds wherever you could get them. In time, more First Warders received food stamps and government cash assistance than did Second Warders. The First Ward, the local "us folks," rationalized this as something the government owed them from past persecutions. The tension between the visions of the competing factions became stronger, more evident, and more emotional through the years.

Unmaking of the Community: The Creation of a Post Hoc Theological Rationale

Every community differs in how best to accommodate individual needs within its long-term goals. How this accommodation is institutionalized highlights the weight given to communitarianism versus individuality. The accommodation never completely eliminates more tacit, albeit alternative, values that coexist on the margins of society. It is the leadership's ability to mediate these often-conflicting domains that enables the resolution of potentially violent conflicts over the satisfaction of material needs within an ethos that highlights spiritual fulfillment.

The most frequently invoked explanation of the 1984 Split was a disagreement over theology. The issue is presented thus: Should only one man lead the community as its divinely inspired and adored prophet or should the community be led by a consensus among a council of divinely called men? Our investigation found that although justification of the "one man doctrine" was advanced during the Split, it was not elucidated and perfected as a theological doctrine of the fundamentalist people until after the community divided into contentious and separate wards. For example, a 51-year-old man told us, "We never heard anyone talk about the 'one man doctrine' until after we divided."

To clearly juxtapose these two positions, two doctrinal references are given here.

> The first is: "...and I have appointed my servant Joseph to hold
> this power in the last days, and there is never but one on earth at
> a time on whom this power and the keys of this priesthood are
> conferred."[47] This "one man doctrine" holds that God's prophet is
> the "one" referred to and no one else can direct the affairs of the
> Work or receive manifestations of His mind and will. President Leroy
> Johnson was considered by all to be their prophet; to some, he may
> have been more their god as, over the years, the doctrine took on an
> aspect of infallibility of the prophet.

In response, the Second Ward's position states that the verse above refers only to the power or key to call and ordain other apostles, as explained in the writings of Joseph W. Musser. As far as the equal authority of the apostles, they quote from a revelation to Wilford Woodruff in 1880:

> And while my servant John Taylor is your President, I wish to ask the rest of my servants of the Apostles the question, although you have one to preside over your Quorum, which is the order of God in all generations, do you not, all of you, hold the apostleship, which is the highest authority ever given to men on earth? You do. Therefore you hold in common the Keys of the Kingdom of God in all the world.
>
> You each of you have the power to unlock the veil of eternity and hold converse with God the Father, and His Son, Jesus Christ and to have the ministrations of angels.
>
> It is your right, privilege, and duty to inquire of the Lord as to His mind and will concerning yourselves and the inhabitants of Zion and their interests.[48]

The two positions seem clear, but the different explanations had far-reaching consequences. An examination into the motivations behind individuals' decisions to separate over this issue found something remarkable: Most people sided with their respective families. If their father supported "the one man doctrine" then almost all of his sons and many of his daughters did so too. For the most part, divisions within a family occurred between siblings. Daughters for the most part stayed with their husbands and accepted their position on the doctrine, while sons mostly sided with their fathers. There were some exceptions, with some families ending in legal divorce. Some plural wives, on both sides, sought and received a religious release from marital covenants. The family names were represented on both sides after the Split.

The First Ward consisted mainly of Barlows, Johnsons, Jessops, Jeffs, Steeds, Zittings, and most of the prominent families from Salt Lake City and Canada. They supported the position on the "one man doctrine" held by apostles Leroy Johnson and Rulon T. Jeffs.

The Second Ward consisted mostly of Hammons, Timpsons, Zittings, Williamses, Knudsons, Dockstaders, and some of the prominent families from Salt Lake, and one family from Canada. They supported the position of the "Priesthood Council" doctrine held by apostles J. Marion Hammon and Alma A. Timpson. Approximately 80 percent of the original community went into the First Ward, and 20 percent went into the Second Ward.

Once the theological discussion began in earnest, everyone became engaged with the details and justification. What had been for most a moot issue—no one doubted the president's right to administer with whomever he called to assist him—now became the subject of lively debate. In this way, the post hoc theological debates arose out of the need to prove to themselves as well as others the legitimacy of their actions.

A Counterexplanation: The Importance of Material Factors

It is our position that the motivation for the 1984 Split arose out of a long-standing struggle for social standing, power (both economic and political), and access to limited material resources in the community. The Split was first and foremost a political disagreement over social and material entitlements, more than a debate over theological principles. To provide support for our position, we need to highlight who would lose or gain from the expected transformation of political leadership.

From 1935 to the 1980s, the Colorado City leadership wore two hats—one was concern with spiritual matters and the other with social and community matters. In the 1960s a separation in roles had emerged that resulted in Leroy Johnson, the revered community spiritual and religious leader, stepping into the role of presidency of the polygamist movement across the West, Canada, and for a time Mexico, and Marion Hammon acting as community director of Colorado City/Hildale and being responsible for implementing Priesthood Council policies.[49]

Marion Hammon, the second in Priesthood Council authority, in adopting this appointment, downplayed but never abandoned the spiritual persona. His sermons generally addressed issues of the community, being socially responsible, paying debts, getting along socially and in the family, and being respectful and obedient to Priesthood Council authority. In every way, Hammon saw himself as advancing the priesthood ideals that would turn Colorado City from a backward community into an intentional fundamentalist settlement worthy of being called "a community of Saints." But, as noted before, Leroy Johnson and Marion Hammon functioned as a team. Johnson was the president, the spiritual advisor, and prophet of the community. Hammon was its civic leader. Many First Ward residents complained that, as civic leader, Hammon did not follow the directions of Johnson but acted too independently.

Hammon was opposed by rival elite families, most notably (and openly) the Barlows, Fred Jessop, and others. By the end of the 1970s, the resentment, on both sides, between Marion Hammon and the "Barlow boys" was well known. Fred Jessop had begun to side more openly with the Barlows and sympathized with their complaints. Hammon had a profound respect for President John Y. Barlow that extended to his family, but he began to change his opinion of the Barlow sons after he was called to direct the community affairs in 1942, and again in 1958. After numerous difficulties, Hammon began to perceive them as less dedicated to priesthood principles and more as opportunists who used a hierarchical religious and communal discourse to advance their own personal interests. Although married to one of their sisters, he did not have much use for the Barlow brothers. "Great Big Elders," he called them. "You can't do anything with them, and you can't do anything without them."[50]

He knew Fred and many of the Jessop clan sympathized with them. When asked if he knew Fred wasn't entirely converted to the Priesthood Council efforts, why give him so much authority? Hammon said, "He was there. He was willing. We used him."

There has been no way of determining the amount of money dedicated to the Priesthood Council leadership in the way of tithing during the time period of this study. Tithing, a tenth of one's income, had been collected only since the administration of John Y. Barlow. Its stated use was to help the poor and meet the expenses of the Priesthood Council. It was understood and accepted by the community that the tithes were used for the upkeep and maintenance of the president and his family. Those who objected to this use of the money had long since left the community and the Work.

Many times, Second Warders, who associated with outsiders perhaps more than First Warders, remarked that Leroy Johnson traveled with dozens of people in his train. It became common knowledge among the community that he paid all the expenses of those traveling with him. Cynically, many Second Warders called it "the Gravy Train." Many of those traveling with President Johnson were apparently living off tithing and the storehouse, something reprehensible to Second Warders.[51] It became clear that if Hammon succeeded to the presidency, people would be expected to work to support their families, and the storehouse would be used to help only the truly needy. The Barlows and Jessops suspected that he would reorganize the board of trustees of the UEP with members who would not sympathize with their interests. If he succeeded, many people who had grown accustomed to the extra entitlements would have seen their lifestyle seriously undermined.

Decline of Priesthood Council Influence

Johnson now resided in Colorado City, although he retained residences in Salt Lake City and elsewhere. Giving advice to members of the Work and overseeing the religious activities filled his time. His health began to deteriorate; he was past 90 years of age. When complaints about Hammon's administration of the community became frequent, he finally relieved him of responsibility.[52]

The problem of administering the community became too much for President Johnson. Utilizing the political savvy of Fred Jessop, he turned more and more of the administration over to him. In 1985, Colorado City was incorporated as a legal Arizona town. Dan Barlow was nominated as the town mayor and duly elected. Jessop handpicked the city council. Similar events took place earlier in the twin city of Hildale, Utah. The mayor of that city, Lynn Cooke, a long-time resident, resented Jessop's directives, especially those that skirted legality. David Zitting replaced him. Fred Jessop now controlled the community politically.

Leroy Johnson's problems became compounded when he developed a severe case of shingles that aggravated a chronic back problem. His age plus his illness made meeting with the Priesthood Council difficult. As Johnson grew more feeble, he began taking higher and higher doses of the painkiller Percocet. Those unfavorable to the Jessop-Barlow faction feared that the narcotic distorted his judgment, and it was for this reason Del Timpson told them to leave him alone. Those who favored the Priesthood Council doctrine believed that the Brethren were still directing the affairs of the community. They soon found out they were not.

The "one man doctrine" had spread throughout the Work. At this time, the Priesthood Council consisted of Leroy S. Johnson, J. Marion Hammon, Rulon T. Jeffs, and Alma A. Timpson. Jeffs, at first a strict adherent to the historical position of the Priesthood Council, eventually supported the Jessop-Barlow faction, and Hammon and Timpson continued with the Priesthood Council doctrine. Without President Johnson, some held, the Priesthood Council had no authority to meet and decide anything. Although Hammon and Timpson continued to meet and discuss community issues, their decisions had no binding authority. Only the prophet could receive the Word of God.

As Johnson's mind and body declined, Fred Jessop and the Barlow sons seemed to take control of community policies and activities, advancing their own interests, agendas, and religious doctrines. They became, in effect, his gatekeepers and controlled access to him. Also, in becoming his gatekeepers, they controlled the kinds of information given to him. As time went on, Second Warders were convinced they also influenced his judgment in favor of a different religious doctrine that impacted the way the community and the Work were governed.

Supporters of Fred Jessop invoked Brother Johnson's name to advance the "one man doctrine" that would justify the transfer of governance from the Priesthood Council to "the one man" who was held as the believers' living prophet. All the apostles had accepted the idea of the senior apostle administering the affairs of the work since the days of Joseph Smith. Hence they had no problem accepting the change of administration of community affairs from Hammon to Johnson. But they could not accept that he would remain as sole judge of religious doctrine and could change what was considered the Word of God at will. In fairness, Johnson never claimed he could. But in 1984, this doctrine, advanced by his supporters, not only changed the political and economic governance of the community, but also the historical religious doctrines of the Priesthood Council.

For Second Warders, the motivation to advance the "one man doctrine" was obvious: J. Marion Hammon, the next in seniority to become leader of the Priesthood Council, had shown himself dangerous to many long-time elite Short Creek families and their personal interests. To undercut his religious and political authority, and thus the control of economic resources of the UEP, a radically different theology had to be introduced in order to bypass the conventional line of succession.

In 1984, Johnson finally dismissed Hammon and Timpson from all leadership positions. He stated there would be no Priesthood Council until the Savior came. He ordered them to resign from the board of trustees of the UEP and for Hammon to return the deed of the Academy land and building; this they did.[53] They now realized that something integral to the community had died and could not be renewed. They directed their supporters to say or do nothing that might be construed as rebellion to Johnson's direction and administration. The Lord was sifting his people, they said. They would stand back and let it happen. They sat in the audience with the other members while Fred Jessop and the Barlows sat on the stand with President Johnson.

A few months later the community formally split into two separate wards. Brother Johnson had released the two apostles to continue their work while he worked with the people of the community and in other places. Rulon Jeffs, the only other member of the Priesthood Council, worked with him.

The Second Warders were declared apostate and were served with eviction notices from their homes in the community because the property of the UEP could only be for the use of true believers. The threatened residents filed a lawsuit to clarify residents' position in regard to the improvements made to the land. This held the evictions in check while the issue was pursued in the courts.

The court decided the UEP owned the land and improvements and that members could not sell them. However, eviction constituted unjust enrichment on the part of the UEP. As long as Second Warders wanted to live in their homes, the First Ward could do nothing.

In 1986, President Johnson died. Rulon T. Jeffs, his designated successor, became the prophet of the First Ward, the newly formed Fundamentalist Church of Jesus Christ of Latter-Day Saints (FLDS). The Second Ward members were excommunicated as apostates. They responded by saying they had never been members of that particular church and thus could neither be apostates nor excommunicated. Jeffs, in declining health, governed the community until his own death in 2002.

During Rulon Jeffs's administration, his son Warren Jeffs performed most religious leadership duties, while Fred Jessop continued in the political and civic leadership position in much the same relationship as had existed between Johnson and Hammon. When Rulon died, Warren Jeffs assumed all the leadership positions and Fred Jessop, now aged, retired. Warren Jeffs began the Eldorado, Texas, community and, although currently in prison, continues to govern and is regarded by the First Ward as their true spiritual as well as political leader.

In sum, the growing friction between elite families over social standing, political power, and economic/material privilege resulted in continuous struggles for dominance that ultimately transformed the meaning of community unity, family solidarity, and religious salvation.

The Remaking of Two Communities

A classic debate between two nineteenth-century social theorists, Karl Marx and Max Weber, revolved around how much weight should be given to material versus ideological factors. Weber, who never disagreed that material factors exerted a strong and, at times, dominating influence, also thought that ideas, under the right circumstances, could influence and guide social change. We have argued that the rationale behind the Split had less to do with theological difference and more to do with material factors. However, once the Split had taken place, the rationale or justification for the Split exerted a compelling influence and forced the two communities to place different weight on those values concerning individual agency and obedience.

The philosophies of community that emerged would have different consequences for practices of public speaking, gathering in fellowship, and interacting with the outside world. In many ways, the philosophies rested upon competing notions of authority, individuality, and community. "The tension about authority and community," John Bowen points out, "plagues all Christian movements that attempt to structure themselves around the ultimately unknowable grace of God."[54] In a case in the 1980s, a division within a Baptist church pitted more individualistic North Carolina farmers against more urban Virginia townspeople. In the end, "the issue came down to who makes the rules and who has access to the Word of God."[55] This also held true for the Colorado City division.

Mormonism has always embraced two important values—agency, or free will, and obedience to priesthood authority. The two values are given different weight at various points in Mormon history and in the fundamentalists' communities. In the aftermath of the 1984 Split, the Wards came to different definitions of agency, a nineteenth-century idea taken from American transcendentalism. The First Ward people regarded agency as obeying willingly the directions of the prophet. After the Split, the Second Ward came to view agency as a more open concept that involved free choice of personal matters and taking the resultant consequences. Social and political standing, however, remained as they did before: determined by the degree to which one accepted the authority and vision of the religious hierarchy.

First Ward Views

In contrast, the Split resulted in the retrenched isolation of the First Ward characteristic of the old Short Creek community. First Ward residents removed their children from the public schools, fearing spiritual and cultural pollution through contact with unbelievers (e.g., Second Ward apostates, dissidents, or those who renounced the religion, and those who were never members) and put them into home schools or private schools. This practice is common throughout Utah, however. Believing that the Apocalypse would occur soon, the First Ward withdrew all students, about 1,200 in number, from all schools. The Utah schools, Phelps Elementary and Middle School, closed and the district sold the buildings to the UEP. The Arizona public school district went into financial collapse and receivership. For a time, students attended private parochial schools with a curriculum focused on religious beliefs. During the time that Warren Jeffs was a fugitive, the First Ward children were homeschooled.

The First Ward, seeking spiritual purity, also began to withdraw themselves from association with those outside their faith, including, in some cases, former family members as well as associates. They quoted the Bible admonition that whoever is unwilling to sacrifice friends and family is unworthy of the Kingdom of God. The UEP could no longer evict residents, but the newly formed FLDS Church could disfellowship and excommunicate those not in harmony with the Prophet. Excommunicated First Ward residents, mostly men, felt they were being expelled and exiled from the community, and many moved away. In some families, teenage children were disfellowshipped and their families, attempting to maintain spiritual purity, asked them to leave the family home and reside elsewhere.

The origin of the "Lost Boys" is found in this movement. This group of young men sued for loss of beneficial interests as beneficiaries of the UEP trust. The trust, reorganized in the late 1980s, refused to respond to the suit, and the "Lost Boys" won by default. However, the attorney general of Utah asked the court to rule that failure of the UEP board to defend the trust property constituted a breach of fiduciary responsibility and to place the UEP in receivership. The court agreed. The receiver, Bruce Wisan, replaced the board of trustees. By that time, Jeffs encouraged his followers to begin building communities in Texas, Colorado, and South Dakota.

The loss of the UEP devastated the community. Under Wisan's receivership, the community has suffered serious economic setbacks in businesses as well as residential property. The First Ward continues to assert the UEP as a religious trust rather than a business trust. Wisan, they claim, is assisting the state in destroying the community.

Second Ward Views

In 1985, Second Ward residents purchased 960 acres of land south of Colorado City. They began work on a new high school and community center. Later, some residents began to build homes on the property. On September 26, 1986 (the centennial celebration of the 1886 revelation to John Taylor), J. Marion Hammon dedicated the land as a new intentional fundamentalist community named Centennial Park.

The tension over authority and individuality impacted the reorganization of the First and Second Ward as communities. The more the First Ward embraced a doctrine of unquestioned obedience, or what some negatively referred to as "totalization of outlook," the more the Second Ward embraced the importance of personal choice and responsibility, including wider freedom of exploration and expression. Some members even allowed their youth to attend religious services of other denominations in order to appreciate their own theology. The priesthood sermons often ended with the admonition to "think about it" and less often with "you must do it."

One point of diversion between the two communities concerns the status of women. Family unity and harmony are highly important and continue to be stressed by the leadership. However, one woman said, "I could not breathe as a woman until the [Centennial Park movement] was called." Admittedly members of a conservative patriarchal society, many women felt repressed during the period from 1935 to 1970. Beginning from the 1960s to the mid-1980s, that feeling gradually evolved until the 1984 Split. By that time, two philosophies were extant in Colorado City. The First Ward postulates that a woman should obey her priesthood head in all things. The Second Ward philosophy holds that a woman obeys her husband or father only as he obeys Christ, a doctrine first enunciated by Joseph Smith. Women are just as accountable for their actions and decisions as men. No woman must follow her husband blindly.

Second Ward families, like families everywhere, are concerned that their children embrace the values that have defined their community. The period immediately following the Split was dedicated to a renewal of faith and commitment to the historical goals of the Priesthood Council. New apostles were called to guide the community.

Their commitment to formal education and their wider involvement in mainstream culture led the Second Ward in different paths from their First Ward relatives. The Second Ward people constructed a new building for the Colorado City Academy, their private high school. They organized a public charter school, named Masada Charter School, a K-9 school with about 400 students enrolled. The Colorado City public school system, a K-12 school, continued serving students in the area. It has about 400 students enrolled.

Social and Cultural Contrasts

The Split impacted the social structure and culture of the two communities. This is readily apparent in statistics reflecting the age of first marriage. Agrarian societies around the globe overwhelmingly prefer early marriage. A cultural survival of this practice can still be found in state laws that allow young women (with parental consent) to marry as early as age 16. Until recently, when Utah and Texas changed their statutes, a young woman was allowed to marry as early as 14 years of age. In New Hampshire the age is 13, the youngest in the United States.

During the Depression of the 1930s and into the 1940s, early marriage among fundamentalists was common, with 14 to 16 being the age of first marriage among women and 16 to 18 among men. The Priesthood Council was not particularly pleased with this custom, and during the 1960s and 1970s encouraged young women to complete high school before marrying. Hence the age at marriage changed to 18–19 for young women, and 19–21 for men.

The Second Ward marriage statistics reflect this trend, as most young women complete high school and begin a college education before marriage.

The age of marriage ranges from 19–21 for young women and 21–27 for young men, who complete a work mission of three years and begin a college degree or vocational career. Some earlier marriages occur, but the leadership does not encourage the practice due to pressures from state officials; and, more important, they want young people to be committed to the religion before marriage. In our research, we found one recent marriage of a girl, 17, to a 27-year-old man, a first and legal marriage for both. Additionally, two teenagers, 15 and 16 years old, separately asked for the Brethren to marry them, only to be told they were too young and to wait until they were of legal age.

No discussion would be complete without an examination of the practice of plural marriage among these communities. The media have portrayed a community where young girls are forced to marry elderly men and young men are "run off" to reduce competition for available women. Our investigation has not confirmed this practice. The mean number of years between a man's first marriage and his entering "the Principle," or a second marriage, is about 10 years. On average, most men become polygamists in their thirties and have only two wives or "mothers." Since the 1990s, only about one-third to one-half of households are polygamous. For a man to enter "the Principle," the other wives should give their consent. A great deal of thought, prayer, and discussion is given to first and plural marriages. Among the Second Ward, thoughts of force or coercion run counter to their philosophy of agency. As in other matters of their lives, the Will of the Lord is sought through prayer and consultation with religious leaders.

Ascertaining marriage patterns, with any degree of accuracy, among the First Ward has been almost impossible. Based on newspaper reports and conversations with friends associated with the First Ward people in Colorado City, marriages of young (under 18) women do occur. However, it is not at all clear whether these are polygamous marriages, legal marriages, or what age the husbands have been. In our research, early marriage is neither promoted nor common among First Ward membership, as has been asserted in the media. Such early marriages as do occur may only be artifacts of political alliance building. What degree of force or coercion accompanies First Ward marriage has been impossible to determine. Women who have recently authored books claim that this happens, active First Warders adamantly deny it. The disagreement is essentially one of validity and representation and requires a more neutral scholarly investigation.

Another striking difference between the two communities is seen in their views of education. The First Ward tends to de-emphasize formal, classroom-centered education in favor of home-centered and vocational training. Since some women become registered nurses or teachers, college training does occur among them. Degrees among men range from medicine and engineering to education and business.

Both Wards feel that many aspects of mainstream culture are immoral (e.g., X- and R-rated movies, premarital sex, clothing styles). Most members of the communities participate as interested spectators and, at times, disgruntled critics of national and international events. Contemporary fundamentalists are not like the Hutterites, who disapprove of and strive to withdraw from mainstream American culture. Among the Second Ward people, life is to be enjoyed, and they do not hesitate to partake of life's delights (e.g., drinking coffee and alcohol—very un-Mormon things to do; visiting nearby national parks; shopping at the mall; or feasting at all-you-can-eat $12.99 buffets in Mesquite, Nevada). Common dinner topics range from religious issues, current events, entertainment, politics, and changes (good and bad) in American culture, to the benefits of flax seed oil and homeopathic remedies for preventing or treating illnesses.

Aware of the outside world, but at the same time opposed to its evils, many fundamentalists often seek validation from the world. Not ashamed of their beliefs or practices, they actively defended themselves when the media broadcast negative images and sensationalized information of the raid on the Eldorado, Texas, compound. Wives organized a letter-writing campaign, held media interviews, and journeyed to state capitals to testify before legislative committees and courts about the benefits of plural marriage. The Centennial Park Action Committee (CPAC), engaged in dialogue with the two states' attorneys general and established workshops and support groups to deal with abuse. The Second Ward has worked proactively to address social issues as part of their effort to establish an intentional religious community. The First Ward organized two web sites, www.Truth-WillPrevail.com and www.CaptiveFLDSchildren.com, which promote their viewpoint.

Until recently, the First Ward remained relatively mute. Its members may be victims of their own ideological tenets, which stress withdrawal and indifference to the external world. When confronted with forces that demanded a response, they were unprepared. Their inability to respond effectively was further compounded by Warren Jeffs's seemingly relentless purging of potential rivals. Without experienced leadership, the community stalled. The incarceration and conviction of Warren Jeffs left a political void. In the end, the legal takeover of the UEP, combined with leadership problems and efforts to build communities elsewhere, contributed to the near collapse of Colorado City as a dynamic religious community.

Conclusion

In 1986 the Colorado City–Hildale fundamentalist polygamous community divided, primarily along family lines. The two factions, called wards, formed new communities based on each's peculiar vision of the people who began this intentional community. The First Ward people, who interpreted the vision as a collection of related families, became more ultra-orthodox with a single leader assisted by trusted associates lower in authority. Lines of political authority are traced from this single leader, but blur thereafter. There exists no recognized line of succession. Their religious values emphasize strict obedience to the prophet's word.

Although many members of the Second Ward still reside in Colorado City, the Second Ward began a new intentional community, based on their vision of a religious community directed by divinely called and inspired men. Scripturally supported religious doctrines form the basis of community policy. Lines of political authority are drawn from the president of the Priesthood Council, formerly known as the Council of Friends. Policy is set by consensus among the members of the Council. Secondary leaders are men of authority among the members. Succession is determined by seniority of ordination of the Council members.

The relative role of the individual changed as a result of the division. The First Ward members stress strict obedience to the non-negotiable directions of the prophet, while the Second Ward members emphasize personal choice and its resultant responsibility. The passing of Rulon Jeffs enabled his son Warren Jeffs to assume the role of prophet and church leader in the First Ward, as there was no clear line of succession. He set in motion new policies and practices never seen before in Colorado City (e.g., devaluing education and personal choice, stripping wives and family from a man in order to humble him, emphasizing first-cousin marriage). These policies and practices were implemented after the 1984 Split and were never part of Second Ward doctrine.

As noted above, the most remarkable difference between the two wards is their respective positions concerning the importance of priesthood leadership. The Second Warders continued the idea of priesthood authority as a council of apostles, each equal in authority but ranked by seniority of ordination. Opposed to that, the First Warders embraced the "one man doctrine" of there being only one "key holder," who was God's only representative on earth. In time, other values and policies emerged as each community attempted to redefine itself along the lines of the original vision of community and often in opposite terms to each other. Over the last few years, the Second Ward leadership has begun a return to the importance of embracing the long-time Mormon value of obedience to ordinated authority, albeit of one's own will and choice. Harmony and good will continue to be goals of each community. The motivation for the discussion is the community's renewed effort to implement and live according to the tenets found in the philosophy of the United Order and a community of true believers.

The idea of a United Order extends back to the nineteenth century; it is a form of Christian socialism in which everyone shares and tries to assist his or her neighbor in the quest to achieve a higher form of spiritual enlightenment unhindered by material concerns. To achieve this vision, the leadership of both communities teach their members to be less assertive of individuality and to adhere more to harmony and unity in achieving community goals, both of which conform to fundamental Christian ideals.

It remains to be seen how successful the Second Ward leadership will be in steering its membership between the twin and often-competing values of individual choice or agency and the desire to belong to a greater whole. In the end, an unintended consequence of this prolonged introspection may be that the Second Ward is transforming itself from "public secret" into a more open, focused, and thus viable intentional community.

NOTES

We thank the following people for their encouragement, insights, and suggestions: Frieda Beagley, Nelda Beagley, Lara S. Burton, Boyd Dockstader, Melanie Bistline Hammon, Sadie Hinson, Cardell Jacobson, Joseph Thorton (deceased), Dr. Don D. Timpson, and John Williams.

1. Colorado City, Arizona, is one of six polygamous communities found in western North America and northern Mexico. Each community is separately governed and maintains only nominal, if any, contact with each other. The population of Colorado City is listed in the 2000 Census as being around 3,200 but was actually more like around 8,000, with the median age being 12 years old. Many residents have relocated to polygamous communities elsewhere, most notably Eldorado, Texas. Currently there are about 6,500 people living in and around Colorado City. Unlike nineteenth-century Mormonism, where an estimated 10 to 20 percent of the families were polygynous (Lawrence Foster, *Women, Family and Utopia*, Syracuse: University of Syracuse Press, 1992), in 1996, more than 45 percent (158 out of 350 Colorado City families) form a polygynous household. Because people practice Big House polygamy, as opposed to each wife having her own house, the houses range in size from three-bedroom mobile trailers to huge 35,000-square-foot mansions that are in various stages of completion or renovation.

2. Louis Kern, "Communal and Utopian Impulses Are as Old as American History," in *Women in Spiritual and Communitarian Societies in the United States*, eds. W. Chmielewski, Louis Kern, and Marlyn Klee-Hartzell (Syracuse: Syracuse University Press, 1993), 201–220.

3. L. Sargent, "Dreams and Other Products of Nineteenth-Century Communities," in *Intentional Communities* (Rutledge MO), No.90 (1996): 165–171.

4. Ibid.

5. Kern, "Communal and Utopian Impulses."

6. Sargent, "Dreams."

7. *Doctrine and Covenants*, Sec. 13.

8. *Doctrine and Covenants*, Sec. 27; B. H. Roberts, *A Comprehensive History of the Church of Jesus Christ of Latter-Day Saints* (Provo, Utah: Brigham Young University Press, 1957).

9. *Doctrine and Covenants*, Sec. 84: 63–64.

10. Joseph W. Musser, *Journal of Joseph W. Musser*, unpublished manuscript.

11. *Doctrine and Covenants*, Sec. 107.

12. *Doctrine and Covenants*, Sec. 107: 8–9.

13. *Doctrine and Covenants*, Sec. 107: 64.

14. Musser, *Journal*.

15. Joseph W. Musser, ed., "Statement of Lorin C. Woolley, 1929," *Truth Magazine* 14 (1948): 149–152.

16. Musser, *Journal*.

17. Musser, "Statement of Lorin C. Woolley, 1929," 149–152.

18. C. Hardy, *Solemn Covenant: The Mormon Polygamous Passage* (Urbana and Chicago: University of Illinois Press, 1992).

19. Ibid.

20. Ibid.

21. Benjamin Bistline,*The Polygamists: A History of Colorado City* (Self published, Ogden Kraut Publisher [UT], 2004).

22. Hardy, *Solemn Covenant;* Paul Bohannan, *All the Happy Families* (New York: McGraw-Hill, 1985).

23. The issues between the fundamentalists and the LDS Church go beyond just plural marriage and include other fundamental doctrines of Mormonism. For additional information on these differences see Joseph W. Musser, *A Priesthood Issue* (Truth Publishing Co.), 5:179–89 (1 January 1940) Salt Lake City, UT.

24. Martha Sonntag Bradley, *Kidnapped from That Land: The Government Raids on the Short Creek Polygamists* (Salt Lake City: University of Utah Press, 1993). 110.

25. Joseph F. Smith, *Teachings of the Prophet Joseph Smith* (American Fork, Utah: Covenant Communications, 1976), 83–84).

26. Bistline, *Polygamists*.

27. Ibid.

28. Ibid.

29. Ibid.

30. Ibid.

31. Ibid.

32. There are more than 8,000 people, including 2,000 children, who live in 186 of the more established North American intentional communities (1990 Dictionary of Intentional Communities). One hundred forty-two of those groups are rural, or have rural and urban sites.

33. Bistline, *Polygamists.*

34. T. Earle, *How Chiefs Come to Power: The Political Economy of Prehistory* (Stanford, CA: Stanford University Press, 1997).

35. Bistline, *Polygamists.*

36. Ibid.

37. Ibid.

38. Ibid.

39. Ibid.

40. Ibid.

41. Ibid.

42. Ibid.

43. Fred M. Jessop fostered close ties with the offspring of one of the community's most prominent founders, John Y. Barlow. He favored the sons of Martha, his sister, whose eight sons came to be called "the sons of the prophet." In time, they came to dominate positions within the town. As youths, the Barlows lived with Fred Jessop. Due to the Barlows' lineage—offspring of the respected John Y. Barlow—Fred Jessop was able to borrow status from this affiliation with the "sons of the prophet." The affiliation between the Barlow sons and Fred Jessop proved to be mutually beneficial as Jessop moved strongly into a position of power within the community. In time, through Fred Jessop's assistance, they would occupy important leadership positions in the town. They controlled the Colorado City Improvement Association, a shadow corporation that owned several buildings in the community leased to the school and other agencies.

44. The sermons of LeRoy S. Johnson were published from Colorado City, Arizona, but no publisher is noted. Documents in possession of Heber B. Hammon.

45. Bistline, *The Polygamists.*

46. Ibid.

47. *Doctrine and Covenants,* Sec. 132: 7.

48. Joseph W. Musser, ed., "Four Hidden Relevations," *Truth Magazine* 14 (1948): 145.

49. Bistline, *Polygamists.*

50. Ibid.

51. Ibid.

52. Ibid.

53. Ibid.

54. J. Bowen, *Religion in Practice: An Anthropological Approach to the Anthropology of Religion* (Boston: Allyn and Bacon, 2002).

55. Ibid.

Chapter 3

Twenty Years of Observations about the Fundamentalist Polygamists

Ken Driggs

Over the past 20 years, I have forged friendships with and personally observed members of the Fundamentalist Church of Jesus Christ of Latter-Day Saints (FLDS). During this time, I have enjoyed extensive contact with both the leadership and the members of the FLDS community, headquartered in Colorado City, Arizona, and Hildale, Utah. I have become intimately aware of their worship, teachings, and family and community life.

I approach this subject as a sixth-generation member of the Church of Jesus Christ of Latter-Day Saints (LDS) with two generations of polygamy on my family tree.[1] I am also a criminal defense lawyer with an interest in how cultural minorities are treated in the courts, and I have a graduate degree in legal history with an emphasis on the experience of the FLDS.[2] My association with the FLDS began in the late 1980s. I happened to view a couple of television programs about the FLDS. Since I had grown up in the South, not Utah, I had not even heard of this group.[3] The programs sparked my interest and I determined to find out about them.

Historically called Short Creek, the twin communities of Colorado City and Hildale are located just off Arizona Highway 389 on the Arizona Strip, an area of high desert cut off from the rest of the state by the Grand Canyon. It is beautiful country. The nearest cities of any size are St. George and Hurricane, Utah.

My desire to learn more about the FLDS people led me to Colorado City on January 2, 1988. I showed up uninvited and was turned over to Mayor Dan Barlow,[4] a son of the late John Y. Barlow.[5] Mayor Barlow introduced me to his brother Sam Barlow. These initial meetings began a long friendship with the brothers and their families.

Later that year I began working on a master of law degree (LL.M.) at the University of Wisconsin. My major professor, Dr. Dirk Hartog,[6] suggested a thesis about a mean-spirited 1955 Utah Supreme Court decision terminating the parental rights of a Short Creek plural wife named Vera Black, *In re Black,* 283 P.2d 887 (Utah 1955). I threw myself into the project, locating Vera and her children for interviews through Sam and Dan. This brought about a long-term friendship with Vera's extended family.

My associations with the community grew when Dixie State College president Doug Adler invited me to speak about my research on polygamy at the college's January 1990 Statehood Day—commemorating Utah's admission as the 45th state on January 4, 1896.[7] Dixie State College is located in St. George, Utah, relatively close to the FLDS communities. I was surprised by the number of the normally reclusive fundamentalist Mormons who were in attendance at my presentation. (The FLDS are easily identified by their dress.) In the next few days, several FLDS men and women made it a point to introduce themselves to me as I visited the Short Creek area. Some even wanted me to meet their families. Many of my closest Short Creek friendships flow from that Dixie College appearance.

Over the next few years my circle of fundamentalist Mormon contacts spread to other fundamentalist Mormon groups outside of the FLDS. These included the late Owen Allred, leader of the Apostolic United Brethren (AUB).[8] Another is Marianne Thompson Watson, a University of Utah history graduate and AUB member who has published her history.[9] I also worked with attorneys representing FLDS interests,[10] including three times when I was retained as an expert witness—although one St. George judge refused to allow my testimony.[11]

Since the uninvited visit in 1988, I have visited fundamentalist Mormons, especially the FLDS, all over the West. I have attended their religious services and funerals, discussed history and belief with them, was given access to historically important documents, and at times informally advised them. More important, I slept in their homes, ate at their dinner tables, played with their children, and watched them grow up. I photographed family and community gatherings, and in general have been invited into much of their day-to-day lives.

The reader should know that with such intimate exposure comes friendship and appreciation. I do not agree with many of their beliefs and customs, and I'm sure they would not make the choices I do. I do not see them as sinister and, based on my own observations, I reject the stereotypes and collective condemnation that have often been leveled at them. In the words of sociologist Thomas F. O'Dea, "I have striven throughout to combine intellectual objectivity with intelligent human sympathy."[12]

The April 2008 raid on the Yearning for Zion (YFZ) Ranch outside Eldorado, Texas, renewed my interest in the group—and did so dramatically. I had never been to Eldorado, but I followed news accounts of its development and viewed images posted on the Internet. I was especially interested in the building of the first FLDS Temple, which looked surprisingly like the main LDS Church's 1877 St. George, Utah, Temple.[13] I participated in numerous news interviews about the FLDS, many of which started with some stunning misinformation from reporters and so-called experts. Because of this rampant lack of awareness and misunderstanding, I have decided to bend my personal rule about not discussing what I learned through being invited into the personal lives of my FLDS friends. What follows are my personal observations about the fundamentalists, specifically the FLDS community.[14]

The Physical Community at Short Creek

Short Creek was the original name of the town that is now the adjacent towns of Hildale, Utah and Colorado City, Arizona. It is a mile or mile and a half long stream bed running out of the Vermillion Cliffs, through the two towns, and then into the high desert south of the community. It is dry the majority of the year. The area was first settled by Europeans in 1912, when Mormon cattle rancher Jacob Lauritzen arrived in the area. He built the first water ditch, a three-mile undertaking from a nearby canyon. He later brought in his wife and seven children and his brother-in-law. A 1914 Utah government publication described Short Creek: "a small settlement is being built up there, which has a school and post office. It is on the proposed Yellowstone-Grand Canyon highway, and dry farms from 'Dixie' to Kanab."[15]

Fundamentalist Mormons first arrived in Short Creek in 1935, when about 40 families moved to the area.[16] The appeal of the site was its remoteness; it was viewed as a "refuge for the Saints."[17] The community was so isolated that power lines were not brought into the community until 1959.[18] It took three more years for the road between Hurricane and Short Creek to be paved.

In 1963 a University of Utah graduate student visited the community and attempted interviews but found no one willing to talk to him. He counted 31 houses and 8 mobile homes on the Utah side, and another 25 homes and 6 mobile homes on the Arizona side.[19]

Physical Presentation and Dress

FLDS people have a distinctive dress that makes them stand out, especially the women.[20] Faithful men do not wear beards and always have short hair.[21] Faithful women do not cut their hair, do not wear makeup or jewelry, and generally adopt a distinctive old fashioned hairstyle. Much of this is not by edict but by community custom. I have known women in good standing in the community who wore some makeup and jewelry, who wore pants, cut and styled their hair, and did not follow the prevailing customs. These included people in polygamous families. I have never, however, seen a visible tattoo or body piercing on an active FLDS member.

The late FLDS prophet Leroy Johnson had little tolerance for the popular fashion of larger society. He was distressed that "the daughters of Zion would walk the streets of our great and glorious city of Salt Lake as harlots; and you will not be able to tell the face of a Saint from a Gentile." He frequently preached against long hair on men and said "the women's hair is her glory...and there are certain ordinances of the Priesthood that she will need beautiful hair in order to perform."[22]

From the time of Joseph Smith, the main LDS Church has used undergarments now referred to as "temple garments." Their use is considered a measure of religious devotion, a commitment to modesty, and the wearer has, in the past, been promised protection from physical danger while wearing them.[23] Over the years the garments used by the LDS Church have undergone considerable change, covering less of the body.[24]

In August 1936 Joseph W. Musser challenged the LDS temple garment design changes and temple ordinance practice adopted by the LDS Church. *Truth,* the monthly fundamentalist magazine, acknowledged "[t]his is a delicate subject" because the "nature of the ceremonies pertaining to Endowments, is such to preclude an exposition of them through public print..." Observing generally that there had been changes in both temple ordinances, in the interest of time, and in the cut of garments, in the interest of fashion, *Truth* wrote of "the displeasure the Lord feels toward" the LDS Church leaders who initiated these changes.[25]

Fundamentalist Mormons consider these changes to be a retreat from the modesty originally taught to Mormons, and an example of the LDS Church's compromise with the world. They refer to their religious undergarments as "priesthood garments" and believe the proper cut extends to the wrist and ankles, and includes a collar, in the style of garments used by the LDS Church until as late as 1920. Because of this older style cut, FLDS dress always involves long sleeves and shirts buttoned at the collar for men and long dresses, high collars, and long sleeves for women. These garments are considered sacred, and I have observed some discomfort in FLDS members whom I was photographing while they had their sleeves rolled up working in the kitchen or yard, revealing some of the white of their garments. These garments are worn by FLDS children as well as adults. It is common to see little girls playing in "prairie dresses" with long pants underneath them.

When Warren Jeffs and his traveling party were arrested by a Nevada highway patrolman in August 2006, he was not wearing dress that conformed to such "priesthood garments."[26] This caused considerable comment among fundamentalist Mormons with whom I spoke.

In the aftermath of the YFZ raid in April 2008, there was some puzzlement in the press about the community's disdain for red clothing or decoration. One of the Mormon sacred texts is the *Doctrine and Covenants,* in which one section describes the return of Christ the Savior, who would be clothed in red.[27] At some point FLDS prophet Rulon Jeffs had recommended that his flock not use red out of respect for the Savior, and it became one of the customs of the community.

Women, Marriage, and Families

For me, one of the most inaccurate and offensive aspects of media coverage of the raid on the YFZ Ranch was the portrayal of women. It is true that, as Martha Bradley put it, "The powerful male world of fundamentalist Mormonism does not exist without the supportive and obedient female."[28] However, "obedient" can be a loaded term. It should not be read as pliant.

During the YFZ events in Texas, an FLDS woman named Maggie Jessop published a column in the *Salt Lake Tribune* under the headline "I am an FLDS woman and I am entitled to the same rights as you."[29] Her indignation was evident from the beginning of her essay:

> So, you want to hear from the FLDS women, huh? OK, you asked for it. However, I may not have it within my psychological or emotional capacity to communicate appropriately due to the widespread "fact" that I belong to an uneducated, underprivileged, information-deprived, brainless, spineless, poor, picked on, dependent, misled class of women identified as "brain-washed." But, I'll give it my best shot.

Jessop further observed, "If someone is different, people get suspicious, perhaps even jealous, and assume the worst." She then commented, "I used to think anyone in this country was innocent until proven guilty, but, no, I am guilty because the media and the government and the religious bigots think or say or hear or suspect I am immoral and abusive. Good grief!"

Maggie Jessop sounds like women I have often encountered among the FLDS. Many have strong personalities. They are not people who are going to be easily pushed around by anyone, including husbands or prophets. I encountered several college-educated women, including some whose college education was paid for by church leadership to meet community needs. They were articulate, well spoken, thoughtful, and committed to an FLDS life.

I watched the CNN interviews with a group of FLDS women whose children had been taken in the Texas raid. I had the same reaction most viewers probably did, that they came across as terrified and not very independent. But these were people without much media experience, and their children had just been ripped from them; nevertheless, I couldn't help but reflect on the many FLDS women I knew who would have presented much stronger, more assertive personalities.

Regarding marriage practices, one young woman explained to me that when a woman reached an age at which marriage was appropriate, her "priesthood head," usually a father but possibly other men in that role, would "turn her in to the priesthood." At that point the prophet would determine a suitable mate, who would be presented to her. I was told that both the prospective husband and wife had a right of refusal, but there are social pressures which might compromise that right.[30] This form of arranged marriage is called "placement marriage." Some couples I know who were faithful and committed to the community left me with the strong impression that they would always be monogamous.

It was apparent from my firsthand observation that some brides were 16 or 17, but I did not observe it to be the norm. I personally knew of only one marriage to a 14-year-old, and that took place in the 1950s. Other leaders told me that the community kept track of family relationships to avoid incestuous relationships. Willie Jessop, who has recently been the public spokesman for Warren Jeffs in church leadership matters, has pledged that they will now comply with state laws on underage brides. Other fundamentalist Mormon groups have generally disavowed such marriages.[31] I remember talking with a group of FLDS young women about how the law may regulate these marriages, saying that I believed plural marriages to "minors" did not have any legal protection. One married woman in her early twenties, a plural wife, asked me "What is a minor?" When I explained, she responded, "I guess I was a minor." I do believe that some in the community do not understand such lines drawn by the law.

On coming of age, young men prepare themselves for marriage. A leader in the community under Rulon Jeffs explained "work missions" to me: young men went out into the world to work, turning most or all of their income over to the church. Upon their return they were assigned a United Effort Plan (UEP) lot to build on and a "worthy wife." Most outsiders view these "arranged" marriages as offensive and counter to our culture's expectations of individual freedom.

In 2008 I was interviewed for a program on MSNBC on mind control. The premise of the program seemed to be that there were no independent minds among the FLDS, that all had been brainwashed by a closed cult, had been isolated from the outside world since birth, and were incapable of making decisions for themselves. Thus, they all needed to be rescued by a more enlightened larger society. The premise was that there was a near complete lack of free will and access to the larger world, which is preposterous based on my observations. I regard that theory as ridiculous. It ran completely contrary to my own observations.

At one point after the 2008 Texas raid, authorities suggested that a great many of the seized children showed signs of violent physical abuse. They quickly seemed to retreat from this. I have been around a great many small children with their parents and cannot recall seeing a child spanked even once. Generally, little kids seemed comfortable with me and did not hesitate to play with me. I have watched many of those children grow up. I have seen nothing that even hints at a culture of physical child abuse, or evidence that children were taught to fear all non-FLDS people.

Another issue in the news involves the so-called "Lost Boys." "Lost Boys" is the term applied to young men supposedly expelled by the FLDS in great numbers in order to free up potential young wives for the older patriarchs who run the community.[32] I have no doubt that some young men have left the community, or perhaps have been kicked out by their parents for acts that were viewed as rebellious. I think that is inevitable in any socially conservative community with strict behavior norms, be they Seventh-day Adventist, Southern Baptist, Amish, or Latter-Day Saint. However, I think the numbers routinely reported for the FLDS are wildly exaggerated. I have never observed such a thing and do not accept that adolescent males are cast out by older patriarchs in order to free up young girls for plural families.

Schools and Education

I know many FLDS members who are college educated, both men and women. They are not art history or poetry majors, however; education is approached in very practical terms.

Colorado City has a public school system, funded by Utah and Arizona. However, in 2000, Warren Jeffs, speaking on behalf of his father, counseled their flock to pull their children out of public school. Enrollments dropped dramatically and children were educated in a series of church-affiliated academies or were homeschooled.[33] I toured some of those academies and know women who taught in them. I was told that the move came about because they objected to curriculum limitations imposed by the state. Mayor Dan Barlow told the *Salt Lake Tribune*, "The [public] schools have been reducing enrollment for several years as people have taken on the responsibility of educating their children." Close observers outside the community suggested to me that a major motivation was internal disputes, that many paid school employees had withdrawn from the FLDS and were considered irritants.[34]

One of my FLDS friends, an elementary school teacher, described how she got her college degree. She became a plural wife at a relatively young age and had a number of children as part of a large family. It happens to be a family with strong women, where the daughters generally struck me as assertive, independent personalities. The community's leadership decided they needed college-trained school teachers to meet their needs. My friend and some others were offered the opportunity to have their college expenses paid by the FLDS if they would become teachers. Some of my friend's children were still young and at home, but she was not worried about their welfare; her sister wives took care of them during the weeks while she was away at Southern Utah University in Cedar City, Utah. She came home on the weekends. At college she shared an apartment with other women from the community who had also been called on these education missions. It worked out well for my friend, and she was delighted at the opportunity to get an education while serving her community. She taught first in one of the public schools and later in one of the private academies near her home.

I have heard similar stories about other FLDS college graduates. The community has a doctor and more than one dentist who got their degrees in this way. The understanding for all was that they would return to the community and share their newly acquired talents.

In 1991 the FLDS tried to establish Barlow University, which they hoped would attract fundamentalist Mormons and religious conservatives of all stripes, but it did not last long. The late Louis Barlow, then administrator and a friend of mine, claimed 200 students when the university opened, and he had ambitious future plans.[35] I toured the two-story building that housed it and found it to be more vocational school than anything, but with a heavy emphasis on computer skills. Mohave Community College also has a substantial branch campus located in Colorado City.

Church Meetings

Until recently, the main public worship service among the FLDS was a two-hour Sunday afternoon gathering, similar to LDS sacrament meetings. Between 1988 and 2003, I attended 20 or 25 such meetings both in Colorado City and at the Alta Academy in the Salt Lake Valley.

The Johnson meeting hall in Colorado City looks like a very large LDS ward building, complete with the combined main seating area and recreational space with a curtained performance stage at one end and speaker's podium at the other. It has ample balcony seating. Classrooms and offices surround the main meeting hall. One wall has a large mural of historic Lee's Ferry on the Colorado River, where Johnson grew up.

Their religious meetings are generally not open to the public. I always made arrangements in advance when I attended. If I walked into the building unescorted, I would be intercepted by ushers, who always seemed to know who I was once I introduced myself. Once I figured out the customary dress, I tried to present myself in conformity with that, but I have a beard, which made me stand out. On a few occasions I was introduced from the stand, which I took as a kind of signal to members that I was trustworthy.

Attendance at Colorado City ranges from about 1,500 to 2,500. I was told the meeting hall could seat about 5,000. The more modest Alta Academy generally included several hundred worshippers. Meetings always started and ended promptly. They were quiet and orderly, much more so than my LDS wards. Rarely did I hear fussy children, even though they surrounded me.

Members of the LDS Church would find these meetings familiar but different. Worshippers would sit in the same metal folding chairs that any LDS member will be familiar with. A choir would sing some traditional LDS hymns, while the congregation sang most, using the green hymnals published by the main LDS church. Both men and women would speak, although decidedly more men. Opening and closing prayers were always delivered by men. Joseph Smith, Brigham Young, and other historic Mormon prophets would be quoted. Most speakers would bear their testimonies, usually without knowing in advance that they would be called upon to speak, but they were mostly from the same cluster of men in leadership roles. Talks would draw from the four LDS standard works—the Bible, the Book of Mormon, the Doctrine and Covenants, and the Pearl of Great Price—along with the sermons of Leroy Johnson and Rulon Jeffs. Testimonials of the leadership and the religious importance of plural marriage were usually part of these talks. The 1953 Short Creek Raid would often be spoken of as evidence that they were God's chosen people and would always have their faith tested by persecution. (I am certain the April 2008 Texas raid will have an even greater importance in the folklore of the FLDS community.)

The Sacrament was not administered as in LDS or AUB Sacrament meetings.[36] The prophet was in attendance at every Sunday afternoon meeting I attended. He conducted but rarely spoke. At the conclusion of the meeting, the custom was for the congregation to line up and greet their leader, usually shaking hands, on the stand. This could take an hour.

The last such meeting I attended was December 1, 2002, after Rulon Jeffs' death. The meeting was conducted by a very frail 92-year-old Fred Jessop, a counselor in Rulon Jeffs' administration. Mayor Dan Barlow was the first speaker and testified to his belief that Warren Jeffs was the next prophet. Next Warren Jeffs asked a woman, identified as Naomi, a widow of Rulon Jeffs, to speak. A very attractive blond in her mid- to late twenties, she began by testifying that "I am nothing without the priesthood." She reported marrying Rulon Jeffs in 1993 and that it was his wish that she marry Warren Jeffs after his passing. The FLDS believe this is a biblical custom. Finally, Fred Jessop spoke, also testifying to Warren Jeffs'calling as prophet.

One of the oddest things to me was a large group of young women seated in the congregation in a block directly in front of the speakers. Each wore identical sky-blue traditional dresses with identical hair styles. I guessed about a hundred were in the group. They were not addressed or explained in any way that I detected. I had never seen that before. The meeting concluded with the usual line of worshippers filing by Jeffs and the other leaders on the stand, shaking hands, myself among them.

Formerly, the FLDS also conducted a kind of combined worship and community meeting on Saturday mornings, also in the Johnson meeting hall. After opening prayer the local bishop, the late Fred Jessop when I attended, would discuss community work that needed to be completed and would make assignments. Drainage ditches needed to be cleaned, the many green irrigated city parks needed to be maintained, the small community zoo needed work, homes needed repair, water master Joe Jessop, Jr., needed help with wells, and generally the community needed to be kept up. These tasks would be assigned, mixed in with religious messages.

Larger community projects would also be coordinated in such meetings. When fire destroyed one of the town's main employers, a cabinet factory, the community quickly repaired the plant in order to meet production requirements. At another time the community pitched in together to build the "24-hour house," a large two-family home that was built from the ground to completion in a single round-the-clock day.

Priesthood and seminary meetings for the youth were conducted at other times. Sunday school was generally conducted in individual homes. They have their own church seminary program of religious instruction for high school age young people, using modified LDS Church materials.

Public meetings were suspended when Utah and Arizona authorities began arresting men for polygamy-related crimes, culminating in the indictment of Warren Jeffs, followed by the offer of a $10,000 reward for information leading to his capture.[37]

An FLDS Journal of Discourses

In the nineteenth century the teachings of LDS leaders were recorded by clerks and published in a series called the *Journal of Discourses,* which included sermons from 1852 to 1885. In a pre-electronic media age, such a series gave rank-and-file members access to the teachings of their leaders. The series fell out of use, in part because the LDS Church came to disavow some of the teachings they contained. Fundamentalist Mormons used their monthly magazine, *Truth,* to reproduce many of those problematic sermons and in the 1950s republished the *Journal of Discourses.*[38]

Similarly, fundamentalist Mormons recorded the sermons of their leaders. In the 1980s the FLDS published a typescript series with the teachings of Leroy S. Johnson and a few by John Y. Barlow.[39] The custom was continued with the sermons of Johnson's successor, Rulon T. Jeffs.[40] The sermons of Jeffs' son and successor, Warren Jeffs, have likewise been recorded and no doubt will be published in the same way, if they have not been already. I have heard tape recordings and seen typed transcripts of his sermons. These volumes can be found in just about every FLDS home. It is common for FLDS members to listen to audio tapes and other recordings of the sermons of their leaders.[41]

The UEP and the Division of the Community

Fundamentalist Mormons not only saw Short Creek as a refuge from criminal prosecution, but also as a place to restore United Order living. The United Order was a generic name for the varied forms of religious communalism practiced by Mormon pioneers in Utah Territory but discarded in the twentieth century.[42] However, during the 1930s, the largely poor fundamentalists were feeling the pressure of the Great Depression. The ravages of the Depression made a return to some kind of United Order attractive.[43]

As early as 1936, the community decided "to organize a Co-operative enter-prize [sic] according to the laws of the land and work under direction of the Higher Priesthood body."[44] In October 1936 a Declaration of Trust was filed in the Mohave County Courthouse in Kingman establishing the United Effort Trust. The trust held title to a sawmill, some farm equipment, and land given "for the purpose of building up the Kingdom of God" through the building of a physical economic community.[45] The group had earlier begun experimenting with a services exchange.[46]

There were constant interpersonal conflicts with living the United Order, but it continued into the 1940s, when it was finally dissolved. After a year of deliberation a new trust was organized in November 1942 as the United Effort Plan (UEP). In 1942 the UEP was to be administered by not less than three nor more than nine trustees, initially consisting of John Y. Barlow, Joseph W. Musser, Leroy Johnson, Marion Hammon, and the accountant Rulon T. Jeffs. The trust instrument provided that "[t]he purpose and object of the trust shall first be charitable and philanthropic, its operations to be governed in a tru [sic] spirit of brotherhood" through "all kinds of legiti-mate business ventures."[47] Hammon had recently arrived to the community with a new group of fundamentalists and was appointed manager of UEP properties.

The UEP survived the 1953 Short Creek raid (see chapter 1 in this vol-ume) and the generation of fear that followed. The community was further tested, severely, by internal divisions. As Leroy Johnson aged, his leadership was challenged by Marion Hammon and Alma Timpson, resulting in a split in the community. That break was complete on May 13, 1984, when followers of Hammon and Timpson held their first separate priesthood meeting, which Brian Hales called "an alternative organization." On September 27, 1986, they dedicated a meeting hall of their own.[48] They came to be known commonly as the Second Ward (though the leaders prefer the term "The Work") and began building a nearby new community called Centennial Park City, which, by 2003, had nearly 2,000 people.[49]

The Community Today

In the last 20 years, the United States census reflects significant growth in the overwhelmingly FLDS communities of Colorado City, Arizona, and Hildale, Utah. The census web site put the population of Colorado City at 2,426 in 1990, 3,334 in 2000, and 4,807 in 2007. Hildale was found to be 1,325 in 1990, 1,895 in 2000, and 1,982 in 2007. The total of both communities was 3,751 in 1990, 5,229 in 2000, and 6,789 in 2007. See chapter 6 in this volume for a more detailed demographic description of the community.

Today the community is aggressively irrigated and dotted with green parks and playgrounds. Large communal agricultural plots are spread around the community with families assigned portions for growing crops. A dairy operation is located in the center of town. A small shopping district has developed, which includes a gasoline station–convenience store, a large general store, small cafes, and some light industry. A newer commercial district has sprung up on either side of Arizona Highway 389. A nearby high school and two elementary schools in town have mostly fallen into disuse. All of this is nestled amidst some breathtaking scenery of red rock and high desert.

The Internal Debate in FLDS

I believe that throughout fundamentalist Mormon history, and especially among the FLDS, there has been internal debate about engagement with the outside world. Should the religious community retreat into their own bubble, withdrawing from the outside world? After all, fundamentalist Mormons accuse the LDS Church of selling out to the outside world, of compromising doctrine and sacred practices in the interest of acceptance, status, and getting out from under legal pressure. Additionally, from their perspective, the outside world has often persecuted them and has made little effort to understand their beliefs and culture.

In the time I have been going to Colorado City, that isolation has changed dramatically. There are now signs on the highway identifying the town and paved roads into it. A small motel,[50] the Mark Twain Restaurant, a franchised oil change business, a branch bank, a convenience store–gas station–fast food combination, and other businesses all sprang up on both sides of the highway. All recognize that money is money, whether it comes from the pockets of the FLDS or the non-believing tourist. The town even constructed a small airport, with government matching funds, to meet its needs.[51]

In May 1992 the Mormon History Association (MHA) held their annual meeting in St. George. It brought one of the largest turnouts MHA had ever enjoyed, including some FLDS members. A bus tour of the old Short Creek was arranged. So many participants signed up that three buses were chartered, each with an FLDS representative and historian guide. I was one of those guides. The groups toured major public buildings and sites. One stop at the fire station included cookies and lemonade. It represented a significant reaching out by the FLDS and reflected their growing confidence.

By the 1990s fundamentalist Mormonism all over the West were feeling more comfortable in an increasingly tolerant world. The *Salt Lake Tribune* called the 1990s "something of a golden era for Colorado City and polygamists in general."[52] A *New York Times* reporter wrote "they have begun a virtual public relations campaign to achieve tolerance, respect, a greater following, and ultimately legal protection. They are speaking at university forums, granting interviews to reporters and forming alliances with groups they once condemned."[53] Even the LDS Church–owned *Deseret News* reported in 1991 that "[f]or the most part, polygamists are a law-abiding, quiet lot who don't flaunt their violation of state law and so aren't bothered by legal authorities."[54] A 1994 *Arizona Highways* writer observed that "today, with a hotel and restaurant, Colorado City has decided to live with the outside world instead of fearing it. It seems like a town sure enough of the good in its lifestyle to be able to withstand alternatives displayed by passersby."[55]

Dan Barlow was mayor of Colorado City from its incorporation until his abrupt resignation and excommunication by Warren Jeffs in January 2003. The *Deseret News* noted that Mayor Barlow's "gentle nature and friendly style endeared him to many outsiders, and he often served as a spokesman for the FLDS Church."[56] Mayor Barlow often explained to me the need to find employment for the many FLDS young people. He and others recognized that jobs were necessary to the life of the community. Many FLDS commuted to Hurricane and St. George, but there were few jobs near their homes. Barlow understood that education and networking were essential to the success of the community. As mayor he reached out to the larger world, becoming active in Republican politics and small municipality organizations. He learned how to deal with the press and present a non-threatening FLDS face.

Until the administration of Warren Jeffs, the community had been trending toward increased engagement with the outside world. The incorporation of the towns of Hildale and Colorado City, which brought access to state and federal monies, were at the beginnings of that reaching out. The economic growth in the towns and the pursuit of non-FLDS dollars were a direct result of this opening up. Mayor Barlow increased the engagement with the outside world by becoming available to the mass media. It appears this came with the approval of their prophet, Rulon T. Jeffs, a college-educated man who lived most of his life in the Salt Lake City area.

When Warren Jeffs returned to the community, he came down on the side of those who opposed integration with the outside world. Speaking for his elderly father, and then as prophet in his own right, he moved the FLDS away from the outside world. In the name of his father, he urged all FLDS to gather in historic Short Creek. A great many returned from the Salt Lake Valley.

Religious Conflict, Leadership, and the Rise of Warren Jeffs

Leadership of the FLDS has evolved in recent history. In the early 1950s the main body of organized fundamentalist Mormonism split into two groups over a succession dispute. Initially, most of the fundamentalist Mormon world looked for leadership from a seven-member Priesthood Council, with the senior member by ordination calling new members. (There was internal debate as to whether these new callings had to be approved by the Council or could be made unilaterally.) From 1935 until his death on December 29, 1949, the leader was two-time former Mormon missionary John Y. Barlow.[57]

With Barlow's death, Joseph W. Musser, long-time editor of *Truth* magazine (a monthly fundamentalist Mormon magazine published from 1935 to 1956) and the premier intellectual of the movement, would have been next in line. However, Musser was disabled by a series of strokes and wished to designate Rulon Allred, a naturopathic physician, as his successor.[58] The rest of the Priesthood Council refused to follow Musser. By 1952 this impasse resulted in Musser calling an entirely new council. Long-time fundamentalists tell me that less than a third of the community followed the new Musser Priesthood Council and more than two-thirds stayed with the old Council.[59] The old Council eventually looked to Short Creek resident and junior Council member Leroy Johnson as its leader. This group evolved into the FLDS. The Musser group became the Apostolic United Brethren, lead by Allred after Musser's death in 1954.[60]

Under Johnson and, after his death at age 98 in 1986,[61] his successors Rulon Jeffs[62] and Warren Jeffs, the FLDS ceased to maintain a Priesthood Council. They came to recognize a "one man doctrine," which views a single individual as the prophet and presiding officer without checks from a larger body. Most recently, the FLDS has taught that their leader would designate his successor at or near his death.[63]

As late as 1998, Rulon Jeffs lived in a four-acre estate near Salt Lake City, which housed a large home, the Alta Academy school, a nursery, and a church meeting hall. The entire property was valued at $2.9 million. Jeffs reportedly commuted by Lear jet to Colorado City to preside over Church business. The property was sold, however, and he moved with his reported 20 wives to Colorado City amid rumors of a prophesied Book of Revelations–style end of the world during which 2,500 FLDS members would be lifted to heaven. FLDS leaders had often made such end of the world predictions, although Colorado City mayor Dan Barlow has dismissed the rumors.[64]

When Rulon Jeffs died in September 2002, the outside world was not immediately informed that he would be succeeded by his son, Warren Jeffs. The *New York*

Times incorrectly reported that "[h]is death leaves a void in church leadership that could take years to fill." Within the community, the transition was almost immediately understood. While some have dissented, the majority of the FLDS remained loyal to the son, who had been his father's spokesman for a few years.[65]

I have known Warren Jeffs casually since the 1990s, when he was headmaster of the Alta Academy in the Salt Lake Valley. Cable television has portrayed him as a charismatic, controlling figure able to dominate his community by force of will. In my view, the truth could not be much further from that. Jeffs is a rather bland, gangly, stooped, sometimes socially awkward individual. He is, in my opinion, a poor monotone speaker more apt to put you to sleep than hold your rapt attention. He rarely gestures, rarely raises his voice, and never shows any flash. He dresses plainly. He is neither physically nor personally imposing.

That is not to say that Jeffs is not respected in his community. Those who follow him respect him deeply. They believe he is a prophet, chosen by God to lead his community and make intimate decisions for them. He speaks in a religious language that is familiar to the FLDS community. He is respected because of the religious office he holds, not because of his personal qualities. This is the same respect that members of the LDS Church hold for their prophet, whom only a few have ever met. The pope is similarly revered by most Catholics, as are many Protestant leaders by their religious communities. Jeffs, like his father and Leroy Johnson before him, is respected because of who his followers believe him to be. Much of it is pure projection. They believe they should "follow the prophet" and they want to do so for reasons that make sense to them.

To understand this, outsiders must focus on the community, not on individual leaders. Warren Jeffs, however flawed, is the current leader of a religious community that has existed for several generations; it is not the recent creation of a charismatic individual like David Koresh. Thus far, the majority of FLDS have remained loyal to him in spite of his 2007 conviction, concerns about his mental competency, and lengthy prison sentences.[66] In 2010 the Utah Supreme Court unanimously overturned that conviction in a way that makes retrial unlikely.[67] He still has serious charges pending in Texas.

Recent Conflicts

The early conflicts over communalism and the United Effort Plan have continued. This division spilled over into bitter litigation as the majority tried to expel dissenters from UEP property. The dissenters, in turn, argued that their contributions to the UEP over the years were investments, buying shares of UEP stock, while the majority said, no, those were charitable contributions that the donors could not recapture. After a lengthy bench trial, the matter ended up in the Utah Supreme Court. The state supreme court affirmed the essential charitable nature of the UEP but awarded life estates to some of the residents.[68] One result of the suit was that signs sprung up in front of nearly all community businesses and homes identifying them as UEP properties.

In 2004 Brent Jeffs, a nephew of Warren Jeffs, sued the UEP, alleging that Warren Jeffs, Leslie B. Jeffs, and Blaine B. Jeffs had sexually abused him in the 1980s at age five or six.[69] Two years later, Leslie Jeffs and Blaine Jeffs were dropped as defendants.[70] The UEP was also sued in spite of the fact that Warren Jeffs had no official role with the UEP at the time of the alleged sexual assault, though he did at the time of the suit.

Jeffs apparently instructed FLDS lawyers not to answer the suit.[71] Without a response, the plaintiffs would have won by default and all of the UEP's $100 million in assets would have been in jeopardy—including the homes of many FLDS members. The Utah trial court finally acted to protect UEP residents by removing Jeffs and the other trustees and appointing a conservator.[72] There was considerable resistance among UEP residents to the conservator. Gradually the conservator has pushed the UEP to a non-religious nature. Individual residents were given the opportunity to buy their homes outright, effectively withdrawing from the cooperative.[73] By the time of this writing, the UEP takeover was characterized as a "mess" by Utah's attorney general.[74]

Following the takeover, FLDS representatives began purchasing large tracts of land in Texas, which eventually became the Yearning For Zion (YFZ) Ranch, at least 60 acres in Colorado,[75] and 140 acres outside Pringle, South Dakota. *USA Today* reported that the South Dakota community contained less than 200 people on land and buildings worth about $4.5 million.[76] Some who followed the FLDS believed that Jeffs was building a new UEP with his most dedicated followers. I see this branching out as directly connected to the secularizing of the UEP.

A Theory on Reactions to the FLDS

A community of several thousand people is going to have some incidence of domestic violence, of child abuse, of sexual molestation, of ordinary crime. Community leadership is not exempt from this reality of human nature. After a long career as a criminal defense lawyer, I know better than to believe in any perfect society. Additionally, there will always be people who fit the stereotypes of both submissive women and domineering men. Stereotypes do develop from actual types of people.

It is a mistake, however, to seize upon the occasional bad actors, dysfunctional families, or predators as being representative of a community of thousands. It is especially dangerous to make such assumptions about a community that is not ready to open itself up to the leering or the curious. Yet that is what we have done. There may be no greater example of such a sweeping stereotype than the April 2008 Texas CPS raid of the YFZ Ranch.

As a culture, we have a hard time understanding individual or group decisions that we would not make and do not understand. "They must be crazy; they must be enslaved," we think to ourselves. "There is something wrong with this picture." Sometimes we set about defining how they are crazy. They must be brainwashed. They are mentally ill. They are imprisoned. And we are always doing this through our own worldview, adopting the thinking of our personal culture.[77] We did that with gays, once defining homosexuality as deviance and mental illness. Even as this book is being written, our whole country is struggling to understand Islamic society. We are not willing to believe that faithful Islamic women would willingly wear a chador as an act of piety. This prejudice certainly adds to the difficulties that Muslim Americans have living in American society.

Today American society simply does not understand religiously based polygamy and the culture it comes from. We do not understand the choices, we are offended by the cultural language, and we are quick to see it as deviant or predatory somehow.

The FLDS are not going away. Mass prosecutions, community invasions by heavily armed law enforcement such as the misguided Texas assault, and seizure of their children only deepen their sense of persecution and community solidarity. The most effective agents of change have been education and exposure to the outside world. The kind of pressures brought in the twenty-first century can be very counterproductive for that goal, making the FLDS more reclusive.

NOTES

1. My great, great-grandfather Shadrack Ford Driggs was married to my great, great-grandmother Elizabeth White and to Celia Taylor. My great-grandfather Apollos Griffin Driggs was married to Cornelia Pratt, Mary Melvina Kimball, my great-grandmother Elizabeth Alston, and Eliza E. White. Both were prosecuted for polygamy; Apollos went to prison in 1887. *Driggs: History of an American Family* (Phoenix: Driggs Family Association, 1972), 44, 79; see a variety of newspaper clippings about the 1886–1887 prosecution of Apollos Driggs, Bishop of the Sugar House Ward, in the A.T. Schroeder Collection, Scrapbook #3, at the Wisconsin Historical Society Archives in Madison, Wisconsin.

2. My 139-page thesis was entitled "'There Must Be No Compromise with Evil': A History and Analysis of the Utah Supreme Court's 1955 Decision in *In Re Black, 283 P.2d 887* (Utah 1955)." A version of it was published as "Who Shall Raise The Children? Vera Black and the Rights of Polygamous Utah Parents," *Utah Historical Quarterly* 60 (Winter 1992): 27–46. Vera Black was one of the three wives of Leonard Black. They had eight children, seven at the time of this case. The two oldest, Orson, 17, and Lillian, 12, testified in the juvenile court termination of parental rights proceedings.

3. I had seen a *60 Minutes* piece about internal disputes over their communalism and a really bad 1981 TV movie, *The Child Bride of Short Creek*.

4. See Dan Barlow's account of the 1953 Short Creek Raid, where he was one of the defendants, in David Isay, "Dan Barlow: Fundamentalist Mormon and Mayor of Colorado City, Arizona," in *Holding On* (New York: W. W. Norton, 1996), 169–173.

5. Barlow was born in Panacea, Nevada, on March 4, 1874. He died in a fundamentalist Mormon–owned home on 2157 Lincoln Street in Salt Lake City on December 29, 1949. He was called to the original fundamentalist Mormon Priesthood Council by Lorin C. Woolley in March 1929. For information on John Y. Barlow as a leader of this community see Brian C. Hales, *Modern Polygamy and Mormon Fundamentalism: The Generations after the Manifesto* (Salt Lake City: Greg Kofford Books, 2006), 239–288. Hereinafter cited as Hales.

6. Note Hendrik Hartog, *Man and Wife in America: A History* (Cambridge, MA: Harvard University Press, 2000).

7. My lecture was published as "One Hundred Years after the Manifesto: Polygamy in Southern Utah Today," *Dialogue: A Journal of Mormon Thought* 24 (Winter 1991): 44–58.

8. Owen and I became very good friends. I found him to be a warm, unpretentious, genuine, gentle, thoroughly nineteenth-century man. I made a point to fly to Utah to attend his funeral after his death at age 91, on February 14, 2005. Brooke Adams, "Followers, Critics Profess Respect for Polygamist Leader," *Salt Lake Tribune*, February 17, 2005. Much of my research of newspaper coverage of the FLDS was done online where page numbers often are not present. I provide page numbers where available but attribute to the article with or without page numbers.

9. See Marianne T. Watson, "Short Creek: 'A Refuge for the Saints,'" *Dialogue: A Journal of Mormon Thought* 36 (Spring 2003): 71–87 and "The 1948 Secret Marriage of Louis J. Barlow: The Origins of FLDS Placement Marriage," *Dialogue* 40 (Spring 2007): 83–136.

10. For many years Salt Lake City attorneys Rod Parker and Scott Berry represented Short Creek interests. Rod was instrumental in turning the tide of public perception after the April 2008 Texas raid on the Yearning for Zion (YFZ) Ranch. Jennifer Dobner, "Police Well Armed for Raid on Polygamist Sect," *The Intelligencer*, April 16, 2008, A8; "PR Storm Unusual for Polygamous Sect," *Washington Times*, April 21, 2008, A3; Brooke Adams, "Fix 'Slanderous' Claims, FLDS Says," *Salt Lake Tribune*, June 18, 2008. We often talked about the issues that come up in their representation and about our many mutual friendships in the community.

11. See *Holm v. State*, 2006 Ut 31, 137 P.3d 726, 749 (Utah 2006) and Elizabeth Neff and Pamela Mason, "Court Rejects Polygamy Defense," *Salt Lake Tribune*, Wednesday, May 17, 2006, A1.

12. Thomas F. O'Dea, *The Mormons* (Chicago: University of Chicago Press, 1957), vii.

13. Temples are new for Fundamentalist Mormons. They do not see the physical location of a religiously sanctioned marriage as being important as long as it is under priesthood authority they recognize. However, with the LDS Church's extension of the priesthood to African Americans in 1978 the FLDS regards their temples as tainted. Both the AUB and the FLDS have built temples since that time.

14. Among my fundamentalist Mormon friends are independent women of all ages, married and single. While there are always people who fit the media and public images, these women in particular have defied the stereotypes of this religious community (see Mary Batchelor, Marianne Watson, and Anne Wilde, *Voices in Harmony: Contemporary Women Celebrate Plural Marriage* (Salt Lake City: Principle Voices, 2002)). This was part of an increasingly public defense of their lives. Their book was followed by the effective Centennial Park Action Committee, a group of Centennial Park plural wives who also reached out publicly to challenge the stereotypes (see Elise Soukup, "Polygamists, Unite!," *Newsweek*, March 20, 2006, 52).

15. See generally: *Under the Dixie Sun: A History of Washington County* (Panguitch, Utah: Washington County Daughters of the Utah Pioneers, 1950); *Facts and Figures Pertaining to Utah* (Salt Lake City: State Bureau of Immigration, Labor and Statistics, 1915), 167–168.

16. Alexander J. Wedderburn Jr., "Polygamy Again Causes Half-Amused, Half-Bitter Arizona-Utah," *Washington Post*, September 29, 1935, 9B.

17. See generally, "Short Creek: A Refuge for the Saints." See also Ken Driggs, "'This Will Someday Be the Head and Not the Tail of the Church': A History of the Mormon Fundamentalists at Short Creek," *Journal of Church and State* 43 (Winter 2001): 49–80.

18. Benjamine G. Bistline, *The Polygamists: A History of Colorado City, Arizona* (Agreka, LLC: 2004), 122.

19. Marshall Day titled his unpublished 1963 master's thesis concerning Short Creek "A Study of Protests against Adaptation," which is an apt description of what brought about fundamentalist Mormonism.

20. "Second Coming Dress Code," *Washington Times*, April 22, 2008, A10; Brooke Adams, "FLDS Fashions for Kids Sold on Enterprising Web Site," *Salt Lake Tribune*, September 30, 2008.

21. Note that male applicants for admission to the LDS Church–sponsored Brigham Young University must sign a written pledge to abide by these same grooming standards.

22. As quoted at *Sermons of Leroy S. Johnson*, 57.

23. "Early on, the garments were seen as protecting those who wore them. This idea was underscored by the circumstances surrounding the deaths of Joseph and Hyrum Smith in the jail at Carthage, Illinois. Neither Joseph, Hyrum, nor John Taylor had been wearing their garments. Willard Richards, who had, escaped unscathed.

Johns David Buerger, *Mysteries of Godliness: A History of Mormon Temple Worship* (San Francisco: Smith Research Associates, 1994), 146. Growing up Mormon in the Deep South in the 1950s, I was often told of the divine protection that came with wearing garments.

24. In 1923 LDS Church leaders authorized changes in garments to shorten the sleeves and legs, replace strings with buttons, eliminate collars, and other changes. This was vigorously opposed by more traditional Mormons. Further modifications were authorized in 1936. Buerger, *Mysteries of Godliness*, 150–154.

25. *Truth* (August 1936): 33–36, 44–45.

26. Brooke Adams and Lisa Rosetta, "FLDS Leader Jeffs Captured; Future of Leadership Cloudy," *Salt Lake Tribune*, August 30, 2006; Kirk Johnson, "Leader of Polygamist Mormon Sect Is Arrested in Nevada," *New York Times*, August 30, 2006, A11; David Kelly, Gary Cohn, and Don Woutat, "Polygamist Sect Leader Captured in Traffic Stop," *Los Angeles Times*, August 30, 2006, A1.

27. *Doctrine and Covenants*, 133: 48 reads "And the Lord shall be red in his apparel, and his garments like him that treadeth in the wine-vat."

28. Martha A. Bradley, "The Women of Fundamentalism: Short Creek 1953," *Dialogue: A Journal of Mormon History* 23 (Summer 1990): 15–37, at 16.

29. Maggie Jessop, "I Am an FLDS Woman and I Am Entitled to the Same Rights as You," *Salt Lake Tribune*, May 9, 2008.

30. See "The 1948 Secret Marriage of Louis J. Barlow: The Origins of FLDS Placement Marriage."

31. Brooke Adams, "Crackdown Brings Unease to Some Polygamists," *Salt Lake Tribune*, July 17, 2005, A8; Owen Allred, "Polygamist Communities Support Women Making Own Marital Decisions," *Salt Lake Tribune*, February 25, 2001, AA6.

32. Erik Eckholm, "Boys Cast Out by Polygamists Find New Help, " *New York Times*, September 9, 2007, A1; Hilary Groutage Smith, "The 'Lost Boys': Outcasts Find a Friendly Refuge," *Salt Lake Tribune*, March 14, 2004, G6.

33. "Polygamists Are Leaving Public Schools," *Deseret News*, August 2–3, 2000, B2; Mark Shaffer, "Town Split by Mormon Fight," *Arizona Republic*, August 29, 2000, A1; Robert Gehrke, "Polygamist Sect Growing More Reclusive," *Deseret Morning News*, September 17, 2000, 51A; Julie Cart,"Parents Heed 'Prophet,' Keep Kids Out of Schools," *Los Angeles Times*, October 10, 2000, A1.

34. Greg Burton, "Polygamists Pull Kids from School," *Salt Lake Tribune*, August 2, 2000, B1.

35. Joe Garner, "Barlow University's Opening Fulfills 30-Year Dream," *Rocky Mountain News*, February 17, 1991, The West 93.

36. In AUB sacrament meetings the sacrament is blessed and passed by the adult Melchizedek Priesthood, not the youth Aaronic, as in the LDS Church. It would be presented directly to individual members by the priesthood holder, not passed down the aisle as is the LDS custom. With the AUB, sacrament water was presented in goblets that each congregant drank from, as was the nineteenth-century custom in the LDS Church. The small paper or plastic cups I grew up with in LDS sacrament meetings were introduced around 1918 in response to the influenza pandemic.

37. Pamela Mason, "Jeffs Is Focus of FLDS Crackdown," *Salt Lake Tribune,* July 17, 2005, A1; Andrew Murr, "Polygamist on the Lam," *Newsweek,* May 22, 2006, 37.

38. See *Sermons of Leroy S. Johnson,* 52–53.

39. *L. S. Johnson Sermons,* 7 vols. (Hildale, Utah: Twin Cities Courier Press, 1983–1985, 1990).

40. *The Sermons of President Rulon Jeffs.* 7 vols. (Hildale, Utah: Twin Cities Courier Press, 1996).

41. I have only heard tapes, but given the technology skills I observed in the community, I assume other devices are used. A great many people in the community are very computer literate and have advanced technical skills.

42. See Leonard Arrington, *Great Basin Kingdom: An Economic History of the Latter-Day Saints, 1830–1900* (Cambridge, MA: Harvard University Press, 1958); and Feramorz Y. Fox, Leonard Arrington, and Dean L. May, *Building the City of God: Community and Cooperation Among Mormons* (Salt Lake City: Deseret Book Company, 1976).

43. Note Wayne K. Hinson, "The Economics of Ambivalence: Utah's Depression Experience," *Utah Historical Quarterly* 54 (Summer 1986): 268–285.

44. *Diary of Joseph Lyman Jessop.* 3 vols. [N.p.: n.d.] vol. 1, November 12, 1910, to April 12, 1928; vol. 2, January 1, 1934, to April 21, 1945; vol. 3., May 15, 1945, to April 4, 1954. See February 18, 1936.

45. Declaration of Trust, Recorder's Record of Mohave County, Kingman, Arizona, 307, dated October 12, 1936 at 307.

46. Journals of Joseph White Musser. Originals in the LDS Church Archives. 1895–1911 are handwritten and catalogued as MS 1862; 1920–1944 are typescript and cataloged as MS 2899. I also have a photocopy of the original given to me by a fundamentalist Mormon source. See December 29, 1935.

47. Declaration of Trust of the United Effort Plan, Recorder's Record of Mohave County, Kingman, Arizona, dated November 9, 1942, at 597.

48. The date was not an accident. Most fundamentalist Mormons believe that on September 26–27, 1886, LDS Church president John Taylor had a visitation from Jesus Christ and Joseph Smith, Jr., instructing that religiously based plural marriage be continued without regard to what position the institutional church might take. See Lynn L. Bishop, *The 1886 Visitations of Jesus Christ and Joseph Smith to John Taylor: The Centerville Meetings* (Salt Lake City: Latter-Day Publications, 1998).

49. Hales, 328; Hilary Groutage Smith, "Centennial Park: Sharing the Wealth," *Salt Lake Tribune,* March 14, 2004, G6.

50. The Hildale motel was owned by Richard Holm, who was later excommunicated and removed from the community by Warren Jeffs. Brooke Adams, "Thou Shalt Obey," *Salt Lake Tribune,* March 14, 2004, G1.

51. See Lynette Olsen, "Colorado City Airport Soars to Best in State," *Daily Spectrum,* May 13, 1992, 1.

52. Tom Zoellner, "Polygamy on the Dole," *Salt Lake Tribune,* June 28, 1998.

53. Dirk Johnson, "Polygamists Emerge from Secrecy, Seeking Not Just Peace But Respect," *New York Times,* April 9, 1991, A8.

54. Bob Bernick, Jr., "Is Altering Utah's Constitution's Ban on Polygamy Worth the Fight?," *Deseret News*, September 11–12, 1991, 8D.

55. Lisa Schnebly Heidinger, "Colorado City: A People on the Cusp of Time," *Arizona Highways*, August 1994, 36–44.

56. Nancy Perkins, "Colorado City Mayor Quits after FLDS Action," *Deseret News*, January 12, 2003.

57. Barlow was an LDS missionary in both the Northern States and Eastern States Missions, 1895–1897. In 1918–1919 he was again an LDS missionary in the Northwestern States Mission, at a point when he was married and 44 years old. Barlow was released from his mission on February 6, 1919, after it was learned that he had taken a plural wife in the Darlington Branch, Lost River Stake, Idaho. He was honorably released. See Manuscript History of the Northwestern States Mission, LDS Church Archives.

58. Rulon Allred was born on November 29, 1906, a son of Bryon Harvey Allred, Jr. He was murdered on May 10, 1977, by followers of Ervil LeBaron. On Rulon Allred and his murder see: Dorothy Allred Solomon, *In My Father's House: An Autorbiography by Dorothy Allred Solomon* (New York and Toronto: Franklin Watts, 1984); Ben Bradlee Jr., *Prophet of Blood: The Untold Story of Evril LeBaron and the Lambs of God* (New York: G.P. Putnam's Sons, (1981); and Dorothy Allred Solomon, *Predators, Prey, and Other Kinfolk: Growing Up in Polygamy* (New York: W.W. Norton, 2003).

59. In 1944 press accounts put their total number at 2,500. "Religion: Fundamental Polygamists," *Newsweek*, March 20, 1944, 86. In 1956 their number was set at "upwards of 5,000 persons in polygamous families in Utah." "Judges Decide Procedure On Custody of Cult Tots," *Salt Lake Tribune*, January 26, 1956, 12.

60. See Ken Driggs, "Imprisonment, Defiance, and Division: A History of Mormon Fundamentalism in the 1940s and 1950s." *Dialogue: A Journal of Mormon Thought* 38 (Spring 2005): 65–95; "Religious Cult Leader, 82, Succumbs after Illness," *Salt Lake Tribune*, March 31, 1954, 26.

61. Steven Daniels, "Polygamists Bury 'Uncle Roy': 5,000 Attend Colorado City Rite," *Arizona Republic*, December 1, 1986, B2; Ron Bitton, "Polygamous Leader Passes On," *Sunstone*, January 1987, 11.

62. Jeffs was born on December 6, 1909. He was educated as an accountant and after passing the state examination in 1942 worked as a CPA. He died on September 8, 2002, at age 93. See Hales at 271, 335.

63. See Rulon Jeffs, *History of Priesthood Succession in the Dispensation of the Fullness of Times and Some Challenges to the One Man Rule. Also Includes Personal History of President Rulon Jeffs* (Hildale, Utah: Twin City Courier Press, 1997). This book traces the leadership of the Priesthood as the FLDS views it: Joseph Smith, Jr., Brigham Young, John Taylor, John W. Woolley, Lorin C. Woolley, John Y. Barlow, Leroy S. Johnson, and Rulon T. Jeffs.

64. Tom Zoellner and Greg Burton, "'Deliverance' Day for Polygamous Group," *Salt Lake Tribune*, November 28, 1998, 1A; and Angie Parkinson, "Apocalyptic Prediction May Be Circulating in FLDS Church," *The Spectrum*, September 7, 2000, A1.

65. Michael Janoesky, "Mormon Leader Is Survived by 33 Sons and a Void," *New York Times,* September 15, 2002, A16. This reporter wrote that Jeffs was survived by 19 or 20 wives, 60 children, and a great many grandchildren.

66. Gwen Floria, "Some Members of Polygamy Sect Fleeing as Law Closes In," *USA Today,* April 13, 2006, 3A; Andrew Murr, "Polygamist on the Lam," *Newsweek,* May 22, 2006, 37; Kirk Johnson, "Leader of Polygamist Mormon Sect Is Arrested in Nevada," *New York Times,* August 30, 2006, A11; Andrew Murr, "The Polygamist's Life," *Newsweek,* September 11, 2006, 25; Nancy Perkins, "Judge Orders Jeffs to Stand Trial; Subpoena of Reporter Quashed," *Deseret News,* May 26, 2007, B1; Brooke Adams, "Judge Says Jeffs Fit for Trial," *Salt Lake Tribune,* May 26, 2007, A1; Kirk Johnson, "Case Against Polygamist Goes to the Jury in Utah," *New York Times,* Saturday, September 22, 2007, A11; "Sect Leader Is Guilty in Rape Case," *USA Today,* Wednesday, September 26, 2007, 3A; Brooks Adams, "Force-feeding Resumes as Jeffs Refuses to Eat," *Salt Lake Tribune,* August 4, 2009.

67. *Utah V. Jeffs,* no. 20080408 (Utah Supreme Court, July 27, 2010), Motion for Rehearing Pending. See also Dan Frosch, "Polygamist Sect Leader's Rape Convictions Are Overturned," *New York Times,* July 28, 2010, at A11.

68. *Jeffs et al. v. Stubbs et al.,* 970 P.2d 1234 (Utah 1998).

69. Linda Thomson, "FLDS Leaders Facing Abuse Suit," *Deseret News,* June 30, 2004.

70. Brooke Adams, "Brothers of FLDS Leader Dropped from Suit," *Salt Lake Tribune,* April 14, 2006.

71. The FLDS defaulted in other civil suits during the same time frame. Pamela Manson, "Polygamous Leader Ruled in Default in Suit," *Salt Lake Tribune,* March 12, 2005.

72. Linda Thomson, "Judge Grants an Order to Suspend FLDS Trustees," *Deseret News,* May 28, 2005; Jennifer Dobner, "Polygamist Sect Leader Removed from Church Trust," an Associated Press story dated June 22, 2005; Nancy Perkins and Leigh Dethman, "FLDS Trust Stuck in Limbo," *Deseret News,* August 3, 2005; Leigh Dethman, "Judge Delays FLDS-Trustee Decision," *Deseret News,* August 6, 2005.

73. Timothy Egan, "Polygamous Settlement Defies State Crackdown," *New York Times,* October 25, 2005, A16; Brooke Adams, "CPA Making Few Friends as Trust Overseer," *Salt Lake Tribune,* May 28, 2007, A1.

74. Brooke Adams, "State Wrestles with UEP Trust Costs as Bills Pile Up," *Salt Lake Tribune,* August 10, 2009, A1.

75. "Sect Buys Mancos 'Hideaway,'" *Durango Herald,* October 24, 2004; Lisa Church, "Colorado Town Not Too Concerned with FLDS News," *Salt Lake Tribune,* October 25, 2004.

76. William M. Welch, "Pringle, S.D., Keeps Watchful Eye on Polygamist Sect," *USA Today,* April 28, 2008, 2A; Nate Carlisle, "Reclusive, Yet Neighborly: FLDS Settle into South Dakota's Black Hills," *Salt Lake Tribune,* April 7, 2006.

77. For example, see Andrea Moore-Emmett, "Behind the Cloak of Polygamy," *Ms.,* Summer 2008, 46–49.

Chapter 4

History, Culture, and Variability of Mormon Schismatic Groups

Janet Bennion

This chapter provides a brief examination of the history, culture, and lifestyles of contemporary Mormon fundamentalists living predominantly in the Rocky Mountain West, including Mexico and Canada. I explore the roots of contemporary polygamous living, shedding light on the differences between the four major fundamentalist movements, including the Fundamentalist Church of Latter-Day Saints (FLDS) and the Apostolic United Brethren (AUB), both of which were originally one group from 1930 to 1955. The data is drawn from nearly two decades of anthropological fieldwork (1989–2008).

The State of Texas raided the Eldorado Yearning for Zion (YFZ) ranch, operated by the FLDS, separating over 400 children from their parents and putting them into state protective services. The raid cost the State of Texas and the U.S. government approximately 8 million dollars within the first 20 days of the siege. In retrospect, this expensive raid pitted two altruistic causes against each other: the desire to stop suspected child abuse through underage bride trafficking, and the desire to uphold the group's constitutional right of the freedom of religion. This seizure also brought a third cause to light, a cause spurred on by various polygamy scholars and fundamentalist advocates, like Anne Wilde of Salt Lake City, designed to educate the public and government about the rich diversity of polygamist lifestyles, and to protest against the attempts made by government to enact policies against entire communities, as was done in Short Creek, Utah/Arizona (1953), Island Pond, Vermont (1985), and Eldorado, Texas (2008). This chapter is designed to answer the call of this third and vital cause. I examine the variability and complexity in Mormon fundamentalism by focusing on the visionary beginnings of the North American Anglo experiment in polygamy. I then describe the rich cultural expressions of the thousands of people who believe that plural marriage is a divine calling.

History and Evolution

Although many orthodox Mormons seek to distance themselves from contemporary expressions of their ancestors' historic past, plural marriage is an ethnographic reality within the Mormon culture and will remain so for many years to come. Polygamy first arose in the Mormon context in the 1830s when Joseph Smith decided to restore plural marriage to the earth. He married several women and may have had children with some of them.[1] Later in 1890 the Church of Jesus Christ of Latter-Day Saints (LDS) discontinued the practice in order to gain statehood for Utah. Fundamentalists, however, believe that John Taylor (third prophet of the LDS Church) received a revelation in 1886 to continue polygamy. According to the fundamentalists' beliefs, Taylor had been taking refuge in the Woolley home when Jesus Christ and Joseph Smith appeared to him in the evening of September 26th. Based on that vision, Taylor confirmed five men (including John Woolley and his son, Lorin, and my own ancestor, George Q. Cannon) to be Apostles of God with the exclusive mission of keeping "celestial marriage," or polygamy, alive. Prior to his death, John Woolley confirmed Lorin to carry on this quest. Lorin C. Woolley[2] and his Council of Friends (John Y. Barlow, J. Leslie Broadbent, Charles Zitting, Joseph Musser, LeGrand Woolley, and Louis Kelsch) established a sub rosa movement, which Woolley led from 1928–1934. The movement relied on early Brigham Young doctrines of communalism and plural marriage; its adherents established themselves in an area known as Short Creek on the Utah-Arizona border. They believed the location was consecrated by Brigham Young, who said it would be "head not the tail" of the Church,[3] and that it would become a gathering place for many exiled polygamists. Contention and different interpretations over who would be the "one mighty and strong"[4] caused four factions to break from the original Short Creek gathering: the FLDS, the AUB, the LeBarons, and the Kingstons. All of these groups were associated with the original Short Creek sect, and they share common threads of kinship, marriage, and core beliefs.

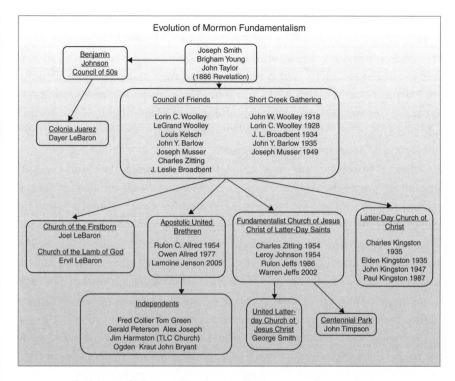

FIGURE 4.I. Evolution of Mormon Fundamentalism

To understand the split, one must go back to 1934, when Lorin C. Woolley died. J. Leslie Broadbent assumed the leadership until his death in 1935, after which John Y. Barlow became prophet until his death in 1949, when Joseph Musser took control. Another group formed in Colonia Juarez, in northern Mexico, where many Mormons fled during the 1885–1887 polygamy trials in Salt Lake City. A handful of families, led by Alma Dayer LeBaron, kept the "principle" of polygamy alive. LeBaron claimed to have received the priesthood keys from his uncle, Benjamin F. Johnson, a member of the Council of Fifty[5] of the early LDS Church, who received them from Joseph Smith. He later established Colonia LeBaron, in Galeana, Mexico.

Fragmentation of the Council

In 1952, the Short Creek priesthood council split apart. Joseph Musser sought to bring Dr. Rulon C. Allred, a naturopath, into the Council of Friends.[6] This was vetoed by the council, so Musser and Allred started a new group called the Apostolic United Brethren. Leroy S. Johnson and Charles Zitting remained in Short Creek and created the FLDS church, which has become the second largest fundamentalist sect with around 8,000 members. It has branches in Hildale, Utah; Colorado City, Arizona; Eldorado, Texas; Mancos, Colorado; Pringle, South Dakota; and Bountiful, British Columbia.[7] When Leroy Johnson died in 1986, Rulon Jeffs took over with a tyrannical "one-man" rule. Dissenters Marion Hammon and Alma and John Timpson built a new community in nearby Centennial Park, Arizona, calling themselves "the Work." A further split occurred in 2002 when Winston Blackmore broke off from the "Jeffs rule" and settled in Bountiful, British Columbia.

Upon Musser's death in 1954, Allred was named the "uncontested" prophet; by 1959, the AUB grew to 1,000 members with the help of Joseph Lyman Jessop and other converts, who met in Owen Allred's home in Bluffdale, Utah. The Allreds had joined the LeBarons during their exile but fell into disagreement with them about who should be the prophet. The LeBarons believed that Joel LeBaron was the "one mighty and strong." In 1955, LeBaron had established the Church of the First Born of the Fullness of Times as a sanctuary in the Chihuahuan Desert, away from "the sinners and corruption of the modern world."[8] Around this same time, Harold and Ray Blackmore of the FLDS group started a colony near Creston, British Columbia. Despite the splits, the various groups have intermarried for many decades, creating hundreds of grandchildren and great grandchildren who are linked to the two prominent kingdoms.

Another branch of the AUB, known as Pinesdale, is located in the Bitterroot Mountains of western Montana. The community has a school/church, city hall, library, and main street. The primary means of support comes through construction work.[9] Other branches in Utah include: Bluffdale (headquarters), Cedar City, and Mona and Santaquin (called "Rocky Ridge," a 225-acre subdivision with around 50 families). They also have orders in Germany, the Netherlands, and Ozumba, southeast of Mexico City. In the 1970s, with new converts and births the AUB grew to about 3,000 members. Today it is the largest fundamentalist group, with nearly 10,000 members. In 1976, after Rulon was killed by a female assassin sent by Ervil LeBaron, his brother Owen took the helm. In 2004, after Owen's death, Lamoine Jensen became prophet. Recently, Lamoine has developed intestinal cancer, leading several others to seek the presidency.

Still another group developed in 1935. Charles Kingston and John Y. Barlow created the Latter-Day Church of Christ. Most members of the group live along the Wasatch Front in Utah. Also known as the Kingston clan, they practice polygamy, often marrying within the extended family to underage girls as young as 13–15 years of age. Paul Kingston is the current prophet. The

Kingstons have about $150 million in security, gambling, mining, and other development investments.

Paul Kingston, 58, is a CPA and attorney with 40 wives and an unknown number of children. He believes that plural marriage allows a man to achieve glory through as many wives and children as possible. He encourages his wives to nurse for only a few months so they will be ready to conceive again earlier. Kathleen Tracy[10] estimates that some of his wives have 16 children, and that he may have as many as 300 children. In his youth he was student body president of South High in Salt Lake City, Utah; a Boys' State representative; and a law student. In spite of his many accomplishments, Paul appears to prefer to remain secretive and isolated. His cousin, Carl, on the other hand, enjoys the public light and serves as the group's primary legal counsel. Carl has several wives and 30 children. He has represented his relatives in a variety of legal cases. Reportedly, the girls were considered "old maids" in the Kingston clan if they were not married by age 17.[11] Some in the group have been sued for welfare fraud; the group's assets were estimated at $70 million in 1983.

In 1986, when Rulon Jeffs took over the FLDS, dissenters Marion Hammon and Alma and John Timpson built a new community, "The Work," in nearby Centennial Park, Arizona. This offshoot group has about 1,500 people. They still practice a form of arranged marriage, but they dress in slightly more contemporary clothing and live in large homes and are funded by both the priesthood community and government funding.[12]

Another sect split in 1990 from the Centennial and FLDS sects. Called the Nielsen/Naylor group, with around 200 people, they live in Salt Lake City. In 1990, a group of FLDS women fled from the various sects, initiating a series of investigations into polygamy in Colorado City and Bountiful, British Columbia. The Creston Royal Canadian Mounted Police (RCMP) launched an inquiry into the life of the Bountiful residents.

A further split occurred in 2002, shortly after Rulon Jeffs had a series of strokes. Rulon was succeeded by his son Warren. In 2003, Warren Jeffs purchased land in Colorado and Texas, and in 2004 he excommunicated 21 FLDS men. In 2005, the Arizona grand jury convicted Jeffs of child sex abuse. Two civil suits were also brought against him in Utah for expelling young men (the "Lost Boys") and sexually abusing a nephew. Further lawsuits were brought against him relating to misusing United Effort funds, whereupon the Utah State government seized FLDS assets, including land and homes in Bountiful. Jeffs escaped to Canada to avoid arrest and was later found near Mesquite in Nevada with $50,000 in cash, computers, and disguises. In 2007, Jeffs was convicted as an accomplice to rape and is currently serving a prison sentence in Utah. Even in prison, however, Jeffs still has considerable influence in the group. He has assigned Bill and Merrill Jessop to oversee the organization in his absence.[13] The group thrives on land deals, various in-house industries, and machine shops that sell airplane components to the government, which may seem ironic as their bigamist practices are considered a Class C felony.[14]

As noted earlier, the FLDS, with approximately 8,000 members, has branches in southern and northern Arizona, Eldorado, Texas, but also in other states including at least one in Canada. The average man has three or four wives and an average of eight children per wife.[15] It is the Bountiful branch that is under scrutiny by the International Human Rights Law of Canada for its practice of marrying underage girls. It was founded in the 1950s and now has about 1,000 people. The Eldorado compound, at the Yearning for Zion (YFZ) Ranch, was raided by the state of Texas in 2008 because of accusations of abuse. The YFZ ranch is located in the desert of West Texas on 1,700 acres with a large white temple, a school, a clinic, many huge homes, and a few factories.

The FLDS has gained the reputation of being the most rigidly patriarchal Mormon fundamentalist group in existence, yet, it has the same roots as the AUB. The prophet typically rules with an iron fist and ostracizes those who oppose him. He has the power to assign people where to live and whom to marry. He also can reassign these resources at will. Jeffs requires people to avoid wearing red (the color belonging to Jesus) and requires women to keep their hair long so they can use it to bathe the feet of Christ when he comes again. He also forbade people from using the word "fun." The community is isolated from the outside world and forbids any access to technology such as cable TV, the Internet, and newspapers. Members started questioning Jeffs' motives in 2004 when he began taking other men's wives and ousting their husbands. Because of his powerful position and the potential for increasing their status, many women agreed with this arrangement and stood by him. Some had little choice in the matter. He also alienated many members when he ordered a group of teenagers to spy on people and search their homes for evidence of sin and dissent. Jeffs' use of power, along with the excommunication, led about 50 families to leave the group.

One other small group is ULDC (United Latter-Day Church of Jesus Christ), whose early leaders were George Woolley Smith, Heber Gerald Smith, and Steven H. Tucker. George W. Smith came from early Mormon polygamous stock, stating that his status as priesthood key holder came directly from his grandfather (the same story is told of Joel LeBaron). Smith joined other underground polygamists in Short Creek, then moved his group to Nebraska, after which he and his 12 wives moved in several directions. A few live in

California, a handful in Wyoming, and the rest live in northern Utah. After his death, Smith was succeeded by his son Heber.

Another independent, Jim Harmston, who is not affiliated with any group, is known for drawing women from other polygamist movements to his fold. His church, called the True and Living Church of Jesus Christ of Saints of the Last Days (TLC) was founded in Manti, Utah, 130 miles south of Salt Lake, with about 400 people. Manti is a poplar-lined small Mormon town, surrounded by mountains, with a huge white LDS temple in the center of town. It is a quiet place with no billboards or traffic and a very low crime rate. In 1994, Harmston, a property developer, and his first wife sought to restore their church before the Second Coming of Christ.[16] Harmston said he was confirmed with the Melchizedek priesthood by Enoch, Noah, Abraham, and Moses, by the laying on of hands. He preached plural marriage, consecration, and "mortal probations," a concept similar to reincarnation. Harmston taught his flock that he was the reincarnation of Joseph Smith and that he could beam himself up to various planets in the night.

Harmston governs his church through the Quorum of the Twelve, a group of a dozen men who have 40 wives among them. Many of their wives are well educated, with college degrees. In fact, one polygamist's wife was a reporter for the *Chicago Tribune* who fell in love with the lifestyle and stayed. Local Sanpete County officials state that the polygamists are peaceful, honest, law-abiding citizens who work hard.

By 2004, Harmston had married 21 women, among them a mother and daughter. In 2006, however, he was accused of racketeering and fraud when members failed to see Jesus and the world did not end as he predicted. He was excommunicated by his own group. By 2008, Harmston was down to eight wives, and many of the other members of the Quorum had lost their wives and children and left the group.

Many unaffiliated independent polygamists also live in and around the West. This includes Tom Green, Roy Potter, Addam Swapp, Fred Collier, Ogden Kraut (deceased), John Singer (deceased), John Bryant, Alex Joseph (deceased), and the Lafferty brothers. Many independents follow the blueprint of the character Bill Henrickson in the television series *Big Love*. They do not defer to any prophet or priesthood leadership but seek to build their autonomous family kingdom and live freely with the mainstream world. Fred Collier and Ogden Kraut are well-known authors of books about the virtues of fundamentalism. Some independents, such as the Laffertys and Addam Swapp, are serving prison terms. Dan and Ron Lafferty murdered Brenda and Erica Lafferty, their sister-in-law and her daughter, stating that God ordered them to do so. John Singer died in an FBI-led shoot-out in 1979.

Ideology

Fundamentalist beliefs are identical to mainstream Mormon ideology in many ways: the evolution of God concept, the Atonement and Resurrection, the use of core scriptures such as the Bible, Book of Mormon, Doctrine and Covenants, and the Pearl of Great Price, the belief in a patrilineally established kingdom of heaven, the three degrees of glory, the Word of Wisdom, and various Mormon cultural rules such as avoiding caffeine, having a food supply in case of emergency, etc. They have links to common pioneer ancestors who crossed the plains and were persecuted for practicing plural marriage. My own great-great-grandfather, Angus Cannon, and his brother, George Quayle Cannon, were Mormon pioneers and were arrested in the 1880s for polygamy. Most twentieth-century LDS leaders like the Romneys, Kimballs, and Bensons have polygamous roots. Mormons and polygamous groups also agree on other issues. Both function in a male-dominated hierarchy in which men hold the priesthood and women and children learn to respect and obey their "priesthood head." Both have a male prophet who is the conduit for direct revelation from God. Women are designed to develop tabernacles for spirit children. Like the LDS, the fundamentalists' religion is a complete lifestyle; one cannot just go to church once a week, but must practice each day to put one's faith into action through "good works." Both also believe in modesty, hard work, patriarchy, eternal families, and community and that they are the Chosen People belonging to the true Joseph Smith–inspired faith. Additionally, both feel that God is an exalted man and that if His children are worthy, they can themselves become gods and goddesses of their own worlds.

One difference between mainstream and fundamentalist Mormonism is that Sunday activities do not last three hours in the offshoot groups, but are typically broken up into meetings throughout the week, as it was in the LDS past. Many meet in their own homes for services, with the father leading the sermon and administering the sacrament, reading from the scriptures, and the mother leading the singing. A further difference is in their association of the "fullness of times" with plural marriage, as a prerequisite for attaining the highest glories of the Celestial Kingdom. This marriage is performed only by the "one mighty and strong" who is "to set in order the house of God."[17] Fundamentalists also favor God's laws over civil laws, seeing welfare fraud and bigamy as minor necessary steps to obtain the higher mandate of providing for large numbers of children.[18]

Believing that God's laws never change, fundamentalists feel that missionary work should be conducted without "purse or script." They also insist that blacks should not have been given the priesthood. They disapprove of the 1927 and 1990 changes to the LDS temple rites and garments.

Fundamentalist Doctrines and Practices

Though the Fundamentalist groups vie with each other over leadership, most share the same theological dogmas. Here, I detail some of the important unique doctrines.

Plural Marriage

Polygamy is said to remove the evils of modern society, which include single motherhood, single career women, and widespread divorce. Polygamists believe that for every righteous man, there are at least seven righteous women.[19] Fundamentalists refer to Mosiah Hancock, a friend of Joseph Smith, who dreamed that in the Pre-Existence there was a grand arena where Christ preached to all the spirit children. He laid out his plan of salvation and gave the floor over to Satan, who lured away one-third of the congregation (all males). This left a dearth of males, exactly one male to seven women, who agreed to follow Christ and further paved the way for contemporary plural marriage. Fundamentalists believe that God himself had at least two wives, Eve and Lilith, and that Christ was married to both Mary Magdalene and her back-burner sister Martha. A common witticism among polygamists is that you can always find a Mary, the bossy favorite, first wife, and a Martha, the dishwasher, diaper-changer, stay-at-home wife, who takes residence in the attic or basement of the first wife's home.

Plural marriage is considered to be the supreme kingdom building tool, bringing more spirit children into this Estate (this life), exponentially, than is possible through monogamy. For example, one patriarch who helped Rulon C. Allred establish the AUB, Joseph Lyman Jessop, had three wives, Winnie, Beth, and Leota, who had collectively 39 children, 273 grandchildren, and approximately 950 great-great-grandchildren, all of whom defer to their apical ancestor as Lord and Ruler. His descendants believe that Jessop will eventually evolve to become a king and a god, just as God was once a man. This concept was taught by Joseph Smith at the 1844 funeral of a man named King Follett. The address was later reconstructed by several people who heard it delivered.

Brigham Young saw polygamy as a way to restore the "fullness" and return to the Garden of Eden's "state of being." It is a divine principle, Joseph Musser argues, "dedicated by the Gods for the perpetuation of life and birth of earths,"[20] washing away the filth of the "daughters of Zion."[21] Many suggest that if polygamy were adopted in the United States, it would wipe out prostitution, infidelity, homosexuality, spinsterhood, childlessness, and other types of sexual sin.

Law of Consecration

Fundamentalists also adhere to the United Order and Law of Consecration; this practice requires that every family donate their surplus to the bishop's store-house (or bank) containing investments, cash, building supplies, and food-stuffs. This is then divvied out to those in need by the Brethren. The FLDS use the United Effort Plan (UEP, worth $100 million), whereas the AUB uses the United Order, both subsidiary organizations that control and redistribute property and businesses in the form of stewardships.[22] Both groups homeschool their children from kindergarten through sixth or eighth grade, with public high school as an additional option. The FLDS, LeBaron, and Kingston groups do not encourage young women to continue after junior high, however.

The AUB United Order somewhat resembles the Israeli *moshav*, in promoting individual industry while maintaining a communally protected economy. Each man is given an economic stewardship, such as a dairy, orchard, or construction business. Those who have close ties with the Brethren or have "blood families" are the ones who get the most lucrative stewardships; this system thus often alienates younger, "rogue" males. Some may have jobs outside the priesthood, such as working in the fireworks industry, selling Book of Mormon tapes, or practicing naturopathy. The wives are also given in-house stewardships such as working in accounting, textiles, teaching, child care, and food preparation. Some wives also hold outside jobs in law, business, education, or sales.

New members in both the AUG and the FLDS are asked to consecrate all their properties and assets to the order to be "worthy to have their names written in the book of the law of God."[23] A side effect of the belief in consecration and polygamy is a psychological predisposition toward anti-government sentiment, mistrust of "Babylon" (the outside modern world), and isolation. Some groups adopt non-secular education (homeschooling) and do not allow women to take jobs outside the community.

The patriarchs of some households are not permanent residents. They spend time with their other wives and work outside community. Nevertheless, they can exert enormous control over their wives and children and typically preside over three or four wives and 20–40 children. The families exhibit great variation in their living arrangements. For example, in some families the women live in separate dwellings and meet all together only once a week. In others, up to five or six wives live under one roof and share bathrooms, kitchen, and dining areas, with a separate bedroom for each wife. Some homes are quite small split-levels or modular prefabs, with a full basement to accommodate second wives.

Others can range in size from 10,000 to 12,000 square feet. These larger homes are typically found in Centennial Park, Arizona, and Eagle Mountain, Utah. Jim Harmston, prophet of the True and Living Church, bought and restored a bed and breakfast in Manti, Utah, for his large, eight-wife family. It has 11 bedrooms and five bathrooms with a communal kitchen/living area. Steve Butt, one of the few non-Mormon polygamists, lives in Circleville, Utah. He also remodeled a structure for his family. He renovated an old LDS church for his three wives and six children. The church's massive kitchen remained the same, but the wives' bedrooms were rebuilt from existing Sunday School classrooms. The pews and "chapel" area are used for family meetings and entertainment centers.

Gender and Sexuality

The gender dynamics of fundamentalists are segregated based on religious and economic function. Men and boys are expected to be "kings in the making," taking up the mantle of religious priesthood leadership, economic steward-ship, and head of household. The fathers are the conduits for God's law in the family. They are in charge of the spiritual development of their families. Some groups (FLDS, Kingston) require that a man have three or more wives to enter the kingdom (seven is a "quorum"), whereas others (the current LeBaron, AUB) suggest that some men are not meant to be polygamists.

Although women play no role in the formal priesthood scheme, they may, if worthy—and if married to a high-ranking Melchizedek priesthood holder—tap into his power when they are with him. By and large, females are expected to bear and raise a "righteous seed" for their husband's kingdom. In addition to raising up a "seed," women are to be spiritual leaders in their household. They are second in command to their husbands. In 1854, LDS Apostle Parley P. Pratt established the following Rules of Conduct that are considered appropri-ate guidelines by polygamists today:

> Men should be leaders and counselors to women and children and
> rule with wisdom.
>   Men should have good judgment in their selection of women
> for their kingdoms; fancy pretty women with no talents are like the
> dew-drops which glitter for a moment in the sun, dazzle the eye, and
> vanish. Men should look for kind and amiable dispositions; for mod-
> esty and industry; for virtue and honesty; for cleanliness in apparel
> and household; for cheerfulness, patience, and stability; and genuine
> spiritual righteousness.
>   Men should call their wives and children together frequently and
> instruct them in their duties to God and to themselves. Men should

pray with them often and teach them to invite the Holy Spirit in their midst.

A woman should unite herself in marriage with a man, submitting herself wholly to his counsel and letting him govern as the head. She should not rebel against the divine patriarchal order of family government to protect against condemnation.

Each mother should correct her own child and see that they don't dispute and quarrel. The husband should see that each mother maintains a wise and proper discipline over her children, especially when young; it is his duty to see that all children are obedient.

Let husbands, wives, sons, and daughters, continually realize that their relationships do not end with this earth life, but will continue in eternity. Every qualification and disposition, therefore, which will render them happy here, should be nourished, cherished, enlarged and perfected, that their union may be indissoluble, and their happiness secured both for this world and for that which is to come.[24]

Gender roles vary greatly between groups. Some households and families are actually run and organized by the wives, and others have a more patriarchal style of structure in which the husband's word is absolute law. Where they believe in male supremacy, the appropriate behavior of husbands and wives is that of ruler and subject, respectively. This is based on the teachings of Joseph Smith.[25] Husbands must be instructional and dominating, and wives must be obedient and respectful. Further requirements for women are summarized in Genesis 3:16: "Thy desire shall be to thy husband, and he shall rule over thee." Women should "respect and revere themselves, as holy vessels, destined to sustain and magnify the eternal and sacred relationship of wife and mother." A wife is the "ornament and glory of man; to share with him a never fading crown, and an eternally increasing dominion."[26] Musser also wrote that a man "shall fight the physical battles in protection of his loved ones, and bring into the home the necessaries of life." The wife "adorns the home, conserves the larder and renders the habitation an earthly heaven where love, peace, affection, gratitude, and oneness shall abound, she the queen and he the king."[27]

Women belonging to the FLDS or Kingston groups generally experience more gender inequality than in the AUB and the twenty-first-century Le-Baron groups. In these latter groups, women have the right to marry whom they choose, work outside the sect in the mainstream in a field of their choice, and dress the way they wish. Contrary to the AUB beliefs, the FLDS holds that plural marriage is absolutely required to attain the celestial kingdom. This puts enormous strain on young men in the wife-hunting process. Members of these groups generally adhere strictly to the nineteenth-century dress code. They rarely use technology, and they use the prophet's revelation to determine who will marry whom. Often this results in young teenage girls being "eternally covenanted" to much older men. Women are often described as being isolated, financially dependent, uneducated, and married off in their young teenage years as "stepford wives on the prairie."[28] FLDS wives are subordinated to their husbands under the "law of placing," where a young girl is assigned to a husband by revelation from God to the prophet, who elects to take and give wives to and from men he deems worthy, often his own kin. Women wear their hair long, braided with a Gibson girl hair-sprayed wave in front. They are modest and wear neutral, pastel colored, homemade dresses with long skirts and puffy sleeves. Under the skirts they wear trousers or thick stockings and modest boots or shoes.

Rulon Jeffs of the FLDS provides an example of these practices. Current estimates are that Jeffs married 75 wives.[29] His son, Warren, currently has 60 wives.[30] This marriage pattern contributes to the lack of available brides for young men and increases their alienation. In all, Jeffs ousted 400 FLDS teen boys for trivial offenses like dating or listening to rock music in order to deal with the bride shortage.[31] In 2004, apparently in an effort to further reduce the competition for wives and to rid the community of rebellious "rogue" males, Dan Barlow and 20 FLDS men were excommunicated and stripped of their wives and children, who were reassigned to other men.

The AUB theology, on the other hand, does not require that one be a polygamist to enter the kingdom of heaven. As Dee Jessop of Pinesdale states: we can't all have multiple wives, in fact, "most Pinesdale kids grow up to be monogamists."[32] Further, the AUB does not allow underage marriages. In 2001, Owen Allred, who married eight wives, spoke in favor of laws preventing the use of intimidation or force to get a girl to marry against her will. The AUB require that young women be at least 18 years of age and that she have full right to denounce a partner. If a woman is dissatisfied with a current man, she goes to the Brethren and explains his faults. Following Brigham Young's rules, she then has the right to pick a man who is more righteous and more financially stable than her last. Allred women are "allowed" to be leaders in their own right, get jobs, attend colleges, and gain a release (divorce) from any unfavorable alliance.[33] Because of their lenient practices, their 35 percent divorce rate is much higher than what you would find in other groups.[34] The AUB also tries to honor the Law of Sarah, which requires the first wife's permission to select a new wife. During the marriage ceremony, she also gives the new wife by hand to her husband, as Sarah did with Hagar. Owen Allred stated that each wife should be treated fairly and that a man cannot allow privileges to one wife that he does not allow to the other wives.[35] In addition, AUB women's clothing runs from modest pioneer style to modern. The women are allowed to choose their hairstyle. In short, women have more freedom. In Pinesdale, for example, clothing typically reflects the old farm-family style of Montana with practical work garb and modest church-wear. In the Bluffdale, Utah, branch, however, contemporary fashions are acceptable. Most groups have respect for women with long hair, considering it to be a virtue.

Among fundamentalists, native or "born in" women have vastly different experiences than convert women, who tend to come in from the main LDS world. The convert women are most attracted to the AUB to achieve mobility, career advancement, or college education, and to have greater decision-making powers in the home and community. Converts are typically raised in the secular world where women's rights, feminism, and self-actualization for women are not only allowed, but expected. Some female converts actually increase their status when joining fundamentalism by escaping their troubles in the mainstream Mormon Church. As Rex Cooper[36] points out, single women, single mothers, divorced and widowed women, and unmarriageable women are often socially and economically deprived of the resources available to the rest of the larger society. Women who convert are typically drawn to polygamy to find a husband, bear children, make friends, and access priesthood resources tied to their salvation. The women are baptized and integrated into an already established polygamous network with access to valued resources. For example, Bonnie, a convert from Rocky Ridge, says she loves her polygamous lifestyle, in spite of the fact that she has lost three jobs because of discrimination. She, her co-wife, and her husband and children live in a suburban subdivision of 50 homes in the Rocky Ridge order. She said she was attracted to the idea of bonding with women as well as with her husband and was friends with her co-wife before her conversion. She states that it is usually the women more than the men who tend to be the biggest advocates of polygamy—the men are the shy ones.[37]

Other female converts, in contrast, become dissatisfied because of abuse, abandonment, poverty, or jealousy. Intervention and disengagement are difficult, as they are trained to believe that the outside world is both spiritually and temporally dangerous. They are threatened with the loss of their children if they leave, and they know that children can be kidnapped by patrilineal relatives. Women are also told that they will not survive economically on the outside, which is often true. As women, they are financially dependent on the order for their basic needs. Some are told they will be damned and tossed out of their family kingdom, or that their skin will turn dark, as they believe Cain's was.

"Born-in" or native women often have contempt for converts, as the converts can be slow to acknowledge the "right of their husband to wear the pants in the family." Likewise, the new women are considered "women's libbers." Born-ins have been raised with the father-adoration perspective and never dispute a man's visions and needs, even when the husband is abusive or domineering. They follow the command of Warren Jeffs in his speech to young women that "a woman's desires should be to her husband."[38] Born-in women are more often sequestered in the home and community without driver's licenses or permission to work outside the boundaries of the sect. From a patriarchal standpoint, it is easier to control women who are uneducated.

At the same time, the role fulfillment and dedication to family of "born-in" women can keep them content in their nineteenth-century gender roles. The promise of their role as handmaid to their husband's kingdom and that they will rise to queenly status keeps them satisfied. Their role as mother is highly esteemed by others. According to one FLDS "born-in" wife, people should respect women's religious rights to rear their children in a safe, isolated community, away from the corruption and evils of the outside world. Still other polygamous women are "independents"—those who do not affiliate with any organized polygamous group. They, like converts to the organized groups, tend to be more highly educated, independent-minded, modern, and blend into the mainstream. They dress and act like typical orthodox LDS members and even attend the local LDS Church, disguising themselves as single mothers. One "born-in" woman, seventh daughter to a council member, left the group with her husband and co-wives to live out their lives in another state as independents. She is now the manager of the family business and works outside the home (she shares child care with her two co-wives).

Contrary to the Viagra-popping image portrayed by HBO, standard Mormon fundamentalists do not necessarily celebrate sexuality. It is often seen as a necessary evil—a force men must learn to control and from which pregnant, lactating, and menstruating women must be protected. Because a woman's single most important role is motherhood, a task associated with celestial rewards and kingdoms of glory, barrenness is seen as the reproach of God or a curse on the woman and her husband.

However, some of today's independent polygamists feel that sexuality is a requirement for reaching eternal glory. Jim Harmston, for example, believes that when his wives have sex with him, it is like taking the sacrament.[39] According to one of his wives, he believes that when a person reaches orgasm it is like witnessing the Holy Spirit, and this should occur as often as possible.

Contrary to what many monogamists often think, however, Harmston's brand of sexuality is an anomaly. For most fundamentalists, polygamy is not a way to live out a sexual fantasy, nor is it practiced by lustful elderly men. The general rule is that there simply isn't the time or energy for men to become polygamous "playboys." Most fundamentalists are Puritanical in that they view sex as necessary for childbearing. Many view it quite practically, considering the workload and extra expense associated with additional children. Many men hesitate to take on another wife, but are cajoled into it by their wives, who desire to live the "fullness."

Abuse, Blood Atonement, and Racism

All groups contain some abuse, just as in monogamy. Yet the number of complaints and convictions in the FLDS and Kingston groups far exceeds the few cases in the AUB or LeBaron colony. Despite a few notorious accusations of sex abuse[40] and money laundering issues, the AUB is currently considered by law officials to be one of the more "progressive" groups.[41] They generally cooperate with the government and provide autonomy to their women. The AUB also follows more closely the LDS Church doctrines and practices. Like the main LDS Church, they have a primary,[42] a relief society, a young women's organization, and priesthood for all males 12 and older; they blend in with the LDS mainstream in clothing, occupation, and lifestyles.[43] Many current-day LeBarons also allow more gender equity.

Other groups, in contrast, have a reputation for abuse. In the FLDS group, for example, Rodney Holm was convicted in 2003 of unlawful sexual conduct with a 16-year-old girl. In 2007, Warren Jeffs was convicted of contracting a sexual alliance between a 14-year-old, and an 18-year-old, and of raping a male minor. Also, in 2005, ten FLDS men were indicted for sexual contact with minors.[44] The FLDS also has the world's highest incidence of fumarase deficiency, a genetic disorder resulting from cousin marriage between the descendants of Joseph Jessop and John Y. Barlow. The deficiency causes encephalopathy and mental retardation.[45] In the Kingston Clan, Jeremy Kingston was sentenced in 2004 for taking his 15-year-old cousin as a fourth wife. John Kingston was also accused of beating his daughter because she would not remain in a marriage to his brother. John Kingston also has had children from three half-sisters.[46] His brother, David, was charged with "incest and unlawful sexual conduct" with his 16-year-old niece, who was also his fifteenth wife.

A related concept that leads to abuse is the idea of blood atonement. This doctrine teaches that certain sins aren't covered by Jesus' atonement insurance plan. To attain salvation, the doctrine states, people must spill their own blood so that the "smoke thereof might ascend to heaven as an offering for their sins."[47] The AUB practiced blood atonement under the direction of John Ray in the 1970s, but since his death it is no longer practiced. Under the leadership of Warren

Jeffs, however, members are required to atone for grievous sins with physical punishment or even the sinner's death. Ervil LeBaron also practiced blood atonement in Colonia LeBaron during his reign of terror in the mid-1970s.

All sects have discriminated against blacks, who are labeled as being "marked by the blood of Cain." The FLDS removed a Polynesian from their midst, stating he was too dark to have the priesthood, and the AUB removed Richard Kunz (a phenotypic white, genotypic black male) from his position on the Priesthood Council. Yet, while the FLDS frowns on interracial marriages, the AUB allows both Hispanic and Polynesian mixed alliances.

Sample Family Profiles

The experiences of polygamists are rich and varied, and most are ignored by the larger Mormon culture as peripheral. Yet, they are hardly outside the Mormon experience. Most converts continue to raise their children in accord with Mormon doctrine and traditions. They strive to live the "eternal round." They strive to be the perfect Mormon family, and they feel that plural marriage polishes them like diamonds, meriting the greatest glories. To illustrate the variability, I present three family profiles, whose names are changed to protect their identities.

Rod Williams, a former Secret Service agent, converted to the AUB around 1985. He and his wife (Ann) were members of the mainstream LDS Church (having met and married in Washington). They became attracted to the values of the Bluffdale fundamentalist congregation: food storage, anti-government sentiment, distrust of the modern, wicked world. Rod further wanted to expand his family kingdom, which was easier in the AUB than among LDS. After a few years of living in their split-level home in Bluffdale, Rosa, a 30-year-old, strong-willed, educated Hispanic woman, began to attend AUB meetings and approached Rod about joining his family. Rosa, having served in the military for six years, wanted to settle down, have children, and be a part of a strong family kingdom. She liked Rod's laissez-faire style governance, which allowed her freedom to pursue her career and continue her outspoken ways without rebuke. Furthermore, she got along well with Ann, a nurturing and loving woman, whom she knew would help take care of her children while she attended school. Rod had a thriving immigrant rescue business and after a few years became close to a few members of the council. He began taking trips with the AUB to the Holy Lands, where he met his third wife, Emily, 17, who was a born-in daughter of a respected councilman.

When I met the three wives in their Draper suburban home, I was reminded of my own Mormon sisters—busy with dinner, getting their many kids bathed for Sunday School, and gossiping about shopping purchases and new members of the ward. They shared common goals and tasks. They were soccer moms and Relief Society presidents. They chauffeured their kids around in their sport utility vehicles to music lessons and day camp. They hosted chaotic, jubilant, Family Home Evening events on Monday nights. They even had approximately the same number of kids. But Rod's wives rotated work among the wives rather than putting it on the shoulders of one wife. This arrangement allowed Emily to earn her business degree and Rosa to earn her master's degree in sociology. They set up a rotation schedule that enabled Rod to visit Ann one night, Rosa, the next, and Emily the third night. After a few years, Ann began working as an administrative secretary, Rosa as a social worker, and Emily and Rod ran the family business. During all the years in Draper, the family relied on Ann's health insurance, which covered herself, Rod, and all the children, but not Rosa and Emily's health needs.

After being in the group for 12 years, Rod became disillusioned with the AUB, recognizing, as some converts do, that their access to the high priesthood powers and kingdom building resources was limited to their ability to forge strong ties with the brethren. Rod offended the hierarchy with his accusations against them and was soon expelled for alleged heresy. He and his wives were ostracized. His adult children, however, were allowed to stay in the group as long as they followed Owen Allred and disassociated themselves from their father. Rod, his wives, and his underage children became independents. They still believed in plural marriage, but no longer associated with the AUB. He, along with another former "Allredite," became part of an investigation of money laundering against the AUB "iconoclastic muckraker" John Llewellyn. For nearly a decade, Rod assisted Virginia Hill in her attempt to regain a few million dollars allegedly stolen by the AUB. Needless to say, the AUB leadership has great contempt for Rod and his family.

Rod and his family eventually left Utah. They currently live in the Pacific Northwest in a 5,000-square-foot home in the woods.

Rod's second wife, Rosa, recently left the family after discovering that she was a lesbian. In all, Rod and his three wives produced a relatively "small" polygamist family: 13 children, 40 grandchildren. He has now formally left fundamentalism entirely, and has nothing to do with Mormonism. He states that he is now in a "consensual sexual relationship" with his two wives. Having removed all religious association with polygamy, he believes that he is uniquely designed to live with and love more than one woman.

By contrast, the Marvin Jessop family is a very powerful entity in the Allred Group; Marvin may be in a position to take up the presidency if Lamoine does not survive his cancer. Four of Marvin's five wives have remained loyal to him for many years. Marvin holds court in Pinesdale. He and his brother, Morris, act as the official priesthood leaders representing the interests of the AUB, but not necessarily those of the new prophet, Lamoine Jensen. Marvin is the grandson of Joseph Lyman Jessop and the colleague of founder Rulon C. Allred. As a "born-in," Marvin has longevity and controls the construction stewardship upon which the town relies. In fact, ironically, it is their extended family that builds many of the LDS churches in the Intermountain West.[48] Although some women are occasionally sent into Hamilton to apply for welfare as single mothers,[49] none of Marvin's wives do so. They are well cared for in the group. Each has her own stewardship and calling. Marvin and his first three wives were all born into polygamy, and they all live in Pinesdale. His first wife, Sharon, born into a family of 45 members, was Marvin's high-school sweetheart. She lives in a separate home. The third wife, Mary Ann, shares a large duplex with her birth sister. The second wife, "Mona," died of cancer some years ago. She grew up in the Mexico group with ties to the LeBarons. The fifth wife, "Katie," the only convert to the group, left around 1985. Many years ago, one of Marvin's brothers died, leaving a wife, "Eleanor," and a few children. Honoring the law of the levirate, Marvin married Eleanor and adopted her children. The same kind of arrangement occurred when his grandfather, "Jay" Jessop, died. His wife Leota and her two children were given to his brother as a third wife. Marvin's first wife, Sharon, who screens any visitors to the community, is the true leader of the extended family. She now works in the construction business, keeps records and oversees all family affairs, including the settling of disputes among the wives, the budgeting, and the rotation of Marvin's visiting schedule. Marvin is usually traveling to Mexico, various other orders, and Salt Lake City on priesthood business. He also heads a construction company and is often on the road to oversee projects. He typically sees each of the three Pinesdale wives, when he is in town, once every three days. On some occasions, when a wife is lactating, menstruating, or is not in the mood to be near her husband, she will call the first wife to keep Marvin at her place a few days longer, forgoing her turn to be with her husband. In some cases, when a wife is trying to get pregnant, women will adjust their visits to meet her needs. In emergencies, the wives rally to help support each other. For example, before Sharon's hysterectomy, she divvied up her 13 kids among the remaining two wives. When I visited her co-wife in the winter of 1989, she had four of her own, plus six of her co-wife's children to care for. The women share child care, bulk purchases, food preparation and preservation tasks, and various church callings that range from watching children in the primary to teaching Sunday School. Sharon mentioned that while Texan polygamists were being split apart, their life in Montana went undisturbed. In Pinesdale, polygamy has thrived for

40 years. It is a refuge where religious freedoms are protected. Although she is content to remain with Marvin and her other two wives, Sharon has severed her ties to the AUB for "personal reasons."

Yet another case, also found in the AUB, is a story of a bright Brigham Young University (BYU) graduate, "Bill Mason," who began to ask questions about the "mysteries" and was referred to a friend of a friend in the group. He and his wife, "Jill," began attending cottage meetings. They soon converted to the group. Jill then told her best friend, also a BYU student, about the "Work" and sought to convert her. She promised her that her husband would love her forever and they could bear and raise their children together, eventually growing old as lifelong companions. After (Yvonne's) conversion, and the subsequent endowment ceremony where Jill placed Yvonne's hand in her husband's hand, Jill knew she would be tied to her BYU girlfriend for eternity as a friend, sister, and wife. She told me that "Yvonne and I were roommates at BYU. When she wrote me about the lack of good men down in Provo, I told her to come on up to Montana and I'd hook her up to my husband." Although Jill and Yvonne both live in Pinesdale, Bill spends his time traveling between Montana and Utah to visit his other wives and to take care of priesthood business as one of the 10 AUB councillors. In all, Jill and Yvonne see their husband only six months of the year. This forges a strong emotional and economic bond between them.

Another family experiencing relative success is that of Ariel Hammon in Centennial Park.[50] Hammon is 32 and his first wife, Helen, is 30. This is one of the rare "peer" marriages in fundamentalism. Hammon and Helen have seven kids. His second wife, Lisa, who is 20, has two. They all live in a cramped, 1,400-square-foot cottage, which was provided by the community. When the family expands, the community has promised they will help build an addition.

Ariel met his first wife in high school but could not date her, as unauthorized courtship is strictly prohibited by their beliefs. Helen approached her father and church leaders about her interest, and without Ariel's knowledge, Helen and the patriarchy formulated a betrothal plan. Not long before the ceremony, Ariel was propositioned by the council and he accepted their divine authority. For his second wife, Lisa, it was the same process of council-approved betrothal without dating. She was very interested in him, and it didn't bother her that he was married to Helen. She consented to the match.

Another polygamist family is the Alex Joseph clan of Big Water, Utah. I met his wife, Elizabeth Joseph, at the gay-polygamy[51] forum in the Salt Lake library. I find her to be strong and outspoken. A documentary was made by Ted Mikels about their lives entitled *Alex Joseph and His Wives*. The film describes how Alex, a former cop, became a polygamist in the Allred Group and eventually took 12 wives (surprisingly from non-Mormon families). He and his wives started their own town in Big Water, introducing libertarian ideals to all new citizens. Alex eventually was investigated for charges of selling drugs and engaging in illegal real estate deals.[52]

Non-Mormon Fundamentalism

Not all polygamists are associated with Mormonism. Steve Butt and his three wives and five children live in Circleville, Utah.[53] They call themselves Christian polygamists who believe in continuing the legacy of Abraham. Ten years ago, as a monogamist, he worked, ironically, as a "cult exit" counselor in Maine, where he helped young people who had been abused in non-traditional religious movements. One of his patients became his second wife and they moved to Utah. The headquarters of their church, called the Be Free Patriarchal Christian Church, ministers to about 1,000 people in the nation. They hope to first convert Mormon polygamists, then proselyte among other Christian churches throughout Utah and California. Each of Steve's wives has her own bedroom. Steve rotates each night, starting with his first wife, Diane, 51, who has two children, then his second wife, Merry-Ann, 44, and his third wife, Dawn, 32, who has three kids. Butt doesn't want to be confused with the FLDS group that practices sex abuse; he states that his lifestyle is not about oppressing women, but about liberating them. The father is to be the strong patriarchal leader, but that doesn't mean the wives are slaves. The husband provides "headship" so the women can fulfill their potential. The women say they love the lifestyle because they are in charge of their own activities in the home. They enjoy each other's company as sisters.

Conclusion

From the historical roots of Mormon fundamentalism one can see that polygamists have a great deal in common with mainstream members of the LDS church. They share the same early doctrines and values. Many share ancestors who crossed the plains with Brigham Young. They read the same scriptures and have many similar cultural beliefs. Obviously, there is dispute over priesthood authority and the vital contrast between present-day revelation disavowing polygamy in the mainstream church versus the concept that the "gospel never changeth" among fundamentalists.

The media has helped mold our images of fundamentalists, heavily underscoring the horrors of polygamy. The media neglect the reality of everyday lives that might be considered boringly normal by most readers. It is vital to acknowledge the full diversity and complexity of Mormon fundamentalism as it continues to grow and develop in the United States. One venue that is helping the public to view polygamy as a somewhat normal and positive lifestyle is the sitcom *Big Love,* written by two openly gay writers, Mark Olson and Will Scheffer. Although a little heavy on the sex angle, the show is remarkably accurate. It has even been praised by polygamists as helping the public acknowledge fundamentalism as a viable alternative.

This chapter has provided a historical and cultural guide for social workers, government officials, and media representatives to prevent future cross-cultural misunderstandings that can lead to violence and sieges. Once people understand the full history, culture, and variability in lifestyles of fundamentalists, they can make better judgements about policy on polygamy as it impacts women and children.

NOTES

1. Todd Compton, *In Sacred Loneliness,* (Signature Books: Salt Lake City, UT, 1997).

2. John W. Woolley proclaimed that John Taylor gave him, George Q. Cannon, and three others the priesthood keys to perform plural marriages. Woolley then passed that authority to his son Lorin.

3. Ken Driggs, 'This Will Someday be the Head and Not the Tail of the Church': A History of the Mormon Fundamentalists at Short Creek," *Journal of Church and State* (January 1, 2001). FLDS Women Speak, 2008, www.youtube.com/watch?v=cDDXY5KHMqA.

4. The "one mighty and strong" is a reference to revelation received by Joseph Smith and sent to his follower W. W. Phelps. It is recorded as scripture in the church's *Doctrine and Covenants* 85: 7: "And it shall come to pass that I, the Lord God, will send one mighty and strong, holding the scepter of power in his hand, clothed with light for a covering, whose mouth shall utter words, eternal words; while his bowels shall be a fountain of truth, to set in order the house of God, and to arrange by lot the inheritances of the saints whose names are found, and the names of their fathers, and of their children, enrolled in the book of the law of God"; Joseph Smith never revealed the identity of the "one mighty and strong," and it has been used by many schismatic Mormon sects to justify their claims of authority.

5. The Council of Fifty is a little-known organization established by Joseph Smith in the early 1840s. Its function was basically governmental; it was to serve as the head of a theocracy when the events of the last days destroyed the nation's government. The Council of Fifty was apparently extinguished in the LDS church when its last member, the LDS prophet Heber J. Grant, died in 1945. See D. Michael Quinn, "The Council of Fifty and Its Members, 1844 to 1945," *BYU Studies 20, no. 2 (1980): 163–198,* <http://byustudies.byu.edu/shop/pdfSRC/20.2Quinn.pdf>.

6. The Council of Friends is an organization established in the FLDS priesthood hierarchy. It originally consisted of seven high priests who governed the church. It can be viewed as roughly equivalent to the LDS Church's Council of Twelve Apostles.

7. The Bountiful branch is under scrutiny by the Canadian officials for underage marriages of girls who had been smuggled across the border.

8. Janet Bennion, *Desert Patriarchy* (Tucson: University of Arizona Press, 2004); Verlan LeBaron, *The LeBaron Story* (El Paso, TX: Keels, 1981).

9. Ironically, it is their extended family that builds most of the LDS churches in the Intermountain West.

10. Kathleen Tracy, *The Secret Story of Polygamy* (Naperville, IL: Sourcebooks, 2001).

11. Michael Janofsky, "Young Brides Stir New Outcry on Utah Polygamy," *New York Times,* February 27, 2003, A01.

12. Hildale/Centennial Park residents receive substantial amounts in federal housing grants , food stamps, and welfare. Please see Tom Zoellner, "Polygamy on the Dole: Welfare aids the illegal lifestyle of many families in Utah-Arizona border community." *Salt Lake Tribune.* June 28, 1998.

13. Brooke Adams, "Jeffs Preaching Will Be Dissected Word by Word," *Salt Lake Tribune,* August 30, 2007.

14. Randi Kaye, "Pentagon Paid $1.7 Million to Firms of Polygamy Bosses," CNN, 2008, 4–18. www.cnn.com/2008/US/04/17/polygamy.pentagon/index.html.

15. Irwin Altman and Joseph Ginat, *Polygamous Families in Contemporary Society* (Cambridge: University of Cambridge Press, 1996).

16. Becky Johns, "The Manti Mormons: The Rise of the Latest Mormon Church," *Sunstone* (June 1996): 30.

17. *Doctrine and Covenants* 85: 7.

18. Brian Hales, *Modern Polygamy and Mormon Fundamentalism: The Generations after the Manifesto* (Salt Lake City: Greg Kofford Books, 2006).

19. Isaiah 4:1.

20. Joseph Musser,*Celestial or Plural Marriage* (Salt Lake City: Truth Publishing Company, 1944).

21. Isaiah 4:4.

22. The AUB may suffer financially in the next few years as they lost a civil law suit filed by Virginia Hill that, along with interest, could cost them $18 million (Civil suit, 2003).

23. LeBaron, *LeBaron Story.*

24. Parley Pratt, "Rules of Conduct," *The Seer* (London: 1854).

25. Musser, *Marriage.*

26. Ibid.

27. Joseph Musser, *The Inalienable Rights of Women* (Salt Lake City: Truth Publishing Company, 1948).

28. Rebecca Walsh, "Feminists Waffle in FLDS Case," *Salt Lake Tribune.* May 25, 2008.

29. Nancy Gibbs, "The Polygamy Paradox," *Time Magazine,* Sept 20, 2007.

30. Wade Goodwyn, et al., "Warren Jeffs and the FLDS," NPR, May 3, 2005.

31. Ted McDonough,"Lost Boys Found," *Salt Lake City Weekly*, September 23, 2004.

32. MNS, "Pinesdale Resident Disturbed by Recent Events in Texas," Montana's News Station, April 22, 2008, 2.

33. Leigh Dethman, et al., "Polygamist Owen Allred Dies," *Deseret Morning News*, February 16, 2004.

34. Janet Bennion, "Abbas Raptus: Exploring Factors Contributing to the Sexual Abuse of Females in Rural Mormon Fundamentalist Communities," *Forum on Public Policy: A Journal of the Oxford Round Table*, (Fall 2007); Janet Bennion, *Women of Principle: Female Networking in Contemporary Mormon Polygamy* (Oxford: Oxford University Press, 1998).

35. Hales, *Modern Polygamy*.

36. Rex Cooper, *Promises Made to Fathers* (Salt Lake City: University of Utah Press, 1990).

37. Mencken also writes that it is men who more often object to polygamy, not women (1918).

38. Adams, "Jeffs Preaching."

39. Julian Borger, "Hellfire and Sexual Coercion," *The Guardian*. June 30, 2005.

40. Joseph Thompson and George Maycock were accused of sex abuse in the 1990s, while Chevrol Palacios was arrested for underage marriage in 2002.

41. John Llewellyn, *Polygamy under Attack* (Salt Lake City: Agreka Books, 2004).

42. Primary is a religious-based children's program in the Mormon Church, typically held after school. It is the LDS parallel of the Catholic Catechism.

43. The bishop is the leader of each branch, but there are also AUB councilmen living in each branch to help provide priesthood authority. They are known to use some religious and educational material published by the LDS Church in their sermons and coursework.

44. Kirk Johnson, "Case against Polygamist Goes to the Jury in Utah," *New York Times*, September 22, 2007.

45. John Dougherty, "Forbidden Fruit," *Phoenix New Times*, December 29, 2005.

46. CNN, "Man Sentenced for Marrying His 15-year-old Cousin," January 26, 2004.

47. Brigham Young, *Journal of Discourses* 13 (1856–1869): 56–61.

48. In my early fieldwork (1998), I was told that most of the Allredite building contracts were for the construction of new LDS wards (chapels) in Utah, Idaho, and Oregon.

49. Llewellyn, *Polygamy*.

50. Harry Phillips and Joseph Diaz, "Polygamists Practice Big Love in Arizona," *ABC News*, August 14, 2007.

51. In the early 1990s I was asked to speak at a forum about alternative marriage and sexuality at the Salt Lake City public library, hosted by both lesbian women and polygamist wives, both of whom were outspoken advocates for Right to Marry laws.

52. Ted Mikels, *Alex Joseph and His Wives* (1976). A documentary written by Ted Mikels and William Thrush.

53. Hannah Wolfson, "Polygamy without Book of Mormon," Associated Press, in *Phoenix Republic*, July 19, 1999.

Chapter 5

Differing Polygamous Patterns: Nineteenth-Century LDS and Twenty-First-Century FLDS Marriage Systems

Kathryn M. Daynes

Polygamy is all the same. Many thought that as they watched children being hauled away from the FLDS Yearning for Zion (YFZ) Ranch in white First Baptist Church buses. And too often those who heard the Texas Child Protective Service's accusations that all the children were being abused made this facile assumption. In fact, various polygamous groups' practices diverge, depending on the rules and customs prevalent within the group. That is the case among contemporary polygamous groups, as well as those in the past. Polygamy as lived by members of The Church of Jesus Christ of Latter-Day Saints (LDS) over a century ago differed in many of its rules and practices from those of today's Fundamentalist Church of Jesus Christ of Latter-Day Saints (FLDS). Moreover, nineteenth-century culture and legal systems differed from those of the FLDS in the twenty-first century.

To be sure, there are some similarities, even though the dominant culture in contemporary America values egalitarian marriages that differ substantially from the nineteenth-century definition of marriage with its emphasis on different gender roles.[1] Plural wives, both then and now, were perceived by other Americans as abject women held in submission by tyrannical husbands and their prophet. In the nineteenth century, Congress appropriated money to build a home in Salt Lake City for women who wanted to escape from polygamy. Few came.[2] Similarly, current FLDS wives have been called "brainwashed," and Carolyn Jessop's best-selling book is entitled *Escape*, but most wives who left the YFZ ranch with their children in April 2008 are adhering to their religious beliefs while living outside the ranch.[3] Safe Passage, a program funded by the federal government in 2004 to help polygamous wives, assisted 1,300 people before it was ended in 2007, and 15 women sought shelter at the DOVE Center in St. George, Utah, during the last year of funding.[4] In both eras, some women did protest their polygamous lifestyle by leaving their communities, but most remained loyal to their beliefs. Even Jessop's daughter Betty returned to her church after living outside the FLDS community for three years with her mother.[5] Strange as it may seem to most Americans, the loyalty of FLDS members to their beliefs runs deep.

Clearly, polygamy poses challenges not faced by monogamists, especially in living arrangements and interpersonal relations among spouses. But generalizations are difficult because so many factors are involved. The number of wives a husband has, whether all wives live in the same household, the number of children in the household, the ages of the wives, geographic location of the family, household income, personalities of husband and wives—these are just some of the factors impacting the daily lives of polygamous families. Too many factors influence family life within polygamous families to generalize about the quality of life within them, either in the past or now.

In both eras, church leaders stressed the leadership of husbands in the home and the importance of wives' obedience. In 1861 Brigham Young advised women "not ask whether you can make yourselves happy, but whether you can do your husband's will, if he is a good man." The next year he added, "Let our wives be the weaker vessels, and the men be men, and show the women by their superior ability that God gives husbands wisdom and ability to lead their wives into his presence."[6] Similarly, in 1998, Warren Jeffs was also emphatic when he advised women to "obey your husband in all things in righteousness." While he stressed that the obedience was conditional on righteousness, women were also advised to "build up your husband by being submissive," even if the husband was inexperienced and untrained. (Note that to ensure that the church's teachings are not misconstrued, these quotations are taken from documents Warren Jeffs submitted to the court in his defense.)[7]

While these injunctions are much alike, the general American contexts in which they were expressed differ considerably. The FLDS injunctions to wifely obedience contrast strikingly with America's current views of women and even with current LDS views, which emphasize mutuality in relationships. In the nineteenth century, ideas about women were changing in general, so a wide range of views existed. Nevertheless, however oversimplified may be the mid-nineteenth-century "cult of true womanhood" as embodied in purity, piety, domesticity, and submission, these traits were valued by large numbers of Americans.[8] Injunctions for women to be submissive were not so jarring to nineteenth-century ears as they are today.

Education, Occupations, and Leadership

How these injunctions played out in practice in the two societies is difficult to determine. Most LDS plural wives a century and a half ago had limited opportunities for education; unlike today, that was the situation for the large majority of American women. At that time, most American as well as LDS women worked in service jobs, in light manufacturing, or—most likely—in their own homes. If they lived on farms, as many did, they worked in their farmyards and gardens. On the other hand, in 1869 Brigham Young encouraged education and a variety of occupations for LDS women:

> [W]e have sisters here who, if they had the privilege of studying,
> would make just as good mathematicians or accountants as any man;
> and we think they ought to have the privilege to study these branches
> of knowledge that they may develop the powers with which they
> are endowed. We believe that women are useful, not only to sweep
> houses, wash dishes, make beds, and raise babies, but that they
> should stand behind the counter, study law or physics, or become
> good bookkeepers and be able to do the business in any counting
> house, and all this to enlarge their sphere of usefulness for the ben-
> efit of society at large. In following these things they but answer the
> design of their creation.[9]

Young believed women were the intellectual equals of men, a view not universally shared in nineteenth-century America.

When the University of Deseret in Salt Lake City opened in 1868, almost half the students were women. At that time, less than one percent of U.S. women aged 18 to 21 were enrolled in college. Moreover, with Brigham Young's blessing, some LDS plural wives, like Ellis Shipp, Margaret Shipp Roberts, Romania Pratt, and Martha Hughes Cannon, earned medical degrees in the eastern United States and subsequently established Deseret Hospital in Salt Lake City.[10] LDS plural wives were teachers as well as writers and edited their own newspaper, *The Women's Exponent.*[11]

Perhaps more surprising is the prominence of LDS plural wives in the nineteenth-century woman suffrage movement. Eastern newspapers floated the idea that Utah women should be given the vote so they could cast off their own shackles. The Utah legislature called their bluff and gave women the vote in February 1870, only two months after Wyoming, the first state or territory to do so. Much to the chagrin of Easterners proposing the idea, Utah women voted overwhelmingly with their husbands. Utah women had to fight to retain the vote in the face of anti-polygamists' opposition, and after Congress passed the Edmunds-Tucker Act in 1887 disenfranchising Utah women, they had to fight to regain their right of suffrage. When their vote was restored in 1896, Dr. Martha Hughes Cannon became a candidate for the state legislature and was the first woman elected to a state senate in the United States.[12]

Information about FLDS women today is less abundant, coming mostly from those who have left the church. While these are important accounts of the authors' experiences within the community from their perspective, they must be used with care and not as strictly accurate representations of the entire community. Nevertheless, they can indicate the opportunities available to FLDS women. Carolyn Jessop, mother of eight who left the FLDS church and wrote a best-selling book about her experiences, earned a bachelor's degree and became a teacher in the public schools. She wanted to become a pediatrician, but Leroy Johnson, the FLDS prophet, only gave her permission to go to college to become a teacher. He simultaneously arranged her marriage to Merril Jessop, so she was attending school while bearing children, and her continued attendance was at her husband's sufferance.[13] Other FLDS women are teachers and nurses, although most women work at service or sewing jobs. Many are stay-at-home moms. Marrying at age 14, Elissa Wall, the woman whose testimony helped convict Warren Jeffs, only finished the ninth grade and then worked in various service jobs.[14]

In 2001, after Warren Jeffs ordered children to stop attending public schools and to go to private ones, opportunities for women's education and consequently their ability to become professionals were curtailed. Nevertheless, FLDS women proved resourceful after the April 2008 raid of the Yearning for Zion (YFZ) Ranch by setting up a web site selling their handmade fashions. Like women everywhere, FLDS women have a range of personalities. Terry Secrest, an Austin social worker dealing with FLDS women who were relocated to central Texas, commented, "Each woman has her own personality. Some are funny. Some are quiet. All seem strong and independent."[15] But stereotypes die hard, now as in the nineteenth century.

While it is clear that FLDS women are not the browbeaten women often depicted in the press, LDS women in the nineteenth century were not only actively encouraged to get a good education but also to become leaders in their fields. Although the education and work of many LDS women were comparable to most American women, some, including some plural wives, achieved considerable recognition for their leadership and accomplishments.

Choice of Spouses

Differences exist between the nineteenth-century LDS and current FLDS women despite their similar basic beliefs about marriage. For both, the revelation received by Joseph Smith and recorded in the Mormon scripture *Doctrine and Covenants* 132 is the justification and doctrinal foundation for plural marriage. Important as that document is for understanding the religious underpinnings of eternal marriage, with its corollary of plural marriages, it gives no guidance about how polygamy should be implemented. In the absence of such regulation, nineteenth-century Latter-Day Saints created a fairly permissive system that allowed latitude in age and choice of spouse, with the limitation that women could marry only one man at a time. Although today's FLDS marriage system has its roots in the earlier LDS marriage practices, it has evolved into a rather rigid system in which marriages are arranged by their prophet.

A significant difference is the amount of choice given women in selecting their husbands. Nineteenth-century LDS women could choose whom to marry, although, as was the custom elsewhere, men generally proposed marriage and women chose whether to accept. For example, in the 1870s 15-year-old Anna Maria Isaacson fell in love with a 21-year-old bachelor, Edwin Whiting. Her polygamous parents preferred her to marry "some older man who had already proved himself, had a wife or two and was ready to provide for his families." She refused several offers of plural marriage, and at age 18, with her parents' blessing, she married the man she loved.[16]

While parental consent was ideal, it did not outweigh the woman's choice. When 17-year-old Ann Cook showed a preference for William Kilshaw Barton, a man who already had a wife, her father objected to the couple keeping company. Later, Brigham Young visited the community and told her father that she had the right of choice, and with her father's acquiescence, Ann became William's second wife on October 10, 1864.[17] A few women even proposed marriage. In 1852, widow Emmeline Woodward Whitney wrote church leader Daniel H. Wells, asking him to consider her lonely state and "return to her a description of his feeling for her" and expressing a wish to be "united with a being noble as thyself." Later that year she became his fifth wife.[18] A few young women felt pressured to marry, but the pressure was exerted by their parents, not the church. Brigham Young stressed a woman's right to choose her husband: "When your daughters have grown up, and wish to marry, let them have their choice in a husband,...you shall have your own agency in the matter, even as I want mine."[19] Uncertain which suitor to marry—a bachelor or a much-married church leader—Adelia Belinda Cox wrote Young in 1862 asking for advice. He suggested she marry the younger man, which she did, remaining a lifelong monogamist.[20]

Although revering Brigham Young, FLDS prophets began arranging marriages about a half century after the Latter-Day Saints had officially ceased sanctioning new plural marriages. Before the late 1940s, FLDS men had wide latitude in whom to court and marry, although they asked for permission to do so from church leaders.[21] Those practicing polygamy were excommunicated from the mainstream Church of Jesus Christ of Latter-Day Saints, and among the FLDS, family governance under patriarchal leadership became prevalent in the first part of the twentieth century. Fathers, who had a greater natural concern for their daughters' feelings than church leaders, gave consent for marriages. But arranged marriages, or the placement system as it is called, shifted power from families to church leaders and then to the one dominant leader, a shift that was one of the causes of the split within the fundamentalist community between those who followed Rulon Allred and those who became FLDS.[22]

Until a young woman is placed, she is not supposed to have any relationship with a boy or man. Placement begins when a young woman, usually between the ages of 15 and 20, feels herself ready for marriage. She discusses this with her parents, and then her father takes her to see the prophet, the only person who can place her with a husband. Under inspiration, as the FLDS believe, the prophet then assigns her a husband. The prospective husband is informed, and the marriage usually takes place soon thereafter, often within a couple of hours to a week. The women believe that marriage is too important a decision for them to make a mistake in their choice of spouse, so they rely on their prophet with his inspiration to arrange their marriages. One young FLDS woman said that "there is a lot of romance in not knowing who you're going to marry until the last moment." When the marriage is ordained by God through the prophet, they believe the couple will come to love one another.[23]

While this is the general practice, it is not always followed. Carolyn Jessop writes that when she was 18, against her wishes her parents informed her that in two days she would marry Merril Jessop as his fourth wife. Elissa Wall's placement was more harrowing, although the marriage was monogamous. Her stepfather informed her when she was 14 that the prophet had placed her with her cousin Allen Steed. Not only was she too young, she protested, but she also bore a marked dislike toward Allen. She appealed to the prophet at the time, Rulon Jeffs, but his counsel to follow her heart was overruled by Jeffs' son

Warren. Both these women eventually left the FLDS community, and Wall's testimony against Warren Jeffs was crucial in his conviction in 2007.

Some young couples got around the placement system by having sex with each other and then confessing their sin. The prophet would tell them to have a civil marriage and repent. In a year, if the prophet felt they had repented, they could be rebaptized and sealed to each—sealing being the marriage ceremony believed to be essential for salvation.[24] By the time Warren Jeffs became the leader in 2003 and began excommunicating men for trivial or unknown reasons, this avenue to choosing one's mate was likely considerably curtailed or closed completely. One former member claims that the placement system originated partly in response to the intense competition for wives between already married men and bachelors. Not surprisingly, young women often preferred unmarried men for partners.[25]

Latter-Day Saints women in the nineteenth century also preferred marrying single men, which partly explains the trend for fewer new marriages to be plural ones as that century advanced. The LDS Church tried to retain its young men within the fold, resulting in decreasing numbers of polygamous marriages.[26] Among the FLDS, on the other hand, arranged marriages can reward faithful unmarried men while ensuring that married men deemed worthy may marry additional wives. Still, a relatively contained population attracting few converts, such as the FLDS community, results in a relatively even sex ratio among the young.

Opponents of the FLDS church claim that young men are expelled from the community for trivial reasons so that more brides are available for the remaining men. Three of seven men who won a settlement against the FLDS in 2007 claimed they were expelled from the community for trifling reasons: smoking, wanting to go to public school and play sports, watching unapproved movies, associating with apostates, and talking to girls. The FLDS, however, contend that these allegations of expelling the so-called "Lost Boys" for trivial reasons—or to reduce competition for wives—are ridiculous.[27] Whether these young men are leaving of their own accord, as some LDS boys also did over a century ago, or are expelled, it appears more males than females leave the community.

Still, there is likely a dearth of potential brides in the FLDS community, which generally believes a man must have a minimum of three wives in order for all of them to attain the highest level in heaven. Although in the nineteenth century some LDS thought three wives were necessary for exaltation, most apparently did not. About two-thirds of those who entered plural marriage in the pioneer period had only two wives at any one time. In contrast, the FLDS Bishop's Record with information current as of 2007, taken from the YFZ ranch in April 2008, lists 24 polygamous families. Of those 24, only slightly more than one-third of the families had just two wives, while the remaining almost two-thirds included three or more wives, just the opposite of the earlier LDS population.[28]

Although this list may not be representative of the general FLDS population, the presence on the list of almost 3.5 married women for every married man indicates a skewed sex ratio. Moreover, of the 37 families listed as family groups, 65 percent are polygamous. In a stable population, such a high prevalence of polygamy is unsustainable.[29] Besides the loss of some young men from the community, another source of wives is from younger women. In a population with a high birthrate, each successive age cohort is larger than previous ones. For example, there will be more young women at ages 15 to 20 than there are men at ages 25 to 30.

Single men in the nineteenth-century LDS community, competing in the marriage market for wives with already married men, married in higher percentages than in the United States. But almost half of them (47.7 percent) who first married from 1847 to 1869, when the percentage of new polygamous marriages was highest, found wives by wedding women five or more years younger than themselves. That is, men married women from a younger age cohort, which had more females than in their own. In contrast, the 12 monogamists listed on the FLDS Bishop's Record were on average only 2.75 years older than their brides, and only one was more than five years older than his wife. Today's FLDS placement system seems to result in smaller age intervals between men and women marrying for the first time than did the free-choice marriage market of the earlier period.[30]

Just as polygamous men in the nineteenth century often married as second- and higher-order wives women whose ages differed considerably from their own, so do the FLDS today. Polygamous husbands on the Bishop's Record are on average about 12 and a half years older than their wives. Then 67-year-old Wendell L. Nielsen, believed to be the first counselor to Warren Jeffs, was more than 20 years older than over half of his wives. His youngest wife was 24. No young women 15 or younger are listed as married, but five of the eight 16-year-olds are, four of the five 17-year-olds, and one of the three 18-year olds. One 23-year-old is the only unmarried woman older than 18. Of the 16 women between ages 16 and 18, 62.5 percent are married, and half of those married are polygamous wives.[31] Because both polygamists and monogamists marry women from the same pool, it is not surprising that young brides are found in both types of marriages.

While the average marriage age cannot be calculated from the Bishop's Record, it appears to be younger than 18. Elissa Wall was 14 when she was placed in a monogamous marriage in 2001, but the other women whose ages she mentioned in her autobiography are in their later teens. In 1953, FLDS women married at about age 16, but this rose to 19 by 1988.[32] It appears to have declined again under Warren Jeffs' leadership, although how much is presently disputed. In the nineteenth century, women in Utah also married fairly young, although generally not quite so young on average as today's FLDS women. An in-depth study of Manti, Utah, for example, found that those born before 1852 married on average at 20 years, while those born from 1852 to 1870 or immigrated from 1870 to 1887 married on average at 21. A study of St. George, Utah, concluded that the average female marriage age from 1861 to 1880 was similar to Manti's at 19.4 years. To be sure, during the Mormon Reformation of 1856–1857, when the percentage of plural marriages was at its height, the average age declined to 16.5 years in Manti. It rose steadily thereafter, however, as the percentage of new plural marriages declined.[33]

Social and Legal Culture

More significant than the differences in marriage age between the two groups is the contrast between the two social and legal cultures in which they lived. After the American Revolution, the general consensus was that couples should have wide latitude about age in their marital choices. Legislation, supported by judicial decisions, adopted the English common law minimum ages of 12 for females and 14 for males, although minors needed parental consent until age 21. In the 1830s a few states began raising the age requirements. In 1854, however, the Massachusetts Supreme Judicial Court issued a writ of habeas corpus to the mother of a 13-year-old girl who had married against her mother's wishes and told her she must release the young bride. Because legislation did not specifically declare such youthful marriages void, the justices viewed the law to be "directory" rather than compulsory.[34] It was into this legal culture that Mormon polygamy was born.

During the mid-nineteenth century, however, laws slowly began changing. In contrast to the previous century, Victorian middle-class parents saw children as "tender innocents" needing protection. Children were kept at home longer, prolonging childhood.[35] A number of states began to increase the minimum marriage age to 16 for females and 18 for males. By 1906 only 17 states or territories retained the common law marriage ages, but only 12 states had enacted into law the minimum age sixteen or above for women. The majority required parental consent until age 18.[36] Nevertheless, the trend toward higher minimum ages for marriages continued. By the first decade of the twenty-first century, almost all states mandated a minimum age of 16 for women, but even those states allowing younger marriages hedged those marriages with parental consent and judges' orders.[37] In contrast to a century and a half earlier, state legislatures believed that the state had an interest in the age at which individuals married and enacted laws accordingly.

In both eras, however, the general American practice was to marry on average at ages considerably higher than the minimum ages embodied in statutes. Because not all states required registration of marriages in the nineteenth century—South Carolina, for example, did not so require until 1911—the average age of marriage in that period is not precise.[38] The average for those from middle-income families during that century in the North was early twenties, although it was lower in the South and newly settled areas in the West.[39] Anyone who spends much time researching in marriage records or federal censuses, however, will find a fair number of women marrying below the age of consent, even as young as 15 or 16.

The situation is considerably different today. After reaching its nadir in the 1950s and 1960s, the average age of marriage has climbed steadily, until in 2006 it was almost 26 for women and 27.5 for men.[40] In an age when women have many educational and occupational opportunities and men and women prefer being somewhat established before wedding, the marriage ages for both have been rising. Whereas in the nineteenth century LDS marriage ages were within the law and only slightly younger than their contemporaries, the general practice of FLDS women marrying before they are 18 is clearly outside the mainstream of current marital practice, and at least a few marriages, such as Elissa Wall's wedding at age 14, are outside the law.

Conversion or Closed Community

Another difference in the practice of polygamy between the LDS and FLDS groups is the type of women who became polygamous wives. The FLDS community is mostly a contained population with few converts. Wives are therefore drawn from among women who have in general been lifelong members of the community. FLDS values have been instilled since birth, and the lifestyle is often the only one they know.

It was significantly different in nineteenth-century Utah. With the influx of many converts, the LDS population grew rapidly. Some of the converts were single women whose fathers were dead or who did not live in Utah, while others were widowed or divorced women. Many of these women became monogamists, but women in those situations disproportionately became polygamous wives. A study of 444 polygamous wives showed that about one-third were never-before-married women who came to Utah alone or with family members but no father. Another third were women who were widowed or had been divorced, while most of the remaining third of polygamous wives were daughters of polygamous families. Among the never-before-married immigrant women, almost half (47.6 percent) in the pioneer period before 1869 became plural wives, although that percentage dropped to a third (32.8 percent) in the 20 years before 1890.[41]

What two-thirds of women who became polygamous wives shared was the absence of a male breadwinner in their households. In the difficult years of first settling the semi-arid Great Basin lands, immigrants, particularly those women with little financial self-sufficiency, were considerably more likely than other women to enter polygamy. They believed in plural marriages as a religious doctrine, but they had economic motives as well. In nineteenth-century American society, men owned and controlled most economic assets, and Utah was no exception. Most occupations available to women in Utah, as in the United States—seamstresses, teachers, and servants—earned little. Single women were barely able to eke out an existence. Plural marriage gave women a moral right to some of their husbands' resources. It also gave them a home and family. In poverty-stricken pioneer Utah, plural marriage was the major means of caring for previously indigent women.[42]

Economic opportunities today are strikingly different from those of the nineteenth century. A contemporary single woman is no longer consigned to poverty, genteel or otherwise. Although a woman still earns only about three-quarters of what a man earns, she is no longer dependent on men for a livelihood, as she generally was 150 years ago. There is no reason to conclude that economic reasons loom large as motives for entering plural marriage in the FLDS community, as they did for pioneer polygamous wives. Rather, some in the FLDS community depend on government programs to help support their families. In 1998, according to the *Salt Lake Tribune*, Colorado/Hildale, home of the largest FLDS community, ranked among the top ten towns with populations greater than 2,000 in the Intermountain West that were dependent on Medicaid and WIC, government programs providing medical care for the poor and food for indigent women and their children. Also a third of the town's residents received U.S. Department of Agriculture food stamps, a figure that escalated to between 65 and 80 percent by 2002.[43]

Economically, the LDS and the FLDS societies are at opposite poles: the nineteenth-century LDS helped support some disadvantaged women through plural marriage, while the FLDS appear to help support some plural wives by relying on government programs. At the YFZ ranch, however, the FLDS used no government funds. They did not even send their children to public schools. But the cost to the state of Texas for housing the children taken away from FLDS parents was about $5.3 million.[44]

In contrast to FLDS marriages, nineteenth-century LDS plural marriages served a significant social purpose, women chose their husbands as did other Americans, and LDS marriage ages were not far from the American mainstream.

Divorce

In the nineteenth century, the Utah rate of divorce was high. Divorce laws in the United States were becoming more lenient over the nineteenth century, and the divorce rate at that time was the highest in the Western world. Utah divorce laws were lenient enough that in 1875 some lawyers in Chicago, Cincinnati, and New York turned a few counties of Utah Territory into divorce mills. Utah never intended its laws to apply to those out of state and three years later enacted more stringent laws. Utah residents also utilized the divorce laws, of course. A study of Payson, Utah, shows that 6 percent of monogamous marriages there ended in divorce. In Utah County from 1852 to 1887, only 8 percent of petitions for divorce were not granted, unlike in the eastern United States, where stringent laws permitted few divorces.[45]

Plural marriages were not civil marriages, however, so divorces granted from plural marriages were ecclesiastical, not civil. Although church leaders tried to resolve marital problems, any wife who insisted on an ecclesiastical divorce—called a cancellation of sealing—received one. No woman unhappy in her marriage was trapped there. Yet most women were committed to their marriages. In an in-depth study of divorce among nineteenth-century Manti polygamists, 17.8 percent of plural marriages ended in divorce. Women who were not first wives, however, were more likely to end their marriages; almost one-fourth (24.6 percent) were divorced. Not surprisingly, the minority of plural wives who married at ages 17 or younger experienced higher rates of divorce; 36 percent of those who married young ended their marriages. While these rates were certainly higher than elsewhere in the United States at the time, they are lower than in the United States in the twenty-first century. In 2004 37.5 percent of men and 40.7 percent of women ages 50 to 59 had experienced a divorce, while in 2001 42.0 percent of men and 39.5 percent of women those ages had been divorced.[46] The comparisons to the nineteenth century are not exact, however, since information about divorce is currently gathered and calculated differently than it was then.

When an LDS plural wife divorced in the nineteenth century, she was free to choose her subsequent status: single, monogamous, or polygamous. Divorced women chose all three, with a surprising 22 percent of women in the Manti study again entering a plural marriage.[47] Clearly it was their particular marriage, not plural marriage in general, that those women rejected.

Today's FLDS women are also freed from unhappy marriages. There are no available statistics about the prevalence of divorce, or "reassignment" as it is called, although it appears to be considerably less than in the nineteenth-century LDS community. Wall claims that "it is extremely rare for a couple to request a release from a marriage that was revealed by God through the prophet," although her autobiography does not evince wide observation of her society beyond her own family.[48]

The evidence is not abundant, but it appears that the unhappy wife must convince the prophet that the marriage is too dysfunctional to continue or that the husband is no longer worthy to have her as a wife. As in the nineteenth century, all of a man's marriages except the first are religious ones and so must be their dissolution. Elissa Wall's mother, Sharon, complained to the prophet, Rulon Jeffs, about problems in her family. He told her to take her children to her childhood home. After a few months, a reconciliation was effected, and Sharon and her children returned to the Wall household. As part of the reconciliation, however, the first wife was told to move elsewhere. Despite what seemed like a fresh start, problems escalated, and Sharon again complained to the prophet. This time she moved her family to Hildale/Colorado City, where she was "reassigned" as the wife of Bishop Fred Jessop. While this story is told by a person with negative views of the FLDS church, it shows that the church leaders did try to reconcile a couple with marital problems but did reassign the unhappy wife to another marriage when those problems continued.[49]

Elissa Wall herself, however, was not allowed to separate from her monogamous husband, even though she approached the prophet several times. In her view there was too much counseling in an attempt to save her marriage when she only wanted to be released from it. In contrast, in the trial against Warren Jeffs in which Wall was the chief prosecution witness, Jennie Pipkin testified that she complained to the prophet about her husband's unwanted sexual advances and was given a release. But couples who had a difficult time in the early years of their marriage were apparently expected to make the best of it. One young woman who called the first couple of years of her marriage "hell" worked hard with her husband to make the marriage into a happier one, and the marriage stayed intact. One motive for trying to make the marriage work was that a "release" often meant a "reassignment" to another marriage. When Warren Jeffs asked Carolyn Jessop if she wished to be released from her unhappy marriage, she replied she did not. She feared that she would be placed in an even worse marriage.[50] But that Jeffs asked the question seems to indicate that the opportunity to be released from an unhappy marriage is probably greater than "extremely rare."

Perhaps some of the reassignments are in fact unwanted. When an FLDS man is excommunicated or deemed unworthy of his family, his wives are reassigned, and initially he may not have visitation rights with his children. Apparently not all women who were directed to leave their husbands did so, at least in the past. In the 1990s the first wife of Elissa Wall's father refused to leave him when his three wives were released from him. Under Warren Jeffs' leadership, excommunications, even of well-respected church members, became more frequent than previously, and although the men claimed they did not know why they were being excommunicated, their wives were reassigned to other husbands, although not always immediately.[51] In the nineteenth century, wives of those who apostatized were granted divorces, and the cancellation of sealing came after the woman requested it. One woman remained with her polygamous husband for 15 years after he was excommunicated.[52] LDS women in the nineteenth century chose whether to divorce their husbands, even if their husbands had been excommunicated.

In short, the nineteenth-century LDS marriage system allowed considerable choice for women: choice of their spouses, choice in the type of marriage, and choice in whether to remain in the marriage. It also provided financially for economically disadvantaged women without breadwinners in a poor pioneer society.

The FLDS marriage system differs in all these ways. Women are placed in marriages by their prophet, and while they can ask to be released from unhappy marriages, their prophet will probably reassign them to another marriage. It is more difficult to assess the economic advantages—or disadvantages—of polygamy for these women, but the dependence of considerable numbers on government programs indicates that polygamy plays a significantly different role economically for FLDS women than for pioneer LDS plural wives.

The Influence of Statutes and Law Enforcement

While there are many differences between polygamy as practiced by the LDS in the nineteenth century and the FLDS in the twenty-first, there are many similarities in the reactions of their surrounding social and legal cultures. In both cases, the reaction was hostile, at times extremely so. And in both cases lawmakers believed that the current statutes were inadequate for addressing the perceived problem and enacted new ones. In the nineteenth century, polygamy was a crime, but successfully prosecuting it was hampered by the statute of limitations and the difficulty of providing substantial enough evidence to secure a conviction. In 1882 Congress passed the Edmunds Act, which made unlawful cohabitation a misdemeanor.[53] The prosecution had to show only that during a specified period a man visited two or more women reputed in the community to be his wives; no sexual relationship needed to be proven. Almost 900 indictments for unlawful cohabitation were found from 1886 to 1888 alone. Far more served in prison for that misdemeanor than any other crime meant to punish plural marriage—polygamy, adultery, and fornication.[54]

Similarly, to aid in the prosecution of current polygamists who married underage females, both Utah and Texas enacted laws to raise the minimum age to 16. Utah raised the age from 14 to 16 in 1999, and Texas did so in 2005. Mark Shurtleff, Utah's attorney general, testified in favor of Texas changing its marriage-age law after the FLDS began building its community near Eldorado, Texas, in 2003. Shurtleff's policy has been to prosecute abuse within polygamous communities rather than to prosecute polygamy itself. He has tried to develop open relationships with polygamists so that those communities will report problems and underage brides will come forward.[55]

The government changed the laws in both eras, but of course the nature of the laws were different. Over one hundred years ago, American mores demanded the abandonment of polygamy, but the subsequent century changed society and law in the United States. Polygamy may be no more accepted now than previously, but sexual behavior between consenting adults is. And the laws and practices believed necessary to protect the Victorian child have long since been expanded to protect adolescents. So while there are still some prosecutions for polygamy under bigamy statutes—note Tom Green in Utah and the current bigamy indictments in Texas—the emphasis currently is on preventing underage marriages.[56]

The differences in the laws enforced made some noteworthy differences in the nature of law enforcement. A century ago, men were punished after individual trials; in 2008 children as a group were taken into custody by the state, and the hearings for the individual cases came after the children were first taken away from their homes. Despite vigorous law enforcement in the 1880s, federal deputies and prosecutors wanted to avoid making more martyrs than necessary. Older men were spared from prosecution much more often than younger men. In St. George, for example, only 19 percent of polygamists 65 years or older were arrested, in contrast to 47 percent of those who were younger.[57] While the prosecutions of the 1880s disrupted families, many in the community were affected only indirectly, not directly as were almost all families in the YFZ Ranch. Agencies such as Child Protective Services do not operate under the same rules as prosecutors, but their potential to create widespread anguish in a community is great. Despite the differences between the two periods, however, the goal of government was to break up families: in the 1880s by either extracting a commitment from polygamists to live with only one wife or sending them to prison, and in 2008 by taking away all the children.

In both periods, these two groups suffered considerable disruption to their societies beyond the prosecutions for polygamy-related crimes. In 1887 the Edmunds-Tucker Act mandated that the U.S. attorney general institute proceedings to take into possession all LDS church property over $50,000 not used exclusively for worship. As the confiscation of the property went on apace, the United States Supreme Court upheld the escheatment under the Edmunds-Tucker Act in *The Late Corporation of the Church of Jesus Christ of Latter-Day Saints v. United States* in 1890. The same year the Supreme Court also upheld an Idaho "test oath" requiring potential voters to swear that they belonged to no organization advocating polygamy. All Mormons, not just polygamists, were thus disenfranchised. In the wake of that decision, Congress took up a new measure, the Cullom-Strubble bill, which would also have disenfranchised Utah Mormons. These actions not only disrupted LDS society but also threatened their ability to protect themselves through political means.[58]

But the coup de grâce was the fear that their temples would be confiscated, the buildings in which the LDS people performed their most sacred ordinances believed to be essential to their eternal exaltation. As houses of worship, the temples were unlikely to be confiscated under the Edmunds-Tucker Act, which exempted buildings used exclusively for worship, but the possibility that the temples outside of Salt Lake City, which were owned by local corporations, might be confiscated under the Morrill Act of 1862 was suggested by Judge John W. Judd on September 18, a week before the Manifesto of 1890 was issued.[59] Feeling constrained both by events and by inspiration, the president of the LDS Church issued what is called the Manifesto on September 25, 1890. He declared his intention to submit to the laws of the land and to use his influence on fellow Latter-Day Saints to do likewise.[60] Change was not immediate. Prosecutions of polygamists continued, and the church was pushed into further concessions. In the end, however, American society achieved its goal of the church's officially renouncing further support of polygamous marriages. In return, the church retained its temples, which were more essential to the church's religious mission than were its former marital practices.

Congressional acts and judicial decisions had been successful in eliminating polygamy from the LDS Church, but they were markedly unsuccessful in abolishing it entirely, as the various polygamous groups currently in and around

Utah abundantly show. Like men and women in the nineteenth century, FLDS polygamists have gone to prison as punishment for their marriages—with the same effect. Those who suffered at the hands of the judicial system became revered martyrs and more dedicated to their religious principles.[61]

The raid on the Yearning for Zion ranch and the subsequent taking away of all the children will undoubtedly have the same effect. It has disrupted both families and also the church. To preserve their families, a core FLDS value, the church was willing to modify a practice that once was deemed crucial. Previously, the FLDS had claimed that the prophet's revelations were fundamental; obedience to the prophet was key. When the prophet "placed" a girl in a marriage, the couple married soon thereafter, sometimes within hours of the placement. The girl's wishes or her age were apparently not considerations. But under the catastrophe of losing their children, two months after the raid the church promised its own obedience to the marriage-age law: "In the future, the church commits that it will not preside over the marriage of any woman under the age of legal consent in the jurisdiction in which the marriage takes place. The church will counsel families that they neither request nor consent to any underage marriages."[62] The statement was published the day after Judge Walther vacated her order giving Texas Child Protective Services managing conservatorship over the FLDS children. While the concession was made too late to have an effect on the Texas Supreme Court decision to return the children to their parents, it is nevertheless part of the process by which the FLDS church will renegotiate its position in relation to American society.

Whether the FLDS church adheres to its statement about underage marriages probably depends on the centrality of the belief in their prophet's inspiration about who should marry whom and when. Just as federal officials continued arresting and imprisoning polygamists after the 1890 Manifesto, today Texas officials are taking few chances, despite the FLDS statement. The state has asked 63 FLDS girls between the ages of 10 and 17 to complete individual counseling sessions to educate them about marriage laws and sexual abuse. Noncompliance could jeopardize dismissal of a girl's case. And, as of October 2008, one 14-year-old girl, allegedly married at age 12 to Warren Jeffs, has not been released from state custody.[63] While past actions are being punished, as the growing number of indicted and convicted FLDS men in Texas shows, the state is equally concerned with prevention of future underage marriages. The church's statement is insufficient; it will have to prove enduring to be effective, just as the Latter-Day Saints found in its long and difficult journey from a polygamous to a monogamous marriage system.

As Sarah Barringer Gordon's work perceptively shows, the two sovereigns of church and state potentially produce "conflicted loyalties, especially those that trap the believer between religious command and temporal authority."[64] The histories of these two churches illustrate that the conflict between these two sovereignties is ongoing, and they highlight the difficulty that the dominant American culture experiences in dealing with groups whose religious values and practices are in marked contrast to its own. Religious freedom is embodied in the Constitution, but at least at some levels the intention in both these cases was not only to change individual behavior but also to alter these churches' conduct. In the nineteenth century, Congress dissolved the corporation of the LDS Church and confiscated many of its resources. In today's Texas, Child Protective Services and the judge of the district court sought to undermine the FLDS church by taking away every one of its children, cutting off its next generation from the church.

Both the nineteenth-century LDS and the current FLDS examples reveal the limits of dissent in the land of liberty. The tension between church and state is ongoing, but the history of the LDS Church illustrates a long-term positive outcome. Its conflict with the state forced it to order its religious priorities, choosing those most fundamental to its mission. While retaining its uniqueness, the church adapted to American society and even flourished within it. Like the LDS in the nineteenth century, the FLDS church has had to make a concession to a deeply held value of American society, and the church has promised to avoid future underage marriages. Just as the LDS church a century earlier, the FLDS conceded a practice abhorred by American society to retain practices the church valued more: it gave up prophet-mandated underage marriages for the state's acquiescence in their practice of plural marriage. Whether this FLDS concession will have a long-term effect within the church or on its relationship to American society, only the future will tell.

NOTES

1. The literature on changes in the dynamics of American family life over time is large. See, for example, Steven Mintz and Susan Kellogg, *Domestic Revolutions: A Social History of American Family Life* (New York: Free Press, 1988); Nancy A. Hewitt, *A Companion to American Women's History* (Malden, MA: Blackwell Publishing, 2002), 392, 429.

2. Gustive O. Larson, "An Industrial Home for Polygamous Wives," *Utah Historical Quarterly* 38 (Summer 1970): 263–275; Peggy Pascoe, *Relations of Rescue: The Search for Female Moral Authority in the American West, 1874–1939* (New York: Oxford University Press, 1990), 24–30, 61–68, 87–90.

3. Carolyn Jessop, with Laura Palmer, *Escape* (New York: Broadway Books, 2007), 409; Sara Corbett, "Children of God," *The New York Times Magazine,* July 27, 2008, 39.

4. Ben Winslow, "Federal $$ to Help Victims of Abuse in Polygamy Is Cut," *Deseret News* (Salt Lake City), November 5, 2007, http://findarticles.com/p/articles/ mi_qn4188/is_20071105/ai_n21088725/print?tag=artBody;co11, provided by ProQuest Information and Learning Company, accessed July 30, 2008. The Safe Passage Program was ended because the U.S. Justice Department did not renew the grant to continue outreach within the polygamous communities.

5. Jessop, *Escape*, 411–412.

6. B. Carmon Hardy, "Lords of Creation: Polygamy, the Abrahamic Household, and Mormon Patriarchy," *Journal of Mormon History* 20 (Spring 1994): 119–152; *Journal of Discourses*, 26 vols. (London: Latter-Day Saints' Book Depot, 1854–1886): 9: 38 [April 7, 1861] (first quote); *Journal of Discourses*, 9: 308 [June 15, 1862] (second quote).

7. Warren Jeffs' Teachings, Feb, 20, 1998, 71, Defendant's Exhibit 061500526, No. 16, *State of Utah v. Warren Steed Jeffs* (2007), Court Filings, Evidence, Loose Sheets 2, http://www.utcourts.gov/media/highprofilecourtcases/archives/Loose%20 sheets%202.pdf, accessed July 15, 2008 (first quote); Leroy S. Johnson, Vol. 4, 1642, October 15, 1978, in *Light and Truth*, 197, in "Specific Duties and Counsel to Daughters; Responsibility Resting Upon Parents," Friday, January 30, 1998, Defendant's Exhibit 061500526, No. 28, ibid. (second quote).

8. Barbara Welter, "The Cult of True Womanhood, 1820–1860," *American Quarterly* 18 (Summer 1966): 151–174; also see essays in "Women's History in the New Millennium: A Retrospective Analysis of Barbara Welter's 'The Cult of True Womanhood, 1820–1860,'" *Journal of Woman's History* 14 (Spring 2002): 149–173.

9. *Journal of Discourses*, 13: 61 [July 18, 1869].

10. Maureen Ursenbach Beecher, "Women's Work on the Mormon Frontier," *Utah Historical Quarterly* 49 (Summer 1981): 276–290; Jill Mulvay Derr, Janath Russell Cannon, and Maureen Ursenbach Beecher, *Women of Covenant: The Story of Relief Society* (Salt Lake City: Deseret Book Company, and Provo, Utah: Brigham Young University Press, 1992), 106–108; Claudia L. Bushman, ed., *Mormon Sisters: Women in Early Utah*, new ed. (Logan: Utah State University Press, 1997), 58–61; Mary R. Clark and Patricia Lyn Scott, "From Schoolmarm to State Superintendent: The Changing Role of Women in Education, 1847–2004," in *Women in Utah History: Paradigm or Paradox*, ed. Patricia Lyn Scott and Linda Thatcher (Logan: Utah State University Press, 2005), 223–231; Terryl Givens, *People of Paradox: A History of Mormon Culture* (New York: Oxford University Press, 2007), 98–99.

11. Jill C. Mulvay [Derr], "Zion's Schoolmarms," in *Mormon Sisters*, 67–87; Carol Cornwall Madsen, *An Advocate for Women: The Public Life of Emmeline B. Wells, 1870–1920* (Provo, Utah: Brigham Young University Press, and Salt Lake City: Deseret Book, 2006), 34–66.

12. Madsen, *An Advocate for Women;* Carol Corwall Madsen, ed., *Battle for the Ballot: Essays on Woman Suffrage in Utah, 1870–1896* (Logan: Utah State University Press, 1997); Kathryn L. MacKay, "Women in Politics: Power in the Public Sphere," in *Women in Utah History*, 360–381.

13. Jessop, *Escape*, 72–73.

14. Benjamin G. Bistline, *Colorado City Polygamists: An Inside Look for the Outsider* ([Scottsdale, Ariz.]: Agreka LLC, 2004), 96–97; Elissa Wall, with Lisa Pulitzer, *Stolen Innocence: My Story of Growing Up in a Polygamous Sect, Becoming a Teenage Bride, and Breaking Free of Warren Jeffs* (New York: William Morrow, 2008), 124, 175, 206, 228–229, 251. One must be careful when using works by those who have left a group and have an agenda to discredit it. But one can often see the outlines of the society if one notes events in the penumbra of the author's major assertions and arguments.

15. "Polygamists Are Leaving Public Schools: Fundamentalist Families Are Urged to Teach Their Kids," *Deseret News,* August 2, 2000, B2; Jaimee Rose, "Mothers in Polygamous Sect Selling FLDS Fashions Online," *The Arizona Republic,* July 2, 2008, http://www.azcentral.com/news/articles/2008/07/02/20080702FLDSDress. html, accessed July 30, 2008; Andrea Ball, "Polygamist Sect Work Takes a Toll on Social Workers," *Austin American-Statesman,* May 8, 2008, http://www.statesman. com/news/content/news/stories/local/05/08/0508stress.html, accessed July 30, 2008 (quote).

16. Annette W. Farr, *The Story of Edwin Marion Whiting and Anna Maria Isaacson* (Provo, Utah: J. Grant Stevenson, 1969), 120, 124 (quote), 125–127.

17. William Kilshaw Barton, *Copy of Diary and Missionary Journal of William Kilshaw Barton, Pioneer of 1852* (Salt Lake City, n.p., n.d.), 12–13.

18. Emmeline B. Whitney to Daniel Wells, March 4, 1852, Emmeline B. Wells Papers, LDS Church Archives, cited in Patricia Rasmussen Eaton-Gadsby and Judith Rasmussen Dushku, "Emmeline B. Wells," in *Sister Saints,* ed. Vicky Burgess-Olson (Provo, Utah: Brigham Young University Press, 1978), 459. For a discussion of marital choice, see also Kathryn M. Daynes, *More Wives Than One: Transformation of the Mormon Marriage System 1840–1910* (Urbana: University of Illinois Press, 2001), 61–65.

19. Fred C. Collier, ed., *The Teachings of President Brigham Young,* vol. 3, *1852–1854* (Salt Lake City: Collier's, 1987), 292. For a similar comment by Brigham Young, see *Journal of Discourses* 6: 307 [April 8, 1853].

20. Leonard J. Arrington, *Brigham Young: American Moses* (New York: Alfred A. Knopf, 1985; reprint, Urbana: University of Illinois Press, 1986), 315.

21. Marianne T. Watson, "The 1948 Secret Marriage of Louis J. Barlow: Origins of FLDS Placement Marriage," *Dialogue: A Journal of Mormon Thought* 40 (Spring 2007): 84; Bistline, *Colorado City Polygamists,* 78. Bistline dates the change from the late 1950s, but Watson convincingly shows that the change took place in the previous decade.

22. Watson, "The 1948 Secret Marriage of Louis J. Barlow," 84–91.

23. Watson, "Secret Marriage," 86. Jessop confirms that a woman may have only two hours from the time she is informed of her placement and her wedding. Jessop, *Escape,* 75.

24. Jessop, *Escape,* 72–76; Wall, *Stolen Innocence,* 123–180; Bistline, *Colorado City Polygamists,* 92.

25. Bistline, *Colorado City Polygamists,* 78.

26. Daynes, *More Wives Than One,* 102, 11.

27. Brooke Adams, "Partial Settlement of Suit Involving FLDS: Lost Boys Win Cash, Land," *Salt Lake Tribune*, April 6, 2007, http://www.religionnewsblog. com/17897/lost-boys-win-land-cash, accessed July 28, 2008; Bistline, *Colorado City Polygamists*, 91–92; Donald Richter, "The Truth about the 'Lost Boys,'" *Truth Will Prevail*, June 13, 2008, http://www.truthwillprevail.org/archive.php, accessed July 28, 2008.

28. Wall, *Stolen Innocence*, 9, 19; John Dougherty, "Polygamous Leader of Mormon Is Sentenced in Utah," *International Herald Tribune*, November 27, 2007, http://www. iht.com/articles/2007/11/21/america/20cndjeffs.php, accessed July 23, 2008; Annie Clark Tanner, *A Mormon Mother: An Autobiography* (Salt Lake City: University of Utah Library Tanner Trust Fund, 1991), 73; Daynes, *More Wives Than One*, 130; Father's Family Information Sheet, Bishop's Record, Petitioner's Exhibit No. 4, Court Documents, http://web.gosanangelo.com/pdf/BishopsList.pdf, accessed July 23, 2008.

29. Davis Bitton and Val Lambson, "Demographic Limits of Polygyny," copy in author's possession.

30. Kathryn M. Daynes, "Single Men in a Polygamous Society: Male Marriage Patterns in Manti, Utah," *Journal of Mormon History* 24 (Spring 1998): 106–109; Father's Family Information Sheet, Bishop's Record, Court Documents. Thirty-five percent of the young men born from 1852–1869 and marrying when the percentage of polygamous marriages was declining married women five or more years younger than themselves, still much higher than the 8 percent of monogamists listed on the Bishop's Record.

31. Jessie L. Embry, *Mormon Polygamous Families: Life in the Principle* (Salt Lake City: University of Utah Press, 1987), 34–36; Father's Family Information Sheet, Bishop's Record, Court Documents.

32. Wall, *Stolen Innocence*, 14, 36, 41, 82, 123, 138, 287, 399; Martha Sonntag Bradley, *Kidnapped from That Land: The Government Raids on the Short Creek Polygamists* (Salt Lake City: University of Utah Press, 1993), 99–100.

33. Daynes, *More Wives Than One*, 96–97, 106–108; Larry M. Logue, *A Sermon in the Deseret: Belief and Behavior in Early St. George, Utah* (Urbana: University of Illinois Press, 1988), 56.

34. Michael Grossberg, *Governing the Hearth: Law and the Family in Nineteenth-Century America* (Chapel Hill: University of North Carolina Press, 1985), 106–108.

35. Mintz and Kellogg, *Domestic Revolutions*, 58–60; Paula S. Fass and Mary Ann Mason, eds., *Childhood in America* (New York: New York University Press, 2000), 2 (quote).

36. Grossberg, *Governing the Hearth*, 141–144; S. N. D. North, comp., *Marriage Laws in the United States, 1887–1906* (Conway, AR: Arkansas Research, 1993). The author appreciates the help of the Center for Family History and Genealogy, Brigham Young University, for the analysis of these laws.

37. Marriage Laws of the Fifty States, District of Columbia and Puerto Rico, Cornell University Law School, Legal Information Institute, http://topics.law.cornell. edu/wex/table_marriage, accessed August 4, 2008; Marriage Laws in the USA, http:// www.coolnurse.com/marriage_laws.htm, accessed August 4, 2008.

38. Research at the Archives, South Carolina Department of Archives and History, http://archives.sc.gov/information/vital/marriage.htm, accessed August 4, 2008.

39. Grossberg, *Governing the Hearth*, 106; Daynes, *More Wives Than One*, 96–98.

40. Median Age at First Marriage, 1890–2006, Infoplease, http://www.infoplease.com/ipa/A0005061.html, accessed August 4, 2008.

41. Daynes, *More Wives Than One*, 98, 116–127.

42. Daynes, *More Wives*.

43. "Gender Gap Widening, Census Data Shows," Info.com: U.S. Government Information, http://usgovinfo.about.com/od/censusandstatistics/a/paygapgrows.htm, accessed August 5, 2008; "Tom Zoellner, "Polygamy on the Dole," *Salt Lake Tribune*, June 28, 1998, A1; James Thalman, "Children Eligible for Welfare," *Deseret News*, May 18, 2008, http://deseretnews.com/article/1,5143,700226972,00.html, accessed August 5, 2008.

44. "Ex-polygamists Tell Court They'll Take Kids," CNN, May 20, 2008, http://us.cnn.com/2008/CRIME/05/20/polygamist.retreat.ap/index.html?iref=newssearch, accessed August 5, 2008.

45. Daynes, *More Wives Than One*, 143–149, 161–162; Kathryn M. Daynes, "Breaking the Seal: Analysis of Cancellations of Sealing by Brigham Young," paper presented at the Mormon History Association Conference, Killington, Vermont, May 26–29, 2005; Lisa K. McCasline, "The Civil Side of Divorce in Utah County," paper presented at the Mormon History Association Conference, May 26–29, 2005.

46. Daynes, *More Wives Than One*, 162–167; U.S. Census Bureau, Detailed Tables—Number, Timing and Duration of Marriages and Divorces: 2004, Tables 1 and 3; http://www.census.gov/population/www/socdemo/marr-div/2004detailed_tables.html : accessed March 19, 2010).

47. Daynes, *More Wives Than One*, 167–168.

48. Wall, *Stolen Innocence*, 189.

49. Wall, *Stolen Innocence*, 18–19, 54–65, 88–103.

50. Wall, *Stolen Innocence*, 186–190, 206–208, 248–252, 401–406, 189 (quote); Nicholas Riccardi, "At Jeffs' Trial, An Inside Look at His Church," *Los Angeles Times*, September 23, 2007, A-16, http://articles.latimes.com/2007/sep/23/nation/na-flds23, accessed July 28, 2008; Marianne T. Watson, "The Secret Marriage of Louis J. Barlow: A Story about the Origins of the FLDS Arranged Marriage System," paper presented at the Western History Association Conference, Scottsdale, Arizona, October 12–15, 2005; Jessop, *Escape*, 279.

51. Wall, *Stolen Innocence*, 18, 118, 284–285; Bistline, *Colorado City Polygamists*, 197; Pamela Manson and Brooke Adams, "Ousted FLDS Leader Louis Barlow Dies," *Salt Lake Tribune*, May 25, 2004, C10.

52. *Journal of Discourses*, 24: 171 [John Taylor, May 19, 1883]; Jens Christian Anderson Weibye, "Reminiscences and Journals" [ca. 1862–1893], typescript of MS 4723 Box 3 FD 1–4, March 16, 1870, Historical Department, The Church of Jesus Christ of Latter-Day Saints, Salt Lake City, Utah; Sanpete County, Utah, Probate Record, 1884–1890, Book B, December 22, 1885, microfilm of MS, Family History Library, Salt Lake City, Utah.

53. U.S. Statutes at Large, 22:47, March 22, 1882, 30–32.

54. Sarah Barringer Gordon, *The Mormon Question: Polygamy and Constitutional Conflict in Nineteenth Century America* (Chapel Hill: University of North Carolina Press, 2002), 156–161, 275; Rosa Mae McClellan Evans, "Judicial Prosecution of Prisoners for LDS Plural Marriage: Prison Sentences, 1884–1895," (Master's thesis, Brigham Young University, 1986), 24–39; Stan Larson, ed., *Prisoner for Polygamy: The Memoirs and Letters of Rudger Clawson at the Utah Territorial Penitentiary, 1884–87* (Urbana: University of Illinois, 1993), 209–231.

55. *West's Utah Code Annotated* (2004) §30-1-2; *Vernon's Texas Code Annotated* (2003) §2.102; Kirk Johnson, "Texas Polygamy Raid May Pose Risk," *New York Times,* April 12, 2008, http://www.nytimes.com/2008/04/12/us/12raid.html, accessed April 12, 2008.

56. Brook Adams, "Polygamist Tom Green Out of Prison, Now What?" *Salt lake Tribune,* August 8, 2008, http://www.rickross.com/reference/polygamy/polygamy679.html, accessed October 16, 2008; Paul A. Anthony, "Three More Sect Men Surrender," *San Angelo Times,* October 1, 2008, http://www.gosanangelo.com/news/2008/oct/01/three-more-sect-men-surrender/, accessed October 16, 2008.

57. St. George 1880s Polygamy Database. This database was constructed from names drawn from tithing records of the four wards in St. George. To be included, a man had to be in polygamy between 1885–1891 and donate funds for at least two years in that period. Tithing Records, CR 104 9, various reels, Church History Department, Church of Jesus Christ of Latter-Day Saints, Salt Lake City, Utah (used by permission). The men's marital status was determined by searching Ancestral File, International Genealogical Index, Pedigree Resource File (all at http://www.familysearch.org), 1880 and 1900 U.S. censuses, Utah Burials Database (Utah Division of Archives and Records Service http://history.utah.gov/apps/burials/execute/searchburials), and biographical accounts of the individuals listed in the tithing records. The database includes 52 polygamists.

58. U.S. Statutes at Large, 24: 375, March 3, 1887, 634–641; Gordon, *Mormon Question,*185–187, 206–220, 225–228; Leonard J. Arrington, *Great Basin Kingdom: An Economic History of the Latter-Day Saints, 1830–1900* (Lincoln: University of Nebraska Press, 1958), 360–386, 400–403; *Late Corporation v. United States,* 136 U.S. 1 (1890).

59. "Informal Discussion," *Deseret Weekly News,* September 27, 1890, 461.

60. Daynes, *More Wives Than One,* 214; Thomas G. Alexander, *Mormonism in Transition: A History of the Latter-Day Saints, 1890–1930* (Urbana: University of Illinois Press, 1986), 12; Doctrine and Covenants, Official Declaration.

61. See, for example, *Journal of Discourses,* 26: 151–157 [John Taylor, February 1, 1885]; Remarks by Sam Barlow, FLDS Priesthood Meeting and Conference, April 13, 2002, Utah Court Documents, Evidence—Loose Sheets 2, September 26, 2007, http://www.utcourts.gov/media/highprofilecourtcases/archives/Loose%20sheets%202.pdf, accessed 16 July 2008.

62. "FLDS Makes Concessions Regarding Plural Marriage Rules," *Salt Lake Tribune,* June 3, 2008.

63. Brooke Adams, "Texas Officials Say They Want to Help At-Risk Girls and Sexual Abuse Victims Face Emotional Issues," *Salt Lake Tribune*, October 11, 2008, http://www.sltrib.com/ci_10696387?IADID=Search-www.sltrib.com-www.sltrib.com , accessed October 18, 2008; Brooke Adams, "FLDS Girl Should Remain in State Custody, Say State Welfare Officials," *Salt Lake Tribune*, October 17, 2008.

64. Gordon, *Mormon Question*, xiii.

PART II

Social Scientists Examine Polygamy and the Seizure of the FLDS Children

Chapter 6

Demographic, Social, and Economic Characteristics of a Polygamist Community

Tim B. Heaton and Cardell K. Jacobson

As other chapters in this volume document, the general public knows little about the Fundamentalist Church of Jesus Christ of Latter-Day Saints (the FLDS). The other chapters have focused on the history and religious aspects of the FLDS and other polygamous communities. Here we focus on the social and demographic characteristics of the FLDS community.

The isolation and remoteness of these communities, along with their own reclusiveness, allowed these communities to grow in relative anonymity. The media images of the raid on the FLDS community in Eldorado, Texas, provided many outsiders their first view of fundamentalist polygamists. The images were at the same time surprising and odd. Few men were shown. When shown, the men appeared to be typical of other men who live in rural areas of the country. Attired in jeans and shirts, they fit in easily. The women in the videos, however, seem to be out of the mid-nineteenth century. They dress in long pastel dresses with full sleeves. The images were, by today's standards, at best quaint. Then there was the hair—mounds of it piled on top of the head. The media also showed children, a lot of children, with the girls also dressed in the old-style clothing.

Naturally, the media and people around the world were fascinated by the polygamists. The media focused on the raid, the strangeness of the group, and the practice of polygamy. They did not describe the origins of the Texas group and its relationship to other groups, nor did they describe the social and demographic characteristics of the FLDS community or the polygamist groups in general.

Obtaining information about the community is difficult. The Texas authorities removed 463 children and placed them in the foster care system. Neither the Texas authorities nor the media provided details about the ages of the children, the number of boys and girls, or the number of men and adult women in the community. Later the authorities identified several of the children as being adults and the number of underage children was reduced to 439.

Little is known about the socioeconomic characteristics of the community. We rely on the census data from the 2000 census to provide at least some description of the community that lies along the southern border of Utah and spills into northern Arizona. In the year 2000 the Eldorado group was part of the larger community located in "Shortcreek," a community originally established along the Utah-Arizona border. The area is now composed of two cities: Hildale, Utah, and Colorado City, Arizona. The FLDS in Texas likely reflect the composition of the larger community from which they emigrated. We use census data to examine the social and demographic characteristics of the larger group.

The practice of polygamy, high fertility, and selective in-and-out-migration,[1] combine to produce unusual, even unique, demographic and social characteristics within the polygamous communities. The physical isolation of the community further isolates the workforce. Some residents travel outside the area for economic and labor opportunities, but this further skews the social and demographic characteristics of the community.[2] We use aggregated data from the two communities on their separate sides of the border to provide a profile of the total community. We report results from the state of Utah for a comparison.

Age and Sex Composition of the Community

The population of the United States grows as a result of immigration, but also from natural increase (the number of births minus the number of deaths). The population, even without immigration, is growing slowly. This modest growth rate, combined with the selective immigration of primarily younger people, results in a somewhat younger population than would otherwise be the case. One quarter (25.7 percent) of the population in the United States was under age 18 in the 2000 Census. In contrast, Utah has a somewhat higher birthrate than the nation as a whole; nearly a third of the children (32.2 percent) in Utah are under the age of 18. By comparison, the percentage of the Hildale–Colorado City community is double that of the State of Utah: 61.6 percent of the population is under the age of 18. Or stated differently, more than six out of ten people in the town are minors.

A young age structure in a community presents difficulties in current American society. The adults must provide child care, schooling, and other child-related services. Job creation for young adults becomes critical. If sufficient jobs are not available, the residents may be forced to migrate temporarily or permanently to other locations for employment. A third option is the farming and ranching industries that many of the FLDS have chosen. Such environments provide the isolation from the larger society that members want, while at the same time they provide labor-intensive jobs for some of the young adults. As Bennion notes in her chapters in this volume, many young men also work in construction industries in southern Utah and other adjacent areas.

One mitigating factor for job provision is that the FLDS Hildale–Colorado City area is small. The United States Census reported 232 households in Hildale in the year 2000 with a total of 1,895 people. Colorado City, on the other side of the border in Arizona, was larger, with a population of 3,334. By 2007 the estimated population of the two towns was 6,789 (http://www .census.gov/). The offshoot FLDS group in Eldorado, Texas, by comparison, is still much smaller. All 463 individuals initially identified as children at the time of the raid were removed; the number of adults was likely only about

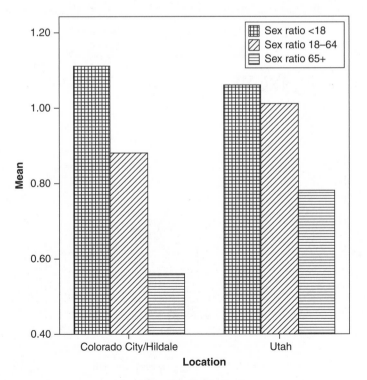

FIGURE 6.1. Sex Ratios by Age
Source: 2000 Census

100. Many of the men in the area built the homes and the "temple" located at Eldorado. Others were involved in the farming activities in the community.

The sex ratios of the communities are highly skewed. The ratios for the Hildale–Colorado City area (by age groups) are reported in figure 6.1. Normally, populations have roughly the same number of males as females, but younger age groups tend to have a slightly higher number of males than females. In the United States, about 105 males are born for every 100 females (sex ratios are computed as the number of males per hundred females). Males tend to die younger than females do, however, so the sex ratios tend to decline in later age groupings. In the "Shortcreek" community, the ratio of males to females for the children (those under the age of 18) is slightly higher (1.11) than in Utah as a whole (1.06). This variation may be a random variation. More likely, however, the ratio is the result of young married females overstating their age to the census enumerators to avoid the appearance of underage marriage.

The sex ratios for the adults and the elderly in the community are much different, however. Both groups show a clear shortage of males. Among those aged 18–64 there are only 88 men for every 100 women, compared to a nearly even ratio of 1.01 in Utah generally. Among the elderly, 65 years of age and older, there are only 56 men for every 100 women in the polygamist community, compared to 78 males per 100 females in Utah. The decline in the sex ratio in Utah

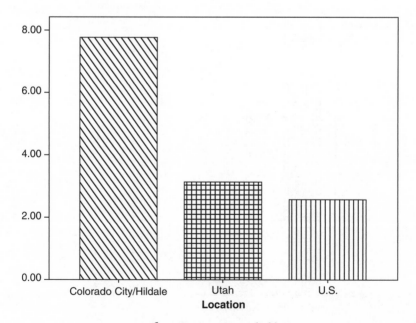

FIGURE 6.2. Average Household Size
Source: 2000 Census

is normal; the steep decline in the polygamous is not. The differences in the sex ratios among the older groups may result from selective recruitment of women into the group, thus increasing the number of women relative to men. Some men also are forced out of the group either because they fail to follow the leadership or because the leaders want to reduce competition for wives. Young men who are forced out are sometimes referred to as the "Lost Boys" (see the Bennion chapters in this volume). Finally, some of the men may have been working and living out of the community at the time the census was taken. These sex ratios are not surprising in a polygamous community. The practice of polygamy would seem to preclude universal marriage. Nevertheless, universal marriage can happen in such communities for several reasons. First, the banishment of some competing men, either as young men or as adults, allows for the reassignment of wives to other men. Second, a rapidly growing population means that each successive generation has more women than the previous generation of men. Thus, universal marriage can happen as older men marry younger women. The FLDS community has over three times more people in the late teenage years (ages 15–19) than it has in the 35–39-year-old group. If men aged 35–39 marry women aged 15–19, then each man could have at least three wives. For such a pattern to continue, however, the community must grow rapidly through high birthrates and conversion. In reality, the practice likely creates limited marriage opportunities for some men. The senior men have control of marriage and dictate who can marry whom. When preference is given to the more senior men so that they can have multiple wives, some younger men cannot compete and may leave the community—the "Lost Boys."[3]

Household Composition and Marital Status

Consistent with a high birthrate, the households in Hildale–Colorado City are large. The average household has 7.75 people, compared to 3.13 in Utah and 2.59 in the United States (see figure 6.2). Nearly three-quarters (74.6 percent) of the households in Hildale–Colorado City are composed of married couples with children. Only a few of the households are headed by females. By comparison, even in the family-oriented state of Utah, 35 percent of households include a married couple with children under 18. The other households in Utah are composed of single-parent families, individuals, or most commonly, husbands and wives whose children have left home.

Only 2.9 percent of the FLDS aged 15 and over reported that they were separated or divorced at the time of the census (compared to 9.3 percent of the population in Utah). Despite the high percentage of family households in

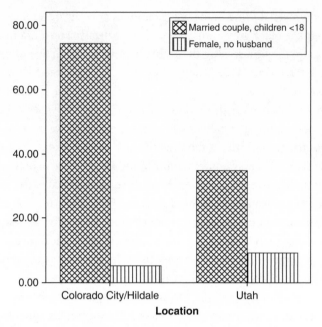

FIGURE 6.3. Household Composition
Source: 2000 Census

the FLDS group, most live in what the census terms "rental units." More than three in five (62.8 percent) live in such units (compared to 28.5 percent in Utah as a whole). In fact, these rental units are simply homes owned by the FLDS Church.[4] Sometimes the homes have been built and donated to the Church.

Education and Economic Status

Educational attainment in small communities is often lower than in more urban areas. Residents often remain in the community and work, rather than attending college or other advanced educational opportunities that require commuting or moving. This is true in Hildale–Colorado City, where the educational levels are somewhat lower than in Utah and the United States. Although a majority of the FLDS population aged 25 and older completed high school (71.5 percent, compared to 87.7 percent in Utah and 80.4 percent in the U.S.), only a small fraction complete a college degree. The community has a high school, which allows most of the residents to complete high school without leaving the area. Fewer than 5 percent of the FLDS have completed a bachelor's degree, however. This is strikingly lower than the percentage in Utah and the nation who have completed

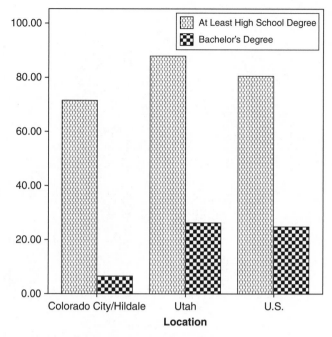

FIGURE 6.4. Educational Status of Population aged 25 and Older
Source: 2000 Census

college; more than 25 percent of all people in Utah have completed college and nearly that many in the nation have completed college (see figure 6.4).

Educational attainment is usually related to the occupational structure and the kinds of jobs that individuals have in their adult lives. The polygamous communities vary from this normal pattern. Since few members of the polygamous communities complete college, the men tend to have more agricultural and construction jobs. In the FLDS community, about half the workforce is engaged in white collar (business, professional) jobs and about half in blue collar (manual labor, manufacturing) occupations. In contrast, over three-fourths of the labor force in Utah works in white collar jobs. Less than one percent of the workforce is engaged in agriculture in the FLDS community and the same is true in Utah in general (see figure 6.5). Self employment, on the other hand, is slightly higher (8.9 percent) in the community than in Utah (5.8 percent).

Furthermore, a smaller fraction of the Hildale–Colorado City population over age 16 is in the civilian labor force than is the case for Utah. This is largely because females in the FLDS community are less likely to work for pay. Unemployment, however, is relatively low in the community (2.2 percent in the community, compared to 5.0 percent in Utah in 2000).

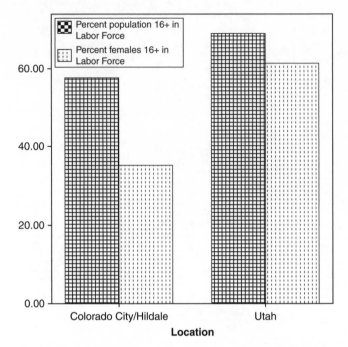

FIGURE 6.5. Labor Force Participation aged 16 and Older
Source: 2000 Census

Given these factors, overall income is comparatively low in the polygamist community. The median family income is 37 percent lower than in Utah. The incomes of both the males and females are lower in Hildale–Colorado City than in the state of Utah. These lower incomes reflect the isolation and location of the city in a lower-income part of the state. The relatively low educational levels and the limited occupational training also limit the opportunities for high-paying jobs.

The ratio of female-to-male income for full-time workers in the FLDS community is also lower than in the state of Utah. In Hildale–Colorado City, males earn 49 percent more than females do, whereas men in the state of Utah earn 20 percent more than women do.

Perhaps ironically, income inequality in Hildale–Colorado City is quite high. Overall incomes are low, but a slightly higher percentage of families earn over $100,000 per year (4.7 percent) than is the case for Utah (3.6 percent). This ratio results in the high inequality.

The low incomes and large families combine to create a high poverty rate in Hildale–Colorado City. Nearly one-third of the families fall below the official poverty level for families their size (compared to only 6.5 percent in Utah). Thus, more

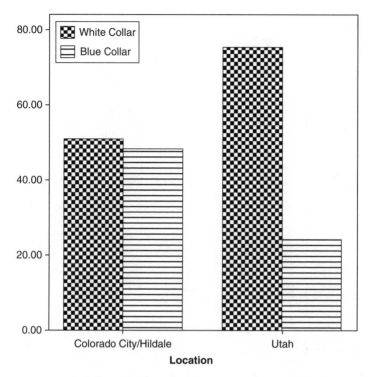

FIGURE 6.6. Occupational Status of Labor Force aged 16 and Older
Source: 2000 Census

families receive public assistance. Supplemental Security income is also higher in the polygamist community (4.4 percent, compared to 2.8 percent in Utah).

Racially, the community is overwhelmingly white (98 percent compared to 89 percent in Utah and 75 percent in the U.S.). The percent that identify as Hispanic (who can be of any race) is also very low (2 percent, compared to 9 percent in Utah and 12.5 percent in the U.S.).

In sum, the polygamous community known as Shortcreek and subsequently officially named Hildale, Utah, and Colorado City, Arizona, exhibits several interesting characteristics that distinguish it from other communities in both Utah and other parts of the country. Some of these are the result of the isolated location. Others reflect the theological beliefs and practices of the polygamous community. Still others reflect a combination of the choices and dogma. Clearly, the isolation and lower educational levels limit job opportunities since the local job market is composed primarily of construction trades and agricultural pursuits. The lower educational levels, however, also reflect the decision of the leaders to limit access to outside influences that might undermine the community and its peculiar religious perspectives. Likewise, the emphasis within the Church to have many

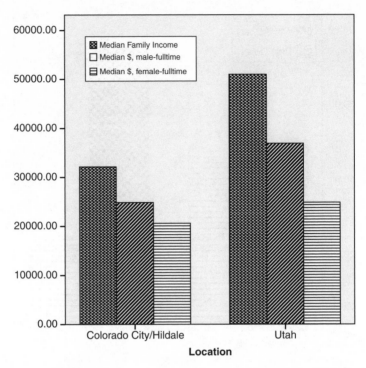

FIGURE 6.7. Median Family Income of the FLDS Community and Utah by Family Type
Source: 2000 Census

babies and to have the women stay home with the children limits the income they
might otherwise provide to the families and the community more generally.

The emphasis on early marriage and the pronatalist stance produce a
group that is young in comparison to the others who surround the community, even as it tends to rely on governmental aid. Ironically, women seemed
to be converted to the lifestyle more than men (see the Bennion chapters in
this volume). As Miles[5] and chapter 7 in this volume show, women can find
the lifestyle rewarding. This may seem to be at odds with the view that polygamy is all about sex. As these authors show, it is not. Nevertheless, this selective recruitment also skews the population. The practice of polygamy and the
heavy emphasis on marriage also results in relatively low divorce rates. Family relationships within polygamy are also somewhat different. Since many
families live together within larger homes, the women form strong relationships with each other, and the children often form strong bonds with half
brothers and half sisters that would not prevail in the larger society. The children also establish strong relationships with other mothers and aunts. The
social demographics of the society are unusual. While any group is susceptible
to abuse, these polygamous arrangements can also provide strengths that are

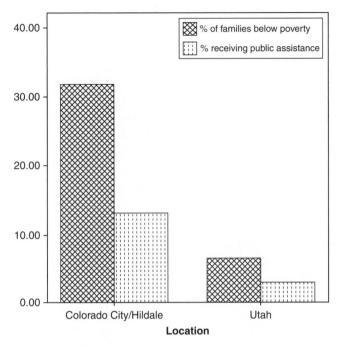

FIGURE 6.8. Percent of Families below the Poverty Line and
Receiving Public Assistance

absent in other parts of society. The demographics discussed in this chapter
show the family arrangements; they cannot, however, show abuse or strength.
We leave those discussions to others in this volume.

NOTES

1. The leader of the group, Warren Jeffs, reportedly expelled several men from
the group as recently as 2004 and reassigned their wives and children to other men.
Some news articles refer to the young men and boys who were forced out as "Lost
Boys." They are often described as having few social skills or abilities to function in the
larger society.

2. While some members of the community are not members of the FLDS group,
the community is dominated by the FLDS. Those not members of the FLDS are often
ostracized and pressured to leave the community. This is especially true of those who
have been expelled by the FLDS.

3. Jon Krakauer, *Under the Banner of Heaven: A Story of Violent Faith* (New York:
Doubleday, 2003).

4. The source of this information is a former employee of the County Assessor's
office in Washington County (the county containing Hildale, Utah).

5. Carrie A. Miles, "Polygamy and the Economics of Salvation," *Sunstone
Magazine*, August 1998.

Chapter 7

The Many Faces of Polygamy: An Analysis of the Variability in Modern Mormon Fundamentalism in the Intermountain West

Janet Bennion

Polygamous Mormon women's lives are now paraded on prime-time television through the HBO series *Big Love,* featuring a Viagra-popping Utah businessman and his three wives living in suburbia. This series provides the first televised portrayal of the contemporary polygamist lifestyle. In spite of its overemphasis on sex, which often confounds the real issues for women in these movements, the series has the potential to awaken the mainstream to the realities of the lives of women in polygamous marriages. Not surprisingly, many prominent Mormons, such as former presidential candidate Mitt Romney and former LDS prophet Gordon B. Hinckley, express concern about the negative publicity it can bring to mainstream Mormonism. This concern informs public policy, which acts to alienate plural marriage through a "don't ask, don't tell" strategy that has multiple effects: (1) it allows polygamists to fade into the background, away from the evils of Babylon and government scrutiny; (2) it makes it harder for polygamists to solicit public support and acknowledgement for legalization; and (3) it makes it easier for abusive polygamists to thrive under the cloak of isolated, rurally circumscribed regions.

My purpose here is to dispel some of the media-driven, ethnocentric myths and tap into the rich and varied experiences of polygamous women, who are often marginalized by the mainstream. This effort will provide evidence that there are many faces of polygamy, not just those depicted by Jon Krakauer[1] and Carolyn Jessop.[2] Furthermore, "abuse" itself is a culturally relative term, often used by the media and government protection agencies in a biased fashion to warrant raids and discrimination against small nontraditional religious movements. Polygamy does not in itself, as Oprah Winfrey suggests, perpetuate "third-world Taliban-type abuse,"[3] nor do all groups require that their women be treated like property, good only for breeding and child rearing. On the contrary, there are ample illustrations of female autonomy, achievement, and contentment within a polygamous context. In short, I follow columnist Rebecca Walsh's recent counsel,[4] that a true feminist defends other women's right to choose how they wish to make love, marry, and raise their families.

My remarks are drawn from 15 years of anthropological fieldwork conducted in three environments: the AUB (Allreds) of the Bitterroot Mountains of Montana; the AUB and surrounding independent polygamists of the Salt Lake Valley of Utah;[5] and the LeBaron group of Galeana, Chihuahua, Mexico.[6] I have lived and worked with 22 extended polygamous families and interviewed more than 355 individuals about their conversion to the movement, their living arrangements, and their lifestyles. I also draw upon my own history as a descendent of nineteenth-century Mormon polygamy from the Cannon, Bennion, and Benson lines.

Rationale: Why Study Polygamy Now?

In April 2008, the State of Texas raided the Eldorado Yearning for Zion ranch, separating 463 children from their parents—the largest government seizure of children in the history of the United States. This rash, traumatic measure was initiated by a telephone hoax of a young woman from Colorado who was not connected in any way to the sect. Texas officials and the FBI placed the children into foster care which, ironically, has often been associated with abuse.[7] Texas officials ignored the history of other failed raids of religious movements: Island Pond, Vermont, where the governor approved the removal of 112 children from the Twelve Tribes commune in 1985; and Short Creek, Utah/Arizona, where 236 children were removed from their mothers in 1953.[8] Each case led to public outcry and a U.S. Supreme Court ruling that such raids are unconstitutional. In the Island Pond case, government officials worried that the children were being beaten. In the Eldorado case, authorities sought evidence of underage girls being forced into polygamous marriages. The Texas officials took cotton swab DNA samples of children and mothers to determine parentage and placed them in a variety of housing situations. The state neglected to acknowledge the damaging cultural shock that the FLDS children experienced in foster care. The FLDS children had been taught to fear such modern government institutions and the "outside" world. In the end, Texas authorities admitted that the raid was focused, not on individual cases of sex abuse, but on the entire FLDS culture.[9]

Governments have repeatedly attempted to investigate polygamous lifestyles and intervene in alleged cases of abuse. Prior to the Eldorado fiasco, the arrest and trial of FLDS prophet Warren Jeffs for his alleged abuses against underage women, including his niece of 14, whom he forced to marry her cousin of 18, provided fodder for media outlets.[10] Before the Winter Olympics in Utah in 2002, the State of Utah arrested polygamist Tom Green and convicted him of marrying a 13-year-old girl.[11] While most Intermountain states have used the "mutual-consent abandonment" policy, in which each side acts as if the other does not exist, both Utah and Arizona are initiating dialogue between law enforcement and sect leaders wherever possible.[12]

Furthermore, the Canadian and U.S. governments are currently struggling to cope with larger numbers of Muslim and Mormon fundamentalist citizens who believe it is their religious right to practice polygamy. Although polygamy is a felony in the United States, between 38,000 and 60,000 individuals practice Mormon polygamy in the Intermountain West.[13] The number of Muslim polygamists is expected to increase as Islam continues to grow in the United States and Canada.[14] In addition, attention is being given to alternative marriages. In 2003, the Supreme Court decriminalized sodomy, which helped polygamy causes by implying that the court should stay out of the bedroom. Law professor Jon Turley called openly for the legalization of bigamy and same-sex marriage, stating that though he finds it offensive, it should not be illegal.[15]

Current U.S. policy has adopted Canada's approach, which asserts that the practice of polygamy violates women's right to "equality within marriage and the family."[16] Yet the United States does not actively prosecute unless evidence of abuse or welfare fraud is provided. The International Human Rights (IHR) faculty in Canada instructed the Justice Department to institute an anti-polygamy law based on a series of assumptions about harmful conditions perpetrated against polygamous women. In short, any polygamous families that migrate from the United States to Canada in search of religious freedom will soon be at risk of arrest. This result is based solely on Cook's work, which uses the sources of international law identified in

Article 38 of the Statute of the International Court of Justice (I.C.J.) as a guiding framework. They found polygamy to

> violate women's right to freedom by requiring obedience, modesty, and chastity codes that preclude women from operating as full citizens and enjoying their civil and political rights. Further, women can often be socialized into subservient roles that inhibit their full participation in family and public life. The physical, mental, sexual and reproductive, economic, and citizenship harms associated with the practice violate many of the fundamental human rights recognized in international law.

I argue that the studies cited by IHR to support their assumptions lack substantive evidence of abuse and are also ethnocentric. Most of the studies are based on sensationalized, nonrepresentative cases and do not reflect the prevalent condition of family life. In fact, the only ethnographic, long-term data on women's lives cited in the report was my work, which offered insight into the relative benefits of polygamy: "indeed the networking Janet Bennion outlined in her scholarship on contemporary Fundamentalist Mormon polygamy signals that this type of social framework is already being utilized by women" and that increased scholarly discourse on the topic can help "women within the Fundamentalist Mormon communities to re-define religious doctrine that subordinates them while still being able to embrace faith components that are normatively valuable."[17] Also missing from the IHR report was well-documented evidence that many plural families around the world are prone to be "well-functioning."[18]

I challenge the IHR assumptions and the existing media-driven paradigm that polygamy uniformly "violates women's right to equality within marriage and the family."[19] It is essential to examine the full and variable impact of polygamous family life on the health and well-being of women and children based on satisfaction levels, sexuality, economic activities, living arrangements, leisure and autonomy, financial stability, socialization, and the presence or absence of abuse. I predict that polygamy is not, per se, the ultimate and inevitable cause of abuses against women and children. The following conditions, when combined with polygamy, may produce a greater risk for victimization of abuse and violation of human rights: (1) father absence or low father parental investment,[20] (2) isolated rural environment or circumscription,[21] (3) absence of a strong female network,[22] (4) overcrowding in the household,[23] and (5) male supremacist ideology.[24] The results of this current examination and other future studies of contemporary polygamous lifestyles may help identify the presence of abusive conditions, which can then inform policy for the protection of victims and the prevention of future abuses. On the other hand, such studies could show a lack of abuse, which can inform policy on legalization rights and procedures and anti-discrimination laws for the protection of alternative family forms.

Literature Review

Only a handful of scholars have examined Mormon fundamentalism. Irwin Altman focused on the complexity of relationships among a few key AUB families and examined the struggle for families to fit into a polygamous structure using Victorian, monogamous psychological frameworks.[25] William Jankowiak[26] investigated the father adoration concept in polygamous relationships in the FLDS group. Robin Fox[27] and Phillip Kilbride[28] were both interested in showing the relative benefit of polygamy to offset the crises of American modernity in which women are drawn to alternative marriage forms to cope with socioeconomic obstacles. These studies applaud adaptive measures taken by polygamists to share resources and provide protection from urbanity. My own research explores the ironic ascendance of women in rigid patriarchal communities. In the Montana Allred branch[29] and Colonia LeBaron in Mexico,[30] I record female conversion experiences and find that many women are attracted to the commune for socioeconomic support. Women report that they are fleeing a difficult life in the mainstream where their status as divorcees, single mothers, widows, and "unmarriageables" limits their access to good men and also access to the economic and spiritual affirmation that comes from a community of worship. In "Abbas Raptus,"[31] I describe six sensational cases of arrests of perpetrators from various polygamous groups and analyze factors contributing to father-daughter abuse. The following conditions are typical in these cases: rural environments, frequent absences of the father from the home, lack of a female network present in circumscribed housing, overcrowded households, and the presence of "father worship."[32] Combined with the adoration of the father was a strict code of obeisance required of all children and wives. Punishment for breaking this code was the blood atonement, which was a physical whipping or cutting of the skin to atone for the sins against the father. It is this final study of cases that led me to believe that a thorough investigation of polygamy must be made to clarify whether only a few miscreants are guilty of abuse or whether all polygamous families contain abuse.

During my research among the Salt Lake AUB, in 2000, I was asked to speak at an American Civil Liberties Union–sponsored panel with two polygamous women and two lesbian women to help clarify the reasons why certain Mormon women are attracted to alternative sexual lifestyles. First, women are often drawn to fundamentalism for socioeconomic reasons: a home, a family, and the female network inherent in big polygamous structures. Men are often attracted to polygamy for political and religious reasons: to gain a family kingdom and a calling as high priest of that kingdom. These are the patterns of conversion predominantly among people in their thirties and forties. However, there are some young, college-aged Mormons who are also drawn into fundamentalism, particularly from BYU, who are bored of the "milk" they get in the LDS experience often associated with a shallow social emphasis. They hunger for the "meat" they find in fundamentalism, representing the deeper doctrinal and spiritual dialogue associated with the "mysteries." Ironically, most converts are not interested in polygamy but in adherence to purer doctrine.[33] Like Roy Potter, a Mormon who joined fundamentalism in 1979, most converts come from the LDS Church.[34] Potter was angered over the changes to original doctrine and for being censured by the LDS Brethren.[35] Converts, like Potter, are not actively proselytized by polygamous groups, but are mostly drawn to writers like Ogden Kraut and leaders and friends from the AUB, whose beliefs most closely resembles the LDS experience but provide the doctrinal "meat" they are seeking. Fewer converts seek to join the more restrictive FLDS group, as it is remote from jobs and cities, and the clothing and behavioral rules are not appealing. Furthermore, most FLDS members are born and reared in the group. Likewise, few converts join the Kingston Clan as it requires new families to fully submit to the Kingston family rule. At one time, under Ervil's rule, the LeBaron group actively sought converts from other fundamentalist groups, but that effort failed during his "killing spree" in the mid-1970s.

The four major fundamentalist groups are all tied to the original movement initiated by Lorin C. Woolley in the early 1930s. This movement is based on a vision purportedly received by John Taylor that polygamy should continue to be practiced as an eternal principle. From that sub rosa movement sprung the four separate movements:

- The Fundamentalist Church of Jesus Christ of Latter-Day Saints, originally set in Short Creek, on the border of Arizona and Utah; led by LeRoy Johnson, who then appointed Rulon Jeffs, who called his son Warren to the presidency;
- The Apostolic United Brethren, also known as the Allred Group, whose first prophet was Joseph Musser who then appointed Rulon C. Allred, who then gave the seat to his brother Owen, who then bequeathed it to Lamoine Jensen;
- The Latter-Day Church of Christ, also known as the Davis County Corporation, founded by John Ortell Kingston, son of Elden Kingston,

who broke away from Musser's leadership in the 1950s, eventually relinquishing his title as the "one mighty and strong" in 1987 to his son Paul Elden Kingston; and

• The LeBaron order, formally known as the Church of the First Born of the Fullness of Times, was established in 1955 as a sanctuary in the Mexican desert, by Joel LeBaron based on the vision that was given to his father, Alma Dayer LeBaron.

Examining Viability and Impact

Just as one can never paint all marital forms with one brush, likewise, within polygamy, it is folly to assume that all women have the same experience. Although there are many faces, the press broadcasts only the ugly ones. Within one month, while visiting the West, I witnessed three different styles of polygamy. While driving from Cedar Breaks, Utah, I stopped at Yankee Meadow Reservoir, where I saw an FLDS extended family comprised of two men, their five wives, and seven kids. They had arrived in two brand new Chevrolet minivans for a pleasant afternoon of fishing. Three of the women were wearing pastel pioneer dresses, with one dressed in a unique camouflage pattern. While the women fished and gutted the catches, the men relaxed in the shade, talking. The next family I saw, while shopping in Spanish Fork, Utah, was an AUB patriarch and his five wives, varying in ages from 18 to 35, from the Rocky Ridge order. Their style of dress was modern, with brand-name shoes and fancy colors, albeit quite modest (dresses and long-sleeved blouses). The women's hair was long but done up in creative braids and buns. The husband had blond hair and blue eyes and was in his forties; the three women were of various ages from their twenties to forties. The seven children also had blond hair and blue eyes. Lastly, while traveling to Seattle, Washington, I met a family of one businessman, an independent, and his two wives, and five of their 23 children. The man and his first wife were in their sixties, both dressed in modern, almost hip, attire, whereas the young wife was still in her thirties, dressed in a long conservative skirt and a long-sleeved blouse with a fish-tail braid trailing down her back. She looked nearly identical to Nicki, Bill Henrickson's second "born-in" wife on *Big Love*.

Because forms vary, each polygamous family must be evaluated in its own cultural context. Only certain types of polygamy may be at high risk for abuse. Accusations of these high risk candidates must be followed up with investigations on a case-by-case basis instead of targeting an entire religious community or cultural enclave. Further, definitions of "contentment" or "abuse" may

be vastly different from culture to culture. Even in this paper I may be tread-
ing on dangerous ground with assumptions about positive or negative impact.
I will try to pair my definitions with the factors provided by the International
Human Rights (IHR) Document about satisfaction, autonomy, and abuse, but
the communities themselves may not agree with this pairing. They may see an
underage bride as fully appropriate to the lifestyle and values of their particular
beliefs, whereas the individualistic mainstream may call this behavior outrageous and abusive.

Positive Impact

The IHR document, like the media, focuses only on negative traits, such as lack
of freedom of choice and autonomy, presence of subordination, deference to
patriarchal mandate, and the presence of abuse. Al-Krenawi, an international
expert on social work and mental health, gives characteristics of a successful
polygamous family that are more helpful in defining positive impact. These
include: (1) religious sanction of polygamy (God's wish or destiny); (2) equal
allocation of resources among families; (3) separate households for each wife;
(4) maintaining an attitude of respect toward the other wife; and (5) open communication among all wives, siblings, and among children and other mothers.[36]
I focus on four traits or features that have a clear positive impact on women and
children (mirroring both IHR and Al-Krenawi's criteria): (1) viable alternative;
(2) republican motherhood and empowerment; (3) female solidarity and friendship; and (4) sustainability and libertarianism.

Viable Alternative

Some Mormon women experience more individual satisfaction within the
dynamics of a polygamous family than they could in any other marital form.
This may account for the high rate of female (versus male) conversion.[37] Pro-
polygamist advocates like Anne Wilde say it can be seen as a "viable alternative
lifestyle between consenting adults."[38] Anthropologist Phil Kilbride states that
plural marriage can help rebuild a strong sense of family for specific groups of
Americans, especially in times of socioeconomic crisis.[39] He asks, is monogamy
so perfect? Many monogamous women suffer from being under the thumb of
a dominant man with no one else nearby to help them. He points out that at
least polygamist women have their co-wives to talk to and help potentially protect them from a tyrannical husband. According to Adriana Blake,[40] polygamy
may be essential in our future, as there is a skewed sex ratio in America in

favor of women: for every 100 men, aged 45, there are 200 single women. She thinks a return to plural marriage could be the best alternative to divorce and may provide husbands for women, fathers for children, and an end to loneliness. With an overabundance of unmarriageable women, more women will be willing to be linked to a good "alpha" male, even if they have to share him; "women prefer half or quarter of a good man to whole of a third rate man."[41] One FLDS woman said she is married to an older man because "there are only a few good men out there and if you don't share your good man with a sister wife, she'll have to marry a jerk."[42]

Besides reducing divorce rates and providing single women with more options, some advocates provide evidence that polygamy enhances family life by providing more loving parents for child care. For example, during the recent raid, many FLDS children were asked to identify their mothers. They replied that they had many mothers who cared for them.[43] There are also intense friendships forged within the large, extended family network. Jankowiak found that when children are raised in polygamy, they develop sibling solidarity.[44] This phenomenon refers to the bonds that develop between full and half siblings relating to inclusive fitness.

Republican Motherhood and Empowerment

"Republican Motherhood" was founded in the early Mormon suffragette movement and was directed by outspoken polygamous women such as U.S. senator and doctor Martha Hughes Cannon.[45] It allowed benefits for women in the private and public realms of life and it was encouraged by Brigham Young to advance careers in business and politics: "Women are useful, not only to sweep houses...but they should stand behind the counter, study law or physics, or become good bookkeepers...all this enlarges their sphere of usefulness for the benefit of society at large."[46]

Polygamous women also increase their "republican motherhood" status with the number of children they bear. Joe Jessop's first wife, who bore 14 children, for example, is considered a "queen among women." June, an AUB naturopath and midwife, who has birthed 1,300 children, enjoys enormous prestige, as she facilitates the migration of spirit children to their mothers. Other than motherhood, empowerment may also come from the power of choice. Mary, from the AUB and the wife of the mayor, for example, was once married to a councilman and found him to be emotionally disturbed. She demanded a "new and improved" husband and the priesthood gave her the choice among all the men in town. She chose a wealthy man, the mayor, who had two kind and gentle wives. She is known as "a libber" for her willingness to speak her mind and provide her children with protection. Another example of empowerment is "Emily," a businesswoman with a bachelor's degree who runs the family's six-figure operations. She is an independent second wife, no longer pledged to any group, but she enjoys "top dog" status as the family's primary breadwinner. Rarely does anyone in the family, including her husband, disagree with her decisions. Other women described their control of the reproductive schedule and the financial budgeting. A further example is Donna Baird, the administrative director of the AUB who for many decades oversaw the financial and religious organization of the sect under the leadership of Owen Allred. I have never met a tougher lady. She is the check and balance of the group, reminding councilmen and members alike when they are in the wrong or in need of her fine-tuned adjustment to their moral characters.

Another form of empowerment comes from participation in religious ritual. Women described their access to healing powers and feminist ideologies that the mainstream church long ago abandoned, such as using the priesthood to bless one's child and praying to Heavenly Mother.[47]

Female Solidarity and Friendship

Polygamous women enjoy autonomy and freedoms associated within a huge female economic network established between married women of the patrilineage. When faced with a challenge, such as a husband who gets "out of line," women may unite in opposition against him. For instance, one woman said that her husband wasn't spending enough time with her son and that he also forgot her birthday. The other wives joined her in "boycotting" their husband—barring him from access to food and sex for a week. These women say they feel sorry for monogamous women who are with their husbands "24/7." Within polygamy, and with the help of co-wives, they argue, one can gain respite from their husband and engage in individual pursuits in education or careers.

Additionally, women voice satisfaction in the "Law of Sarah" ceremony, which covenants women to each other for eternity. Ideally, the first wife agrees to link the second wife not only to her husband, but also to herself, in this life and the next. Through this eternal bond, women are encouraged to work together economically, socially, and spiritually, and in some rare cases, sexually. These bonds are enhanced through the common feature of women courting other women as future co-wives. While a guest in the LeBaron group, for example, one co-wife engaged me in deep conversation and, after I had left the group, continued to "court" me as her husband's potential fourth wife, stating that we had a great deal in common. In an AUB family, a third wife of one of my best informants had prodded her husband to propose to me, in spite of the fact that I was already happily married. She remarked that I would be a great intellectual and financial asset to the family and that, furthermore, she liked me. On another occasion, a woman expressed her wishes for me to marry into the family because we agreed politically.

This friendship/courtship network is vital, especially during the prolonged absences of husbands. Women develop a strong interdependence with each other that creates a large repertoire of domestic and mechanical skills such as dry-walling, fishing, plowing, and herding cattle (all typically male activities). "If one wife can't fix it, the other can," is a commonly spoken concept. Few monogamous women experience this type of shared skill-set. One example of the female network is the "Ben Sampson" family of Pinesdale, Montana, where four women—all skilled in different areas—worked together for the maintenance of the whole family. One wife was skilled as a nurse and worked part-time at the Hamilton hospital. Another woman, trained in child development, was a key figure in the care of the family's 24 children. A third wife, schooled in elementary education, helped at the local Montessori school. And the fourth, an excellent cook, stayed home to help the second wife with the children.

Yet another example of female solidarity is "David" LeBaron's family in Colonia LeBaron near Galeana, Mexico. David, son of Verlan and Irene LeBaron, constructed three homes with his own hands for each of his wives and 22 children. Together, they raise a variety of crops from tomatoes to alfalfa. They run cattle and a dry-wall business in the Midwest. He and his sons work in the United States and send money home to his three wives, who form a tight-knit survival group during his absence. Now, through the use of cell phones, they can communicate freely for aid and support in their daily needs, from shopping in Casas Grandes to canning peaches. They take turns with caring for the childen, teaching at the local school, and tending the livestock. They live only a few miles apart and so are able to share tasks easily. All three wives married David of their own volition and feel free to move across the border as they wish.[48]

Finally, the best example of economic networking is the Alex Joseph family of Big Water, Utah. Alex Joseph joined the Mormon Church in the 1950s and later the fundamentalist Allredite fold in Pinesdale. He convinced four Missoula students to marry him (none of whom was connected to Mormonism). He left the Allreds to build the community of Big Water in 1983 and organized the Confederate Nations of Israel.[49] Joseph became famous through his wives' notoriety. While he fashioned himself as a writer, salesman, scholar, and manager, his seven wives were all professional career women: lawyers, accountants, businesswomen, and teachers and provided the vast bulk of resources for the family's needs. At the same time, they also obtained college degrees, bore and reared children, and built careers.

Libertarianism and Sustainability

Polygamists often voice their heavy reliance on isolation from the outside world and freedom from oppressive government as a major component of their conversion. They seek freedom to live a religious code without interference, yet they pride themselves in also being good citizens of the United States. In Big Water, for example, Alex Joseph and his wives became libertarians, convincing all other members of the town to follow suit and abolish all town property taxes.[50] In Pinesdale, they pride themselves on their freedoms and independence and have one of the lowest tax rates in the nation because they believe in taking care of their own roads, buildings, water systems, and law enforcement. Many adopt sustainable living and self reliance. They subscribe to *Mother Earth News* and *Home Power* magazines to learn better ways to live "off the grid," away from heavy dependence on expensive water, oil, and electricity. In fact, many polygamists are against the war in Iraq, which they believe was initiated by an over-reliance on foreign oil. They favor alternative energy to heat their homes, and they follow subsistence strategies such as herbalism, beekeeping, hunting, and grinding their own wheat. One family installed a windmill, solar panels, and a thermal heating (radiant floor) system 25 years before it became popular. They also typically heat with an oil-barrel old-fashioned wood stove and drink from well water. During a forest fire in the Bitterroots, many families picked the morel mushrooms fertilized in the ash of the fire and sold them for profit to various outside businesses. They also are very keen on food storage. They store valuables such as toilet paper, whole grains, wood, water, and canned fruit.[51]

Negative Impacts

Not all stories of polygamists' lives are contented, productive, and positive, as the media is fond of illustrating. I observed some of this negativity when I met a woman named "Beth." She had been physically abused by her husband and feared for her children's welfare. She sought to leave the Allred group but was told that if she tried to do so, her husband's "pure-blood" family would kidnap her children, confiscate her possessions, and jeopardize her salvation. She decided to stay until her youngest child graduated from high school. In a similar case, a woman who was seeking asylum from a bad marriage in the mainstream Mormon Church (her husband announced, after four children, that he was gay) fell in love with a man who had two other wives. They all got along famously until her husband showed favoritism toward the senior wives' children, neglecting to provide resources and attention to the other wives' sons and daughters. One of the older sons of this same senior wife also began sexually abusing the new wife's young daughter. This woman soon left the group and went back into the mainstream Church.

There have been many stories of women escaping the difficulties in polygamy. For example, Debbie Palmer wrote about her experience in the Bountiful, British Columbia, FLDS community, where she was forced to marry a 70-year-old leader at age 15.[52] Dorothy Allred Solomon wrote about the secrecy, poverty, imprisonment, and raids she endured as a daughter of Rulon C. Allred.[53] Irene Spencer, of Mexico, wrote how she married her sister's husband, Verlan LeBaron, who then took eight additional wives. He had a total of 58 kids, and she felt he treated her as "just a number." FLDS member, Carolyn Jessop, who, at age 35, escaped from polygamy with her eight children, wrote about her difficulties.[54] She was a sixth-generation Jessop with a domineering father and a frustrated, abusive mother. After middle school in Hildale, she went to public high school and fostered a dream of being a doctor. At 18, however, she was forced to marry Merril Jessop, who was 50 years old and had three wives. She exchanged being raped by her husband for better treatment in the family.

Various other stories of abuse were picked up by the press, such as the 2002 abduction of 14-year-old Elizabeth Smart by Brian David Mitchell, a sidewalk preacher/polygamist. He raped her and claimed her as his second wife. For more than a year the public mourned over her loss, only to find that she was in Salt Lake City, brainwashed into believing that her kidnapper was a good man who should not be harmed. There was also the story of the incestuous and abusive John Daniel Kingston, who married 16-year-old Mary Ann Kingston to her cousin. Another tale was that of Kaziah Hancock, of the FLDS group who, at 15, was married to an elder in the hierarchy and endured what she called 18 years of oppression.[55]

To help discern the factors contributing to these cases of abuse, I catalogue the negative traits, based on the IHR and Al-Krenawi criteria. They fall into two basic themes: (1) elite polygny[1] and (2) physical, sexual, and emotional abuse.

Elite Polygyny

Elite polygyny was first discussed by anthropologist Nakanike Musisi[56] as a method of maintaining reproductive and productive control by a handful of powerful, blood-related patriarchs. This device effectively alienates younger, rogue males, while facilitating the control of all marriageable, or fertile, women in the tribe, including a mechanism of wife capture (conversion) that insures a continual flow of fecund women into the community. I apply this term to some fundamentalists in the Intermountain West who have a negative impact on women and children through the kingdom-building process. Through this methodology, patriarchal control of financial stewardships is first placed in the hands of the reigning Brethren (top pure-blood families, like the Jessops, All-reds, or LeBarons). These stewardships are further funded through the contributions of new converts through the Law of Consecration.

For this control to be maintained, some heads of families will be given favorable stewardships to keep them from rebelling and to be used as officers to protect the rights and properties of the Priesthood Council. Rogue males who cannot access favored stewardships can work for the alpha males, or else they must be disenfranchised through excommunication. In addition, women and children must not be allowed to easily leave the group, as they are the "resources" of the family kingdom. They represent the glory and magnificence of the corporate lineages and therefore are cloistered from the outside world.[57] To achieve this gender segregation, the Brethren use nonsecular education via home schooling and a rural, isolating environment with natural borders; they also restrict them from gaining a driver's license or any outside job that might tempt them from leaving the group. A final strategy is to strip a rebelling woman of her children and her links to her "Savior" on Mt. Zion. This Savior is a woman's representative patriarch in the heavenly family kingdom. Sometimes this can be a father, but in most cases for women, it is the woman's husband, who can open up the gates of the Celestial Kingdom and let her in. He is vital to the woman's salvation, and so her connection to him must be kept intact—even in situations of abuse or domination.

Negative consequences to women and children within elite polygyny include sexual abuse of children, underage marriage, financial abuse (extracting obedience in exchange for food and shelter), megalomania or narcissism, blood atonement, and the alienation of males. In this last category, some individuals are alienated because of competition for valued resources. Excommunications are used to rid the community of excess males who may leave the group and experience depression, drug abuse, or alcoholism. Related to male alienation is insufficient father-son contact and the development of the son's masculine identity. Males may be separated, segregated, and marginalized at puberty because they are direct competition for scarce wives.[58] A further problem with elite polygamy is that it can breed jealousies between wives for the right to their alpha husband's wealth. The wives compete to make sure their sons will be included in his stewardships. Unequal treatment of wives also exists. Sometimes unwanted wives are replaced with younger, more fertile wives.[59]

Warren Jeffs is a perfect example of elite polygyny. He successfully controlled both productive and reproductive resources. In a 1998 sermon, he preached his agenda to young women, stating that the worst thing to happen to a woman is for her to become educated and desire everything. Such a woman will "seek to rule over her husband." Jeffs' words sound like a 1950s marriage manual: women should wake up each morning yearning to please their husband, "rejoicing in his will towards you." Jeffs quotes Brigham Young in stating "the very nature of women in their desires shall be to their husband...completely submit where he shall rule over you...true womanhood is attained through Priesthood."[60] His words teach women to subordinate and defer to men, muting their own voices and desires. If all actions and thoughts are "centered in him," then the men are better able to control the women and financial resources.

Abusive Polygamy

Many of the factors associated with elite polygyny overlap into physical, sexual, and emotional abuses of women and children.[61] These same factors relate heavily to the five-criteria model I used in Chihuahua while investigating evidence of abuse among the LeBarons. Based on the IHR report, Al-Krenawi's criteria, and my own 15 years of experience, I suggest that there are six factors most often associated with the types of abuses found in polygamous communities: (1) isolation/circumscription; (2) lack of a female network; the combination of (3) father absence, (4) overcrowded conditions, and (5) economic deprivation; and (6) male supremacy/patriarchy.

ISOLATION/CIRCUMSCRIPTION. In one Utah Valley study, 95 percent of the abuse cases occurred in a rural environment.[62] Isolation can be used as a means of cloaking sexual and physical abuses against women and children.[63] Remote places are deliberately chosen by abusers to maintain control over their victims. When a woman is isolated, she also experiences circumscription, or the blockage of emigration of disaffected residents by the physical or social environment.[64] In the polygamous cases, the desert's geographic barriers of heat, drought, predators, poor soil, and imposing sierras together create a physical barricade against apostasy and escape. The isolating mountains of the Bitterroot valley of Montana contain these same circumscriptive barriers, particularly for women and children who are isolated in the winter months. People who leave their abusive environment risk hunger, economic hardship, and possibly even death on the outside. This geographic hindrance combines with harsh social boundaries to ensure that people stay put. Fears of ostracism, of losing one's soul, of spiritual death, and of betraying the family also keep people within the group. Women especially face this type of circumscription because they have been raised to value relationships with loved ones and solidarity. They also risk losing their children if they attempt to leave (the offspring of a man belong to his patrilineage in the next life). Thus, if a mother is aware of her daughter's abuse, she is less likely to tell anyone about it for two reasons: her husband and the Brethren would condemn her for it; and she would have to travel a great distance to locate an appropriate sounding board for such a grievance. An example of this concept comes from Warren Jeffs' speech to his young ladies, cautioning them against betraying family in times of abuse:

> What do many people do? They run to their friends or someone they think can give them counsel. You run anywhere else besides your Priesthood head, you could run into trouble...don't ever go beyond your bounds and try to rule over him.[65]

Jeffs' speech provides a local cultural cue that sanctions the abuse of vulnerable individuals by powerful ones—a cue that refuses to see abuse punished.[66]

LACK OF A FEMALE NETWORK. Isolation is closely related to the necessity for women to engage in female solidarity. Where this network is present, such as in Pinesdale, abuses may be more likely to be noticed. In such instances, everyone knows everyone else's business, and the women are "always watching." The network can provide additional child care for women who need to work outside the community and economic aid for women who are not able to work or who have young children at home. It can help reduce the number of hours per day that women must work to provide for their families. This in turn increases opportunities for leisure and contentment.[67] Women are more likely to opt for divorce if burdened by work. If women do not have a protective emotional and a financial safety net, they will be more dependent on their husband for these same resources.

FATHER ABSENCE, OVERCROWDED CONDITIONS, AND ECONOMIC DEPRIVATION. The issues of father absence, overcrowded conditions, and economic deprivation are also intertwined. Randy Thornhill and Craig Palmer[68] write that most male abusers are raised in poverty and use sexual force to gain access to women with good genes. They predict that combating poverty among males will reduce rape. In the case of the Utah Valley perpetrators the abuse occurred in the context of a lower socioeconomic household where the offender was either unemployed or underemployed.[69] In the polygamous cases, most people lived well below the official U.S. poverty level. For example, Thompson and Ray were self-proclaimed scholars with little income. Palacios was in and out of construction work. Ervil and Verlan LeBaron were poor farmers. The women in such households are often dependant on their husband's priesthood stewardships or the charity of the community to gain access to food and clothing for their children. They are not likely to leave an abusive situation unless they have an outside relative who has not disowned them. They need someone who can provide them with economic support as they transition away from polygamy. Others who have jobs are more able to leave the sect. Impoverished parents often express their frustration with their children through beatings, verbal abuse, and sometimes sexual abuse. In an overcrowded, poor household, sibling abuse can be common, and the abuses a father inflicts on his wife and children is often ignored.

In economically deprived families, the father will often travel far from the home for work. He may be absent for long intervals. Under such conditions sexual abuse may occur.[70] A man who is not often present during the imprinting years of his children's lives may become sexually attracted to the girls as they "blossom."

MALE SUPREMACY/PATRIARCHY. Male dominance is also often associated with abusive conditions.[71] In some conditions, when the husband is open to female decision-making and autonomy, women can use a more feminist approach to family structure and policies. This can provide satisfaction and self-actualization for the women. In many homes, however, I discovered cases of alienation, verbal abuse, subordination, and ridicule. Restrictions for females to travel, go to college, or even go to the hospital were imposed. In a few cases, patriarchs would use their priesthood powers to rationalize the sexual abuse of their daughters. Through the vehicle of a patriarchal ideology, the offenders were ultimately responsible for the leadership of the family and control of the household. They were also in charge of the spiritual salvation of their kingdoms and insisted that the family adopt the patrilineal pathway to heaven that ran through them to God. They used their priesthood powers and the biblical blueprint of the Abrahamic Covenant, with its promise of infinite progeny, as the exemplary tool for the selection of child brides and the abuse of their own daughters. Some fathers dominate by coercion; they invoke God's authority to sanction sexual abuse and threaten damnation, the removal of economic resources, and physical abuse to any who challenge them. The victims, themselves, become strongly convinced that their father is justified in raping them, "refusing to equate it with incest."[72] The offenders also required that their children be homeschooled to avoid the "evil" of the secular schools of the mainstream world. This restriction often disadvantaged females over males. For example, many fundamentalists may offer a high school education for the boys who needed rudimentary math and science skills to work in the agricultural and construction industries. But the girls are not encouraged to finish high school and sometimes stop their training after sixth or seventh grade. At that time they are rigorously taught homemaking skills and reverence for male authority in their homes through the examples of their mothers and their mothers' co-wives. They apply these skills early, marrying at 16 or 17.

Based on this analysis of factors, the cultural restrictions on freedom of choice for women are most severe in the FLDS and Kingston Clan. Occasionally, however, the AUB and LeBaron sects will produce abusive patriarchs, who interpret their priesthood authority differently from what is commonly preached in the congregation. During the leadership of Warren Jeffs individual acts of abuse actually reflected the commonly preached male supremacist ethos.[73]

Summary

In this chapter I have examined the variability of plural marriage and illustrated that polygamy, per se, is not uniformly and directly tied to abuses against women and children. In many instances, polygamists have no higher risk of abuse than society as a whole. Only when polygamy is paired with other factors is abuse likely. Governmental actions and intervention should be based on a case-by-case examination. Government agencies should not assume that they understand what is best for communities until they have thoroughly evaluated individual behaviors within the specific cultural context. I also assert that one must gather data on the female experience to fully understand the relative benefits and disadvantages of polygamous family life.

In conclusion, although I have identified cases of abuse, they are still rare in polygamous families. Ironically, in many writings and in the minds of many observers, all Mormon fundamentalists are lumped in one negative pot. The rich variability of lifestyles, beliefs, and behaviors is completely ignored by the public, government officials, and the press. Like any other alternative family form, polygamy does not easily fit into mainstream society. Although I predict that some groups may be at higher risk than the others, this does not mean that entire communities should be held at gunpoint, nor does it mean that all underage marriage is "abusive." In certain circumstances, when a young woman is trained to take on the duties of wife and mother and has full choice in whom she marries, she may not interpret underage marriage as sexual abuse. Further, if Texas is able to target an entire culture because they encourage teenage girls to marry and bear children, will other groups affiliated with child marriage and teenage pregnancy also be seized? In short, why do we send United

States troops against a small Texas community for teen pregnancy when the entire nation is plagued by similar issues?[74] '

Future discourse about polygamy should include an examination of dynamics within monogamous fundamentalist communities, as well. These examinations should be undertaken with the same vigor and intensity that is now being visited upon polygamous groups.

NOTES

1. Jon Krakauer, *Under The Banner of Heaven* (New York: Random House, 2004).

2. Carolyn Jessop and Laura Palmer, *Escape* (New York: Broadway Books, 2007).

3. John Llewellyn, *Polygamy under Attack* (Salt Lake City, Utah: Agreka Books, 2001).

4. Rebecca Walsh, "Feminists Waffle in FLDS Case," *Salt Lake Tribune,* May 25, 2008.

5. Janet Bennion, *Women of Principle: Female Networking in Contemporary Mormon Polygamy* (Oxford: Oxford University Press, 1998).

6. Janet Bennion, *Desert Patriarchy* (Tucson: University of Arizona Press, 2004).

7. National data on child abuse fatalities show that a child is nearly twice as likely to be abused in foster care as in the general population (NCCPR 2008).

8. Martha Bradley, "The Women of Fundamentalism: Short Creek, 1953," *Dialogue: A Journal of Mormon Thought* 23, no. 2 (1990): 15–37.

9. David Fahrenthold, "An Unusual Prosecution of a Way of Life," *Washington Post,* April 27, 2008, A03.

10. Mike Fremd, "Key Witness Testifies in Polygamist Warren Jeffs Hearing." ABC News, November 21, 2006.

11. John Pomfret, "Polygamists Fight to Be Seen as Part of Mainstream Society," *Washington Post,* November 21, 2006, A01.

12. John Dougherty, "Bound by Fear: Polygamy in Arizona," *Pheonix New Times,* May 13, 2003.

13. D. Michael Quinn, "Plural Marriage and Mormon Fundamentalism," *Dialogue* (Summer 1998): 1–68; Richard Van Wagoner, *Mormon Polygamy: A History* (Salt Lake City: Signature Books, 1986); Bennion, *Women of Principle.*

14. Rebecca Cook, "Polygamy and Canada's Obligations under International Human Rights Law," *Department of Justice of Canada* (September 2006); Chris Cobb, "Ottawa Plans for Polygamy Challenge," *CanWest News Service,* Jan 13, 2006.

15. Pomfret, "Polygamists Fight."

16. Cook, "Polygamy and Canada's Obligations."

17. Ibid.

18. Al-Krenawi et al., "Success and Failure among Polygamous Families: The Experience of Wives, Husbands, and Children," *Family Process* 45, no. 3 (2006): 311–330.

19. Cook, "Polygamy and Canada's Obligations."

20. According to Nobel economist Gary Becker, "In polygamous households, the father invests less time in the upbringing of his children." Found in "Should Polygamy Be Legal?" in the Becker-Posner Blog, http://www.becker-posner-blog.com/2006/10/; Seymour Parker, "The Precultural Basis of the Incest Taboo: Toward a Biosocial Theory," *American Anthropologist* 78, no. 2 (1976): 285–305; Janet Bennion, "Abbas Raptus: Exploring Factors Contributing to the Sexual Abuse of Females in Rural Mormon Fundamentalist Communities," *Forum on Public Policy: A Journal of the Oxford Round Table* (Fall 2007).

21. Bennion, *Desert Patriarchy*.

22. Nancy Leis, "Women in Groups," in *Woman, Culture & Society*, eds. Rosaldo and Lamphere (Stanford, CA: Stanford University Press, 1974); Bennion, *Women of Principle*.

23. CRIN, Child Rights Information Network, October 28, 2006, www.crin.org/resources/infoDetail.asp?ID=10931.

24. Bennion, *Desert Patriarchy*; Peggy Sanday, *Female Power and Male Dominance* (Cambridge: Cambridge University Press, 1982).

25. Irwin Altman and Joseph Ginat, *Polygamous Families in Contemporary Society* (Cambridge: University of Cambridge Press, 1996).

26. William Jankowiak and E. Allen, "The Balance of Duty and Desire in an American Polygamous Community," in *Romantic Passion* (New York: Columbia University Press, 1995).

27. Robin Fox, *Reproduction and Succession: Studies in Anthropology, Law and Society* (New Brunswick, NJ: Transaction Publishers, 1993).

28. Phillip Kilbride, *Plural Marriage for Our Times: A Reinvented Option?* (Westport, CT: Bergin and Garvey, 1994).

29. Bennion, *Women of Principle*.

30. Bennion, *Desert Patriarchy*.

31. Bennion, "Abbas Raptus."

32. Jankowiak, "Balance of Duty and Desire."

33. D. Michael Quinn, "Plural Marriage and Mormon Fundamentalism," in *Fundamentalisms and Society*, eds. Martin Marty and R. Scott Appleby (Chicago: University of Chicago Press, 1993); Bennion, *Women of Principle*.

34. Conversely, Quinn mentions that "few current Mormon fundamentalists have ever been baptized members of the LDS Church" (p. 251). I believe he is mistaken; in the early 1990s, the AUB averaged 25–30 families annually, all of whom had been LDS Church members.

35. Quinn, *Fundamentalisms and Society*.

36. Al-Krenawi et al., "Success and Failure among Polygamous Families: The Experience of Wives, Husbands, and Children," *Family Process* 45, no. 3 (2006): 311–330.

37. Bennion, *Women of Principle*.

38. Felicia Lee, "Big Love: Real Polygamists Look at HBO Polygamists and Find Sex," *New York Times*, March 28, 2006.

39. Kilbride, *Plural Marriage*.

40. Adriana Blake, *Women Can Win the Marriage Lottery: Share Your Man with Another Wife* (Newport Beach, CA: Orange County University Press, 1996).

41. H. L Mencken, *In Defense of Women* (New York: Alred A. Knopf, 1918).

42. Brian West, "Former FLDS Member Is Sharing Her Insights on the Sect," *Deseret News*, April 28, 2008.

43. Michelle Roberts, "DNA Samples Taken from Polygamist Children in Texas," AP Service, *Burlington Free Press*, April 22, 2008, 3A.

44. William Jankowiak and E. Allen, "Sibling Solidarity in a Polygamous Community in the USA," *Evolution and Human Behavior* 21, no. 2 (2000): 125–139.

45. Maxine Hanks, *Women and Authority: Re-emerging Mormon Feminism* (Salt Lake City, Utah: Signature Books, 1992).

46. Brigham Young, *Journal of Discourses* 13 (1856–1869): 56–61.

47. Bennion, *Women of Principle.*

48. At present, the small colony lives peacefully in the foothills of Sierra Tarahumara, ignored by mainstream society. David and his wives expressed worry that renegade FLDS members from Texas will flood their area, bringing with them ideas about forced marriage, pedophilia, and restrictive patriarchy. In 2002 a renegade FLDS member named Orson Black arrived with his underage brides and was promptly kicked out of town (Corchado 2008).

49. Quinn, *Dialogue.*

50. Joseph's successor as mayor, Willy Marshall, is an openly gay man who likewise labels himself as a self-reliant, anti-government libertarian.

51. One polygamist called me up one day around the year 2000 and said that he predicted that the Salt Lake Valley would be flooded and that he just bought his family a small truckload of toilet paper to prepare for the emergency. He moved within the month to a large tract of land in the Northwest.

52. Andrea Moore-Emmett, *God's Brothel: The Extortion of Sex for Salvation in Contemporary Mormon and Christian Fundamentalist Polygamy* (San Francisco: Pince-nez Press, 2004).

53. Dorothy Allred Soloman, *Daughter of the Saints: Growing up in Polygamy* (New York: Norton Press, 2004).

54. S. Connelly, "Running from Polygamy," *Daily News* (New York), November 4, 2007.

55. Kaziah Hancock, *Prisons of the Mind* (Salt Lake City: Deseret Blossom Publishing, 1987).

56. Nakanike Musisi, "Women, 'Elite Polygamy,' and Buganda State Formation," *Signs* 16, no. 41 (1991): 757–777.

57. Paradoxically, in spite of its rigid patriarchal nature, elite polygamy has the potential of serving the needs of women who know how to "work the system" to achieve their ascendancy and economic well-being. It does not work well for young male converts and non-favorite male offspring.

58. Michio Kitahara, "Polygamy: Insufficient Father-Son Contact and Son's Masculine Identity," *Archives of Sexual Behavior* 5, no. 3 (1976): 201–209.

59. Dena Hassouneh-Phillips, "Polygamy and Wife Abuse: A Qualitative Study of Muslim Women in America," *Health Care for Women International* 22, no. 8 (2001): 735–348.

60. Brooke Adams, "Jeffs Preaching Will Be Dissected Word by Word," *Salt Lake Tribune*, August 30, 2007.

61. For an account of abuse cases and perpetrator profiles, see pages 164–174 of my recent monograph, Janet Bennion, "Evaluating the Effects of Polygamy on Women and Children in Four North American Mormon Fundamentalist Groups," (Edwin

Mellen Press, 2008). Most accounts of sexual abuse childbride marriage come from the FLDS group (see Bistline 2004; Jessop 2004; Branham 2008; Wall and Pulitzer 2008; Moore-Emmett 2004; Singular 2008; Western 2007; Hancock 1987; and Krakauer 2006). The narrative voices reflect repetitive theme: coercion by priesthood leaders of young, vulnerable, teenage girls. For example, in *The Secret Lives of Saints*, Daphne Bramham describes how Warren Blackmore, former leader of the FLDS branch in British Columbia, "married" and impregnated nearly a dozen teens, some as young as fifteen. In *God's Brothel*, Moore-Emmett describes Laura Chapman's story. Laura was married against her will and saw girls as young as 12 forced to wed their stepfathers. In *Stolen Innocence*, Wall and Pulitzer, recount her struggle against Warren Jeffs who forced her to marry her first cousin at age fourteen. In the Kingston group Mary Ann Kingston reportedly was abused by Ervil LeBaron. Others reportedly engaged in forced sex to "seal" her to him and become her "saviour on Mt. Zion." Some also justified sex with daughters to "obtain a pure bloodline." An independent fundamentalist indoctrinated and "groomed" his 12-year-old biological daughter and 13-year old step-daughter to marry him. When the father was turned into the police by the first girl's mother, the daughter refused to testify against him (Myers and Brasington 2002: 2).

62. Benninon, "Abbas Raptus."

63. Linda Chamberlain, "Domestic Violence: A Primary Care Issue for Rural Women," The Network News featuring National Women's Health Network. Washington, D.C., January/February 2002, www.womenshealthnetwork.org.

64. Robert Carneiro, "The Circumscription Theory: Challenge and Response." *American Behavioral Scientist* 31 (1980): 497–511.

65. Brooke Adams, "Mystery Note: Warren Jeffs May Have Abdicated Polygamist Prophet Role," *Salt Lake Tribune*, April 5, 2007.

66. Of course there are monogamist examples of abuse, related to isolation and circumscription, such as in northern Maine (Zoll 2004), which has high rates of sex abuse, or the remote areas of Midwestern states (Gundy 2006).

67. Michael Kimmel, *The Gendered Society* (New York: Oxford University Press, 2008), 145.

68. Randy Thornhill and Craig Palmer, *A Natural History of Rape* (Boston: MIT Press, 2000).

69. Bennion, "Abbas Raptus."

70. Seymour Parker, "The Precultural Basis of the Incest Taboo: Toward a Biosocial Theory," *American Anthropologist* 78, no. 2 (1976): 285–305.

71. Bennion, *Desert Patriarchy;* Sanday, *Female Power;* Cook, "Polygamy and Canada's Obligations."

72. Wade Myers and Steve Brasington, "A Father Marries His Daughters: A Case of Incestuous Polygamy," *Journal of Forensic Science* 47, no. 5 (2002).

73. Brooke Adams, "Mystery Note: Warren Jeffs May Have Abdicated Polygamist Prophet Role," *Salt Lake Tribune*, April 5, 2007.

74. According to the Centers for Disease Control, the United States has the highest teenage pregnancy rates of any developed nation. In fact, one-third of girls get pregnant before the age of 20. See CDC data at *Teenpregnancy.org*, a site managed by the National Campaign to Prevent Teen and Unplanned Pregnancy. Also found at www.livestrong.com/article/12504-teen-pregnancy-rates-usa.

Chapter 8

"What's Love Got to Do with It?": Earthly Experience of Celestial Marriage, Past and Present

Carrie A. Miles

In 1842, Joseph Smith—the founder of Mormonism[1] and first practitioner of LDS celestial or plural marriage—proposed marriage to Lucy Walker, a 16-year-old girl who had come to live with him and his wife Emma after her mother died. Lucy was understandably disturbed by this proposal. Joseph tried to reassure her, but ultimately confessed, "I have no flattering words to offer."[2]

Scholars have offered many explanations for why a group of Christians in nineteenth-century America should begin to practice a form of marriage then derided as a "relic of barbarism." But it is not clear if any of them explain why an already married prophet of God would propose an illegal marriage to an astonished teenager without professing either admiration, love, or even lust for her. Even less do they explain why a young girl should agree to such an apparently passionless marriage to a man twice her age. Indeed, Lucy herself wrote that Smith's proposition "aroused every drop of Scotch in my veins." Yet she accepted his proposal.

The marriage of Joseph Smith and Lucy Walker took place over 160 years ago, but understanding its basic elements is critical to understanding contemporary Mormon fundamentalism, especially the practice of polygamy. Such continuity should not be surprising. Although Mormon polygamy and "fundamentalism" are generally used as pseudonyms, the term "fundamentalism" does not mean polygamy. It refers rather to those institutions that claim to adhere to the fundamental, basic, or original doctrines of a belief system, whatever the doctrine or system. Thus Christian "fundamentalists" cling to a "fundamental" view of the origins of humankind, one that is at variance with later notions of biological evolution. Fundamentalist Mormons believe that they have the "correct, unchanged principles; the same principles that Joseph Smith taught in the original Mormon Church"[3] and that the LDS Church was wrong in moving away from those original teachings. Thus they preserve or emphasize many aspects of nineteenth-century Mormon teachings about marriage that were lost or obscured in the LDS Church, most significantly those that equate celestial marriage with polygyny.

But how are we to understand the fundamentals of the earthly expression of celestial marriage? Proposals such as Smith's make little sense to people today, for whom there is no reasonable basis for marriage except romantic love and sexual attraction. Even the title of a contemporary television series about Joseph Smith's successors in polygamy betrays the conventional American expectation that marriage is somehow about love or at least lust. This show, *Big Love,* opens to the romantic strains of the Beach Boys' "God Only Knows What I'd Be without You." One man glides smoothly in circles on thin ice, hand-in-hand with his three beautiful wives. The camera comes in close to reveal yearning and devotion in all four faces, implying that theirs is a "big love" indeed. Yet several recent memoirs of actual fundamentalist marriages demonstrate that romantic love and sexual attraction are neither necessary nor sufficient motives for choosing to enter into plural marriage. Love may have nothing to do with celestial marriage.

No doubt that the opportunity to have sex with a number of women provides an obvious and powerful motive for men to accept polygamy. For women as well, polygamy means that they can choose as marriage partners attractive, charismatic, or otherwise high-quality men, regardless of the man's existing marital status. No doubt that Joseph Smith was an extremely appealing man, and this was a big part of women's willingness to enter into celestial marriage with him. Biographies of some of the women, however, reveal that they had no sexual interest in Smith. Sexual motives alone cannot account for the form and persistence of Mormon fundamentalism. To understand plural marriage solely in terms of modern American notions of romantic love or sexuality is to fail to understand it at all. To fully understand celestial marriage as practiced by Mormons early and late, we must do as Lucy, Joseph, his other 32 wives, and thousands of contemporary polygamists do. We must set aside romantic modern notions of marriage based on sex and companionship. For the essential mechanism of celestial marriage is about something entirely different. Indeed, as we will see below, the fact that Joseph Smith chose the term "celestial marriage" to characterize polygamy already gives important information about why thousands of women were and are willing to participate in a system that appears to offer them limited earthly advantage.

In this chapter, I first recount economic thinking on what makes ordinary, earthly polygamy possible. Interestingly, the factors that make polygamy desirable and possible in Africa or Saudi Arabia are not those underlying Mormon fundamentalism. However, we will see, the questions raised by the economic approach to secular polygamy leads to a clearer understanding of religiously based plural polygamy. While on the surface quite different, the mechanism making both earthly and celestial marriage desirable is the same.

The Economics of Polygamy

By the time Joseph Smith began preaching polygamy, Christianity had been struggling for nearly two thousand years to stamp out it and other forms of non-companionate marriage. Prior to the Industrial Revolution in the West (dated to about 1800) and continuing in non-industrialized countries today, marriage was and is based not on romance, but on material need. In pre-industrial economies, people had to produce everything they consumed themselves, including care in illness or old age. They vitally needed children as a source of labor and security. In such economies, having children is the primary purpose of marriage, which is itself a legal contract that virtually every culture has in some form, intended to protect the woman in her role as child bearer.[4] Love often had little to do with choice of partner. Indeed, as the merging of resources from the bride and groom's families, marriage was often considered too important to trust to the vagaries of romantic love. Historically, marriages were arranged by parents without much concern for the feelings of their children. Indeed, under such circumstances it was not unusual to have one or both participants married against their will.[6]

Thus in the pre-industrial, non-Christian world, marriage is more of a market transaction than a source of emotional fulfillment. In such societies, polygamy occurs when individuals or their families decide they would rather have part of a superior spouse than all of an inferior one. Polygyny (one man married to two or more women) is the most common form of polygamy because men vary greatly in the material resources they bring to marriage.[5] After all, if all men were the same, what woman would chose to share her husband and thus give up half of the resources that would be available to her otherwise? All men are not the same, however; one may be a captain of industry, the other a beggar—a difference of millions and perhaps survival versus starvation. Thus, a woman may be better off with part of a rich man, who can support her and her children, than with all of a poor one who cannot. (Even today, there may be plenty of women who would be happy to be Bill Gates's third, fourth, or twentieth wife, if such a thing were legal and Mr. Gates interested.)

In contrast, when a woman's primary function is to bear children, women do not vary as much as men do. A woman may bear one child or twelve, but she doesn't bear thousands. Therefore there is not a corresponding motive for polyandry (one woman married to two or more men), as a woman does not have more children with two husbands than with one, and wife-sharing means that men have to compete with the other husbands for the services of the wife and her children. Hence, while we find that 85 percent of human societies have practiced polygyny, polyandry is very rare (.1 percent).[6]

Polygyny is most attractive to men who desire numerous children or the other things women produce. In some parts of Africa, for instance, polygyny was practiced by the larger landholders because women do most of the farm work. Indeed, in even the recent past, men could not become important or wealthy in Africa without numerous wives and children to provide labor. Where polygyny was/is practiced, it is not considered to be disadvantageous to women, as they would not have married polygamously had they had a better monogamous alternative.

Polygyny is thus accepted and normal where marriage is based on material economic concerns. In fact, polygamy tends to exist formally wherever there are not laws or positive moral positions taken against it. Even when formally forbidden, it occurs informally. Rich men take and support mistresses, for instance, some openly. Informal polygamy is not limited to men, either. Women who are wealthy in their own right may take lovers or marry and divorce a string of husbands (e.g., Catherine the Great, Marilyn Monroe, Elizabeth Taylor, Jennifer Lopez).

The Problem with Economic-Based Marriage in a Christian Context

If polygamy is a common and normal state, then, there is no reason to view Mormon polygamy as depraved, as based on excessive lust, the enslavement of women, or the indoctrination and abuse of children, as it has often been accused of being. Within Christian cultures, however, would-be polygamists face the problem that Christian marriage is not supposed to be based on material consideration. The Christian tradition consistently urged that marriage be entered into only with the willing consent of both parties and that this marriage, once entered, be exclusive ("For this reason, a man shall...cleave unto his wife, and they two shall become one flesh," Genesis 2:24; Matthew 19:6; Ephesians 5:31) and based on mutual love. Polygyny was quickly disallowed within early Christianity, and the church, from early to modern times, fought hard to limit it as well as arranged or coerced marriage. Although the church was not always successful in instilling its values, by the nineteenth century, when Mormon plural marriage came into being, companionate marriage— "the union of two approximate equals, based on mutual respect, affection and the close companionship of husband and wife"—was firmly established as the ideal in the Christian world.[7] Based instead on "considerations of male sexual desire, financial arrangements, and heirship,"[8] polygyny is the antithesis of Christian marriage. Although experiments with alternative, non-monogamous forms of marriage occurred among other Christian groups (such as the Branch Davidians in the late twentieth century, the Oneida colony in the nineteenth, or the sixteenth-century Anabaptists), they were the exception, not the norm, and were soundly decried by the rest of Christianity.[9]

The Exception That Proves the Rule

Like Lucy Walker, young people among the FLDS and other practitioners of plural marriage hold the same hopes for flattering words, romantic love, and companionate marriage treasured by the rest of American society. Indeed, Joseph Smith's marriage to his first and legal wife, Emma Hale, was obviously based on mutual affection, attraction, and even high romance, as she eloped with him contrary to the wishes of her father. What was it, then, that made it possible for Mormons to practice polygamy on such a large scale in a culture that was utterly hostile to the practice?

Here the economic explanation for the prevalence of polygyny in the material world comes into play, but with a small twist. It was certainly not the standard secular motives based on financial concerns that allowed Mormon polygamy. Joseph Smith could not and did not support all (or arguably, any) of the women he married. He had few physical resources to offer them, and from Lucy Walker's account, no emotional sustenance to give either. So the economic explanation is a dead end on this score. But economics is not limited to issues of money. Becker points out that polygyny is a desirable state only when there is an unequal distribution of some resource among men. So if it was not physical resources that made some Mormon women willing to share Joseph with many other women, what was it? What was it that Joseph Smith had to offer women that made sharing part of him preferable to having all of another man? In a more general sense, the question is, What was the resource that some Mormon men, especially Joseph, had a lot of, which other Mormon men had in varying amounts, which some men didn't have at all, and which women can get only in conjunction with a husband?

The answer to this question is found in Mormon doctrine. A central teaching of Mormonism is its expansion of the traditional Christian concept of heaven and hell. In Mormon thought, the eternal state of those human beings who would go to heaven differs, depending on their degree of righteousness and participation in the various rituals of the Church. The highest reward was "exaltation" or "eternal salvation" in the "celestial kingdom." Someone who was exalted would eventually become a god over his own world. Joseph Smith, as prophet, revealed and held the "keys" to the religious rituals necessary to attain this exaltation—baptism, temple endowment, family sealings for eternity, and second anointing.[10] Early Mormonism taught explicitly that the eternal salvation of anyone living during this period would have to come directly or indirectly through him. Smith made these rituals available to both men and women, but the power to save was delegated only to men. Only a man who was himself worthy of exaltation could bring a woman into the celestial kingdom. Women who were not sealed to such a worthy husband could not be exalted.

The masculine power to save was unequally distributed, however. Some men had more of it; some men had none at all. As the focal point of salvation in this period of time, Joseph especially had an unique assurance that he would be exalted. He told Mary Elizabeth Rollins, "I know that I shall be saved in the Kingdom of God. I have the oath of God upon it and God cannot lie."[11] Moreover, Rollins wrote, Smith said that, "It has been revealed to him...that he had the power to save anyone who was sealed to him: 'All that he gives me I shall take with me for I have that authority and that power conferred upon me.' "[12]

What Joseph Smith had in greater abundance than other men, what his followers had in varying amounts, what some men don't have at all, and what women have access to only from a husband, was the ability to "save...in the Celestial kingdom." Women who were "sealed" to an appropriately saved man were assured of the level of exaltation that their husband would enjoy. Here, then, lies the motive for polygynous marriage among the Mormons: according to such theology, it is more to women's advantage to have part of a worthy man's exaltation than to have all of a man with less ability to save. The mechanism allowing polygyny is the same as in non-Christian, pre-industrial countries. The only difference is the variable on which men vary.

The Need for Children and the Subordination of Women

In the nineteenth century, women rarely had identities apart from their husbands. People today might wonder why it is that women were delegated to the role of pawns or property in this celestial scheme. Why would God tie a woman's exaltation to a man or to marriage? Once again, a twist on the basic economic analysis provides the answer. Economist Gary Becker traces the historic sexual division of labor—the pattern of men and women performing different work—to the crucial need for children as a source of labor and security for their parents. A pregnant or breast-feeding woman simply cannot perform certain kinds of work without endangering the child. In consequence, women came to be "domestically specialized," leaving most of the work that required extra-household labor and coordination to men. In such circumstances, men become dominant over women both inside and outside the home.[13]

Although Americans in the mid-nineteenth century were still largely agrarian and retained a strong need for children, the Industrial Revolution was already diminishing the material reasons for large families. It was not the economic need for children that shaped Mormon polygamy and continued woman's subordination to man into the celestial realm: It was theological. Mormon theology teaches that God is the literal father of billions of spirit children, all of whom are waiting for their chance to come to heaven to acquire a physical body. Mormonism, believing itself to be the sole possessor of the path to exaltation, has urged its faithful followers to have as many children as possible in order to put them on that path. Joseph Smith's successor, Brigham Young, taught that,

> There are multitudes of pure and holy spirits waiting to take
> tabernacles [bodies]. Now what is our duty? To prepare tabernacles
> for them; to take a course that will not tend to drive those spirits into
> families of the wicked, where they will be trained in wickedness,
> debauchery, and every species of crime. It is the duty of every
> righteous man and woman to prepare tabernacles for all the spirits
> they can...This is the reason why the doctrine of plurality of wives
> was revealed, that the noble spirits which are waiting for tabernacles
> might be brought forth.[14]

One early leader wrote, "The First Command was to 'Multiply' and the Prophet taught us that Dominion and powr in the great Future would be Commensurate with the no (number) of 'Wives Childin & Friends' that we inherit here and that our great mission to earth was to Organize a Neculi of Heaven to take with us. To the increase of which there would be no end.' "[15] Yet another wrote, "I understand that a Man's Dominion will be as God's is, over his own Creatures and the more numerous the greater his Dominion."[16] (Original spelling retained.)

Salvation

Thus it is no coincidence that the code name for Mormon polygyny is "celestial marriage." The basis for such marriage was neither material wealth nor companionate love, but the unique ability to save held by certain men—an ability that was magnified by possessing numerous progeny. Although those women who left written records of their relationships with Joseph recount their initial resistance to accepting an illegal and seemingly immoral form of marriage, they were, for the most part, won over by assurances that this would guarantee their salvation and even that of their families. For example, one of Joseph Smith's close associates, Heber Kimball, offered Joseph his 14-year-old daughter, Helen Mar Kimball. She later wrote of her marriage to Joseph Smith:

> He [her father] taught me the principle of Celestial marriage, &
> having a great desire to be connected with the Prophet, Joseph, he
> offered me to him…I heard him [Smith] teach…'If you will take this
> step, it will ensure your eternal salvation & exaltation and that of your
> father's household & all your kindred.' This promise was so great
> that I willingly gave myself to purchase so glorious a reward.[17]

Another couple close to Joseph, the Whitneys, married their daughter, Sarah Ann, to Joseph in return for his promise of eternal life for the entire family.[18] This promise was also part of the offer Joseph made to Lucy Walker: Lucy's celestial marriage to Joseph would "prove an everlasting blessing to my father's house, and form a chain that could never be broken."[19]

It appears that Smith used spiritual coercion as well as assurances of salvation to induce women to marry him. Smith's revelation on celestial marriage (recorded as section 132 of the Mormon Doctrine and Covenants) damns those who do not participate in it: "For behold, I reveal unto you a new and an everlasting covenant; and if ye abide not that covenant, then are ye damned; for no one can reject this covenant and be permitted to enter into my glory."[20] No matter how worthy a monogamist may be, the best he or she can expect in the next life is to act as servants or ministering angels to the more worthy polygamists. The negative consequences were not just other-worldly: Joseph told Mary Elizabeth Rollins, who was already married to another man, that their adulterous union was commanded by God, who sent an angel to enforce his compliance with a drawn sword. And if it was not his admiration that drove Lucy Walker to marry Smith, the rest of his statement to her makes clear just what it was: "I have no flattering words to offer. It is a command of God to you. I will give you until tomorrow to decide this matter. If you reject this message the gate will be closed forever against you."[21]

Love and Hierarchy

Since some men would achieve a greater exaltation than others and some men would not achieve exaltation at all, early LDS leaders taught that it was only fair that women be free to choose the man who could best ensure their salvation. Joseph Smith assured Lucy Walker, "A woman would have her choice [of men], this was a privilege that could not be denied her."[22] Joseph's own tremendous ability to save was a powerful factor encouraging women to choose him, regardless of prior obligations. At least 11 of the women Joseph married plurally were already the wives of other men—and continued to live as wives to their first husbands. Mary Elizabeth Rollins reveals that, like the single women who married Joseph, her motivation for a polyandrous marriage was the exaltation Smith offered her. Mary's husband would not join the church and so could not save her. She said, "I begged and pled with him to join but he would not. He said he did not believe in it though he thought a great deal of Joseph....After he said this I went forward and was sealed to Joseph for Eternity."[23] After his death, her husband was sealed to Mary and Joseph as a son.

An 1861 sermon by Brigham Young also demonstrates the power of unequal distribution of charisma in motivating polyandrous marriage. Young said that the doctrine on which he preached was "received...from Joseph the prophet. If a woman can find a man holding the keys of the preisthood with higher power and authority than her husband, and he is disposed to take her he can do so, otherwise she has got to remain where she is...there is no need for a bill of divorcement...If a woman claimes protection at the hands of a man, possessing more power in the preisthood and higher keys, if he is disposed to rescue her and has obtained the consent of her husband to make her his wife he can do so without a bill of divorcement."[24] Such a marriage "is right in the sight of God"[25] (original spelling retained). The divorce rate in nineteenth-century Utah was in fact quite high, especially among polygamists, and it was not difficult for divorced women to remarry. Anthropologist Lawrence Foster observes, "Thus, in Utah, while men could practice polygamy, easy divorce gave women the opportunity for what amounted to serial polygamy."[26]

Finally, men who were not considered to be spiritually worthy were not allowed to keep their wives. When John Hyde was excommunicated in 1857, Kimball said:

> He has taken a course by which he has lost his family and forfeited his Priesthood.... His wife is not cut from this Church, but she is...just as free from him as though she never had belonged to him. The limb she was connected to is cut off, and she must again be grafted into the tree, if she wishes to be saved.[27]

Brigham Young further taught that "if a man forfiets [sic] his covenants with a wife, or wives, becoming unfaithful to his God, and his priesthood, that wife or wives are free from him without a bill of divorcement"[28] (original spelling retained).

Smith and Diminishing Marginal Returns

Joseph Smith occupied an enviable position relative to men whose polygyny is based on material considerations. When it is the superior provision of material resources that attracts women to marry polygynously, the husband experiences diminishing marginal returns at some point. That is, there are only so many wives a man can support, or only so much time and attention he can devote to them. At some point, he stops marrying more wives. In contrast, there was and is no limit to the power to save among Mormon groups that hold this doctrine. On the contrary, these groups explicitly teach that the more women a man has sealed to him, the greater his power to save them, as a man's exaltation increased with the size of his "kingdom." Indeed, Joseph Smith's ability to save was so strong that even death did not diminish it. After Joseph died, 335 women, many of whom he had never met, were sealed to him.[29]

"Put Aside All Desire..."

As plural marriage became institutionalized in Utah, its basis in salvation, not romantic love, became even more obvious. Brigham Young taught:

> Elders, never love you wives one hair's breath further than they adorn the Gospel, never love them so but that you can leave them at a moment's warning without shedding a tear. Should you love a child any more than this? No.

Wives should put aside all desire for the exclusive and romantic company of their husbands. Rather, they should simply "receive, conceive, bear, and bring forth" in the name of Israel's God. They should not be concerned with whether they were loved 'a particle' by their companions. That was not what the principle was about.[30]

Similarly, Lucy Walker, who subsequently married Brigham Young's second-in-command, Heber C. Kimball, after Joseph's death, told an interrogator:

There was not any love in the union between myself and Kimball, and it is my business entirely whether there was any courtship or not. It was the principle of plural marriage that we were trying to establish...and if we had established it, it would have been for the benefit of the whole human race, and the race will say so yet.[31]

Another widow of Joseph Smith, who married Brigham Young after his death, wrote, "[A] successful polygamous wife must regard her husband with indifference, and with no other feeling than that of reverence, for love we regard as a false sentiment; a feeling which should have no existence in polygamy."[32]

Other sources say nothing about romantic love but go straight to exaltation as women's motives for entering plural marriage: In 1844 when William Clayton asked various women to be sealed to him as wives, he recorded in his journal that "Mary Aspen is ready to united to me as her savior, and sister Booth says that she shall not risk her salvation in Roberts hands & wants me to interfere....Jane Hardman...prefers me for a Savior to any one else, so she says."[33] "Sister Booth's" unwillingness to trust her salvation to her husband Robert's worthiness reflects the perception that Clayton held the superior ability to save.

Polygyny and Sex

The unequal distribution of charisma makes sexuality itself only indirectly important in celestial marriage. Mate selection, for instance, may not be based primarily on sexual attraction, although undoubtedly it is a strong motive in many cases. In the first place, sexuality was not a feature of all plural marriages. Joseph Smith and many other church leaders felt it their duty to provide an eternal salvation for older unmarried women and widows. For instance:

Rhoda Richards...remained a 'maiden' throughout her life, although she had been sealed as a living wife to Joseph Smith in 1843 when he

was thirty-seven and she was fifty-nine. She later explained, "In my
young days I buried my first and only love, and true to that affiance,
I have passed companionless through life: but am sure of having my
proper place and standing in the resurrection, having been sealed to
the prophet Joseph, according to the celestial law."[34]

Such marriages were not uncommon and were free of sexual interest.
Indeed, Brigham Young once said that he would no more make some of his
elderly wives a "real wife" (i.e., sleep with one of them) than he would his
grandmother.

Similarly, there are indications that sexual jealously was not an issue in
some cases where one might expect it to be. There is no evidence that Joseph
Smith felt possessive or threatened by his plural wives' continuing to live with
their legal husbands. Indeed, Mary Elizabeth Rollins said she stayed with her
husband Adam Lightner after being married to Joseph because Joseph told her
to.[35] Young's "courtship" of Martha Brotherton is illustrative of this same point.
When Brigham's persuasive powers failed to win the girl, he called in Joseph,
who apparently told her, "...if you do not like it in a month or two, come to
me, and I will make you free again; and if he turns you off, I will take you on."[36]
This case implies that either Young did not mean this marriage to involve
sex (unlikely, as there is no doubt that although Brigham Young avoided his
grandmotherly wives, he did sleep with his more nubile brides), or that the
exchange of marital sexual partners was irrelevant in the celestial scheme of
things. Apparently what mattered was that a woman was celestially sealed to
a man who could save her. To whom a woman was married on earth wasn't
important, because it was clear to whom she belonged in heaven. Similarly,
it didn't matter with which of the husbands a woman slept or which fathered
her children, as, once sealed to Joseph, any children were also accounted to
Joseph's celestial reckoning.

Sex and Succession

After Joseph Smith's martyrdom in 1844, both Kimball and Young each married at least seven of Joseph Smith's plural wives, who were already assured of
exaltation. The explanation usually given for Young's and Kimball's marriages
to Joseph's widows was that this was to provide them with material support,
or to raise up children to Joseph. Material support for Joseph's wives is not an
adequate explanation: many churches support needy widows without marrying them off to church leaders. (Todd Compton's *In Sacred Loneliness,* which

details Joseph's plural wives' struggle to get West with little or no help from Joseph's successor husbands, suggests that it is even an offensive explanation.) Further, not all of these women needed Young or Kimball to support them or to father their children. Some of the wives were young enough to find husbands of their own. Helen Mar Kimball, for example, married a young man, Orson Whitney. Other young plural wives, however, including Lucy Walker, Emily Partridge, and Sarah Lawrence, went immediately back into loveless marriages with either Kimball or Young. The material support explanation also fails to explain why Brigham Young or Heber C. Kimball should marry women like Mary Elizabeth Rollins, Zina Huntington, Prescinda Huntington, and Sylvia Sessions, who had all been married to Joseph but who each had another husband with whom she continued to live, and with whom they continued to meet their physical needs. These women were now the eternally sealed wife of one man and the earthly wife of two others.

The pattern of polygamy as it was practiced immediately after the martyrdom can perhaps be understood as a result of the succession crisis that followed Joseph's death. If plural marriage was based on the unequal distribution of a power uniquely vested in Joseph Smith, so was the priesthood or authority to govern the Church. With the key holder dead, how was the Church to access the power he had once controlled? Michael Quinn writes that Joseph Smith suggested at least eight different ways succession might occur, so his direction on this matter was not decisive.[37] If the basis for succession were to be hierarchy, Sidney Rigdon, as the sole remaining member of the First Presidency, was the logical candidate. If it were to be lineal blood lines, then it should be Joseph Smith's son, Joseph Smith III. If revelation was to determine succession, then whose revelation? LDS doctrine required the person receiving revelation for others to already have the authority to do so. Some people did have revelations at this point and went off with whoever would follow them. Although the Twelve Apostles were sustained as head of church after Brigham Young gave a speech during which some believed they saw his appearance transformed into that of Joseph Smith, apparently even after this event there was still not widespread agreement in Nauvoo that the Apostles should lead the Church.

Although Joseph's authoritative charisma went beyond plural marriage, Joseph had spent much of the last few years of his life establishing that plural marriage was the primary way to tap into it (perhaps in an attempt to bolster a sense of urgency about its adoption). Brigham Young and the Twelve, as the only group among the various contenders who "wholeheartedly accepted plural marriage" and who "had participated in all of the rituals Joseph Smith had secretly introduced,"[38] were really the only ones who could claim this authority. Both Sidney Rigdon and William Marks (a leading contender and the favorite of Joseph's widow, Emma) vehemently denied plural marriage, and so were left out in the cold as far as their claim to this power. Brigham Young and Heber C. Kimball, his second in command, almost certainly married Joseph's widows in order to solidify their claims to his power. Brigham Young married four of Joseph's plural wives within three months of the meeting in which the "mantle of the Prophet" fell upon him. Kimball also married three of Smith's widows in this time frame. Eventually Young would marry eight women who had been sealed to Joseph Smith while he was still alive. Kimball married five or six of the wives Joseph took while living and another four who were posthumously sealed to Joseph. Although obviously not enough to establish Young's succession, these marriages signaled that Brigham Young and Heber C. Kimball shared his most important power. They were both now sealed (indirectly) to Joseph himself, and were qualified to serve as proxies to Joseph's widows if not to his church.[39]

The need to claim Joseph's authoritative charisma perhaps also motivated meetings held throughout Nauvoo in the winter of 1846 in which the general membership was taught the "Principle" of plural marriage. Although it now seems foolhardy in the face of the increasing hostility and threats of violence from Gentile neighbors, the Twelve could not claim an authority that no one knew about. Claiming Joseph's authority meant that they must establish the full meaning of that charisma with the members as a whole by teaching them about the manifestation of that power, plural marriage.

Applications to Contemporary Fundamentalism

Marriage and Hierarchy II

As in the early LDS Church, contemporary Mormon polygamy is not based on the unequal distribution of material wealth. While a few Mormon polygamist men are relatively well-to-do, many plural wives have to support their children and themselves with little emotional or physical help from their over-taxed, much-married husbands. Plural wives who are supported by their husbands often live in crowded communal homes filled with other wives and many children. Irene Spencer, the daughter of a polygamist, makes the common observation that, "polygamist husbands, like my father, were rarely able to support all their wives and children. It was common for subsequent wives...to draw welfare as supposed single moms."[40] The prevalence of plural wives on public assistance as single mothers is discussed in many Utah counties. As the second of an eventual ten wives of Verlan LeBaron, Irene Spencer herself was sent to live in Mexico, where without recourse to even welfare, she lived in abject poverty.

I discuss elsewhere how the mainstream LDS Church's belief in special individuals' unique ability to save has either ceased to exist or, if it persists, has become invisible.[41] Although the reverence of LDS members for high-ranking Church leaders suggests that traces of that inequality persist, the charisma of the modern Church is tied to office, not to the individuals themselves. Gone also are the teachings about a man's exaltation growing with the number of his wives, children, and friends and the self-perpetuating cycle this created. The economic model thus predicts that even if polygamy were legalized, the LDS Church would have no reason or a mechanism to practice it again.

Mormon fundamentalism, however, continues to observe the unequal distribution of charisma that made nineteenth-century Mormon polygamy possible. One smallish polygamous group even calls itself "the Patriarchal Hierarchy." Most of the long-standing groups, including the Fundamentalist Church of Jesus Christ of Latter-Day Saints (FLDS), share a common origin myth that reinforces the special status of certain individuals. These groups claim that in 1886, while in hiding from federal persecution against polygamy, LDS church president John Taylor received a revelation from Joseph Smith stating that the practice of celestial marriage absolutely must continue. He anointed a man named John W. Woolley with the responsibility to continue the practice until the second coming of Christ. The leaders of these consequent groups claim their authority from connections with Woolley's son Lorin. One group known as the Kingstons adds to this pedigree the belief that they are physically descended from Jesus Christ as well as spiritually from Woolley/Taylor. Based on this royal descent, the Kingstons base status within the community on kinship and encourage incestuous marriages to preserve the bloodlines.[42]

One major polygamous group that does not descend from Woolley is the LeBaron clan (The Church of the First Born of the Fullness of Times). The LeBarons claim to hold "special" priesthood authority as spiritual descendents of Joseph Smith, who secretly passed it to their ancestor Benjamin F. Johnson in Nauvoo. Reportedly, Johnson passed that priesthood on to his grandson Alma Dayer LeBaron and specified that this authority was to be passed down to each successor's worthiest son.[43] LeBaron's descendants' murderous infighting to enforce their claims to special authority has landed two of their self-styled prophets in prison for murder.[44]

Also feeding into fundamentalist belief in the extraordinary power of some individuals is a passage from one of Joseph Smith's revelations that quotes God as saying that he "will send one mighty and strong, whose mouth shall utter words, eternal words; while his bowels shall be a fountain of truth, to set in order the house of God."[45] This messianic figure was expected to bring the various fragments of Mormonism (including the LDS Church) back into unity again around the principle of celestial marriage.[46] Various men have claimed to be the "one mighty and strong," to whom all earthly deference is due.

Populating a Celestial Kingdom

As in the secular, pre-industrial motives for marriage, fundamentalist Mormon polygamy today is driven by the desire for children, as seen in the following quotations: "The wives and children sealed to a deserving man while on Earth will assist him in populating the world he is given to rule over in the next link of this godhood chain. The larger his family here, the better head start they'll have there." "Women cannot become gods in their own right. A woman's hope lay solely in being a wife and mother—one of many wives to her husband; mother of many, many children. She thereby contributes to her husband's future kingdom and will ultimately share in his glory as a goddess... A woman is dependent on her husband god to 'pull her through the veil' of death into heaven and divinity."[47] Another writer notes the fundamentalist saying that, "Women are vessels to be worn out in childbirth."[48]

The desire for as many children as possible also partially explains the young ages at which polygamist girls are married. One plural wife wrote, "One fourteen-year-old girl who'd just had her first baby confided in me that she'd never even had a menstrual period until after the baby was born. Her husband had married her at that young age so she could bear as many children as possible. This was important to him because he wanted to become a god with his own kingdom in heaven, where he and his wives and children could be numberless and beget spirit children to populate other worlds."[49] Adding to the urgency motivating earlier childbearing is Mormonism's belief that they are living in the "Latter-Days" and that marriage and childbearing could only be done in this mortal existence. Time was running out, church leaders preached. Christ would return soon—any girl who wanted to marry and have children should do so without delay.[50]

Love Is Not Important

Belief in the superior man's ability to provide salvation, coupled with the desire for many children, contribute strongly to the decoupling of marriage and romantic or companionate love among fundamentalists. Parallel with the material motives for earthly polygamy cited earlier, girls who married polygamously had been taught that "it was better to have a tenth of a good man than a 'worldly' man all to [themselves]."[51] Thus religious belief motivated Irene Spencer to call off her wedding to the non-polygamist LDS man she loved in order to become second wife to Church of the First Born leader Verlan LeBaron. "I wanted to become a goddess and receive the highest exaltation in heaven. Would I throw that away in order to satisfy my small, selfish desires in the present?"[52] LeBaron's position as president of the Quorum of the Apostles in the Church of the First Born made him especially attractive. As only third in command in the First Born hierarchy, however, LeBaron was apparently not always attractive enough. Spencer tells of how a young woman who Verlan wanted to marry turned him down because the woman "wanted prestige and the highest glory she could obtain in exchange for her sacrifices. She snubbed Verlan...and instead asked Joel, our self-proclaimed prophet, if she could become his seventh wife."[53]

LeBaron's sixth wife, Susan Ray Schmidt, writes that girls were advised against or even forbidden to marry young monogamous men who had not yet proven themselves capable of offering salvation.[54] The Kingstons go even further, explicitly teaching that "no church member can reach heaven unless one of his daughters is married to a Kingston leader."[55]

Love as a weak element in marriage is especially true among the Fundamentalist Church of Jesus Christ of Latter-Day Saints, whose leaders "place" or "assign" women in marriage based on revelation by the prophet without consulting the women themselves. Memoirists Carolyn Jessop, the very unwilling fourth wife of powerful FLDS businessman Merril Jessop, and Elissa Wall, whose forced marriage at age 14 resulted in FLDS prophet Warren Jeffs' conviction as accessory to rape, all write of their lack of love or even a passing acquaintance with the men they married. Jessop and Wall were more-or-less arbitrarily assigned (and coerced) to marry men they actively disliked and feared. Jessop cites one of her sister-wives denigrating romantic connections between husband and wife, saying, "A woman who thinks she needs a relationship with her husband is a worldly tradition and it's something she needs to give up."[56]

Among the FLDS, falling in love is even seen as an act of rebellion. Jessop writes, "We were taught that men and women made a covenant to marry each other before coming to earth." Only the prophet could reveal who had covenanted with whom. Therefore, "Falling in love with someone independently of the prophet's revelation was absolutely forbidden, even if it was someone within the FLDS, because that would be a violation of the covenant made to God before birth."[57] A wife's obedience and desire to serve her husband is more important than her love for him.

Andrea Moore-Emmett's collection of biographies of women who left polygamous marriages contains story after story of women agreeing to marriage to men they did not love but whom they felt (for often vague reasons) that God wanted them to marry.[58]

Church of the First Born women were allowed to receive their own revelations of whom to marry, but as Spencer's case showed, even this did not guarantee that love would be a major factor in their marital choices. Susan Schmidt,
who later married Spencer's husband Verlan, was at one point courted by his
brother Ervil LeBaron, along with another girl. Schmidt quotes the other girl as
saying, " 'No! I do not love him. Sometimes I can't stand the man.... The thing
I keep reminding myself of is that he's the Patriarch of God's true church. He's
promised me that I'll begin to love him." Trying to convince Schmidt to join
her in marrying Ervil LeBaron, this same girl reportedly said, "So we're not
madly in love with him. So what? I care more about my spiritual welfare than
about passion and romance...." When the girl finally married Ervil, Spencer
told Schmidt, "She doesn't love him...She can hardly stand him, but he convinced her that she would go to hell if she didn't marry him." Schmidt wrote, "I
knew of other girls in the colony who had married men without being in love.
The brethren had assured them that the proper feelings would come, if they
married a righteous man of the priesthood."[59]

Women as Currency

One of the features of marriage prior to industrial development was its use
to cement business relationships between families. Despite their emphasis
on the spiritual consequences of polygamy, this secular function of marriage
is observed among fundamentalists, especially the FLDS. For example, after
her coerced marriage at age 18 to 50-year-old Merril Jessop, Carolyn Jessop
discovered that she was part of a business deal. Carolyn's father had filed a
lawsuit against Merril Jessop. Jessop asked the prophet, his uncle, to arrange
for him to marry one of Carolyn's father's daughters in order to induce him
to drop it. Merril Jessop also engineered the marriage of his daughters to the
FLDS prophet in order to solidify his own connections with him. "Merril was
beaming," Carolyn Jessop writes of her husband at the wedding ceremony.
"Now he had direct access to the prophet."[60] Carolyn also mentions the power
associated with being the father of a daughter considered worthy of marriage to
the prophet. Similarly, Elissa Wall writes of her family's joy at her 22-year-old
sister's marriage to an FLDS prophet 60+ years her senior, not only because
this marriage assured her sister's salvation, but also because it increased her
family's influence.[61]

Another example of women's use as measures of men's religious status is
seen in the practice of reassigning widows. Just as Brigham Young and Heber
C. Kimball solidified their position as Joseph Smith's successors by marrying
his plural wives, men in both the FLDS and Church of the First Born scramble

to marry high-status widows. "A prophet's widow generally is not allowed to remarry below the status of her husband. She's usually married off to the new prophet."[62] Merril Jessop's next two wives after Carolyn were women who had been recently widowed by the death of LeRoy Johnson, the president of the FLDS. She writes:

> There is tremendous prestige in marrying a former prophet's wife. It demonstrates to the community that after his death, the prophet sent a divine revelation about whom his wife should marry. For a prophet of God—even a deceased one—to have enough confidence and love for a man to give him one of his wives indicates that the man is of exceptional character.
>
> A quick marriage to several of [the deceased prophet's] widows could catapult [men] into leadership roles in the FLDS hierarchy by signaling that these were the men Uncle Roy [the previous prophet] loved and trusted most.[63]

The Law of Purity

If romantic love is not an important part of celestial marriage, what about sex? Of course, outsiders speculate that sex (such as that portrayed in *Big Love*), particularly male desire, is the major motivator for polygamist marriage. However, while sex is obviously a big part of polygamy in general, it seems to provide only a weak motive in particulars. For one thing, many of the fundamentalist groups preserve the nineteenth-century "Law of Purity," which regulates sexual activity within marriage.[64] Spencer writes, "sex had the same singular role within polygamous families that wives had—procreation.... If a husband and wife indulged in sex for any other purpose, they could even commit adultery with each other. Consequently, it was forbidden during pregnancy, lactation, and menses, as well as after menopause." Spencer's memoir is laced with references to her sexual frustrations and arguments with her husband Verlan LeBaron over his strict observance of this law.

Although the Law of Purity does justify polygyny as necessary to meet the sexual needs of husbands of frequently pregnant and hence sexually unavailable women, restricting sex to procreation suggests that Mormon polygamy is not about sensual indulgence.[65] Further, it appears that few polygamist men have the luxury of selecting their wives based on their sexual attractiveness. The demand for numerous wives to fund a celestial kingdom results in a shortage of women. As a result, fundamentalist men are usually willing to marry any woman who indicates an interest in them or who is assigned to them by the prophet, whether or not the man has any sexual or romantic feelings for her. Carolyn Jessop writes about the frustration of some of her sister wives, who were eager to have children, when their shared husband had little interest in having sex with them. FLDS prophet Rulon Jeffs continued to marry young women well past the age when he was capable of sexual relations with them, again to the frustration of the women involved. Notably, however, in both cases, the women were frustrated less by their unfulfilled sexual longing for men several times older than they were, but because without sexual relations they were not able to fulfill their divinely mandated goal of motherhood.[66]

Conclusion

The writers of *Voices in Harmony*, a collection of pro-polygamy essays by plural wives, assure their readers that they have found love and happiness in their plural marriages (although it is often the relationship with their sister-wives that are most meaningful to them). It is striking, however, that the book spends a great many of its 249 pages testifying to belief in the doctrines supporting celestial marriage. Religious belief, especially those teachings that celestial marriage is essential to salvation, appears to be a far more important motivator for marriage than the husband-wife relationship itself.

Immersed as we are in the cultural idea that marriage should be based on romantic love, the whole notion of polygamy makes little sense to modern Americans. It is only when we consider celestial marriage as based on the unequally distributed ability to save that we can begin to understand it. And the desire for salvation—not admiration, flattering words, or sexual attraction—is what polygamist Mormons have said was their motive all along. As Lucy Walker, Brigham Young, and innumerable other Latter-Day polygamists, told us, romance and flattering words were "not what the principle was about."

NOTES

1. The official Church of Jesus Christ of Latter-Day Saints has expressed a preference not to be called "Mormon," but to be referred to by its full name on first usage, with the acronym LDS in following uses. I use the term "Mormon" in this chapter because I am referring not just to the LDS Church but to the broader range of groups that descended from the founding of the LDS Church.

2. Lyman O. Littlefield, *Reminiscences of the Latter-Day Saints* (Logan, Utah: 1888).

3. Susan Ray Schmidt, *His Favorite Wife: Trapped in Polygamy* (N.p.: Kassidy Lane Publishing, 2006), 238.

4. Gary S. Becker, *A Treatise on the Family,* enlarged ed. (Cambridge, MA: Harvard University Press, 1993), 30–31.

5. Becker, 102.

6. Richard Posner points out that informal polyandry—prostitution, in which many men contribute to the support of one woman—is very common. Polyandry is probably mostly informal because, as Becker points out, the purpose of the marriage contract is to protect women in their role as child bearer. Plural husbands don't need this protection, hence no marriage contract. Posner, *Sex and Reason* (Cambridge, MA: Harvard University Press, 1992).

7. Posner, 45. Also Carmon Hardy, *Solemn Covenant: The Mormon Polygamous Passage* (Urbana: University of Illinois Press, 1992).

8. Posner.

9. Lawrence Foster, *Religion and Sexuality: Three American Communal Experiments of the Nineteenth Century* (New York: Oxford University Press, 1981); Sarah Barrington Gordon, *Mormon Question: Polygamy and Constitutional Conflict in Nineteenth-Century America* (Chapel Hill: University of North Carolina Press, 2001).

10. While other strains of Christianity practice baptism, other Mormon rituals are unique to them. The temple endowment is given during attendance at Mormonism's confidential temple ritual; sealing for eternity served the purpose to bind family members together as family past "til death do us part." The second anointing, which took place in the nineteenth century but does not appear to be practiced today, was a second temple ritual.

11. Mary Elizabeth Rollins Lightner, "Remarks by Sister Mary E. Rollins Lightner, Who Was Sealed to Joseph Smith in 1842. B. Y. U., April 14, 1905, She Is 87 Years old." Historical Archives, 3.

12. Ibid.

13. Carrie A. Miles, *The Redemption of Love* (Grand Rapids, MI: Brazos Press, 2006), chapter 3.

14. *Discourses of Brigham Young,* 197.

15. Dean R. Zimmerman, *I Knew the Prophets: An Analysis of the Letter of Benjamin F. Johnson to George F. Gibbs, Reporting Doctrinal Views of Joseph Smith and Brigham Young* (Bountiful, UT: Horizon, 1976; letter written 1903).

16. Joseph Fielding, ' "They Might Have Known That He Was Not a Fallen Prophet': The Nauvoo Journal of Joseph Fielding" (transcribed and edited by Andrew F. Ehat), *Brigham Young University Studies* 19 (1979): 394–402.

17. Helen Mar Kimball Whitney, Autobiography, 1881 (Historical Archives).

18. Rex Eugene Cooper, *Promises Made to the Fathers: Mormon Covenant Organizations* (Salt Lake City: University of Utah Press, 1990), 140.

19. Littlefield.

20. *Doctrine and Covenants of the Church of Jesus Christ of Latter-Day Saints.* (Salt Lake City: The Church of Jesus Christ of Latter-Day Saints), Section 132, verses 4 and 5.

21. Littlefield.

22. Lucy Walker Kimball, "Statement of Mrs. L. W. Kimball," Historical Archives, Church of Jesus Christ of Latter-Day Saints, Salt Lake City, Utah, 1858.

23. Lightner, 1905, 7.

24. Brigham Young, "A Few Words on Doctrine."

25. James Beck Notebooks, 1859–65, Vol. 1, October 8, 1861, LDS archives.

26. Foster, 1981, op. cit.

27. In Cooper, 192.

28. "A Few Words on Doctrine," speech at Tabernacle by Brigham Young, October 8, 1861, Brigham Young addresses, recorded by George Watts, LDS archives. As cited in Todd Compton, "A Trajectory of Plurality: An Overview of Joseph Smith's Thirty-three Plural Wives," *Dialogue* 29, no. 2 (Summer 1996): 24.

29. Thomas M. Tinney, *The Royal Family of the Prophet Joseph Smith, Jr.* (N.p.: Thomas Milton Tinney, 1973).

30. *Journal of Discourses*, vol. 9: 37, 1856; in Hardy, 91.

31. In Hardy, 104.

32. Zina D. Jacobs Smith Young, 1869, cited in Andrea Moore-Emmett, *God's Brothel* (San Francisco: Pince-nez Press, 2004), 101.

33. Cooper, 139.

34. Ibid., 123.

35. Richard Van Wagoner, *Mormon Polygamy: A History* (Salt Lake City: Signature Books, 1986), 39.

36. In Brody, 307.

37. D. Michael Quinn, "The Mormon Succession Crisis of 1844," *Brigham Young University Studies* 16 (1976): 187–233.

38. Cooper, 151.

39. The use of marriage to a king's widow to claim the king's authority has scriptural precedent. In his rebellion against David, Absalom sets up a tent on the roof of the palace and publicly sleeps with David's concubines (II Samuel 16:21–22). After David's death, Solomon regards his half brother Adonijah's request to marry David's concubine Abishag the Shunammite as a declaration of his desire to rule in Solomon's stead (I Kings 1 and 2). As students of Old Testament polygamy, the early Mormon leaders were probably familiar with these stories.

40. Irene Spencer, *Shattered Dreams: My life as a Polygamist's Wife* (New York: Center Street, 2007). See also Susan Ray Schmidt, *His Favorite Wife: Trapped in Polygamy* (N.p.: Kassidy Lane Publishing, 2006).

41. Carrie A. Miles, "Polygamy and the Economics of Salvation," *Sunstone* (August 1998): 44.

42. Moore-Emmett, 67.

43. Ibid., 116. Also Spencer, 44.

44. See http://extras.sltrib.com/specials/polygamy/PolygamyLeaders.pdf for a genealogical chart of the origins of various fundamentalist groups.

45. *Doctrine and Covenants*, Sec. 85: 7.

46. http://www.mormonfundamentalism.com/OneMightyandStrong9.htm. Downloaded on September 11, 2008.

47. Spencer, 10.

48. Moore-Emmett, 95.

49. Spencer, 41.

50. Ibid., 42.

51. Ibid., 306.

52. Ibid., 46.

53. Ibid., 345.

54. Schmidt, 20.

55. Moore-Emmett, 85–86.

56. Jessop, 268.

57. Ibid., 23.

58. Moore-Emmett, 102; see also John R. Llewellyn, *A Teenager's Tears: When Parents Convert to Polygamy* (Salt Lake City: Agreka Books, 2000), chapter 8.

59. Schmidt, 83–84 88, 95, 19.

60. Jessop, 165.

61. Elissa Wall, *Stolen Innocence* (New York: HarperCollins, 2008), 36.

62. Jessop, 119.

63. Ibid.

64. Mary Batchelor, Marianne Watson, and Anne Wilde, *Voices in Harmony* (Salt Lake City: Principle Voices, 2000), 72. Jessop, 178.

65. It also seems that non-member fantasies about sexual activities involving more than one man and one woman are strictly fantasies. *Big Love* has been criticized as shockingly untrue in its portrayal of the husband having sex with one wife within earshot of the others.

66. Jessop, 172.

Chapter 9

Social Scientific Perspectives on the FLDS Raid and the Corresponding Media Coverage

Ryan T. Cragun and Michael Nielsen

News coverage of important events not only documents the facts of the events, but also explores why those events occurred. Media reports on the raid at the Yearning for Zion (YFZ) Ranch ostensibly inform readers of the reasons that the people involved in the raid acted as they did; we learn about people's rationales and motivations as we gain insight into the story. As a result, the media subtly shape public attitudes toward groups and individuals.[1]

A social-psychological analysis of news coverage offers the opportunity to examine how people understand current events, and may warn of potential sources of bias that may color that understanding. In this chapter we examine social-psychological elements found in news coverage of the YFZ ranch. We begin by considering the way that people construe or frame the raid, which provides context, offers an explanation for people's motivations for their actions, and illustrates the attributions that others make concerning their actions. We will see that initially the media relied heavily on the framing of the Texas Department of Family and Protective Services (DFPS) and their agency, Child Protective Services (CPS). Later in the process, the FLDS responded by attempting to reframe the question in terms of civil rights violated by the state.

Social-psychological research on New Religious Movements (NRMs, also known as "cults") is relevant to the YFZ raid and its portrayal in news reports. Concerns over such issues as individual autonomy and obedience to authority in such groups have raised the question of "brainwashing." Those concerns are exacerbated by the strict boundaries that exist between the Fundamentalist Church of Jesus Christ of Latter-Day Saints (FLDS) and the broader, host culture. These illustrate important concepts regarding group membership and its effect on how people judge one another. Finally, we examine some cases of outright hostility toward the FLDS in the media. This type of hostility, while likely a ratings boost, illustrates another important social psychological finding: our tendency to emphasize information that confirms our biases and expectations.

Method

Our primary data source for this chapter is a systematic content analysis of news stories published by the *New York Times,* Fox News, Cable News Network (CNN), the *Deseret News* (in Salt Lake City), and the *Houston Chronicle.* We supplement the content analysis with data from an online survey of Mormons, polygamists whose beliefs affirm the Book of Mormon, and others (N=2433).

We collected every news article published by the above mentioned news sources on their web sites between April 3, the day of the raid, and May 12, 2008. Articles were discovered by searching on the respective web sites of these news organizations for either or both of the following terms: "Texas" and/or "polygamy." Articles were selected for analysis only if they included both terms. Following selection, the articles were coded based on topics and themes using NVIVO 7.

Fox News ran a total of 46 unique stories on the FLDS in Texas between the dates noted above. Of those, 41 were Associated Press stories, which means that the content is neither unique to nor original with Fox News. The remaining five articles or stories on the Fox News web site included two transcripts mentioning the raid from *The O'Reilly Factor,* which is a news commentary show that includes guests who are interviewed; one transcript from *On the Record with Greta Van Susteren,* which is similar in format to *The O'Reilly Factor;* one transcript from *The Journal Editorial Report,* which is a panel of news commentators who discuss news topics; and one story by the "FOXSexpert," Yvonne K. Fulbright, who provides sex advice on Fox News. Her article discussed polygamy's global and historical pervasiveness in light of the raid on the FLDS in Texas and their practice of polygamy.

The other news outlets we examined were CNN.com, the *New York Times,* the *Houston Chronicle,* and the *Deseret News.* The total number of articles on the

TABLE 9.I. Sources of Articles Included in Analyses

	Total Articles	Associated Press Articles	Associated Press Duplicates*
CNN	28	6	5
New York Times	18	I	0
Houston Chronicle	14	6	2
Deseret News	57	6	4
Fox News	46	4I	0

*Duplicates are articles that appeared in two different papers. Most duplicates were between another paper and Fox News; we found no duplicates between other news sources.

raid in Texas is presented in table 9.I. The *Deseret News* ran the most original articles of the newspapers we examined, which is probably a testament to the interest in polygamy among Mormons, its primary audience. Several of these articles were focused exclusively on reminding other media outlets and the world at large that the mainstream LDS religion is not the FLDS and no longer condones polygamy.[2] Between these news outlets, 60 of the articles on this issue were Associated Press articles, 11 of them duplicates reprinted in multiple papers. The duplicate articles were excluded from the analysis.

The Framing of the Raid

Social movements require resources (e.g., people, money, etc.), but to be successful they also require what is called a "collective action frame."[3] Like a picture frame, a collective action frame (or just "frame") marks off a part of the world and draws attention to it.[4] And like the frame of a building, a collective action frame holds things together, providing coherence to symbols, images, and arguments.[5]

Collective action frames include two components: a diagnostic frame and a motivational frame.[6] The diagnostic frame details the problem, while the motivational frame details what can be done about it. The former facilitates agreement, while the latter fosters action.

Often, collective action frames are couched in terms of "injustices"— someone, some group of people, or something (e.g., the planet) is being treated unfairly.[7] Injustice frames compel because they appeal to people's sense of right and wrong and invoke guilt over inaction. Injustice frames are powerful tools in the arsenal of social movements, organizations, and the media.[8]

Both the governmental authorities (Child Protective Services, FBI, Texas Rangers) and the FLDS have employed injustice frames in trying to build support for their actions. We begin by considering the frame of CPS. The earliest framing that appeared in papers spoke vaguely about general concerns for the safety of the children in the FLDS compound. For example, CNN mentioned that:

> Texas authorities are investigating "the safety of children" at a ranch occupied by about 400 followers of polygamist sect leader Warren Jeffs, officials said Friday.[9]

This initial framing is rudimentary but provides justification for the raid. Legally, CPS would not be able to conduct such a raid without justification, but by providing a justification to the media, CPS was already beginning to influence public opinion. The general justification based on children's safety, however, was short-lived. Within a day, CPS provided additional information to the media that gave the public a concrete justification for the raid:

> Law enforcement agencies raided the ranch Thursday night after receiving a report Monday that a 16-year-old girl had been "sexually and physically abused," Azar said.[10]

We can only speculate as to why CPS offered more specific concerns to the media so soon after the raid, but it may be due to concern by the public that generalities like "safety of children" are too vague to justify a raid that included armored personnel carriers and automatic machine guns. The specific claim of child sexual abuse by a caller known only as "Sarah" was sufficient justification for the raid for several days, and the news media was filled with references to this Sarah, even though CPS was unable to find her after having removed the children from the ranch:

> Officials still haven't found the 16-year-old girl whose abuse complaint triggered the massive raid.[11]

When it became known that Rozita Swinton, a previously convicted false reporter of abuse living in Colorado, was possibly the person who had made the initial phone calls, CPS was forced to change their frame once again:

> Child protective services workers insist the girl is unnecessary to their case of child abuse in the FLDS compound. "I think some people have really focused on that (Sarah) but the reality is that her phone call is the reason we went out there, but it was not the reason for the removals," said Greg Cunningham, spokesman for the Texas Department of Family and Protective Services. "The removals happened based on what we saw out there." [Flora] Jessop said Texas child protective services workers found underage, pregnant girls and that is enough to make a possible hoax call moot.[12]

The changing of the injustice frame over time weakened the case of CPS, leading to public criticism of the raid:

> The state's April 3 raid on the YFZ Ranch has been criticized by some
> who believe CPS overstepped its authority when it took all of the children
> and placed them in foster care after finding underage girls were "spiritually
> married" to much older men.[13]

The increasing criticism of CPS as a result of their undermined and changing issue frame tells us something noteworthy about issue frames—they must be consistent and withstand scrutiny in order to retain legitimacy.[14] However, CPS used a multi-pronged approach to justify their actions, including painting their response in the best possible light in the media. CPS stated repeatedly that they were carefully weighing all options and doing what they believed was in the children's best interests:

> The decision to separate children age 5 and older from their mothers
> was made carefully and with input from attorneys and therapists, CPS
> spokesman Marleigh Meisner said Tuesday... It was decided that the
> move was in the "children's best interest," she said, and she later added
> that children who are victims of abuse or neglect typically feel "safer" and
> are more truthful if their parents are not around.[15]

Most of the media outlets we examined were more favorable toward CPS than they were critical. For example, the Associated Press reported that the raid was "justifiable" and "appropriate."[16] The exception was the *Deseret News*, which had a 2 to 1 ratio of criticism to praise for CPS in its articles. Most of the other media outlets[17] were closer to a 1 to 1 ratio or slightly favored CPS.

Criticisms of CPS eventually began to turn to the treatment of the children CPS had in their custody. Reports began filtering into the media about 10 days after the raid that the children and their mothers were living in cramped and unsanitary conditions. There were also allegations that CPS employees were rude and unprofessional. CPS quickly responded to these allegations as well, stating that:

> A number of state agencies are working together to make all the children
> as comfortable as possible, and to meet all their physical, medical and
> psychology (sic) needs while they are in San Angelo.[18]

While the treatment of the children remained under contention, what was uncontested was that there are some polygamists who are "bad" people. The media, intentionally or not, provided a third prong in the injustice frame of

CPS by repeatedly discussing the actions and conviction of Warren Jeffs, the leader of the FLDS. Close to 40 percent of the articles published by these media outlets contained references to Jeffs like the following:

> While mainstream Mormons disavowed polygamy more than a century ago, the sect, led by the now imprisoned Warren Jeffs, believes in plural, arranged marriages that often involve teenage girls and older men... In September, Jeffs was convicted in Utah of being an accomplice in the rape of a 14-year-old girl. He faces additional charges of sexual conduct with a minor, incest and conspiracy in Arizona.[19]

Social-psychologically, the continued references to Jeffs serve a "guilt by association" function, using what is known as the "availability heuristic."[20] The availability heuristic is people's tendency to estimate the likelihood of an event by how readily it is available in memory. Thus, by associating FLDS individuals with their leader, Warren Jeffs, and reminding readers that Jeffs has been convicted of (and continues to be investigated for) sexual improprieties, readers are likely to overestimate the rate of abuse among the FLDS as a whole. The availability heuristic is a common cause of prejudice.[21] Another example of this is attitudes toward Muslims since the September 11, 2001, attacks: for individuals in the United States who did not know a Muslim prior to the attacks, the attacks gave them a specific picture of Muslims. The general dislike Americans hold toward Muslims has continued since September 11.[22]

By associating the FLDS in Eldorado, Texas, repeatedly with Warren Jeffs—while clearly painting Jeffs as a convicted sex offender—the media helped justify the actions of CPS. Despite his imprisonment, Warren Jeffs was, of course, still the spiritual leader of the FLDS. Although it is reasonable to associate the FLDS in Texas with Jeffs, a potential unintended consequence of doing so is increasing prejudice against people who may or may not have been violating the law by associating them with others who have been found guilty of violating the law. This is even more likely to occur in the case of the FLDS. Given that the group is known for violating the norm of monogamy, the leader's conviction is even more likely to color people's evaluations of the group's members. As the Texas Supreme Court[23] indicated, investigations into illegal behavior should be based on the actions of specific individuals and not en masse.

Criticism in the media has not been limited just to Jeffs. Nearly 50 percent of the articles from these media sources include open criticisms of the FLDS, often couched in terms that make the criticism seem as though it is coming from a third party—e.g., "critics say..."—but without citing sources. Criticisms most often focused on the young marriage age (33 articles) or the mistreatment of women and children (15 articles):

Critics say girls as young as 13 or 14 are placed in polygamous marriages to older men.[24]

Women are taught to "keep sweet" and obey their husbands, who hold their "priesthood," or way into Heaven.[25]

Criticism like that above is common in the articles we read, and most of it goes unchallenged except by saying that the FLDS denies charges of sexual abuse.[26] What is sorely needed in these news articles is not necessarily a two-sided argument but data on the actual views of the FLDS and of polygamists in general. Such data are not available, unfortunately, but one study has examined the views of polygamous women more generally. Mary Batchelor, Marianne Watson, and Anne Wilde[27] conducted a survey of 111 women who are polygamous or who support polygamy.[28] In that sample, six were married between the ages of 14–16. Most women in that sample were married between the ages of 17–20 (N=39) or 21–30 (N=35). Because of the grouping of response alternatives and the fact that results are not reported by respondents' specific affiliation, it is impossible to say whether the young marriages were below the legal age of marriage in their state of residence. Even so, Batchelor et al.'s data do suggest that most polygamist women first marry after age 16.

Issue frames provided CPS with justification for its actions, but the injustice frame initially developed by CPS did not withstand scrutiny and had to be modified. The modifications weakened the position of CPS. Even though CPS struggled with its issue frame, the media provided support for the actions of CPS by allowing them a platform to compliment their actions and by tainting FLDS members via association with their convicted spiritual leader, Warren Jeffs. The media have also allowed unqualified criticism of the FLDS without providing data to support the criticisms. In this modern age, however, it is not just the government that is aware of the importance of issue frames; the FLDS developed their own injustice frame.

A Civil Rights Issue?

Just as the CPS did, the FLDS developed an injustice frame to garner public support. The injustice frame of the FLDS was two-pronged. First, the FLDS tried to turn the raid into a debate about civil rights and the prosecution of polygamy, rather than an investigation of child and sex abuse. Second, to support this frame, the FLDS were very critical of CPS, both in the decisions CPS made and the treatment of the FLDS—in particular, the women and children.

About 10 days elapsed before the FLDS articulated an injustice frame that was reported by the media. The mothers talked about the removal of their children as a violation of constitutional rights:

> *The mothers of some of the 416 children taken from a polygamous sect's ranch say that authorities have denied them their constitutional rights and that they want their children back … But at least one woman at the YFZ ranch say [sic] they're being treated like Jews during the Holocaust. "We have been persecuted for our religion," Kathleen said. "We are being treated like the Jews were when they were escorted to the German Nazi camps."* [29]

The claim that civil rights and custody rights were violated drew national attention and brought a representative from the Texas branch of the American Civil Liberties Union, an organization that has defended polygamy in the past, to the custody hearing. The ACLU was sympathetic to their concerns and voiced similar concerns,[30] although it did not file a brief until several weeks after the raid.

The civil rights issue is particularly interesting in light of the fact that government authorities in Utah and Arizona do not prosecute just polygamy despite the fact that it is against the law. The attorneys general of both states have repeatedly stated that they do not have the resources to prosecute polygamy and that it might not actually result in a conviction. For example, Ben Winslow[31] reported that

> *Polygamy is prohibited, but attorneys say constitutional questions regarding religious freedom could make it too difficult to secure a conviction on plural marriage alone, as is the case with court rulings regarding the rights of consenting adults.* [32]

Government violations of civil rights are a serious concern of Americans today. As Charlotte Ryan and William Gamson[33] argue in their discussion of issue frames, people hold multiple frames, even frames that might conflict. Americans despise child sex abuse; thus CPS has generally found support for the raid. But Americans also value their civil rights, specifically those protected by the Bill of Rights. By developing a counter-injustice frame that draws upon a vital element in the worldview of the general public (who are, in a sense, the adversaries of the FLDS), they have built a compelling moral frame. This was heightened by having FLDS women, sometimes viewed to be victims, articulate the frame. This frame drew enough attention that it put CPS on the defensive, forcing CPS to reiterate its injustice frame. As CNN reported:

> *Voss said officials were concerned over the sect promoting "children having children," but added: "It's not about religion, it's about child abuse."* [34]

The injustice frame of the FLDS drew enough support that the media began criticizing the CPS as well. Initial criticisms from the media were similar to those of the FLDS, wondering whether civil rights had been violated. The *Houston Chronicle* reported that:

> The state's April 3 raid on the YFZ Ranch has been criticized by some who believe CPS overstepped its authority when it took all of the children and placed them in foster care after finding underage girls were "spiritually married" to much older men.[35]

But the criticism of the CPS escalated to other areas, including their treatment of the women and children in their custody, as the *Houston Chronicle* reported:

> Barring that, state officials might exert their own undue influence on these vulnerable youngsters, perhaps subtly encouraging them to provide questionable testimony to support the controversial decision to separate parents and offspring.[36]

Also working in favor of the FLDS was the repeated mention in the media that there was little to no resistance during the raid. The FLDS were described as "cooperative" in nine of the articles. Violence did not result from the raid. There were two arrests of FLDS men for minor issues, but the charges were later dropped.[37] What's more, the man who was originally accused in the hoax phone calls, Dale Barlow, was also cooperative and quickly dismissed as a potential suspect.[38] The docility of the FLDS reinforced their claims of victimization.

The FLDS went on the offensive in spreading their issue frame. They developed a web site that serves as a platform for their views: www.captiveflds-children.org. The web site is filled with pictures and videos designed to elicit sympathy from the general public. The media has been critical of the counter-injustice frame of the FLDS, going so far as to interview a law professor who described the web site as part of a propaganda campaign to elicit sympathy.[39] The FLDS, in turn, opened their compound to public scrutiny and appeared on nationally syndicated television shows. Whether the FLDS will pursue their violation of civil rights claims, the efforts of the FLDS to sway public opinion in their favor have been impressive.

Cult-Like Behavior?

The label "cult" is a menacing one for most people, being associated with mass suicides, brainwashing, strange sexual practices, and archaic rituals ranging from torture to human sacrifice. With two exceptions—one reference in the

Deseret News and Bill O'Reilly's discussion in Fox News—the media in our sample refrained from calling the FLDS a cult. Generally the FLDS are referred to as a sect, which is more accurate. Sociologists of religion generally understand the difference as follows: cults tend to have charismatic leaders, form relatively spontaneously (they are not offshoots of existing religions), and have a focus on a novel religious theology; sects may or may not have strong leaders, they branch off existing religions, and the focus is on a return to the "roots" of the religion or a past state of the religion that is seen as more in line with the original aims of the founder.[40]

Based on these definitions, the FLDS is more a sect than a cult: they branched out of an existing religion—The Church of Jesus Christ of Latter-Day Saints—and they advocate a return to the original teachings of the religion, most notably the importance of polygamous relationships.[41] Still, definitions such as these represent ideal classifications. Religious classification is better understood as a matter of degree than as categories of a typology. Thus, while the FLDS have some characteristics of sects, they also exhibit a number of behaviors that are traditionally associated with cults or New Religious Movements (NRMs). Members of the FLDS show a remarkable deference to authority, particularly the authority of the prophet Warren Jeffs, and to a patriarchal power structure. The FLDS also draw distinct borders between those who are FLDS and those who are not, making the distinction between the in-group and out-group particularly salient and important.

Authority, Obedience, and Conformity

Closely tied to power, which is the ability to achieve certain ends (whether or not others want you to), authority refers to one's right to exercise power.[42] There are various types of authority—legal-rational, traditional, and charismatic. Authority in religions can fall into any of these groups. If the leadership is voted in (e.g., Presbyterians), the authority is legal-rational. If leadership passes from parent to offspring or from an existing leader to a chosen successor, the authority is based on tradition. And if authority is based on the personal attributes of individuals— that is, their charisma—authority is charismatic. Among the FLDS, authority is primarily traditional, but also includes a hint of charisma. The leadership of the FLDS passed from leader to chosen successor for generations, eventually falling on Warren Jeffs.[43] Warren Jeffs' personal charisma allowed him to consolidate that power, excommunicating individuals who challenged his authority.

Some of the news stories discuss Jeffs' power over his followers. For example, Jennifer Dobner[44] suggests that:

The FLDS practice polygamy in marriages arranged by the church
president, who is also described as a prophet.[45]

Certainly Jeffs has an inordinate amount of power, indicating that he has combined his traditional authority with charismatic authority. But there is another element of authority in the religion that emerges indirectly in the news articles. Andrew Holden[46] argues that Jehovah's Witnesses are willing to give up near absolute control of their lives to the Jehovah's Witnesses movement because it provides a sense of certainty in an uncertain world. The same can be said of the FLDS, who are willing to divest themselves of power to make their own decisions in exchange for guarantees about their eternal salvation.

The idea of absolute or near absolute control over followers is often considered a characteristic of cults and is sometimes called "brainwashing," a term used in some news reports describing FLDS women. Social scientific research on "brainwashing" has fallen short of demonstrating its use with religious groups.[47] Eileen Barker's[48] study of the Unification Church (sometimes referred to as the Moonies) examines brainwashing at length. According to Barker, people have been brainwashed if their ability to reason based on personal experience is removed and they are unable to control their actions. Many of the media stories relied on more superficial characteristics, such as the women's appearance and manner of speech, to reach the conclusion that they were brainwashed.

The media's use of "brainwashing" is complicated by the failure to distinguish brainwashing from normal socialization processes. Some critics of religion[49] go so far as to argue that all religious indoctrination of children is akin to brainwashing. Most scholars, however, consider religious indoctrination of children to be distinct from brainwashing in that it represents the passing on of tradition; it is a process that occurs in all societies, wherein parents and others teach the society's norms and values to its children and other new members. Additionally, the children will eventually become adults and will be able to decide whether or not to continue in the religion.[50] Thus, there is a fine but distinguishable line between religious indoctrination and brainwashing, and that line hinges upon autonomy during adulthood: if an adult is free to reject a religious philosophy and has control over her behavior, she cannot be considered to be brainwashed. By this definition, despite being subservient to authority, FLDS women are not brainwashed. What people are observing in the FLDS is not brainwashing but deviant social norms: the FLDS do not follow the norms of the larger society, which makes them seem different.[51]

The fact that the focus is on the brainwashing of the women and not the men raises intriguing gender issues. Echoing the CPS frame, most media coverage has cast FLDS women as victims and, either implicitly or explicitly, cast the men as authoritarian predators:

> We intend to show that there has been a practice of grooming or
> conditioning young girls to be the spiritual wives of older men and to
> have sex with them. . . . The male children are at risk because they're being
> trained to grow up to be sexual predators, so it's the potential for abuse.[52]

If it is, in fact, the case that the girls on the ranch are married and impregnated before the legal age of marriage at 16, and the offspring of the women will be kept on the ranch regardless of the actions and decisions of the women, then one could make the case that the women in the FLDS are indirectly forced to remain in the group, leading to pseudo-brainwashing. But that is, of course, a legal question to be determined in court. If the women are able to leave with their children, as Flora[53] and Carolyn Jessop[54] have, this is arguably not brainwashing. Leaving may be very challenging, but this is true for anyone who leaves a religion that is salient in their lives.[55] Leaving a salient religion requires a complete realignment of social relationships, which is emotionally challenging.[56] It also requires a reworking of one's worldview, which is cognitively and psychologically challenging.[57]

The evidence provided by the media seems to indicate that the adult FLDS women are not, in fact, brainwashed but are willful participants in the organization. When given the option of returning to the FLDS ranch or going to undisclosed safe houses, most of the women chose to return to the ranch:

> The women were given a choice: Return to the Eldorado ranch of the
> Fundamentalist Church of Jesus Christ of Latter-Day Saints, a renegade
> Mormon sect, or go to another safe location. Some women chose the
> latter. . . .[58]

Admittedly, this is a complicated scenario. Many of the women may have believed that their best chance of getting their children back was to remain with the FLDS. If reuniting with their children was their primary motivation, their hand was forced and led them to return to the ranch. But Holden's[59] argument that members in highly authoritarian religions value certainty, obedience, and conformity above all else suggests that these women made the decision to return to the ranch of their own accord. By Barker's[60] criteria, these women are not brainwashed—they are devoted, religious acolytes.

While not brainwashed, it is apparent that the FLDS adhere strictly to the authority that they believe gives them certainty in life and the afterlife. This is apparent in their behavior. The women were separated from the children by CPS at times because CPS was concerned they were unduly influencing the children when they were trying to interview them.[61] CPS also confiscated cell phones over what they saw as conformity and authority concerns,[62] believing the women were being unduly influenced by the men via the cell phones.[63] But the women themselves claim they have autonomy, limited though it may be: "Can I leave the premises? Yes," said Nancy, a 40-year-old mother of four, who rises daily at 4:30 A.M. "We have a post office box. We get mail and we take the children to the orthodontist."[64]

The adult women, then, appear to be willing participants in the polygamist lifestyle of the FLDS. But what about the men? If anything, the characterization of the men as sexual predators and the women as unwitting victims is unfair to both sexes. Depicting the men as "groomed predators,"[65] as tyrants and dictators, fails to recognize the existential certainty they gain from their religion. Additionally, the fathering role of the men is largely ignored in the media; there was virtually no discussion of the men wanting their children back. Among the 163 articles in our sample published during the first 40 days of the story, only one mentioned fathers' attempts to have the children returned:

> A church lawyer, Rod Parker, said the 60 or so men remaining on the 1,700-acre ranch had offered to leave the compound if the state would allow the women and children to return with child welfare monitors. The Children's Protective Services agency said it had not seen the letter containing the offer.[66]

While the FLDS are more patriarchal than mainstream U.S. culture, the media depiction of the men and women of the FLDS has been largely biased. The women are depicted as unwitting victims, while the men are depicted as indifferent fathers and sexual predators. Neither depiction is particularly accurate and both overlook the larger motivation for the behaviors of the men and women: their subservience to authority is an exchange relationship that provides immortal salvation for mortal obedience.[67]

In-groups and Out-groups

One aspect of the FLDS depicted well in the media is the nearly tangible barrier between the FLDS and the "outside world," as it is described in many articles. In social-psychological terms, we would consider the extreme distrust of the non-FLDS by the FLDS and vice versa as a classic example of in-group favoritism and out-group prejudice. A large body of literature supports the finding that people develop more positive feelings towards those in their own group, regardless of the criteria used to group people together. At the same time, frequently people judge members of competing groups with animosity, even though under different circumstances they would find they have much in common.[68] To a large degree this in-group–out-group dynamic is driven by the information people have regarding the groups, which is more readily available and more complex for in-groups than for out-groups.[69] This is compounded by mutual distrust and "mirror image perceptions"[70] in which members of both groups view the other suspiciously and as having questionable, even threatening, motives.

This describes the behavior of the FLDS quite accurately and has played itself out in media reports of the raid as well. Numerous news articles mentioned that FLDS "[m]embers are discouraged from contact with outsiders,"[71] as suggested in the following Associated Press story:

> "All these girls are taught from the cradle not to trust anybody from the outside," Shurtleff [attorney general of Utah] said. "Especially the government. We're the beast. We're the devil."[72]

Distrust of outsiders also played out in the custody battle over the children and the criticisms of CPS, as depicted in this Associated Press story:

> Brenda and others were critical of CPS, saying the agency misled them as to what was to happen Monday, weren't told why the children were removed from the compound and given inaccurate messages about opportunities to meet attorneys. "We got to where we said, We cannot believe a word you say. We cannot trust you."[73]

FLDS members' refusal to give their last names when speaking publicly also illustrates the basic mistrust of others:

> For most of these children, we've been given different ages and different names, Goodman said. "We have teenagers who can't tell us their birthdates. Some have answered (that) they don't know. Others have said 'I'm not supposed to tell you.'"[74]

This clear mistrust of outsiders returns us to the discussion of the beliefs of the FLDS. Because there is great emphasis placed on salvation and the next life, and the religion itself is seen as the means to that end, people outside the religion represent potential threats to the ultimate goals of salvation and purity. As CNN reported:

> And the women say the state is placing their children in greater danger by exposing them to things they would have never seen at the ranch. "They are clean and pure," one mother said of the children. "This is the worst thing happening to them. They are learning terrible things from the

questions being asked, things that they have never been exposed to. They have been so protected here."[75]

For many non-authoritarian Americans, being "protected" is actually frowned upon. In order to understand the behavior of the FLDS, however, it is necessary to understand that maintaining distance from outsiders facilitates the realization of their existential goals. Excessive contact with the outside world threatens to make one impure, jeopardizing salvation.

Outright Hostility

In the 163 articles we read in studying the news coverage of the FLDS raid in Texas, we found very few examples of outright hostility toward the FLDS. The hostility we did find usually was from someone interviewed by a reporter or a social commentator. Only occasionally did it come from the reporters themselves.

Conservative media pundit Bill O'Reilly was unrepentant in considering polygamists[76] "brainwashed" and "crazy." On May 2 he stated that:

> *These people go in there, and then they're told by some leadership that you've got to do this to go to heaven, and the rest of America is going you guys are crazy. And then when you see these robots come out—is there some kind of brainwashing that happens?... Should we feel sorry for the people in the Texas cult and your cult, the New Mexico, that's still going on, too? They're still down there in New Mexico doing whatever they're doing. Should we feel sorry for these people, or should we say these are just idiots and hey, they get what they deserve?*[77]

While the data in this chapter illustrates that Bill O'Reilly is not a reliable source of information on the FLDS or other polygamist groups, his show remains the most watched cable news-commentary show with over 2 million nightly viewers.[78]

Uninformed media pundits aside, the news media did express some views that fall into the realm of confirmation bias, a social psychological phenomenon that occurs when people focus on evidence that supports their preconceived beliefs while disregarding evidence that contradicts their views. When people succumb to confirmation bias, they fail to recognize that there is evidence that disconfirms their existing beliefs, or at least calls them into question. One example of this that was reported multiple times by most of the media outlets we examined is described in the excerpt below:

Inside, the three-story temple held hints about possible under-age marriage rites, but no answer to what had happened to the 16-year-old who called the authorities. The authorities found shredded documents, but could not determine when they had been destroyed. The state also found beds on the top floor of the temple, where authorities suspect that older men had sex with under-age girls, court documents released on Wednesday said. In one rumpled bed, authorities found a long strand of hair, the affidavit states.[79]

Only one media source, CNN, ran an article that gave an alternative explanation for the bed—an explanation that appears more plausible than a bed for hurried underage marriage consummation: "Historically, the only use of a bed in a temple is for temple worship itself," said Walsh, who said he has studied the FLDS practices for 18 years. "The worship lasts a couple of hours, so all the temples will have a place where someone can lie down."[80]

Another common concern of individuals involved in the raid that was parroted by the news media was the potential similarity to the Branch Davidians in Waco, Texas, as the following *New York Times* article suggests:

"There was great concern not to have something like Waco," [Texas legislator Harvey Hilderbran] added, referring to the raid on the Branch Davidian compound near Waco in 1993, in which more than 80 people were killed. "So we want to know how to handle it, to have our ducks in a row."[81]

This concern was used to justify the inclusion of nearly 700 individuals in the raid on the FLDS ranch, as well as armored personnel carriers, snipers, and automatic machine guns. But, like the bed in the temple, the evidence should be sufficiently apparent to disconfirm this belief. The repeated references to the underage marriage consummation bed and the Branch Davidians aside, the major media outlets were generally not prone to any forms of outright hostility, Bill O'Reilly notwithstanding.

Heterogeneity and Attitudes of Polygamists

An important facet of news coverage of the FLDS is the potential for confusion to result as charges of underage marriages among the FLDS affect people's views of other, non-FLDS polygamists. There is actually substantial diversity among polygamists, which gets lost in an "out-group homogeneity bias."[82] Humans have a tendency to think of people who are not like them and not in their in-group as being more homogeneous than the people who are in their in-group. A classic example of this is when a white American raised in a rural community with few minorities first encounters a large group of minorities (say, 100 people from China); the white American has a tendency to think they all look similar. Of course, what that white American doesn't realize is that when a person from rural China sees 100 white Americans, he or she will think about them the same way—they all look the same.

Most people (non-polygamists) view polygamists (the out-group) as homogeneous. The assumption is that all polygamists are alike, even though that is not accurate. Information regarding the diversity of practices and views is lacking, perpetuating the out-group homogeneity bias. To address this, it is useful to consider what little data are available.

In a study of people's attitudes toward polygamy, we collected responses from LDS Church members (N=1334), polygamists whose beliefs affirm the Book of Mormon (N=47), and others (N=1052).[83] Although the samples, described in Table 9,2, are not representative and the polygamists are small in

TABLE 9.2. Descriptive Statistics for Polygamists, LDS and Others

Age	Mean	Range	SD			
Polygamists	43.2	18–92	15.5			
LDS	32.6	18–77	13.2			
Other	29.1	18–84	12.3			

Sex	Male	Female				
Polygamists	39.1	60.9				
LDS	45.2	54.8				
Other	32.0	68.0				

Education	Some H.S.	H.S. Diploma	Some College	College Graduate	Master's Degree	Doctoral Degree
Polygamists	0.0	8.5	40.4	27.7	19.1	4.3
LDS	9.6	6.0	28.7	29.3	17.3	9.0
Other	2.7	5.6	53.5	22.1	10.1	6.0

Marital Status	Never Married	Married	Widowed	Divorced	Cohabiting	
Polygamists	15.6	68.9	0.0	6.7	8.9	
LDS	35.2	59.2	0.3	3.8	1.4	
Other	53.7	34.4	0.7	4.7	6.5	

States	Arizona	California	Utah Texas	Not Reported	Other	
Polygamists	14.9	4.3	38.3	2.1	17.0	23.4
LDS	6.0	14.5	26.6	3.2	6.2	43.5
Other	1.2	5.2	1.4	4.1	22.2	65.9

TABLE 9.3. Percent Agreeing That Mormon
Polygamists Are Christian

Group	Disagree	Neutral	Agree	N
Polygamists				
Females	16.7	5.6	77.8	28
Males	17.4	10.9	71.7	18
LDS				
Females	22.7	27.5	49.9	706
Males	15.0	17.4	67.6	592
Others				
Females	50.2	27.3	22.4	651
Males	45.7	24.2	30.1	302

number, the survey data illustrate many of the social-psychological phenomena discussed above concerning the media coverage of the FLDS. Thus, while they await confirmation by more systematic data, the following results are consistent with social psychological theory and research.

Our survey data speak to the question of group boundaries and in-group favoritism. We asked participants how strongly they agree with the statement,[84] "I consider Mormon polygamists to be Christian." The results are shown in table 9.3. Polygamists, not surprisingly, were the most likely to agree that they are Christian, followed by Mormons. Between 50 percent and 60 percent of Mormons consider Mormon polygamists Christians. The non-LDS others were substantially less likely to consider Mormon polygamists Christian (and less likely to consider Mormons Christian; data not shown). While part of the difference can be explained by different definitions of what it means to be Christian between these groups,[85] this pattern illustrates the effort to maintain boundaries. The more similar others are to you, the greater your affinity toward them.[86]

Our survey data also speak to the issue of age at first marriage criticism of polygamists. Table 9.4 presents the responses for the three groups in our survey when asked the minimum ages at which males and females should be allowed to marry with parental consent. In line with mainstream Mormons and the non-LDS in our sample, polygamists believe men should not marry younger than 18. However, the polygamists in our sample said, on average, that women should be allowed to marry with parental consent at 16. While the most common response was 16 (34 percent of polygamists said 16), a majority of polygamists said 18 or older. There are certainly cases in which underage girls have been married to older men, but the polygamists in our survey generally reflected the legal minimum age of marriage in most states.

TABLE 9.4. Minimum Age for Marriage with Parental Consent

	Minimum for Men			Minimum for Women		
	Mean	SD	Mode	Mean	SD	Mode
Polygamists	17.3	3.3	18	16.8	3.6	16
LDS	18.2	1.9	18	17.9	1.9	18
Others	18.3	2.5	18	18.1	2.5	18

TABLE 9.5. Percent Agreeing to "Do Whatever the Lord Wants"

Group	Disagree	Neutral	Agree	N
Polygamists				
Females	27.8	0.0	72.2	28
Males	17.4	2.2	80.4	18
LDS				
Females	8.6	9.4	82.0	722
Males	14.7	11.1	74.2	597
Others				
Females	32.2	14.4	53.4	665
Males	37.4	14.4	48.2	313

Some of the data we collected in our survey confirms that polygamists are authoritarian and obedient in their approach to religion, as discussed above. The survey asked respondents how strongly they agree/disagree with the following statement, "I am willing to do whatever the Lord wants me to do." The results are presented in Table 9.5. The polygamists in the sample were, on average, more compliant to authority than the non-LDS others but about as authoritarian as the LDS respondents. Nearly 75 percent of the polygamists, both men and women, agree that they would do whatever the Lord wants them to do.[87]

Media characterizations of polygamists as patriarchal also warrant investigation with data. We asked participants in our survey to indicate how strongly they agree with the statement, "Women and men should have different roles in society." Both polygamists and LDS churchgoers endorse stricter gender roles than do our other respondents (see table 9.6). This is particularly true for polygamist men, indicating high degrees of patriarchy among polygamists. Related to this, we also asked survey participants how polygamous parents compared to monogamous parents as fathers and husbands (or mothers and wives) (e.g., "Compared to men in monogamous marriages, polygamous fathers are____attentive to their children."). Response options included "more," "equally," or "less." As shown in table 9.7, the non-polygamists tend to think that polygamists—especially polygamist men—are not particularly attentive to

TABLE 9.6. Percent Agreeing That Women and Men Should Have Different Roles in Society

Group	Disagree	Neutral	Agree	N
Polygamists				
Females	17.9	35.7	46.4	28
Males	11.1	16.7	72.2	18
LDS				
Females	33.1	24.1	42.8	717
Males	20.7	24.9	54.4	594
Others				
Females	54.8	21.4	23.8	660
Males	44.6	24.0	31.4	312

TABLE 9.7. Belief that Polygamists Are More Attentive to Family Members Than Are Non-Polygamists

Responding Group	More	Equally	Less	N
Fathers' Attentiveness Toward Children				
Polygamists				
Females	22.2	61.1	16.7	27
Males	20.0	60.0	20.0	18
LDS				
Females	0.7	24.3	75.0	687
Males	3.3	29.5	67.2	570
Others				
Females	2.5	28.8	68.7	643
Males	2.7	45.0	52.3	300
Husbands' Attentiveness Toward Wives				
Polygamists				
Females	44.4	38.9	16.7	27
Males	37.8	40.0	22.2	18
LDS				
Females	1.7	15.2	83.1	686
Males	4.9	23.6	71.4	567
Others				
Females	3.4	17.5	79.1	640
Males	7.4	30.6	62.0	297
Mothers' Attentiveness Toward Children				
Polygamists				
Females	66.7	27.8	5.6	27
Males	62.2	31.1	6.7	18
LDS				
Females	19.9	58.1	22.0	685
Males	19.5	62.6	17.9	569
Others				
Females	16.5	56.6	26.8	641
Males	17.4	58.2	24.4	299

Responding Group	More	Equally	Less	N
Wives' Attentiveness Toward Husbands				
Polygamists				
Females	38.9	50.0	11.1	27
Males	46.7	40.0	13.3	18
LDS				
Females	28.0	32.2	39.8	683
Males	21.9	39.0	39.2	567
Others				
Females	29.4	27.7	42.8	642
Males	23.1	41.1	35.8	299

TABLE 9.8. Percent Agreeing That Teen Boys and Girls Can Leave Polygamy

Group	Disagree	Neutral	Agree	N
Boys Can Leave				
Polygamists				
Females	11.1	18.5	70.4	27
Males	11.1	11.1	77.8	18
LDS				
Females	30.2	29.2	40.6	709
Males	24.5	30.2	45.3	579
Others				
Females	30.7	28.5	40.8	655
Males	25.7	33.2	41.0	307
Girls Can Leave				
Polygamists				
Females	7.1	17.9	75.0	28
Males	11.1	11.1	77.8	18
LDS				
Females	37.4	24.6	38.1	712
Males	36.4	26.3	37.3	582
Others				
Females	30.6	26.2	43.1	656
Males	24.8	34.9	40.4	307

Source: author Nielsen

their family. Polygamists, however, see themselves more positively, illustrating the in-group–out-group bias discussed earlier.

In-group–out-group distinctions are also revealed in people's responses to questions regarding teen autonomy. We asked our participants to indicate their level of agreement with the statements (asked separately for boys and girls), "Teen boys/girls who are raised with polygamous beliefs are able to leave the polygamous lifestyle." Table 9.8 presents the results for our three groups divided by gender. The vast majority of polygamists assert that teens can leave a polygamous lifestyle, while non-polygamists are more skeptical of the claim, although close to 50 percent agree that they can. Polygamists may be authoritarian, and they may believe that leaving the group jeopardizes one's salvation, but they generally claim to grant the ability to leave.

In sum, then, the polygamists in our sample were fairly authoritarian and patriarchal in their attitudes and religious practice, but they believe that members of the group have autonomy. They also exhibit substantial in-group favoritism and bias, which is expected of groups with strict theologies that are living outside the mores of the broader society. The extent to which these patterns are reflected in responses of FLDS churchgoers awaits additional data.

Conclusion

For the most part, the media coverage of the FLDS raid by major news outlets has not been particularly biased, but there are some areas where it has been uninformed and there are patterns that reflect a number of social-psychological phenomena. The media has participated in the efforts of CPS to develop an injustice frame to justify the raid of the FLDS ranch and has supported that effort by highlighting the crimes and conviction of Warren Jeffs, potentially prejudicing readers in the process. However, the media has also served as a medium for the FLDS to develop their own injustice frame that presents the raid as a violation of civil rights.

Media reports we examined accurately described the FLDS as a sect and highlighted its in-group favoritism and out-group distrust. There has not been, however, a very clear or detailed discussion of the authoritarianism of the FLDS or why this is important to them. If anything, the media has raised concerns about the authoritarianism of the FLDS without recognizing its foundations in their theology.

Finally, the media have fallen prey to confirmation bias on some issues; even journalists find answers where they look for them. They also find answers based on the available heuristics. This is evident in the comparison with the Branch Davidians and the assumption that a bed in the FLDS temple could only be used for consummating underage marriages. Neither assumption was supported by the evidence, and more compelling explanations exist but were not widely presented in the media. Applying social psychology to these reports paints a slightly different picture and offers a more nuanced understanding of a volatile situation.

NOTES

1. Robert Entman, "Framing: Toward Clarification of a Fractured Paradigm," *Journal of Communication* 43 (1993): 51.

2. Ben Winslow, "Ex-FLDS Members Try to Counter Claims of Persecution," *Deseret News*, April 15, 2008, http://deseretnews.com/article/0,1249,695270674,00.html (accessed May 13, 2008); Ben Winslow, "Ex-FLDS Members Find Tears, Complaints Ironic," *Deseret News*, April 16, 2008, http://deseretnews.com/article/0,1249,695270759,00.html (accessed May 13, 2008).

3. Rhys H. Williams, "Movement Dynamics and Social Change: Transforming Fundamentalist Ideology and Organizations," in *Accounting for Fundamentalisms: The Dynamic Character of Movements*, eds. M. Marty and R. S. Appleby (Chicago: University of Chicago Press, 1994), 785–833; Robert D. Benford and David A. Snow, "Framing Processes and Social Movements: An Overview and Assessment," *Annual Review of Sociology* 26 (2000): 611.

4. Erving Goffman, *Frame Analysis: An Essay on the Organization of Experience* (Boston: Northeastern University Press, 1986).

5. Charlotte Ryan and William W. Gamson, "The Art of Reframing Political Debates," *Contexts* (2006)5: 13–18.

6. Benford, "Framing Processes and Social Movements."

7. Ibid.

8. Ibid.; Entman, "Framing"; Erving Goffman, *The Presentation of Self in Everyday Life* (Garden City, NY: Doubleday, 1959).

9. CNN, "Agents at Polygamist Ranch Checking 'Safety of Children.'" *CNN.com*, April 4, 2008, http://www.cnn.com/2008/US/04/04/texas.ranch/index.html (accessed May 13, 2008).

10. Bill Kirkos, "Possible Standoff Looms at Polygamist Ranch," *CNN.com*, April 5, 2008, http://www.cnn.com/2008/CRIME/04/05/texas.ranch/index.html (accessed May 13, 2008). Darrell Azar is a spokesperson for CPS.

11. Janet Elliott and John MacCormack, "401 Children in Custody in Polygamist Compound Raid," *Houston Chronicle*, April 7, 2008, http://www.chron.com/disp/story.mpl/side2/5681283.html (Accessed May 13, 2008).

12. Ben Winslow, "Woman Arrested for Colorado Hoax Calls Said Her Name Was 'Sarah,'" *Deseret News*, April 18, 2008, http://deseretnews.com/article/0,1249,695271894,00.html (accessed May 13, 2008).

13. Terri Langford and Lisa Sandberg, "Official: Older Sect Boys May Have Abused Younger Ones," *Houston Chronicle*, May 1, 2008.

14. Benford, "Framing Processes and Social Movements"; Entman, "Framing."

15. CNN, "State Now a Danger to Children, Sect's Mothers Say," *CNN.com*, April 15, 2008, http://www.cnn.com/2008/CRIME/04/15/sect.mothers/index.html (accessed May 13, 2008).

16. Michelle Roberts, "Documents: Sect Married Girls at Puberty," *Fox News*, April 8, 2008, http://www.foxnews.com/wires/2008Apr08/0,4670, PolygamistRetreat,00.html (accessed May 13, 2008).

17. As noted above, when describing the media sources we read, Fox News primarily published Associated Press articles, not original news articles. In the five "original" articles they published on this topic, there was one instance of criticism of CPS and no positive framing of CPS.

18. Ben Winslow, "FLDS Parents Hit with Court Papers for Pending Custody Battle," *Deseret News,* April 14, 2008, http://deseretnews.com/ article/0,1249,695270221,00.html (accessed May 13, 2008).

19. Elliott, "401 Children in Custody."

20. J. W. Sherman, "Development and Mental Representation of Stereotypes," *Journal of Personality and Social Psychology* 70 (1996): 1126–1141.

21. Ibid.

22. Penny Edgell, Joseph Gerteis, and Douglas Hartmann, "Atheists as 'Other': Moral Boundaries and Cultural Membership in American Society," *American Sociological Review* 71 (2006): 211–234.

23. Wallace B. Jefferson et al., *In Re Texas Department of Family and Protective Services, Relator: On Petition for Mandamus,* (Austin, TX, 2008), http://www.supreme. courts.state.tx.us/historical/2008/may/080391.htm (accessed June 5, 2008).

24. Gary Tuchman and Amanda Townsend, "A Dark History Repeats for Religious Sect," *CNN.com,* April 10, 2008, http://www.cnn.com/2008/CRIME/04/10/ polygamist.towns/index.html (accessed May 13, 2008).

25. Ibid.

26. Jennifer Dobner, "Sect Members Say Life 'Normal' on Polygamous Church Ranch," *Fox News,* April 16, 2008, http://www.foxnews.com/wires/2008Apr16/0,467 0,PolygamistRetreat,00.html (accessed May 13, 2008).

27. Mary P. Batchelor, Marianne Watson, and Anne Wilde, *Voices in Harmony: Contemporary Women Celebrate Plural Marriage* (Salt Lake City: Principle Voices, 2000).

28. According to the authors, no FLDS women participated in the study, as they were told not to by the leadership of the religion. Thus, the study participants are non-FLDS polygamist women.

29. CNN, "State Now a Danger to Children."

30. CNN, "ACLU Weighs in on Texas Polygamist Custody Case," *CNN.com,* April 20, 2008, http://www.cnn.com/2008/CRIME/04/20/polygamy.sect/index.html (accessed May 13, 2008).

31. Ben Winslow, "Shurtleff Connects the FLDS Dots," *Deseret News,* April 14, 2008, http://deseretnews.com/article/0,1249,695270178,00.html (accessed May 13, 2008).

32. Ibid.

33. Ryan, "The Art of Reframing Political Debates."

34. CNN, "Witness: Teens at Ranch Said Any Age OK to Marry," *CNN.com,* April 17, 2008, http://www.cnn.com/2008/CRIME/04/17/polygamy.custody/index.html (accessed May 13, 2008).

35. *Houston Chronicle,* "In the Balance," *Houston Chronicle,* May 1, 2008.

36. Ibid.

37. Gretel C. Kovach, "Court Files Detail Claims of Sect's 'Pattern' of Abuse," *New York Times,* April 9 http://www.nytimes.com/2008/04/09/us/09raid.html (accessed May 12, 2008).

38. CNN, "Women Return to Texas Polygamist Ranch," *CNN.com*, April 14, 2008, http://www.cnn.com/2008/CRIME/04/14/polygamy.retreat/index.html (accessed May 13, 2008).

39. Eliott C. McLaughlin, "Experts: Sect Opens Up to Retrieve Children, Hasten Heaven," *CNN.com*, April 28, 2008, http://www.cnn.com/2008/CRIME/04/28/flds.openness/index.html (accessed May 13, 2008).

40. Benton Johnson, "A Critical Appraisal of the Church-Sect Typology," *American Sociological Review* 22 (1957): 88–92; Benton Johnson, "On Church and Sect," *American Sociological Review* 28 (1964): 539–549.

41. Martha S. Bradley, *Kidnapped from That Land: The Government Raids on the Short Creek Polygamists* (Salt Lake City: University of Utah Press, 1993).

42. Richard Bendix, *Max Weber: An Intellectual Portrait* (Berkeley: University of California Press, 1978).

43. Benjamin G. Bistline, *The Polygamists: A History of Colorado City, Arizona* (Scottsdale, AZ: Agreka, 2004); Bradley, *Kidnapped From That Land;* Janet Bennion, chapter 4 of this volume.

44. Jennifer Dobner, "Facts about the Polygamist Sect FLDS," *Fox News*, April 8, 2008, http://www.foxnews.com/wires/2008Apr08/0,4670,PolygamistRetreatGlance, 00.html (accessed May 13, 2008).

45. Ibid.

46. Andrew Holden, *Jehovah's Witnesses: Portrait of a Contemporary Religious Movement*, 1st ed. (London and New York: Routledge, 2002).

47. Meredith B. McGuire, *The Social Context*, 5th ed. (Long Grove, IL: Waveland, 2002); Bernard Spilka, R. W. Hood, Jr., Bruce Hunsberger, and Richard Gorsuch, *The Psychology of Religion: An Empirical Approach*, 3rd ed. (New York: Guilford Press, 2003).

48. Eileen Barker, *The Making of a Moonie: Choice or Brainwashing* (London: Blackwell, 1984).

49. See, for example, Richard Dawkins, *The God Delusion* (Boston: Houghton Mifflin, 2008).

50. Bob Altemeyer and Bruce Hunsberger, *Amazing Conversions: Why Some Turn to Faith and Others Abandon Religion* (Amherst, NY: Prometheus Books, 1997).

51. An alternative view would be to consider the FLDS socialization process in terms of a learned helpless paradigm, in which children learn that it is futile to deviate from the group's norms. Such a view has some support in the context of abusive relationships (e.g., Suraj Mal, Uday Jain, and K.S. Yada, "Effects of Prolonged Deprivation on Learned Helplessness," *The Journal of Social Psychology* (1990): 191–197), but this framework has not been applied to religious groups in the research literature.

52. Kirk Johnson and Gretel C. Kovach, "Dispute on Treatment of Children after Raid." *New York Times*, April 17, 2008, http://www.nytimes.com/2008/04/17/us/17raid.html (accessed May 12, 2008).

53. Eloitt C. McLaughlin, "Ex-sect Members Escape Polygamy But Not Pain," *CNN.com*, April 16, 2008, http://www.cnn.com/2008/CRIME/04/16/polygamy.escapes/index.html (accessed May 13, 2008).

54. Carolyn Jessop and Laura Palmer, *Escape* (New York: Broadway, 2007).

55. Altemeyer, *Amazing Conversions;* David G. Bromley, ed., *Falling from The Faith: Causes and Consequences of Religious Apostasy* (Newbury Park: Sage Publications, 1988); Helen Rose Fuchs Ebaugh, *Becoming an Ex: The Process of Role Exit* (Chicago: University of Chicago Press, 1988); Holden, *Jehovah's Witnesses.*

56. Stuart A. Wright, *Leaving Cults: The Dynamics of Defection* (Washington, DC: Society for the Scientific Study of Religion, 1987).

57. Ebaugh, *Becoming an Ex.*

58. Associated Press. "Polygamist Sect Mothers Forced to Leave Their Children." *Fox News,* April 15, 2008, http://www.foxnews.com/story/0,2933,351272,00.html (accessed May 13, 2008).

59. Holden, *Jehovah's Witnesses.*

60. Barker, *The Making of a Moonie.*

61. Langford, "Official: Older Sect Boys."

62. Jennifer Dobner, "Sect Mothers Appeal to Texas Governor." *Fox News,* April 13, 2008, http://www.foxnews.com/wires/2008Apr13/0,4670,PolygamistRetreat,00. html (accessed May 13, 2008).

63. The FLDS women offered an alternative explanation (Perkins 2008): They claimed the cell phones were confiscated after one of the women called the *Deseret News* to complain about their living conditions. This then speaks to the control of information and the framing issues described earlier.

64. Dobner, "Sect Members Say Life 'Normal.'"

65. Johnson, "Dispute."

66. Associated Press, "Polygamist Sect Mothers."

67. Laurence R. Iannaccone, "Religious Markets and the Economics of Religion," *Social Compass* 39 (1992): 123–131; Rodney Stark and Roger Finke, *Acts of Faith: Explaining the Human Side of Religion* (Berkeley: University of California Press, 2000).

68. Muzafer Sherif, *The Robbers Cave Experiment: Intergroup Conflict and Cooperation* [orig. pub. as *Intergroup Conflict and Cooperation*], 1st ed. (Middletown, CT: Wesleyan University Press, 1988).

69. Patricia W. Linville, Gregory Fisher, and Peter Salovey, "Perceived Distribution of the Characteristics of Ingroup and Outgroup Members," *Journal of Personality and Social Psychology* 57 (1989): 165–188.

70. Urie Bronfenbrenner, "The Mirror Image in Soviet-American Relations," *Journal of Social Issues* 17 (1961): 45–56.

71. Dobner, "Facts."

72. Associated Press, "Officials: Jeffs Hand-Picked Texas Polygamist Compound Members," *Fox News,* April 12, 2008, http://www.foxnews.com/story/0,2933,351018,00.html (accessed May 13, 2008).

73. Associated Press, "Texas Defends Separation of Polygamist Sect Kids From Moms," *Fox News,* April 15, 2008, http://www.foxnews.com/story/0,2933,351389,00. html (accessed May 13, 2008).

74. Lisa Sandberg and Terri Langford, "Official: History of Injuries in Polygamist Sect Children," *Houston Chronicle,* April 30, 2008, http://www.chron.com/disp/story. mpl/life/religion/5742558.html (accessed May 13, 2008).

75. CNN, "State Now a Danger to Children."

76. The interview we reference here was actually with a former member of a different polygamous group based in New Mexico, but Bill O'Reilly used that as a launching point for criticizing the FLDS in Texas, as illustrated in the quote.

77. Bill O'Reilly, "Former Strong City Cult Member Speaks Out—Bill O'Reilly | The O'Reilly Factor," *Fox News*, May 5, 2008, http://www.foxnews.com/story/0,2933,354198,00.html (accessed May 13, 2008).

78. Nielsen Media Research, "January '08 (LIVE+SD) Program Ranker," http://www.mediabistro.com/tvnewser/original/January%20'08%20(LIVE+SD)%20Program%20Ranker.pdf (accessed May 16, 2008).

79. Gretel C. Kovach and Kirk Johnson, "Officials Tell How Sect in West Texas Was Raided," *New York Times*, April 11, 2008, http://www.nytimes.com/2008/04/11/us/11raid.html (accessed May 12, 2008).

80. CNN, "Sect Children Will Stay in State Custody, Judge Rules," *CNN.com*, April 18, 2008, http://www.cnn.com/2008/CRIME/04/18/polygamy.custody/index.html (accessed May 13, 2008).

81. Kirk Johnson, "Texas Polygamy Raid May Pose Risk," *New York Times*, April 12, 2008, http://www.nytimes.com/2008/04/12/us/12raid.html (accessed May 12, 2008).

82. Brian Mullen and Li-Tze Hu, "Perceptions of Ingroup and Outgroup Variability: A Meta-Analytic Integration," *Basic & Applied Social Psychology* 10 (1989): 233–252.

83. The survey was conducted online and participants were solicited by posting links to the survey on a variety of web sites and forums frequented by polygamists, former polygamists, or people with an interest in polygamy as well as several other web sites. Details about the samples and data collection methods are found in (Nielsen, in press).

84. We are aware of objections to the term "Mormon polygamists" but decided to use the phrase because of its frequent occurrence in media reports of fundamentalist groups who reject the LDS 1890, 1904, and 1933 manifestos against polygamy.

85. Armand L. Mauss, *The Angel and the Beehive: The Mormon Struggle with Assimilation* (Chicago: University of Illinois Press, 1994); Jan Shipps, "Christian Century: Mormon Metamorphosis: The Neglected Story," *Christian Century* (1996), http://findarticles.com/p/articles/mi_m1058/is_n24_v113/ai_18612641/print?tag=artBody;col1 (accessed July 14, 2008); Stephen E. Robinson, "Are Mormons Christians?" *New Era* (1998): 41.

86. Michael Nielsen, "Opinions Regarding Polygamy among LDS Church Members: Demographic Predictors," *Archive for the Psychology of Religion* 31 (2009): 261–270.

87. As an interesting aside, the high levels of authoritarianism among the LDS participants play out in the news coverage of the FLDS raid. While the *Deseret News* had more original articles than any of the other media outlets with the exception of the Associated Press (which, of course, is an aggregate of news agencies), there were only three stories that mentioned authoritarian aspects of the FLDS in the *Deseret News*, and most of those references were downplayed. This is consistent with the finding that it requires a questioning and non-authoritarian attitude to see authoritarianism in others (Hunsberger 2006).

Chapter 10

Learning the Wrong Lessons: A Comparison of FLDS, Family International, and Branch Davidian Child-Protection Interventions

Gary Shepherd and Gordon Shepherd

Power always sincerely, conscientiously, in good faith, believes itself right. Power always thinks it has a great soul and vast views, beyond the comprehension of the weak.
> —John Adams, Letter to Thomas Jefferson,
> February 2, 1816

The initial raids by state authorities on the Fundamentalist Latter-Day Saint (FLDS) community in Short Creek, Arizona, in 1935 and 1944 resulted in the arrest and imprisonment of 21 adults for violation of anti-polygamy laws; the 1953 raid resulted in the arrest of about 160 adults, and, additionally, featured the seizure and placement into protective custody of 236 children (see chapter 1, this volume).[1] These raids were all carried out with good law enforcement intentions which, by 1953, also stressed rescuing children from presumed conditions of domestic depravity perpetrated by polygamous adults.[2] The good intentions, but biased assumptions upon which they were based, quickly dissolved into calamitous actual consequences for both authorities and FLDS children, as recounted elsewhere in this volume. The majority of children taken from their homes in 1953 were kept in foster care arrangements for approximately two years, and some of the children were never returned to their parents.[3] The negative impact of these state-compelled, parent-child ruptures was profound for individual family members and for the FLDS community as a whole; bitter memories of the state's action and its consequences have ever since assumed a prominent place in FLDS interpretations of themselves and their embattled relationship to the outside world.

An observation accompanying many reported news stories about the April 2008 removal of FLDS children from their Yearning For Zion Ranch homes in Eldorado, Texas, was that this was probably the largest single protective custody case in United States history, exceeding, in fact, the previous watermark established in the 1953 FLDS police raid. The actual number of children taken in the recent imbroglio was a point of contention, with Texas officials initially claiming that 467 of the individuals removed from the ranch were minors, then later acknowledging that at least 27 of this number were actually adults. Whatever the exact number of children may have been, however, it is rivaled by another publicly unpopular religious group that suffered forced, state removal of at least the same approximate number of their children from community homes scattered around the world in the late 1980s and early 1990s. This group is The Family International (then, simply named The Family, and at an earlier time called The Children of God).[4] Close to 500 minor children under the age of 18 were removed from Family homes in five different countries (Australia, France, Spain, Venezuela, and Argentina) over a period of four years (1989–1993) and placed in state protective custody for periods of time varying from several days to more than a year. All of these children were subjected to varying degrees of physical and psychological examination by authorities (some of it quite severe) to detect evidence of presumed abuse. An additional 140 children in these and several other countries were also intensively examined during this same time period but were not placed into protective custody. Over 100 Family adults were incarcerated in these same countries for periods of time ranging between several days to more than three months.[5]

What was the net result of all these separate investigations following the terrorizing of large numbers of children and adults, mass arrests, imprisonments, custody placements, invasive examinations, and breakup of households? Not a single case against Family adults was upheld in courts of law within the various countries involved. Not one of the more than 600 children examined by doctors and psychologists in these countries was found to have been abused. In every country, in every case, parents and children were released from custody for lack of evidence and eventually reunited.

Superficially, the FLDS and Family International cases may seem quite different. FLDS children were all removed in one batch, from one location, under the authority of one jurisdiction in the United States, whereas Family children were taken from a variety of home locations in multiple different countries over several years' time. The raids against the FLDS and The Family International, however, share several significant, underlying characteristics. Indeed, these underlying characteristics overlap substantially with yet another Texas case—far better known and more tragic than either the FLDS or Family cases— namely, the disastrous Waco, Texas, Branch Davidian episode that unfolded before the world's eyes from February 28, 1993, to April 19 of that same year.[6] Four Bureau of Alcohol, Tobacco, and Firearms (BATF) agents and six Branch Davidian members died in a gun battle that erupted during a botched attempt by BATF to serve a warrant that prominently included charges of child abuse. Later, 21 Branch Davidian children and 53 adults suffered horrible, fiery deaths during the assault carried out by FBI agents on their Mount Carmel home 51 days after the initial clash. Another 21 Branch Davidian children, who were surrendered to authorities by their parents during the siege of Mount Carmel prior to the final tank and tear gas assault, were subsequently placed into state protective custody and eventually into the Texas foster care system.

No one died in either the FLDS or Family cases, and each of the three cases to be examined here differ in particular details. Nevertheless, the broad, underlying characteristics shared by all three groups include the following. First, each group was (and is) a small, heretical, apocalyptic Christian movement with a substantial history of outside opposition. Second, each group emphasizes some form of communal living arrangements as the preferred form of Christian living. Third, each group rejects the materialism, styles and fads, political machinations, and ordinary social involvements of the contemporary world. They all see themselves as a spiritually elect community, set apart and dedicated to serving God and bringing to pass the larger, "end-time" purposes of God's plan for this earth, and they are therefore only marginally integrated in the larger societies where they reside. Fourth, each group is based on the claims of a prophet-founder and is subsequently guided by continuing prophetic leadership claims beyond the death of the founder. Fifth, all three prophet founders of these groups introduced radical teachings and consequent practices, argued to be both biblically based and the product of modern-day revelation, concerning marriage relations and sexuality. Sixth, the most damaging allegation leveled at all three groups by former members and self-proclaimed "cult experts" was that children were being subjected to sexual and physical abuse within their communal home environments. In each case, however, adequate physical evidence from the children and homes in question, prior to the police raids, was lacking. Seventh, all three of these groups were widely and publically stigmatized as "cults" that posed a danger to both the larger community and to their own members.[7] Successful application of the "dangerous cult" label in all three cases, with particular emphasis on the allegation of child abuse, was sufficient to justify extraordinary, armed police intervention in the absence of any other confirmed factual evidence. Concerted crusading efforts by disgruntled ex-group members, self-proclaimed "cult experts," and mental health and social service professionals (abetted by the sensationalizing tendencies of the mass media[8]) played a major role in interpreting and applying the cult label in all three cases.[9]

Elaboration of Religious and Social Characteristics Shared by Branch Davidian, Family, and FLDS Communities

Apocalyptic Movements

The Branch Davidians were and are a sectarian offshoot of Seventh-day Adventism, with a nearly 80-year history of pursuing their version of Christian living while awaiting a fiery end time of history in West-Central Texas. The Family International is a 40-year-old Christian missionary movement, well into its third generation, that has no organizational ties to any denomination or other group, but works assiduously to save as many souls as possible prior to what they anticipate is the near appearance of the Anti-Christ in human affairs and the final tribulations that humankind is then expected to endure before the return of Jesus. The FLDS Church, as recounted in other chapters of this volume, has an 80-year history as a sectarian offshoot of the Church of Jesus Christ of Latter-Day Saints and justifies its communitarian, polygamous lifestyle as necessary preparation for the second coming of Jesus in what are presumed to be the "latter days" of God's grand plan.

Communal Living

The main body of Branch Davidians (approximately 135 people in 1993) all lived in one communal complex at the time of the Mount Carmel raid. (Small numbers of additional Branch Davidian affiliates lived in several other locations in the United States and around the world.) Family International members live in communal homes located in over 100 different countries, with an approximate minimum number of 10 persons and an approximate maximum number of 35 persons living together in any one home. (The overall population of fully committed Family members worldwide has hovered around 10,000 for over a decade.)[10] As a satellite FLDS community, the Yearning for Zion (YFZ) Ranch consisted of multiple communal homes and other essential community buildings with a total population of approximately 800 people. (Most accepted estimates of the total number of current FLDS members are approximately 10,000 people, concentrated primarily in Colorado City, Arizona, and Hilldale, Utah.)

Worldly Rejection

Mount Carmel was located in a rural area approximately ten miles outside the nearest Waco, Texas, suburb. Although adult members often interacted with non-Davidian neighbors and even occasionally with authorities, the bulk of members' time and activities, especially for children (who were home-schooled), was focused in their own, semi-secluded community, where they could more readily carry out their religiously based lifestyle with less distraction and interference.

Likewise, Family International members have regular interactions with outsiders in the larger communities where they establish their communal homes, particularly as a consequence of their full-time missionary activities. However, they prefer, wherever possible, to find homes that provide maximum privacy. They socialize or "fellowship" primarily among themselves, and they do not have conventional salaried jobs (depending instead on a wide range of financial contributions and in-kind services). They watch only news and occasional sports programs on television, create and enjoy their own music and other forms of entertainment, homeschool their children, and indeed birth their children at home with the help of midwives.

FLDS families similarly eschew frequent contact with outsiders and have developed a cooperative economic and social system to enhance self-sufficiency and reduce dependency on outsiders. FLDS people living in other Western states do seek and have employment in nearby towns, but the residents of YFZ in Texas did not. FLDS parents living at the YFZ also homeschooled their children. The YFZ itself, like Mount Carmel, is situated in the country, away from other population centers and is also fenced and gated.

Prophetic Leadership

The Branch Davidians grew out of the biblical interpretations and personal claims to spiritual guidance of Victor Houteff beginning in 1929.[11] Following two previous successors to Houteff, a young but scripturally impressive Vernon Howell, subsequently self-proclaimed as David Koresh—a biblically based messiah for the end-time[12]—assumed prophetic authority in 1987.

The Family International's first incarnation as The Children of God was the result of revolutionary messages preached by a former Missionary Alliance minister, David Berg, to young American hippies in the late 1960s. Berg subsequently also proclaimed himself God's end-time prophet and established a worldwide following of primarily young Christian evangelists who continue to be directed in their endeavors through a complex system of prophetic revelations perfected by Berg's successors—his widow Maria and her now-husband Peter.[13]

Warren Jeffs, the current (albeit imprisoned) prophet of the FLDS Church, is seen by his followers as the latest in a chain of earlier prophet-leaders that eventually merges with the prophetic line of succession claimed by the main Church of Jesus Christ of Latter-Day Saints that stretches back to the founder of Mormonism, Joseph Smith, in 1830.[14] Smith claimed direct revelations from God and Jesus Christ to restore true Christianity to the earth again following a long historical period of corruption and lost priesthood authority.[15]

Radical Marriage and Sexual Practices

David Koresh, in his self-proclaimed role of end-time messiah, claimed exclusive sexual rights to the women among his immediate followers. These rights were based on his interpretation of biblical prophecy that required him to sire a divinely appointed cohort of children, who would subsequently constitute a new ruling "House of David."[16]

David Berg emphasized the primacy of the Law of Love, which he extended into the realm of sexual relationships. Concomitantly, he also introduced the "one wife" doctrine, which promoted sexual sharing among non-married Family adults, and the practice of "flirty fishing," which featured the employment of sexual favors by Family women as a technique to attract unsaved or non-Christian males in order to witness to them of Jesus' saving love.[17]

Finally, Joseph Smith instituted a variant of the ancient Hebrews' practice of polygamy among his closest followers as a requirement for ascension to ultimate celestial blessings. It was the official renunciation of polygamy in 1890 by Mormon leaders that caused the FLDS schism from the LDS mother church. FLDS prophets up to Warren Jeffs have continued to teach the religious necessity of polygamy, encouraged and sanctioned its practice for FLDS followers, and practiced it themselves.

Child Abuse Allegations

Although illegal firearms manufacture was nominally the primary concern of the BATF, child abuse was the first charge listed on the warrant that BATF attempted to serve on the Branch Davidians (even though such a charge fell outside BATF's legal mandate to investigate). This charge also appears to have been the decisive factor in persuading Attorney General Janet Reno to authorize the FBI's subsequent military operations.[18] The one constant charge in all the police raids on Family homes around the world was also child abuse. All of the 600-plus Family children taken from their homes or involved in official investigations were, in each country, subjected to almost immediate physical and psychological testing by doctors and psychologists to discover the expected evidence of abuse. Allegations of FLDS child abuse are primarily connected to marriage of underage girls as plural wives to older men. These allegations are elaborated upon elsewhere in this volume (see, e.g., chapter 8); they were, of course, the necessary and sufficient justification by Texas authorities for the removal of all minor children from their YFZ homes.

Stigmatizing Cult Label

The miniscule Branch Davidian group first came to the attention of federal authorities—as well as to the attention of the media and general public—through allegations of criminal activity made by former Australian members (led by Marc Breault, a leadership rival of David Koresh) to the now-defunct Cult Awareness Network (CAN).[19] CAN affiliates, including especially "deprogrammer" Rick Ross, in turn contacted the Bureau of Alcohol, Tobacco, and Firearms (BATF) and then later provided "expert" advice to FBI authorities who had supplanted the BATF and conducted the subsequent siege of Mount Carmel following the reckless BATF attempt to serve a search warrant through armed force. This military intervention into a small religious community in rural Texas ignited enormous media coverage from all over the world for over 50 days.

CAN was also influential in encouraging and providing aid to a small core of embittered ex-Family members in the United States and networking with other anti-cult organizations (such as FREECOG in the United States, the Association for the Defense of the Family and the Individual in France, Asociación Pro Juventud in Spain, and the Fundación SPES in Argentina) and with former Family members and relatives of continuing Family members in the United States, Europe, and South America. All of the child sexual and physical abuse charges pressed by authorities around the world were predicated on informant claims and copies of old, quasi-pornographic materials published and videotaped by The Family prior to its abandonment of "flirty fishing" and its support of several types of adult-with-minor sexual activity in the late 1970s to mid-1980s. Former members and local "cult experts" in every country where raids against Family homes occurred were routinely interviewed by media representatives before, during, and after the raids to provide an alternately horrified and titillated public with insider insights into the putative perversions of cult life.

The more recent and massive media coverage of the FLDS raid by Texas Rangers and officials of Texas Child Protective Services has made the charges of forced, underage, polygamous marriages of young females (and the attendant felony charges of statutory rape) well-known. It is also well-known that the specific allegations of abuse that triggered the initial raid were the fictitious products of a hoax caller who had no actual connection with the FLDS. Finally, as in both the Branch Davidian and Family International cases, allegations of sexual child abuse by the FLDS were most tellingly and persuasively made by ex-FLDS members. Several of these ex-member critics were authors of subsequently best-selling books about their lives as young polygamous wives and their eventual "escape from the cult." They were interviewed repeatedly by newspaper and TV reporters[20] while Texas authorities and courts tried for weeks to sort out the evidence and decide what to do with the detained children.

To summarize: all three groups were subjected to armed police interventions into their communities based on criminal allegations that emphasized serious sexual abuse of children. These allegations were primarily bolstered by accounts of crusading ex-members and resulted in the removal of large numbers of children from their homes. These groups remain controversial apocalyptic sects that live communally, reject worldly values, are somewhat socially isolated, advocate and practice unorthodox marriage and sexual relationships, are led by prophetic or charismatic authority structures, and have been publically stigmatized as cults.[21]

Summary of Police Raids and Subsequent Outcomes

The police raids mounted against these three groups—triggered and justified by allegations of child abuse that seemed self-evidently plausible within projected cultic environments—resulted in a range of traumatic consequences. Most severe, of course, was the tragic fate of the Branch Davidians. In addition to the horrific deaths of 21 Branch Davidian children, 59 Branch Davidian adults, including parents and grandparents, were also killed. The 12 adults who survived the final FBI assault on Mount Carmel were immediately placed under arrest, convicted on various charges of using illegal firearms and aiding and abetting voluntary manslaughter, and eventually served prison terms ranging from 3 to 14 years. The surviving children stayed in foster care until age 18.

The assault on the Branch Davidians by BATF and FBI agents was far different in execution, resultant violence, and final outcomes than the police raids on Family and FLDS homes, which, in fact, were quite similar to each other in execution and outcomes. The Branch Davidians were heavily armed and fully prepared to engage in self-defense against what they believed to be a biblically prophesized invading enemy.[22] In contrast, The Family is explicitly passivist in both theology and lifestyle, and members have never physically resisted arrest or other actions taken against them by state authorities. The FLDS colony in Texas was also nonviolent in its response to the forced entry of heavily armed Rangers onto its property, even though FLDS theology is not committed to pacifism, and members do own firearms.

Descriptions and analysis of the FLDS raid are detailed in other chapters of this book. But because The Family International's experience is not as well-known in the United States, it is instructive to provide here additional summary details of several of the raids on Family homes in different countries in light of the similar FLDS experience in Texas. Official investigations of Family communal homes producing the most severe consequences—in Spain, Australia, France, and Argentina—culminated in large-scale military-style raids and were all the products of former Family members working with local anti-cult organizations to bring various criminal allegations to the attention of local police and protective service agencies. Outcomes for the residents of the various Family homes raided were all traumatic but varied somewhat in severity. These four cases are summarized below.[23]

The relatively least traumatic of the four highlighted Family cases occurred in Barcelona, Spain, where officials removed 21 children from their communal Family homes in July 1990 and arrested 10 adults on charges of inflicting mental damage on their children, fraud, illegal association (as an alien religious sect), and operating an illegal school. The parents were not imprisoned while awaiting trial and were acquitted approximately a year later by the Barcelona Provincial Appeals Court, during which time, however, their children were detained in state custody. This decision was then appealed by local authorities to both the Constitutional Court and the Supreme Court of Spain but was strongly rejected by both courts in October 1994.

Two years after the Barcelona raid (in May 1992), several Family homes in Melbourne and Sydney, Australia, were subjected to coordinated, large-scale pre-dawn raids by armed police and Department of Community Services personnel. Sixty-five children were taken into state custody in Sydney and 56 children in Melbourne, but parents and other Family adults were not arrested.

A children's magistrate ordered the release of the Sydney children into the temporary custody of their parents within six days of the raids, and the Victoria Supreme Court ordered the same for all children taken in Melbourne. The children were administered various psychological tests and physical examinations, but were generally handled more sensitively than were their counterparts in France and Argentina the following year. The children also were subjected to massive media attention and extensive court appearances while their cases were being adjudicated. Sensational court hearings to determine the validity of charges against parents, including charges of sexual and physical abuse of their children, received continual press coverage for six and a half months in Sydney until a mediated settlement stayed the case for a year. The case was finally dismissed by the New South Wales Supreme Court in November 1993. Family members subsequently initiated a civil suit for wrongful arrest and related damages that was ultimately resolved by the Supreme Court in their favor in 1999 for a compensation of $1.7 million. Meanwhile, Health and Community Services in Melbourne rejected a mediation settlement of their case in 1992 and instituted proceedings to regain custody of the children. This suit was finally settled nearly two years later in April 1994 at estimated costs to taxpayers ranging between $2 and $10 million.

In France, approximately 200 heavily armed police broke down doors of several Family homes in the early morning hours of June 9, 1993, in the cities of Lyon and Éguilles. They dragged 50 adults from their beds into waiting paddy wagons and hauled 90 children into state custody. A number of adults were beaten or otherwise suffered physical injuries during the arrest process.[24] Adults and children alike were terrorized by the aggressive, threatening behavior of police. When taken into custody, children were forced to submit to heavy-handed interrogations and harshly administered and degrading physical and psychological examinations.[25] Nevertheless, finding no immediate evidence to support charges of child abuse, child prostitution, and failure to provide adequate physical and medical care for children, all of the adults in both cities were released from jail after two days. In Lyon, 33 children were released to the custody of their parents after being held for one week. All charges involving these children and their parents were dismissed by the Minor's Court of Aix-en-Provence three months later and were not appealed by local authorities. In Éguilles, however, 47 children were held by the Department of Social Services for 51 days before being returned to the temporary custody of their parents. And the criminal case against 15 parents was pursued for an additional five years until the Tribunal de Grande Instance of Aix-en-Provence acquitted the accused of all charges in January 1999. Even this decision was appealed by the French anti-cult organization Association for the

Defense of the Family and the Individual, but the appeal was rejected by the same court in February 1999.

Officials in South American countries were also aroused to action against alleged Family abuses, beginning with police raids on homes in Buenos Aires, Argentina, in 1989. These raids resulted in the arrest of 13 adults for two weeks on charges of corrupting minors and possession of illegal drugs, and the holding of 18 children in protective custody for over two months. This initial case was subsequently followed by ten additional investigations in Buenos Aires through 1993. Police raids and court cases were also conducted in Nieroli, Brazil, in 1991 and Rio de Janeiro, Brazil, in 1992. Raids in Zulia, Venezuela, in 1992 produced the house arrest of 15 adults for two months and the detention of 21 children for the same length of time. Criminal indictments and trials of ten adults took place in Lima, Peru, in 1990, followed by renewed police and social services investigations in 1993. Back in Argentina, police raids resulted in detained adults and forced examination of children in the city of Rosario, in 1992. As was true elsewhere around the world, all court cases and investigations of Family alleged crimes in these countries eventually exonerated the accused.

But the single worst and most instructive case of the above South American examples began in Buenos Aires on September 1, 1993. Preceded by ten previous investigations of The Family in four years, and goaded forward by the crusading efforts of four former Family members sponsored by the U.S.–based Cult Awareness Network (CAN), federal judge Roberto Marquevich ordered a massive, early-morning police raid on five Family Homes throughout the city. A total of 130 children were scooped up and placed in state custody, while 21 Family adults were arrested and sent to dangerous, maximum-security prisons for both men and women.[26] A laundry list of charges included corruption and prostitution of minors, forced involuntary servitude, illegitimate deprivation of freedom, withholding and concealing persons, illicit association, racial and religious discrimination, and possession and distribution of illegal drugs. The raids and resultant arrests garnered worldwide media attention, including news stories in the *New York Times*[27] and coverage by all of the major U.S. television networks, featuring headlines and story lead-ins proclaiming the breakup of a vicious sex cult.[28] While the case wound its way through the Argentine judicial system, Family children were subjected to repeated interrogations regarding their family life and psychological testing and interviews to determine emotional and developmental impairment. They were also subjected to highly invasive medical examinations, with particular emphasis on gynecological examination of girls, to detect expected evidence of sexual assault.[29] While Family members were in custody, their five homes in two different areas of Buenos

Aires were stripped of articles and possessions of value and then vandalized while supposedly under protective surveillance by police.

On December 13, 1993—three and a half months after the raids—the Federal Appeals Court of San Martin issued a stunning judgment that rejected all charges, berated officials for proceeding without valid evidence and for systematically violating the rights of Family members in a prejudicial manner. The court also declared Judge Marquevich to be incompetent to rule in the case, scorned the testimony of ex-Family members as false and incompatible with independently gathered evidence, and ordered the immediate release of Family adults from prison and their children from state custody. The prosecutor's office subsequently appealed the ruling to the Supreme Court of Argentina, but the Supreme Court rejected this appeal in June 1995. Meanwhile, Judge Marquevich was subjected to impeachment hearings in the Argentina Parliament on charges by the Buenos Aires Bar Association for improper performance of duties, abuse of authority, and false imprisonment of Family members. Nevertheless, virtually all non-Argentine nationals, constituting the majority of Family members, elected to leave Argentina for fear of future reprisals and sought refuge in Family homes located in the United States and other countries around the world.

Lessons to be Learned

What lessons can be derived from this review of state interventions to protect children from presumed adult abuse in the respective communities of the Branch Davidians, Family International, and Fundamentalist Latter-Day Saints? Based on the three cases reviewed, local, state, and federal officials appear to have thought and acted similarly in at least thirteen interconnected ways, summarized below. We believe these constitute errors or negative-lessons of what should not be assumed or done. The first three errors are generated by assumptions about various deviant groups that are perceived to be a problem for law-abiding communities. Errors four through seven are founded on assumptions about religious "cults" in particular that reinforce the first three assumption errors. Finally, errors eight through thirteen are action errors of both omission and commission.

Officials involved in each of the three reviewed instances presumably acted in varying degrees of good faith. But—prior to the raids they proposed, planned, and authorized—these officials all adopted the view that: (1) they were dealing with fraudulent, quasi-criminal groups, (2) that the leaders of these groups were controlling and exploiting their members for selfish purposes through physical and emotional intimidation or through "brainwashing," and (3) that the groups were in fact guilty of the allegations made against them, especially the allegation of child abuse. These assumptions held by officials reflect (4) widespread and strongly held public stereotypes about religious cults. Cult stereotypes are generally reinforced by (5) regular, sensationalized media accounts of various cultic group activities somewhere around the world and are specifically reinforced by (6) presumed accurate insider accounts provided by ex-members of the particular group in question (who frequently have personal grievances to settle or polemical or self-promotional purposes to pursue), and by the (7) opinions and analyses of various entrepreneurial and self-proclaimed cult "experts," who typically are sought to consult about the particular group in question.

One might reasonably suppose that most secular authorities, however jaded some may be, are at a minimum motivated to avoid costly decisions that have the potential to produce greater harm than good and thereby to reflect badly on their judgment; that authorities would therefore not lightly employ armed force against citizens with the object of removing large numbers of children from the care of their parents. Nevertheless, in each of the three cases cited in this chapter, officials did exactly this without entertaining the possibility that (8) members and leaders of the targeted groups might actually be motivated by sincere religious convictions rather than conscious criminal intentions, and that (9) such religious commitment might require a different tactical approach in dealing with these groups. Officials also did not (10) seek more balanced information from scholars, who conduct actual research about the groups in question, and did not (11) seek information about or reflect carefully upon the history and outcomes of previous state-religious group conflicts of the same sort.[30] Instead, officials proceeded with their raids (12) in the absence of unbiased, verifiable evidence and (13) willingly suspended the application of normal legal procedures in so doing.

Unfortunately, the results of these raids have not substantiated the reasons for making them and seriously call into question the judgment of officials responsible for them. Post hoc evidence regarding allegations of Branch Davidian child abuse is, at best, ambiguous[31] and is grotesquely disproportionate to the loss of life, suffering, and other costs that ensued. Children of The Family International were traumatized by the raids inflicted on their homes but not saved from putative abuse, since none was found to have occurred, and all children wound up being returned to their parents. Texas officials' initial claims that 31 minor FLDS females living at the Yearning For Zion Ranch were found to be pregnant or already had babies—prima facie evidence of statutory rape if true—has subsequently been reduced to four girls, and the evidence with regard to these four is still legally disputed as of this writing (late March, 2010).

Meanwhile, all but one of the 440 children (not counting the additional 27 females initially taken but then conceded to be adults) who were removed from their homes have been returned to the care of their parents.

Abuse of children, in all its ugly varieties, is without doubt an enormous, shameful, and vexing social problem throughout the entire world. It occurs in varying degree within every substantial group and population and is fostered by a wide range of psychological, social, cultural, and economic conditions. It has no doubt also occurred, in individual instances, within the Branch Davidian, Family International, and FLDS communities as well. But allegations of wholesale, criminally motivated abuse is a tempting and easy charge to make against alien and marginalized groups. Because the potential consequences of such allegations leveled against an entire community can be so devastating, responsible authorities have a profound obligation to investigate thoroughly and impartially and to weigh carefully the costs versus benefits of massive coercive intervention before committing agencies of the state to irrevocable action.

The thirteen errors identified above—which were consistently perpetuated by authorities in dealing with the Branch Davidians, The Family International, and the Fundamentalist Latter-Day Saints in lieu of thorough, impartial investigation and proportionate response—may all be examined for their logical opposites in order to glean a set of positive lessons for future state-religious group conflicts involving allegations of child abuse. Similar suggestions have been made much earlier, most notably in the aftermath of the Branch Davidian disaster. *Salt Lake Tribune* reporter Brooke Adams, who specializes in covering polygamy news and was in Texas precisely to cover developments in the FLDS child custody case, made this discovery for herself when she picked up a 1995 copy of *Armageddon in Waco: Critical Perspectives on the Branch Davidian Conflict,* edited by sociologist Stuart Wright.[32] Adams read an apropos chapter entitled "Babies Were Being Beaten: Exploring Child Abuse Allegations at Ranch Apocalypse," by sociologists Christopher Ellison and John Bartkowski. At the conclusion of a careful analysis of the issues and events involved, Ellison and Bartkowski proposed a useful set of policy recommendations designed to "avoid future disasters like the conflict at Mt. Carmel." Adams correctly perceived that these recommendations could very well have been applied to the FLDS situation. We see them as complementary, positive supplements to the negative lessons we have summarized above and are as follows:

> Authorities and media representatives should investigate carefully the complex process of claims-making surrounding marginal religious groups and their child-rearing practices. When assessing competing

claims, it is important to link conflicting accounts about the group to the divergent ideological, psycho-logical, and material interests and agendas of the adversarial parties.

"Child abuse" should be defined very carefully, so as to avoid loose and ideologically laden uses of the stigmatizing label. Children who are physically punished, or raised in an unusual set of circumstances (e.g., communally) are not necessarily being abused by their caregivers.

Authorities who must adjudicate the various claims and counterclaims about marginal religious groups should solicit and take seriously the input of social scientists who are familiar with the theology, history, and collective dynamics of such groups.... Child abuse allegations often turn out to be inaccurate for various reasons, and a substantial proportion of such allegations emerge from child custody battles or from other intrafamily or intragroup conflicts.

At each step in the investigative process, it must be the responsibility of authorities to weigh carefully the tradeoffs between the preservation of religious liberty for minority religious groups and welfare of the children. They must avoid taking steps which [are likely to] jeopardize the physical or emotional well-being of the youngsters.[33]

Regrettably, this most recent episode in Texas involving FLDS children shows that none of the above listed suggestions has been heeded at all. Authorities are therefore tragically repeating the same mistakes that a more careful scrutiny of ample historical lessons could help them avoid or at least mitigate. Perhaps the comparisons offered in this chapter, along with the more specific focus on the FLDS experience throughout the rest of this volume, will make some small contribution toward increasing both official and public understanding of these lessons.

NOTES

1. For detailed accounts of all the earlier FLDS raids, see Martha Sonntag Bradley, *Kidnapped from That Land: The Government Raids on the Short Creek Polygamists* (Salt Lake City: University of Utah Press, 1993). For a general history of fundamentalist Mormon polygamy, see Brain C. Hales, *Modern Polygamy and Mormon Fundamentalism: The Generation after The Manifesto* (Salt Lake City: Greg Kofford Books, 2006). See also Ken Driggs, "Imprisonment, Defiance, and Division: A History of Mormon Fundamentalism in the 1940s and 1950s," *Dialogue: A Journal of Mormon Thought* 38 (Spring 2005): 65–95, and also Benjamin G. Bistline, *The Polygamists: A History of Colorado City, Arizona* (Agreka Books, 2004).

2. See Philip Jenkins, *Moral Panic: Changing Conceptions of the Child Molester in Modern America* (New Haven: Yale University Press, 1998), for a social historian's analysis of how public attitudes and legal definitions of child sexual abuse have been generated, shaped, and elevated to a high level in modern America.

3. Ken Driggs, "Who Shall Raise the Children? Vera Black and the Rights of Polygamous Utah Parents," *Utah Historical Quarterly* 60 (1992): 27.

4. For academic sources on both the contemporary Family International and its history as The Children of God, see William Sims Bainbridge, *The Sociology of Religious Movements* (New York: Routledge, 1997); William Sims Bainbridge, *The Endtime Family Children of God* (Albany: State University of New York Press, 2002); James D. Chancellor, *Life in the Family: An Oral History of the Children of God* (Syracuse, NY: Syracuse University Press, 2000); Rex Davis and James T. Richardson, "The Organization and Functioning of the Children of God," *Sociological Analysis* 37 (1976): 321–339; J. Gordon Melton, *The Children of God: "The Family"* (Salt Lake City: Signature Press, 2004); Gary Shepherd and Gordon Shepherd, "Accommodation and Reformation in The Family/Children of God," *Nova Religio* 9, no. 1 (2005): 67–92; Gordon Shepherd and Gary Shepherd, "The Social Construction of Prophecy in The Family International," *Nova Religio* 10, no. 2 (2006): 29–56; Gary Shepherd and Gordon Shepherd, "Grassroots Prophecy in The Family International," *Nova Religio* 10, no. 4 (2007): 38–71; Gary Shepherd and Gordon Shepherd, "The Family International: A Case Study in the Management of Change in New Religious Movements," *Religion Compass* 1 (August 2006): 1–16; David E. Van Zandt, *Living in the Children of God* (Princeton, NJ: Princeton University Press, 1991); Roy Wallis, "Observations on the Children of God," *Sociological Review* 24 (1976): 807–829; ibid., "Yesterday's Children: Cultural and Structural Changes in a New Religious Movement," in *Social Impact of New Religious Movements*, ed. Bryan Wilson (New York: Rose of Sharon Press, 1981), 97–133. For a surprisingly candid history produced by The Family itself, see Samson Warner, *The History of The Family, 1968–1994* (Zurich, Switzerland: World Services, 1995).

5. For a concise summary of all state-sponsored raids of Family International homes during this time period, see Massimo Introvigne, "The Children of God/The Family in Court: A Documentary Legal History," CESNUR (Center for Studies on New Religions) web page at www.cesnur.org. Additional official investigations of Family International homes that did not result in either arrest of adults or placement of children into state protective custody took place in London, England, January 29, 1991; Arneberg, Norway, July 18, 1991; Lima, Peru, July 30, 1993; Los Angeles, U.S.A., July 1993; and Valbo, Sweden, February 1994.

6. For critical assessments of the federal government's siege of the Branch Davidians at Waco, Texas, see Stuart A. Wright, ed., *Armageddon in Waco: Critical Perspectives on the Branch Davidian Conflict* (Chicago: University Of Chicago Press, 1995) and Dick J. Reavis, *The Ashes of Waco: An Investigation* (NY: Simon and Schuster, 1995). For a more recent history and analysis, see the entire issue of *Nova Religio*, Vol. 13, No. 2, 2009, in which five different scholars argue their retrospective views on the tragedy.

7. A long and acrimonious debate has been conducted over the meaning and proper application of the term "cult." See Gary Shepherd, "Cults: Social Psychological Aspects," in George Ritzer, ed., *Blackwell Encyclopedia of Sociology* (London: Blackwell, 2006), and also Benjamin Zablocki and Thomas Robbins, eds., *Misunderstanding Cults: Searching for Objectivity in a Controversial Field* (Toronto: University of Toronto Press, 2001). For more detailed discussions of why many social science researchers have come to prefer the term "new religious movement" in lieu of cult, see Eileen Barker, *New Religious Movements: A Practical Introduction* (London: Her Majesty's Stationery Office, 1989); Lorne Dawson, *Comprehending Cults: The Sociology of New Religious Movements* (New York: Oxford University Press, 1998); James Richardson, "Definitions of Cult: From Sociological-Technical to Popular-Negative, *Review of Religious Research* 34 (1993): 348–356.

8. For analysis of the role played by the mass media in perpetrating cult stereotypes, see Sean McCloud, "From Exotics to Brainwashers: Portraying New Religions in Mass Media," *Religion Compass* 1, no. 3 (2006): 1–15; James Beckford, *The Mass Media and New Religious Movements*, in B. Wilson and J. Cresswell, eds., *New Religious Movements: Challenge and Response* (London: Routledge, 1999), 103–120; and Stuart Wright, "Media Coverage of Unconventional Religion: Any Good News for Minority Faiths?," *Review of Religious Research* (Special Issue: *Mass Media and Unconventional Religion*) 39 (1997): 101–115.

9. The Branch Davidians, The Family International, and the FLDS have all shared and suffered from the generic ethnocentric attitudes and stereotypes of outsiders that are routinely attached to any socially unconventional groups to which the "cult" label has been successfully attached. For sociological development of the general concept of deviant labeling, see Herbert Garfinkle, "Conditions of Successful Status Degradation Ceremonies," *American Journal of Sociology* 61 (1956): 420–424, and also Howard Becker, *The Outsiders* (New York: Free Press, 1963). See specific applications of this thesis to the Branch Davidian case in several chapters of Stuart Wright's edited volume of *Armageddon in Waco,* namely chapters by: Stuart Wright ("Construction and Escalation of a Cult Threat," 75–93), James R. Lewis ("Self-fulfilling Stereotypes, the Anti-cult Movement, and the Waco Confrontation," 95–110), James T. Richardson ("Manufacturing Consent about Koresh," 153–176), and Anson Shupe and Jeffery K. Hadden ("Cops, News Copy, and Public Opinion," 177–204). Specific recent applications of cult labeling that linked both The Family International and the FLDS cases together were generated by several so-called "cult experts," who, in commenting on the unfolding FLDS situation for the U.S. national media, also made references to The Family International as a parallel case, thus putting Family Homes and their children at risk for future state interventions. For example, an interview with sociologist Stephen Kent made comparisons of the FLDS raids to The Family International's 1990s experiences with police raids and the taking of hundreds of their children, alleging that child abuse always did and still continues in The Family, despite the collapse of legal cases against them (Brook Adams, "Polygamy: Where Religious Liberty Ends," *The Salt Lake Tribune*, April 13, 2008). See also self-proclaimed "cult expert" Steven Hassan, making the same linkage to the FLDS and accusations about

254 SOCIAL SCIENTISTS EXAMINE POLYGAMY

The Family in the *Anderson Cooper 360* show and later in the accompanying *Anderson Cooper 360 Blog* for CNN, April 10, 2008.

10. Gordon Shepherd and Gary Shepherd, "World Services in The Family International: The Religious Organization of a Mature Religious Movement," *Nova Religio* 12 No. 3 (2009): 5–39.

11. David G. Bromley and Edward D. Silver, "The Davidian Tradition," in Wright, *Armageddon in Waco*, 43–72.

12. James D. Tabor, "Religious Discourse and Failed Negotiations," in Wright, *Armageddon at Waco*, 263–281.

13. Gordon Shepherd and Gary Shepherd, "The Social Construction of Prophecy in The Family International," *Nova Religio* 10 (2006): 29–56.

14. For an exposition of the many schismatic sects generated in LDS history as a consequence of authority disputes following the assassination of Joseph Smith in 1844, see Newell G. Bringhurst and John C. Hamer, eds., *Scattering of the Saints: Schism within Mormonism* (Independence, MO: John Whitmer Books, 2007).

15. The most recent and thorough scholarly account of Joseph Smith is Richard Bushman, *Rough Stone Rolling* (New York: Alfred A. Knopf, 2005).

16. Bromley and Silver, "The Davidian Tradition," 58–60.

17. J. Gordon Melton, *The Children of God: "The Family"* (Salt Lake City: Signature Press, 2004).

18. Ellison and Bartkowski, "Babies Were Being Beaten," *Armageddon at Waco*, 112.

19. For an account of CAN and its involvement in various "cult" controversies up through its collapse in 1996, see J. Gordon Melton, "Anti-cultists in the United States: An Historical Perspective," in Bryan Wilson and Jamie Cresswell, eds., *New Religious Movements: Challenge and Response* (London: Routledge, 1999), 213–235.

20. See Carolyn Jessop with Laura Palmer, *Escape* (New York: Broadway Books, 2007), and also Elissa Wall with Lisa Pulitzer, *Stolen Innocence: My Story Growing up in a Polygamous Sect* (New York: Harperluxe, 2008). In this same genre, see also Susan Ray Schmidt, *His Favorite Wife: Trapped in Polygamy* (N.p.: Kassidy Lane Publishing, 2006), and Irene Spencer, *Shattered Dreams: My Life as a Polygamist's Wife* (Nashville, TN: Center Street, 2007). Flora Jessop, executive director of the Child Protection Project, although not an author, is an ex-FLDS member who was significantly involved in developments leading to the YZR raid and prominently featured thereafter in many media stories about the raid and FLDS society in general.

21. One significant link between all three of our cases is the psychiatric assessments offered by Dr. Bruce D. Perry, currently senior director of the Child Trauma Academy in Houston, Texas and, in 1993, at the time of the FBI siege of Mount Carmel, director of CIVITAS Child Trauma Programs at Baylor University College of Medicine. Dr. Perry first came to national attention when he and his trauma team conducted forensic interviews and observations of 19 of the 21 Branch Davidian children released from Mount Carmel in February 1993 and wrote a report of findings for the Texas Department of Child Protective Services and the FBI. These findings were widely cited in the media (see for example *Newsweek*, May 17, 1993, 48–54). Although Dr. Perry conflated the traumatic effects of the raid itself with the children's

authoritarian and paranoid upbringing environment and seemed to uncritically accept reports of former members at face value, he found no actual evidence of either physical or sexual abuse present in the children he examined. And he did find fault with the FBI's course of action, saying that "the loss of life could certainly have been mitigated if not entirely prevented," but that instead "the federal government had taken the action most likely to result in a disaster" (Bruce Perry and Maia Szalavitz, "Stairway to Heaven: Treating Children in the Crosshairs of Trauma," *International Cultic Studies Association E-Newsletter* 6, no. 3, 2007).

The following year, Dr. Perry was requested by the Department of Health and Community Services of Melbourne, Australia, to provide a report on the "destructive childrearing practices by the Children of God" (The Family International). This report was solicited as expert opinion to support the state's appeal in the Family International child removal case dating from 1992. Although Dr. Perry had never actually studied The Family nor personally examined any Family children, he nevertheless issued a very critical report of The Family's child-rearing environment and practices, which, he said were likely to result in highly deleterious consequences for the children. These conclusions were based entirely on materials supplied to him by Melbourne Health and Community Services (that had already been rejected as acceptable evidence in the initial Melbourne court case) and generalizations derived from data he had obtained from other "transgenerational, abusive, coercive families," i.e., the Branch Davidians. (A copy of Dr. Perry's report is in the authors' possession.) This report elicited a scathing rebuttal from Dr. Lee S. Coleman, a California psychiatrist who strongly opposes the misuse of psychiatric testimony in criminal cases (copy of "Declaration of Lee Coleman, M.D.," in authors' possession); the state's appeal was denied, as reported earlier in this chapter.

Finally, Dr Perry provided critical testimony in the chaotic 51st District Court hearings in Eldorado, Texas, on April 18, 2008, to decide the custody fate of the more than 400 children taken from their YFZ Ranch homes. Acknowledging that his only knowledge about the FLDS came from what he heard and read in the news, Dr. Perry nevertheless testified that although young FLDS girls say it is their free choice to marry at young ages, they have been indoctrinated to make such choices because "obedience is a very important element of their belief system...the belief system is abusive, the culture is very authoritarian." He did concede that many of the parents seem loving, and that the young boys he played with seemed emotionally healthy. In response to defense questions about whether the FLDS belief system actually posed a danger to the children, his response was "I have lost sleep over that question." Dr. Perry further conceded that "if these children are kept in the custody of the state...the traditional foster care system would be destructive for them" (Associated Press, April 18, 2008). Shortly after Dr. Perry's testimony, Judge Barbara Walther terminated the hearing and ordered that the state continue with its custody of the children, eventually remanding the children into the state foster care system.

22. On the Branch Davidians' preparation for violence, see Catherine Wessinger, *When the Millennium Comes Violently* (New York: Chatham House, 2000).

23. Details about each of the four cases summarized in this chapter—concerning police raids and removal of children from Family homes and subsequent judicial

findings in Spain, Australia, France, and Spain—are taken from copies of court documents, contemporary newspaper articles, sworn affidavits, and personal communications that are in the authors' possession. These include: Findings of Barcelona First Division Provincial Court in the Case of Edward Molinsky vs. Children's Welfare Department, May 21, 1992 (copies of both English translation and Spanish original); Ruling of the Barcelona Constitutional Court, October 3, 1994; Ruling of Minor's Court of Aix-en-Provence, July 30, 1993, and Second Ruling of the Minor's Court, March 3, 1994, in the case of The Children of God and the Department for Social and Sanitary Intervention (English translations); Decision of the Appeals Court of Lyon, July 23, 1993 (English translation); Judgment of the Federal Court of San Isidrio, Province of Buenos Aires in the Case of Cavazza Nicola, Maria Victoria and Others, November 2, 1989 (copies of both English translation and Spanish original); San Martin, Buenos Aires Judiciary of the Nation Appeals Court Ruling in the case of Juan C. and Others, December 13, 1993 (copies of both English translation and Spanish original); New South Wales Mediation Agreement Between the Department of Community Services and The Family; Order of the Supreme Court of New South Wales, Sydney Registry, in the Case of Stuart Hartingdon vs. The Director General of the Department of Community Services, October 31, 1992; Final Ruling of the Supreme Court of New South Wales, November 2, 1993; Supreme Court of Victoria at Melbourne Mediation Agreement Ruling, April 22, 1994; Articles appearing in *El Clarin, Humor,* and in *Pagina/12,* Buenos Aires, from September 3 through December 15, 1993; articles appearing in the *Sydney Morning Herald, The Australian* (Sidney), and the *Daily Telegraph Mirror* (Melbourne), from May 17 through November 6, 1992; Affidavits of Richard Leclerc and Magdalene Coppola given in Condrieu, France, on June 9, 1993; Letters of Sophia Dow and Erica Reyna Cedillo McClendon, written on September 25, 1993. Portions of the above court documents and additional information about the raids are also provided in Introvigne, "The Children of God/The Family," op. cit.

24. Testimony of Richard Leclerc, adult Family Member arrested in June 9, 1993, police raid in Condrieu, France:

"Four men dressed in bullet-proof vests, wearing helmets and carrying automatic weapons, came rushing around the corner of the house, screaming and then headed straight towards me. One of them had an axe, which he swung into the door of our caravan, which immediately flew open. They then grabbed me and dragged me from the caravan across the gravel driveway, leaving my right knee badly bleeding and bruised. Meanwhile, other members of our home were being pushed from the house with their hands handcuffed behind their backs and thrown to the ground. There was screaming and people were being very roughly handled and violently shoved around." (Copy of affidavit in authors' possession)

25. Testimony of Magdalene Coppola, age 18, arrested in police raid in Condrieu, France, on June 9, 1993:

"At 5:30 in the morning I heard this great big bang, then there was all this loud shouting and screaming. I heard the three Mommies upstairs screaming, and I heard a loud thud on the floor as one of the Mommies yelled, "John Paul!" Then this policeman burst into our room wildly swinging his gun around...We asked if we could shut the door to get dressed (we were all girls, ages 11 to 18 years), but they wouldn't let us close the door. We also tried turning on a tape recorder that had songs on it, but they told us to turn it off because it was "brainwashing" us!...They questioned me around noon...They asked me if I'd ever had a sexual relationship with my mother or father, and I said, "of course NOT, that's disgusting!"...I didn't want to take my clothes off, but he had to check me internally for sexual abusement, much to my dismay and shock!" (Copy of affidavit in authors' possession)

26. Account of Sophia Dow, adult Family member, arrested and imprisoned in Buenos Aires raid on September 25, 1993:

"Then they put us in a truck [all the adult females] with our hands chained together and chained to the floor...The truck was pitch black, and we cried all the way to the prison. At last we arrived at the prison and had to go through another complete physical examination, and then we were ushered to our cell. As we walked down the halls, the inmates screamed through the bars: "We're gonna break your bones! Come over here, we're gonna mess you up!"...Please pray for our protection as there are terrifying stories about what happens in the main rooms where the other women inmates all gang up on girls they have condemned...I try not to let my mind run wild with fears, especially after hearing about the horrible accusations they're making about us." (Excerpt from copy of letter in authors' possession)

27. Nathaniel C. Nash, "Argentines Say a Sex Cult Enslaved 268 Children," *New York Times*, September 3, 1993.

28. See Gary Shepherd and Lawrence Lilliston, "Field Observations of Young People's Experience and Role in The Family," in James R. Lewis and J. Gordon Melton, eds., *Sex, Slander, and Salvation: Investigating The Family/Children of God* (Stanford, CA: Center for Academic Publication, 1994): 69–70.

29. Account of Erika Reyna Cedillo McClendon, 20-year-old Family member arrested and imprisoned in Buenos Aires, September 25, 1993:

"After three days, we were told that the children were to be examined physically. We had hoped the children would not need to suffer this...Some of the doctors were very cold and disrespectful of the girls in particular, and many came out of the examinations crying...While they conducted their gynecological exam on me, I felt extremely uncomfortable and humiliated. I felt like an animal whose personal feelings and privacy were of no account. The doors that the doctors used to go in and out of the room led to the waiting room, so almost anybody could see me lying there naked. One of our girls, who is 11, was taken out of the institution to have a second examination. The lady that went to translate for the mother and daughter broke into tears seeing the way they treated the little girl. She said they pulled her vagina open with their hands as if it was a sweater. Five doctors were pulling at her and sticking their fingers in her genitals. She was screaming and trembling the whole time...Who is going to pay for the emotional and psychological damage done to this child? Who are the real abusers here? The parents who love and care for their children or the supposed rescuers who put our children through these horrible atrocities? If you want to see how we live and what we do, our doors are open to you! Come and see for yourself how we operate. Judge Marquevich could have done this, but I suppose, judging from his actions, that he chose to hear only one side of the story, the side of disgruntled ex-members who have a personal vendetta against us, who are out to destroy us! You can't judge any man by the words of his enemies. To judge fairly, you have to hear and see both sides." (Excerpt from copy of a letter in authors' possession)

30. One serious difficulty for reviewing previous episodes involving marginal religious groups (for both authorities and the public at large) is what Stuart Wright calls the "front-end/back-end disproportionality" problem that afflicts most media coverage: "News stories on unpopular or marginal religions frequently are predicated on unsubstantiated allegations or government actions based on faulty or weak evidence occurring at the front end of an event. As the charges are weighed against material evidence, these cases often disintegrate. Yet rarely is there equal space and attention in the mass media given to the resolution or outcome of the incident. If the accused are innocent, often the public is not made aware. People tend to be familiar with the front-end of a story and equate the allegations with proven guilt of the parties involved" (Wright, Stuart, "Media Coverage of Unconventional Religion: Any Good News for Minority Faiths?" *Review of Religious Research* 39, no. 2 (1997): 101–115). Local officials dealing with their own cases in different locations at different times appear as likely to be affected by this problem as the public at large. Wright specifically cites the Family International's experience in the Buenos Aires raids of 1993 as an instructive example.

31. Ellison and Bartkowski, "Children Were Being Beaten," 120–137.

32. "Thoughts at 37,000 Feet over Waco," Brooke Adams Blog, *Salt Lake Tribune*, May 18, 2008.

33. Ellison and Bartkowski, "Children Were Being Beaten," 140–141.

Chapter 11

The International Fight Against Barbarism: Historical and Comparative Perspectives on Marriage Timing, Consent, and Polygamy

Arland Thornton

The removal of the more than 400 children from the Yearning for Zion Ranch (YFZ) of the Fundamentalist Church of Jesus Christ of Latter Day Saints (FLDS) in April 2008 by Child Protective Services (CPS) of the State of Texas was vigorously defended by CPS and emphatically opposed by the FLDS, with all sides expressing considerable emotion. CPS issued a series of public statements saying that the intervention was necessary because middle-aged polygamous men at YFZ were forcing underage girls as young as thirteen into polygamous relationships.[1] CPS stated that this was child abuse, statutory rape, and resulted in early and frequent childbearing. CPS also alleged that even very young girls were being abused because they were taught to enter such relationships and the boys were groomed to be perpetrators of such abuse. The FLDS parents defended themselves by making public statements that they loved their children and that their children loved them and had never been abused. They asserted that marriages were both consensual and formed at appropriate ages. The FLDS alleged that CPS was persecuting them because of their religion, had ignored due process, violated human rights, and abused the children by separating them from their parents.

Although these contradictory and competing messages of abuse, under-age sex, parental love, polygamy, rape, coercion, and violation of human rights dominated the news, another discourse was also heard. This was a discussion of a conflict between a backward, out-of-date group, with the attributes of a tribe in Africa or Asia, coming into conflict with the modern, civilized, and enlightened state of Texas. It was portrayed not just as a story in a small Texas town of claims and counterclaims of abuse, rape, human rights violations, underage sex, polygamy, and religious persecution, but a grand narrative of civilizational conflict between the forces of backwardness and those of moder-nity and enlightenment.

In this chapter I focus on this discourse of backwardness and modernity, of Africans, Asians, and Americans, and how it was important in the inter-pretation of the CPS-FLDS confrontation and may have played a role in the confrontation itself. I do so because for centuries the idea of development, with societies distributed along a continuum from backward to modern, has been influential, and Europeans and Americans have perceived themselves to be at the pinnacle of civilization and those with different customs to be less devel-oped, backward, and even barbaric. Such worldviews have influenced many actions, including the colonization of much of the world by Europeans, the ways in which migrants to the United States were assimilated, and the efforts to "civilize" the native people of Africa, America, Asia, and Australia.

I place the 2008 CPS-FLDS conflict within the context of the nineteenth-century confrontation over the practice of polygamy between the United States government and the mainline Church of Jesus Christ of Latter-Day Saints (LDS) headquartered in Salt Lake City, Utah (often referred to as the Mormons). I discuss how nineteenth-century Mormon polygamy was seen as backward—even barbarous—by the general American public and how this perceived back-wardness played a major role in the vigorous and protracted campaign by the United States to terminate polygamy. The decision by the LDS Church to aban-don polygamy in the late nineteenth and early twentieth centuries and then to actively oppose it resulted in a schism within Mormonism, as several groups, including the FLDS, were established outside of and independent from the mainline LDS Church and continued the practice of polygamy because they believed that it remained a fundamental component of their religion.[2] These polygamous groups—often called fundamentalist Mormons—became the focus of renewed campaigns in the middle of the twentieth century to elimi-nate polygamy.

It is important to note that this chapter is *not* about the behavior of the FLDS people at the YFZ Ranch and whether or not they were guilty of the charges made against them in the Texas raid. This chapter is also *not* about whether the raid itself and the behavior of the Texas CPS during and after the raid were appropriate and justified. The chapter is also *not* about my own views and opinions about the morality or acceptability of polygamy versus monogamy, about the proper legal age for sex or marriage, or about the requirements for consent in marriage. I do *not* offer my own opinions about these topics and leave them to the analyses and opinions of others.

Instead, I discuss how the ideas of modernity, backwardness, development, and progress have been used in the United States and elsewhere for centuries to evaluate people and family life and to motivate and justify public actions and policies toward certain family attributes and the people who follow them. I also discuss how a range of people and institutions—from the U.S. Supreme Court to American public opinion—view marriage timing, consent, and polygamy.

I begin with a discussion of the discourse of modernity and backwardness as it was used by the media to describe the confrontation that exploded in Eldorado, Texas. I then discuss the origins of this developmental discourse and its relevance to arguments and public policy around the world concerning polygamy, age at marriage, and marital consent. The next section of the chapter addresses the historical conflict between Mormonism and mainstream America over polygamy and related matters. I then return to the issues of modernity, backwardness, the Texas Raid, and public opinion concerning polygamy and young age at marriage.

The Discourse about the Confrontation of Modernity and Backwardness in Texas

The theme of modernity versus backwardness, of foreign culture versus American society, presented itself in the media coverage of the CPS-FLDS conflict in many forms. I provide several examples of this developmental discourse in the following paragraphs, with my goal being to illustrate the use of this type of discourse by the media. I make no evaluation of the validity of the various arguments presented in the examples provided.

One reporter, writing in a local Texas paper, noted that the news media "largely focused on the sensational aspects of the 'outsider' FLDS culture...often it seemed, with the zeal of some 19th and 20th Century anthropologists who'd discovered a 'lost' civilization in the South Pacific".[3] Similarly, an interviewer on National Public Radio began his interview with a guest by saying that "The FLDS community has been described as something like a tribe in Papua New Guinea that is untouched by the modern world." He then asked, "Are they really living in the middle of the eighteenth century?"[4]

The *Philadelphia Inquirer,* in an attempt to give some historical perspective on the events in Texas, reported that nineteenth-century Americans coupled polygamy with slavery and condemned both as the "twin relics of barbarism." The *Inquirer* cited the U.S. Supreme Court in the same century as declaring that "Polygamy has always been odious among the northern and western nations of Europe, and, until the establishment of the Mormon Church, was almost exclusively a feature of the life of Asiatic and of African people."[5]

In a similar vein, the *Dallas Morning News* cited a University of Texas law professor, Jack Sampson, as stating that "Religion does not give you the right to sacrifice virgins as the Aztecs used to do."[6] A *St. Helena Star* article observed that "The government [of Texas] knows it's walking a thin line trying to bring the rule of law to an outdated tribal society."[7] And the *Beehive Standard Weekly,* a Western newspaper oriented toward mainline Mormons, asserted simply that "Most Americans do not agree with polygamy and think the FLDS is a backward, even oppressive religion and culture."[8]

The theme of two worlds in collision dominated a *Time* article. On the one hand, the article described an "antique" people with a "bygone style...who have chosen to sit the last century out." On the other hand, wrote the *Time* author, was the "21st century" and "modernity" with its "language of women's rights, of the dignity and self-determination of children, of limits on the authority of fathers—and even on the authority of prophets." The author suggested that these two colliding worlds were so different that "it was as if no common language existed."[9]

This theme also played out in other venues, with the *Houston Chronicle* suggesting that the FLDS women dressed in such a way that "they seemed visions from another age."[10] The *Daily Trojan,* the student newspaper at the University of Southern California, suggested that the children separated from their parents "would have to leave everything they know and enter an alien world of modernity that could possibly give them their most traumatic experience yet."[11]

The *New York Times* wrote that "Watching the polygamists in West Texas come into the sunlight of the 21st century has been jarring, making you feel like a voyeur of some weird historical episode." The article said that it makes one "wonder: who opened the time capsule?" The Texas FLDS "gave us all a glimpse into what a religion was like before it took on the patina of time—with the statues, murals and polished narratives." The article went on to assert that "What you see in Texas—in small part—is a look back at some of the behavior of Mormonism's founding fathers."[12]

The theme of modernity and backwardness was also evident in a response to the *New York Times* article by the mainline LDS (Mormon) Church that had earlier initiated a public relations campaign to convince people that the FLDS in Texas had nothing to do with the LDS. The LDS Church did not dispute the fact that Mormons in the nineteenth century practiced polygamy, but it did try to distance nineteenth-century Mormonism from the charge of backwardness and to associate it with modernity. The LDS posting asserted that in contrast to today's FLDS, the LDS in the nineteenth century were modern as they "strived to move apace with the rapid demands and changes of life and sought to embrace modernity, not thwart it. They sought to take advantage of the ideas and innovations of modern life."[13] In essence, the LDS Church tried to legitimize its nineteenth-century ancestors by asserting that they were modern rather than backward polygamists.

The theme of backwardness emerged in a very different way in a letter to the editor of the *San Angelo Standard-Times* located in Texas. The author, like others, made a connection between modernity and backwardness and the events in Texas, but indicated that it may be the State of Texas that was backward—or in danger of becoming backwards—because it did not adhere to the principles of freedom and the protection of human rights. She stated that "We must all protest this type of gestapo action. We are not a third world country, but if we allow this to happen we are on our way."[14]

I now turn to a discussion of the origins of this developmental discourse about backward and modern places and about Asia, Africa, and the Aztecs. My goal is to show how this discourse is related to the topics of polygamy, age at marriage and sexual initiation, consent in marriage, and the interpretation of the confrontation between the FLDS and the State of Texas.

The Developmental Paradigm and Reading History and the Future Sideways

I begin with the developmental paradigm, a model of social change that can be traced back to Greek and Roman times and was important through most of Christian history. The developmental paradigm dominated much thinking in Europe and America from the Enlightenment of the 1600s and 1700s to the present.

The developmental paradigm suggests that all societies progress through the same natural, universal, and necessary stages of development.[15] Although there were differences in perceptions about the exact stages of development and even in the number of stages, many authors reduced the developmental continuum to two, three, or four broad stages, with the three-step model from savagery to barbarism to civilization being particularly prevalent. In addition to progress along this developmental trajectory, this framework suggested that societies could regress and move backward.

The speed of advancement was believed to vary, so that at any one point in time, societies at different developmental levels could be observed. That is, societies believed to be at the various stages of development from the lowest to the highest were believed to exist at the same time point.

The northwest European proponents of this developmental paradigm regularly placed their region (and its overseas diaspora) at the pinnacle of societal development.[16] This undoubtedly resulted partly from ethnocentrism, but also because of the military and economic might of northwest Europe at the time.[17] Societies least like northwest Europe were designated by these observers to be the least developed.[18] Occupying the lowest positions on such developmental ladders were certain indigenous populations of Asia, Africa, the Americas, and Australia. Other societies were arrayed at various stages between the least and the most developed.

Many people from the 1600s through the 1800s were interested in describing the specific changes that occurred at the various stages along this perceived uniform developmental trajectory. By placing contemporary societies at different levels of development, they believed that they could record the history of societal development by shifting their attention serially from what they believed to be the least through the most developed societies. With this conceptual model, it was possible for scholars to claim that at some time in the past the most developed nations—believed to be those in northwest Europe and in the northwest European diaspora—had been like their less developed contemporaries.[19] With this assumption scholars believed that they could use data from what they perceived to be less developed countries as substitutes for data about the pasts of societies such as northwest Europe that they perceived as more developed. They described the trajectory of development by beginning with what they thought of as the "very young" indigenous societies of Africa, America, or Australia, then progressed through the societies of Asia, then to the societies of central and eastern Europe, and finally to the most "mature" regions of Northwest Europe and North America. I refer to this use of cross-sectional data to make historical conclusions as "reading history sideways" and have shown elsewhere how it was used extensively by scholars in the 1700s and 1800s.[20]

This model also provided a way of reading the future sideways for the people outside the West. This was possible for the practitioners of the model because the West provided a concrete model for change. If the people of the non-West developed and progressed, they would become like the West. Thus, the developmental model and cross-cultural data provided a means for understanding and predicting the future for those outside the West.

Views of Marriage and Marriage Change from Reading History Sideways

Observers have documented a remarkable variety of marriage and social patterns in the societies they have studied around the world.[21] The variations in these patterns have existed both across regions and within regions, and even within specific countries. Despite the substantial within-region differences observed in both northwest Europe and in other geographical regions, scholars have observed that, in general, the social, family, and marriage patterns of northwest Europe were very different from those in many other parts of the world.[22] They found many societies outside northwest Europe where personal autonomy and freedom were limited. They also found societies where polygamy was common, and where marriage was frequently universal and often contracted at a young age, sometimes even in infancy. Arranged marriages were common in many of these societies, often with the new wife and husband having very little, if any, say in the choice of spouse and with little or no opportunity for affection and courtship before marriage. They also had gender relationships within marriage that the scholars of the day interpreted as reflecting low status of women. The marriage and family systems of these societies seemed strange to Western observers, but were understood and endorsed by people living in these societies as normal and proper.

Western observers have generally characterized such marriage systems as traditional, less modern, or less developed. Some of these attributes, such as polygamy, child marriage, and marriages arranged entirely by parents, were sometimes even labeled as savage or barbaric.

By contrast, personal autonomy and freedom in northwest European societies were observed to be more extensive than in many other countries around the world. Also, in northwest Europe the marriage system was monogamous, with the mate-selection process largely residing with the prospective wife and husband. These societies also had less universal marriage, most marriages occurred to mature women and men, and there was extensive affection and couple autonomy in the mate-selection process. Scholars of the era also perceived women's status within marriage as higher in northwest European societies. The marriage attributes of northwest Europe were generally characterized as modern or developed.

With the developmental paradigm and "reading history sideways" methodology, it was easy for generations of observers to believe that the process of development transformed social, family, and marriage patterns from the traditional or backward ones perceived by them to exist outside of northwest

Europe to the developed patterns within northwest Europe. They believed that, sometime before they wrote in the 1700s and 1800s, there had been a great transition that had changed European marriages and families from being like the traditional world outside of northwest Europe to being like the modern families of northwest Europe.[23]

Low and controlled marital fertility was not included in the original conceptualization of modern families in the 1700s and early 1800s. However, the decline of fertility in the late 1800s and early 1900s in northwest Europe and its overseas diaspora, along with continuing high fertility in other regions, brought low and controlled fertility into the modern family package. This also defined high and uncontrolled fertility as traditional or backward.

This developmental model of cross-national differences provided much more than a description of history. It also provided a theory for the changes observed from reading history sideways. The dominant theory of the era was that the modern society in northwestern Europe, with its extensive technology, wealth, cities, education, and military power, was the cause of its modern marriage patterns. An alternate minority view was that the modern marriage system was an exogenous causal force producing a modern society. That is, such things as monogamy, marriages arranged by the couple, and an older age at marriage were seen as factors helping to produce the modern or developed societies of northwest Europe. Both theories, of course, indicated that traditional marriages were not compatible with modern societies; either modern societies transformed traditional marriage, or modern marriage was necessary for the creation of modern societies.

A Developmental Cross-Cultural Model for Evaluation and Public Policy

Important for understanding the role of this model in public policies concerning polygamy and young and arranged marriage is the fact that this developmental model of cross-cultural variation went far beyond providing descriptions and theories of historical change in northwest Europe. It also provided a framework of ideals for the evaluation of society and family structure—that is, a value system. I do not present these arguments about developmental ideals and values as my own values and beliefs, but as the values and beliefs that are derived from the developmental model and its implementation with cross-sectional data. In addition, the point is not whether the beliefs expressed in these propositions are true or false, or whether the values expressed are good or bad. The point is that these propositions provide a system of beliefs and values that can guide and motivate a broad array of family behaviors and relationships. Acceptance or rejection of these propositions can influence how people lead their lives and how governments and the larger public act toward various marriage forms.

The society and marriage patterns of northwest Europe were not only labeled as modern but as enlightened, civilized, and progressive. This model of values also specifies attributes defined as modern to be desirable and to be supported. Societies and marriage patterns elsewhere were defined as traditional—and sometimes as even backward or uncivilized. As such, these societies and marriage patterns were also specified as undesirable and to be opposed.

More specifically, this framework defines the marriage attributes of monogamy, mature marriage, self-selection of spouses, high status of women, and low and controlled fertility as modern, good, and to be supported and sought after. On the other end of the developmental continuum, polygamy, child marriage, parental control of marriage, low status of women, and high and uncontrolled fertility are defined as bad and to be avoided and opposed. In fact, the attributes of polygamy, child marriage, and parental control of marriage are often associated with even more odious and powerful words such as "backwardness" and "barbarity." This labeling of many non-Western family traits such as polygamy, child marriage, and arranged marriage as bad by the developmental framework and its adherents occurred despite the fact that these dimensions of marriage and family life had been accepted, approved, and even encouraged in these non-Western societies for centuries.

Earlier, I noted that the developmental model of cross-national differences had produced a theory indicating that modern marriage and modern society are causally linked, with modern marriage causing a modern society and/or a modern society causing modern marriage. This theory was derived from the definition of both families and societies in northwest Europe as modern and the assumption that their joint occurrence in this region indicated a causal association between modern families and modern societies. This was translated into an action agenda where it was believed that the adoption of modern marriage patterns can help produce a modern society. That is, developmental thinking suggests that the adoption of modern marriage systems—including monogamy, mature marriage, and control over marriage by the prospective spouses—can make society richer and more advanced. The model also suggests that movement toward marriage forms seen as backward, such as polygamy, child marriage, and parental control of marriage, would make society poorer and more backward.

This developmental model also indicated that personal freedom and autonomy were attributes of developed societies and were desirable traits of society. In addition, the developmental model suggested that freedom and equality are fundamental human rights.[24] That is, all human beings have the right to make their own decisions and to choose their own way of life and that all human beings are inherently equal. These ideas of freedom and equality can be important in the drive toward equal rights, respect, and opportunities for women. They can also play a role in shifting norms and laws in the direction of acceptance of divorce, premarital sex, unmarried cohabitation, child-bearing outside of marriage, abortion, and homosexual relations.

One might expect that the principle of freedom in marriage and family matters that would make divorce, premarital sex, unmarried cohabitation, nonmarital childbearing, abortion, and homosexual relations more acceptable would also give individuals and groups additional freedom to have plural wives, marry when they wanted, and to have parents choose spouses. However, influences in this direction are counterbalanced by the fact that parental choice of spouses directly contradicts individual freedom of spouse choice. Similarly, it can be argued that marriages before a certain age cannot involve the individual's consent, as informed consent is impossible before that age. Of course, the age believed to permit free consent can vary across individuals and groups and can change with time.[25] In addition, although it is possible to visualize multiple adult women freely choosing to be married to the same man, polygamous relationships are often argued to be inherently unequal and oppressive to women—an argument that places them in direct contradiction to the principle of equality.

In addition, the use of developmental thinking and principles to restrict—even repress—some forms of behavior in opposition to the ideals of individual freedom was possible because certain principles of the developmental model, including progress itself, often had higher priority than freedom and social equality. Social actions in favor of perceived progress and in opposition to perceived backwardness could be sanctioned by developmental thinking, even if they in some fundamental way violated the principles of freedom and equality.

Opposition to perceived backwardness at the expense of freedom and equality was also facilitated by the belief that development and progress toward a better life were not inevitable outcomes because society could stagnate, or even fall backward. The history of Rome and Greece was believed by many to provide examples of substantial retrogression. There were also some who suggested that the perceived low level of development of Native Americans resulted from a significant backward movement. This motivated many to be energetic in fighting against perceived backwardness or barbarism within the societies of northwest Europe and North America. This vigilance against great leaps backward and the return of barbarism often took precedence over the desire for individualism, independence, freedom, and equality.

Applications of the Developmental Model for Evaluation and Public Policy

Over the past two centuries, and continuing to the present, many governments, institutions, and people have actively opposed several aspects of marriage seen as especially backward—even barbaric—including polygamy, child marriage, and parental control. Western conquerors, colonizers, and missionaries have been effective in spreading Western ideals characterized as modern around the non-Western world. As the custodians of both Christianity and civilization— sometimes confounded as "Christian civilization"—western Europeans and their North American diaspora often perceived that it was their responsibility to spread Christianity and the civilization associated with it around the world.[26] In doing so, they believed they were both fulfilling the command of God and raising others from backwardness and religious alienation from God to civilization and communion with God's church. Thus, they believed that by spreading their Christian civilization and its family and marriage forms they were not only serving God but those who were less fortunate.[27]

Western conquerors, colonizers, and missionaries were not the only ones opposing marriage and family practices seen as traditional and/or backward. In many places, post-colonial governments continued the modernizing mission and implemented reforms to oppose marriage practices they saw as traditional.[28] International organizations such as the United Nations, the international family planning movement, and the international women's movement have also been activists in this cause.[29] Opposition to marriage and family practices seen as traditional or backward also came from indigenous governments striving to avoid Western colonialism.[30] And, in some places, such as China, the opposition emerged from revolutionary governments with the goal of developing their societies.[31] Among the places where these family and marital patterns seen as traditional or backward have been actively opposed, even repressed, have been China, Japan, Thailand, Turkey, and many of the countries of Africa and Latin America.[32]

One observer, writing about Western influence in Africa in the early nineteenth century, stated that "Polygamy was regarded as an uncivilized institution, and therefore to be condemned out of hand....The European consciousness of superiority to the African was a very marked feature of the period."[33] He went on to state, "The fact that polygamy was believed to be harmful to the moral character of the individual was considered sufficient reason for condemning it."[34] Another observer of Africa wrote that "It is probable that...the actual 'victims' of customs which shock the outside world are often oblivious of their own grievances."[35]

At the same time that the United States in the 1800s and 1900s was experiencing substantial campaigns to increase equality and independence in some dimensions of family relationships, other areas of individual and family life were being sharply curtailed. Most important in this regard were the efforts in the United States to control and modify individual and family behaviors identified as especially backward, even barbaric.[36] These included such family practices as very young marriage, arranged marriage, and polygamy.

The fight against perceived barbarism in the United States affected a substantial number of minority groups with family systems outside the mainstream northwest European pattern. Perhaps most affected here were the Native Americans who, for centuries, were the targets of public and private efforts to eliminate what was perceived as savagism—something seen as even worse than barbarism—through the replacement of their social, economic, religious, cultural, and familial patterns through the process of civilization.[37] The mainstream northwest European society in America also made efforts to eliminate the perceived familial backwardness of the Oneida Community and immigrants from southern and eastern Europe—groups that were either initiating new experiments in family living or were maintaining their historical family patterns.[38]

Most relevant for the topic of this discussion is the American campaign of the nineteenth and twentieth centuries to stamp out polygamy among the Mormons. I now discuss the introduction of polygamy into Mormonism and how the discourse of modernity and backwardness was an important element in the efforts of the United States government to eliminate the practice.

Mormonism and Its Conflict with Mainstream American Family Culture

Despite the widespread prejudice against polygamy, the practice was introduced into the LDS or Mormon religion in the early 1800s, when it became a central element of the confrontation between Mormonism and the larger American society. The Mormon Church was established by Joseph Smith in upstate New York in 1830, mostly among northwest European migrants or their descendants. Smith and his followers later moved the new religion to Ohio, Missouri, and Illinois. An early innovation by Smith was the practice of plural marriage, or polygamy—a man marrying more than one wife.[39] The practice was partially motivated and legitimated by the polygamy practiced by some of the patriarchs of the Old Testament. Smith recognized the strong opposition of the American community, including most Mormons, to polygamy and tried to keep the practice of plural marriage secret and limited it to himself and his close associates.[40]

Although not publicly acknowledged, polygamy had become known among many Mormons in Illinois by the early 1840s, where it led to multiple fissures within the Mormon leadership.[41] Opposition to the introduction of this ancient marital practice in America became sufficiently energized in 1844 that a group of dissident Mormon leaders published a newspaper to expose to the larger population several practices of the Church, including polygamy. Smith and his associates then shut the paper down by destroying the press—an action that resulted in his arrest and eventual murder.

Brigham Young, who was also a polygamist, then became the leader of the LDS Church. Plural marriage increased under Young's leadership, but Young recognized that Mormonism and its practice of polygamy would not be tolerated in Illinois, and in 1847 he led his followers to western North America.[42] Parts of this area became the Territory of Utah, and Young was appointed as the first governor.

The Mormons in 1852 made an official public announcement that polygamy was an essential part of their religion.[43] The American reaction to the announcement of Mormon polygamy was swift and strong. There were numerous denunciations of the practice, and it was placed on the agenda for vigorous action to eliminate it. Mormon resistance to governmental actions was equally strong. The result was the meeting of irresistible force and unmovable object that escalated until it had become one of the largest internal confrontations ever managed by the United States government—certainly one against a religious organization.[44]

In 1856 the Republican Party placed in its national platform the desire to eliminate Mormon polygamy, declaring it to be one of the "twin relics of barbarism"—the other relic being chattel slavery.[45] This theme of polygamy as a relic of barbarism continued across subsequent decades.[46] Although the Republicans lost the 1856 election, the Democratic administration believed it was necessary to take action against the Mormons and in 1857 launched a military expedition to Utah to relieve Young of his territorial governorship and to enforce federal authority in Utah.[47] The Mormons initially resisted the United States Army with military force, but then accepted the presence of the army and the new territorial governor, although not budging on polygamy.[48]

In 1862, the first federal legislation was passed against polygamy and was followed in the subsequent three decades by increasingly harsh and powerful legislation and enforcement techniques.[49] By the end of the 1880s, the American crusade against polygamy had disincorporated the LDS Church, was planning to seize Church property, and was barring Mormons from the vote and holding public office. The crusade—labeled as "the raid" by Mormons—had also convicted more than a thousand people for polygamy, had disrupted large numbers of families, had jailed numerous women for refusing to provide testimony, and had motivated many to flee the country or to go underground.

This campaign against polygamy in the United States achieved some success in 1890 when the LDS Church announced that it was abandoning the practice.[50] However, polygamous marriages continued to be performed with the sanction of the mainline LDS Church into the early 1900s, but were then completely abandoned by the mainline Church.[51] Today, the mainline LDS Church vigorously espouses monogamy and actively disassociates itself from polygamy and polygamists.[52] As noted earlier, this resulted in a schism within Mormonism, as several fundamentalist groups were established outside of and independent from the mainline LDS Church and continued polygamy as a fundamental component of their religion. Estimates of fundamentalist Mormons associated with polygamy at the end of the twentieth century exceeded 20,000.[53] More recent estimates put the number at approximately 37,000.[54] These fundamentalist Mormons associated with polygamy include the FLDS and several other groups with beliefs, practices, and organizational structures that can vary substantially from each other and from the FLDS.[55] The FLDS have historically been concentrated in the twin cities of Hildale and Colorado City on the Utah-Arizona border, but recently established the Yearning for Zion (YFZ) Ranch in Eldorado, Texas. (For a description of the various groups and their relationships, see also Janet Bennion's chapters and the Hammon and Jankowiak chapter in this volume.) Though these groups all derive from the main LDS Church in Salt Lake City, none of them are acknowledged as LDS by the mainline LDS Church.

The American Arguments against Polygamy

The confrontation between Mormonism and the larger American public was heated, complex, and lengthy, as it extended over more than a half century and, in addition to polygamy, included several other social, political, and economic issues. These issues were intertwined, and all sides used multiple strategies and made numerous arguments, with the arguments about polygamy and associated family matters alone being numerous and complex.[56] Consequently, I can summarize here only some of the main elements of the debate concerning polygamy and related family issues and illustrate how developmental models and the fight against perceived barbarism played a central role.

The Mormon spokesmen in the nineteenth century argued vigorously and energetically that polygamy was a fundamental teaching of their religion that was sanctioned by the deity. They also argued that their religion—including its sanction of polygamy—was protected by the freedom of religion clause of the Constitution. Furthermore, they suggested that polygamous unions in Mormonism were being made with the consent of the individuals involved, as dictated by the historical marriage principles of Western societies.[57] This meant, the nineteenth-century Mormons argued, that the government should desist in its efforts to eliminate polygamy.

The American public, political leaders, and courts in the nineteenth century accepted the Mormon claim that polygamy was a tenet of Mormon religion, but that was seen by them as a reason to disdain Mormonism itself.[58] The freedom of religion clause in the U. S. Constitution was also recognized by Mormonism's opponents, but they argued that religious freedom did not sanction religious license. The government, they argued, had the right to outlaw immoral and repugnant religious behaviors—practices such as human sacrifice and the burning of widows upon the deaths of their husbands. Scholars, activists, and the United States Supreme Court categorized polygamy with these practices as barbaric and outside of Christian civilization, suggesting that it did not deserve the protection of the freedom of religion clause of the Constitution.[59]

Although the opponents of polygamy lumped polygamy together with human sacrifice and the killing of widows, they made no efforts to demonstrate with empirical evidence from Utah the damaging effects of polygamy on the lives of actual children, women, or men.[60] In addition, when numerous women in Utah publicly pronounced their support of the practice, their appeals did not cause a rethinking of the crusade against polygamy but provided further evidence of how downtrodden and unenlightened the women of Utah were.[61]

The crusaders against Mormon polygamy legitimated and fueled their efforts by arguments from developmental history and the progress of human society.[62] Scholars, politicians, and Supreme Court justices consistently utilized the theories and doctrines of progress and development to justify their laws, judicial decisions, and enforcement practices. As Sarah Barringer Gordon[63] stated:

> Republican antipolygamists believed they were participating in the elimination of state-supported barbarisms....Reformers were committed to the release of fetters on human progress, to the onward march of civilization through the purification of marriage to protect and promote freedom, democracy, and equality—all in a constitutional system that integrated Christianity and political liberty.

In this way the scholars, politicians, and judges of the era suggested that polygamy was an essential element of savagery and barbarism, while monogamy was fundamental to civilized Christian society.[64] As part of barbarism, polygamy was believed to be associated with slavery and the degradation of women. Monogamy, on the other hand, was associated with enlightenment, democracy, and high status of women. In fact, Mormons were seen in as much need of enlightenment as the people of "darkest Africa."[65] In addition, Mormon polygamy was labeled as Asiatic or oriental barbarism and was viewed not only as a threat to future advancement but as a force for the destruction of thousands of years of European progress.[66] This threat to American civilization and progress was seen as serious enough that the president of the United States, Chester Arthur, declared that there was a governmental "duty of arraying against this barbarous system all the power which under the Constitution and the law they can wield for its destruction."[67]

The exercise of the principles that monogamy is good, that polygamy is bad, and that monogamy is causally related to progress and development can perhaps best be illustrated by several important court decisions.[68] The initial United States Supreme Court decision in 1879 that set the foundation for all subsequent decisions ruled that "polygamy has always been odious among the northern and western nations of Europe, and, until the establishment of the Mormon Church, was almost exclusively a feature of the life of Asiatic and of African people."[69] Citing the statements of a contemporary scholar, Francis Lieber, the court stated that "Polygamy leads to the patriarchal principle, and which, when applied to large communities, fetters the people in stationary despotism, while that principle cannot long exist in connection with monogamy."

The Supreme Court had explicitly recognized the arguments of Lieber and drew extensively on his arguments. In more detailed statements than quoted by the Court, Lieber argued:

> ...monogamy is one of the elementary distinctions—historical and actual—between European and Asiatic humanity. It is one of the frames of our thoughts, and moulds of our feelings; it is a psychological condition of our jural consciousness, of our liberty, of our literature, of our aspirations, of our religious convictions, and of our domestic being and family relation, the foundation of all that is called polity. It is one of the pre-existing conditions of our existence as civilized white men, as much so as our being moral entities is a pre-existing condition of the idea of law, or of the possibility of a revelation. Strike it out, and you destroy our very being; and when we say *our,* we mean our race—a race which has its great and broad destiny,

a solemn aim in the great career of civilization, with which no one of us has any right to trifle.[70]

In a similar way, the developmental model was invoked by a judge in Utah in 1884 in sentencing an important Mormon official who had been convicted of polygamy and unlawful cohabitation—a case that Sarah Gordon[71] asserts "marked the beginning of the Raid." The judge, according to Gordon,[72] stated that "The first humans....were promiscuous, until they had gradually progressed to polygamy, and finally to monogamy, which marked the transition from 'barbarism and superstition to civilization.'"

In the Supreme Court case of 1890, which ultimately resulted in the mainline Mormon Church decision to curtail polygamy, the Court ruled that polygamy was "a crime against the laws, and abhorrent to the sentiments and feelings of the civilized world...[a] barbarous practice...a blot on our civilization."[73] The Supreme Court stated further that "the organization of a community for the spread and practice of polygamy is, in a measure, a return to barbarism. It is contrary to the spirit of Christianity and of the civilization which Christianity has produced in the Western world." The Court stated that polygamy was not a religious right, just as human sacrifice and the practice of killing widows among Hindus were not religious rights. The Court further concluded that "the State has a perfect right to prohibit polygamy, and all other open offences against the enlightened sentiment of mankind."

Arguments such as these rang out in the media and the halls of Congress throughout much of the late nineteenth century.[74] The idea that the threat of Mormon polygamy to Western civilization justified the violation of religious freedom and the rights of free choice was the overwhelmingly dominant view in America of the late 1800s.

I mentioned previously that the campaign against Mormon polygamy eventually led the mainline LDS Church and most of its followers to capitulate, but a substantial number of fundamentalist Mormons continued to practice polygamy and continued to be opposed by government agencies. In fact, raids on polygamists continued through the middle of the 20th century.[75] Polygamy again became a judicial issue and reached the Supreme Court where the outcome was the same as in the nineteenth century. Interestingly, the arguments of the majority of the Court replicated those of the nineteenth century, using very similar language from the long heritage of the developmental paradigm.[76] As detailed in Janet Bennion's chapter in this volume, the FLDS in Texas are one of several groups of descendants—both physical and spiritual—of these early-twentieth-century fundamentalist Mormon holdouts who refused to give up the practice of polygamy as the mainline LDS Church had done.

The Developmental Model, Backwardness, and the Texas Raid

I now return to the raid by the State of Texas on the Yearning for Zion Ranch and ask about the role of the developmental model and its value propositions in the raid and its subsequent interpretation and evaluation. My goal here is to consider how the developmental model and the worldview of modernity and backwardness may have influenced the officials in Texas, public opinion toward the raid and the FLDS, and the FLDS themselves. I present information about and from the FLDS that suggests the influence of the developmental model among them. I also discuss how the developmental model and worldview are widespread among the general population, both in America and elsewhere. However, I have not read or heard any discussion by the officials of the State of Texas themselves directly using the language of the developmental model and progress and backwardness. Consequently, I cannot show a direct use of the developmental model in the decisions of the Texas officials. Nevertheless, I will present some reasons why it is likely that the developmental model and its beliefs of backwardness and modernity would have been known and influential among government officials in Texas.

I have already documented the discussion in the media concerning the FLDS being from another age and another place and having backward practices in conflict with the modern world. This was reinforced by frequent references to the FLDS women's "prairie dresses," a symbol that these people were from the nineteenth century or even earlier. This was also reinforced by the frequent references to the FLDS women's distinctive hairdos, which were portrayed with a feeling of exoticism associated with strange and distant places. I hypothesize that such media portrayals reflected a widespread acceptance of the developmental model in American culture, and, in turn, helped to reinforce the ideas and their application to the FLDS.

As I have documented elsewhere, the developmental model has been widely understood and believed for centuries among the educated and elite around the world.[77] My colleagues and I have also documented its widespread belief among ordinary people in such widely disparate populations as Argentina, China, Egypt, Iran, Nepal, and, most importantly for our purposes, in the United States.[78] This documentation of widespread belief in the model in the United States comes from national surveys of the American population conducted in 2006 and 2007.[79] This widespread distribution of the developmental model and its beliefs about backwardness and modernity supports the speculation that the officials of the State of Texas were not immune to this model and its values and beliefs.

I earlier discussed how the developmental worldview and its arguments of modernity and backwardness provided a main intellectual rationale for the worldwide campaigns against certain family practices. This, of course, includes the polygamy raids by the United States government against the Mormons during the nineteenth and twentieth centuries. It is unlikely, although possible, that the worldviews and arguments supporting centuries of family campaigns around the world would have been unknown or without influence in Texas.

Although I cannot directly document the relevance of the developmental model and its values and beliefs for the decisions and actions of the Texas officials, I can point out that their stated rationale for the raid centered on two elements of marriage—young age and the lack of control by the prospective spouses—that have motivated marriage crusaders in the United States and elsewhere for centuries. In addition, it was well-known that the FLDS people on the YFZ Ranch were polygamists. Consequently, even if the CPS officials were unaware of the developmental model and the long history of crusades against polygamy, young marriage, and arranged marriage, they were clearly participants in the continuing action against these practices commonly perceived as backward and contrary to modern civilization.

In considering the role of the developmental model and its views on backwardness and modernity in events and public opinion, it may be useful to mention the expression of some of these same themes by a new anti-polygamy organization, Americans Against Abuses of Polygamy (AAAP), recently established in Richardson, Texas.[80] The homepage of AAAP begins with a welcome to viewers that states: "We are dedicated to informing the public about the truth of modern American polygamy, and the abuses, which are inherent to the cultural practice. Although we do not claim a particular party affiliation, we are proud to stand behind the ideals of the very first Republican Party Platform, of 1856: *'It is the duty of Congress to prohibit in the territories those twin relics of barbarism, polygamy, and slavery.'* Please join us in the effort to protect America's women and children" (italics in original).[81] Another page invites viewers to "Join the growing resistance to barbarism in America. Partner with AAAP to end the abuses of polygamy...."[82] On another page, the executive director of the organization invites people to support efforts "to keep polygamy illegal, as it should be in a civilized society."[83] Thus, the idea of an important conflict between barbarism and civilization seems very much alive and energetic with this particular anti-polygamy group.

As I noted in the introduction, the FLDS launched a campaign after the Texas raid to influence public opinion about themselves and the raid. The FLDS parents told the public that they loved their children and would never abuse them and that their children loved them and needed them. This message of loving and able parents was reinforced by reports from child-care workers who were involved with the parents and their children and who reported the FLDS to be loving parents and to have well-behaved and respectful children. In chapter 9 in this volume, Ryan Cragun and Michael Nielsen also discuss the "framing" of the issues by both the CPS and FLDS.

The public relations efforts of the FLDS also sent the message that the FLDS were not some exotic backward tribe in Africa or Asia or from the eighteenth century. Instead, the FLDS demonstrated in many ways that they were knowledgeable members of the twenty-first century—educated, articulate, and with educated and talented children. Furthermore, they demonstrated that many of them drove up-to-date sports utility vehicles and were sophisticated users of computers, the internet, and other electronic devices. In fact, it was reported that the FLDS use of cell phones was bothersome enough to the CPS workers that they confiscated the cell phones, at least temporarily.

This theme emerged in an Associated Press interview following the raid with an FLDS woman named "Nancy":[84]

"Nancy": "Can I leave the premises [of the YFZ Ranch]? Yes, really, I can leave the premises."

Questioner: "And can you drive your own car?"

"Nancy": "Yes."

Questioner: "And you have your own phone?"

"Nancy": "Yes, and we have like a post office box, and we get mail, and we take the children to the orthodontist."

This implicit, if not explicit, denial of backwardness and assertion of modernity by a twenty-first-century FLDS woman reminds me of a twenty-first-century polygamist man in Kenya speaking at a funeral who stated: "Now although I am a polygamist, I am a civilized polygamist."[85] This Kenyan man was quite happy being a polygamist, but did not want to be tarred as uncivilized. Similarly, the FLDS woman, "Nancy," interviewed in Texas, was quite comfortable appearing on national television as a member of a religious group actively endorsing polygamy, but she was clear in distancing herself from backwardness and in showing that she was immersed in the modern world.

Earlier in this chapter I referred to a guest on National Public Radio who was asked the question, "Are they [the FLDS] really living in the middle of the eighteenth century?" The guest was Brooke Adams, one of the most knowledgeable reporters in the United States concerning polygamous groups, who responded that "I think that is a false perception of this group. They have a number of people who have been to college. They are quite internet savvy as the world now knows with the websites that they have put up to spread their view of what happened to them in Texas. So, I think the idea that they are totally isolated is false."[86]

This "modernity" of the FLDS seems to have both surprised and impressed many observers. One observer reported that an interviewer for a radio program seemed intent on eliciting a statement from a director of one of the facilities serving the FLDS children that the FLDS were "backward and ill-educated." However, the director of the facility insisted that the children were well-educated. In addition, the director explained that each of the girls had her own iPod. The observer reporting this interchange commented, "So much for technological backwardness."[87]

Similarly, a reporter for the *Houston Chronicle* wrote that:

> For women who have shunned the modern world....[they] have become surprisingly adept at navigating it....Connected by cell phone to the attorneys and CPS workers they speak with daily, they have become overnight experts on the ins and outs of Texas family law. They wear out their phone batteries each day, using the phones to determine their children's whereabouts and their legal rights.[88]

Public Opinion Polls About the Texas Raid and Its Aftermath

I now turn to the views of the general public concerning the raid in Texas. These views come from two surveys of the adult population in Utah and one survey of American adults. These surveys provide general views of ordinary Americans about the events in Texas, but, unfortunately, do not tell us why the survey respondents believed what they did. Although it is likely that the opinions expressed in the surveys were influenced by the developmental worldview discussed in this paper, they were undoubtedly influenced by other factors and considerations as well.

In April 2008, shortly after the Eldorado raid, KSL Television and the *Deseret News*, two Salt Lake City institutions long associated with the mainline LDS Church, commissioned a poll of Utah adults about the events in Texas. The poll revealed widespread knowledge of the raid in Texas, as 96 percent of Utahns indicated that they had "heard news stories about the FLDS Church in Texas and the removal of children from the property by law enforcement." Of those who had heard of the action, 62 percent said that it was probably or definitely justified, while only 19 percent said that it was probably or definitely not justified (another 19 percent said that they did not know).[89]

It is impossible to know how much, or even if, public opinion changed as events unfolded in Texas and elsewhere following the initial raid on the YFZ Ranch. It is also impossible to know which, if any, aspects of the FLDS public relations campaign influenced which aspects of public opinion. Nevertheless, the headlines of the *Deseret News* on June 25, 2008, declared that "Utahns change minds on backing FLDS raid." This conclusion was based on a second poll of Utah residents commissioned in June 2008 by KSL Television and the *Deseret News*.

This June 2008 poll was apparently motivated by the rulings in late May 2008 of a Texas appeals court and the Supreme Court of Texas overturning the action of CPS and the Texas district court to remove the FLDS children from their parents and to place them under CPS control. In its review of the actions of CPS and the district court, the Texas appeals court ruled that CPS "did not carry its burden of proof," that the evidence presented to the district court "was legally and factually insufficient to support the findings required" for CPS to maintain custody of the children, and that "the district court abused its discretion in failing to return" the children to the FLDS parents.[90] The appeals court went on to direct the district court to vacate its earlier ruling granting control of the FLDS children to CPS. The Supreme Court of Texas subsequently supported the decision of the appeals court to return the FLDS children to their parents, noting that "On the record before us, removal of the children was not warranted."[91]

In the June 2008 poll, Utah residents were asked their opinions about the decisions of the Texas appeals court and the Supreme Court of Texas to return the FLDS children to their parents. Seventy-five percent of the respondents said that the Court probably or definitely did the correct thing in returning the children to their parents. Only 18 percent said that the Court probably or definitely did not do the correct thing (another 7 percent said that they did not know).[92] It appears likely that at least some Utahns changed their minds about the legitimacy of the original April raid and removal of the children. However, it is possible that the differences between the April and June surveys are the result of different questions being asked, respondents believing that both the original action and the Court decision to return the children were correct, or that there is a general bias of respondents toward agreeing with state action in either direction.

Another view of the public's reactions about the Texas raid on the YFZ Ranch can be obtained from a Gallup poll of the U.S. adult population conducted between May 30 and June 1, 2008, immediately after the May 29 ruling of the Supreme Court of Texas. In that survey respondents were asked to choose which of the following two statements most closely matched their views of the actions of the Texas state officials: (1) that "The officials who removed the children were helping the children by providing protection from possible sexual abuse"; or (2) that "The officials who removed the children were harming the children by separating them from their parents."[93] Sixty-three percent of respondents said the Texas officials were helping the children, whereas 26 percent said they were harming the children (4 percent said both and 7 percent did not express an opinion). Although we do not know national opinions concerning this particular matter before or after May 30–June 1, 2008, these data suggest that at this point the American public was siding with Texas by a margin of almost 2½ to 1.

Although Utah public opinion in June 2008 appeared to support the return of the FLDS children to their parents, Utahns continued to be very suspicious of the FLDS themselves. Eighty-seven percent of Utahns in the June 2008 poll said that the Texas authorities definitely or probably should "continue to investigate the FLDS ranch." On a different question, 49 percent said that they think the FLDS leaders will probably not or definitely not follow the court order, as compared to only 33 percent who said that they think FLDS leaders will probably or definitely follow the court order (another 18 percent said that they did not know). In addition, only 18 percent said that they definitely or probably trusted "the promise of FLDS leaders that there will be no underage marriages" as compared to 74 percent who said they probably or definitely did not trust the FLDS leaders in this regard (another 8 percent said they did not know).[94]

Data, of course, do not speak for themselves, and it is difficult to know how to interpret these survey data about the Texas raid and its aftermath. However, it seems clear that the FLDS were not successful in removing suspicion of their intentions and behavior. At the same time, it appears that they won enough sympathy from at least the Utah public that Utahns generally supported the return of their children. Given the widespread continuing suspicion of the FLDS, it seems likely that this outcome was more the result of the widespread impression that the authorities in Texas had violated human rights and due process than it was the result of widespread acceptance of the FLDS.

It is useful to emphasize again that these poll data provide information only about what people report in response to survey questions and cannot provide information about why people have the beliefs, values, and opinions that they report. This prevents any analysis of how, or if, the developmental model and many other factors may have led people to their views.

U. S. Public Opinion Concerning Polygamy and Young Marriage

I now turn our attention to the views of the American public about polygamy and young marriage in general and ask how the public at the end of the twentieth and beginning of the twenty-first centuries views these issues in general rather than on the raid on the YFZ Ranch in particular. Of particular interest is whether or not the American public today considers polygamy and young age at marriage to be outside the bounds of the acceptable. A related issue is whether the American public applies the principle of freedom of choice to polygamy and young marriage by allowing people to be able to choose when and who they will marry, even if such choices result in polygamous unions contracted at young ages.

To answer these questions, I turn to surveys conducted with the American public that address in at least some ways these issues. Unfortunately, the survey evidence is thin and scattered, which prevents a comprehensive and conclusive evaluation of these questions. In addition, the answers of people to surveys can depend greatly on apparently innocuous differences in wording and in the ordering of questions within a questionnaire. Answers to questions can also depend on the social context at the time the questions are asked. For example, answers to questions about polygamy and youthful marriage immediately following the raid in Texas may be different from answers that would have been given before the raid or substantially after the raid. Nevertheless, I believe that with cautious use of the data, they are sufficient to begin to map out the rough outlines of American public opinion on this issue.

The survey data currently available also do not provide information about why people believe what they believe concerning polygamy and young age at marriage. Answers to such questions will require very sophisticated additional data.

I begin this discussion of general poll data with an August 2006 Gallup Poll that asked Americans to report their views of the state of public opinion on the topic of polygamy. In that poll, 98 percent said that they thought that most Americans oppose it.[95] As I note below, this view is supported by surveys asking people to report their own views on this subject.

A May 8–11, 2008, Gallup Poll of adult Americans addressed the morality of polygamy and a range of other issues by asking survey respondents "whether you personally believe that in general it is morally acceptable or morally wrong." The proportion saying that each of the items is morally wrong is reported in table 11.1.

For our purposes, the most important observation in table 11.1 is that "polygamy, when one husband has more than one wife at the same time," is stated to be morally wrong by 90 percent of Americans participating in this survey. Only three other items received similarly high levels of moral disapproval by study participants; those three items were: married men and women having an affair, cloning humans, and suicide, with 91, 85, and 78 percent, respectively, saying that they are morally wrong. With one exception (cloning animals), all of the other items asked about were stated as morally wrong by less than 50 percent of respondents; these included such things as abortion, the death penalty, doctor assisted suicide, divorce, having a baby outside of marriage, and homosexual relations. Interestingly, many of the items with less than half of respondents viewing them as morally wrong today were vigorously condemned by many in the not-so-distant past. It is remarkable that with this high level of tolerance for so many behaviors that polygamy would continue to be seen as morally wrong by 9 out of 10 Americans. This result suggests that polygamy has not benefited greatly from the dramatic increase in tolerance and the principle of personal freedom that has affected other aspects of personal behavior.

Another perspective on these issues is provided in the May–June 2008 Gallup Poll in which respondents were asked a set of questions "about marriages involving certain types of couples." The respondents were asked for each type of couple whether they think "the decision to marry should be a private decision between the two people who want to marry or if the government has the right to pass laws to prohibit or allow such marriages." The five types of

TABLE 11.1. The Percentage of American Adults Saying That Each Issue is Morally Wrong, May 2008

Abortion	48
The death penalty	30
Doctor assisted suicide	44
Medical testing on animals	38
Buying and wearing clothing made of animal fur	39
Sex between an unmarried man and woman	36
Married men and women having an affair	91
Divorce	22
Cloning animals	61
Cloning humans	85
Suicide	78
Medical research using stem cells obtained from human embryos	30
Having a baby outside of marriage	41
Gambling	32
Polygamy, when one husband has more than one wife at the same time	90
Homosexual relations	48

Note: Data are from May 8–11, 2008, Gallup Poll. The full question is as follows: "Next, I'm going to read you a list of issues. Regardless of whether or not you think it should be legal, for each one, please tell me whether you personally believe that in general it is morally acceptable or morally wrong. How about…?" The survey results reported here were obtained from searches of the iPOLL Databank and other resources provided by the Roper Center for Public Opinion Research, University of Connecticut.

TABLE 11.2. Percentage of American Adults Saying That the Government Has the Right to Pass Laws to Prohibit or Allow Certain Types of Couples Marrying, May–June 2008

Two people of different religions	02
Two people of different races	04
Two people of the same sex	33
One or both people practicing polygamy, that is, having more than one spouse at the same time	66
One or both people under the age of 16	78

Note: Data taken from May–June 2008 USA Today/Gallup Poll. The question wording is as follows: "Next I'd like to ask you about marriages involving certain types of couples. For each of the following, please say whether you think the decision to marry should be a private decision between the two people who want to marry or if the government has the right to pass laws to prohibit or allow such marriages. How about a marriage involving…?" The survey results reported here were obtained from searches of the iPOLL Databank and other resources provided by the Roper Center for Public Opinion Research, University of Connecticut.

marriages asked about and the percentages of survey respondents who believed that the government had the right to pass laws to prohibit or allow such marriages are listed in table 11.2.

Table 11.2 is clear in showing that for most Americans interreligious marriage and interracial marriage are matters for private decision, with only between 2 and 4 percent indicating that government has the right to pass laws concerning them. The data for interracial marriage are particularly interesting because some American states have until recently had laws forbidding interracial marriages. It was only in 1967 that the U.S. Supreme Court ruled that laws outlawing interracial marriages are unconstitutional.[96] The survey results, thus, show a marked trend toward freedom in interpersonal relationships in this area.

Going to the other end of the continuum, table 11.2 reveals that two-thirds of Americans report that the government has the right to pass laws against polygamous marriages. In other words, for these Americans there is no right of privacy for many Americans concerning having more than one spouse. And, more than three-fourths of Americans reported that governments had the right to pass laws to prevent people under age 16 from marrying. Consequently, both polygamy and young marriage were seen by most Americans as being within the realm of government regulation, rather than being totally private decisions.

Some perspective on these data concerning views about the legitimacy of government restrictions on polygamy can be obtained by comparing these results about American views of polygamy with the views of Americans concerning same-sex marriage, which, like polygamy, has been illegal in the Western world for most of its history. Whereas two-thirds of respondents said that it was okay for governments to pass laws against polygamy, only one-third said that it was legitimate for government to pass laws against same-sex marriage.

A random one-half of the respondents in the May–June 2008 Gallup Poll were asked the following question: "In general, do you consider marriage between an adult male and a girl age 17 or younger to be child sex abuse, or not?" Fully 64 percent of respondents said that they considered such a marriage to be child abuse.[97] Clearly, adult men marrying girls (or young women) meets with strong disapproval among the great majority of Americans.

The condemnation of adult men marrying girls is even more widespread if the marriage occurs in polygamous communities. This conclusion is possible because another random one-half of the Gallup respondents were not asked about the marriage of an adult male to a girl, in general, as discussed above, but were asked the following question: "In communities that practice polygamy, do you consider marriage between an adult male and a girl age 17 or younger to be child sex abuse, or not?" The data indicate that whereas a marriage between an adult male and girl age 17 or younger that occurs in the general population is viewed as sexual abuse by 64 percent of Americans, 79 percent say it is sex abuse if it occurs in communities that practice polygamy. It is clear that the combination of polygamy and men marrying girls (or young women) 17 or younger is seen as especially problematic by Americans.

Finally, what do Americans think about prosecuting polygamists? In an older study conducted in 1991 by Princeton Survey Research Associates, American adults were asked the following question: "Some people think a man living with more than one wife should be arrested, since this practice is illegal. Others think he should be left alone to live the way he wants. Which comes closer to the way you think—should he be arrested or left alone?"[98] The public was split almost exactly evenly at this time, with 48 percent saying that he should be arrested and 49 percent saying that he should be left alone, with 3 percent saying that they didn't know.

Conclusions

In this closing section of this chapter, I highlight several of the important points and conclusions from the paper. Before doing so, however, I remind the reader that this chapter is not about the behavior of the FLDS people at the YFZ Ranch in Texas, and whether or not they were guilty of the charges made against them in the Texas raid. This discussion is also not about whether the raid and the behavior of the Texas CPS during and after the raid were appropriate and justified. I offer no opinions about those topics and leave them to the analyses and opinions of others. In addition, although the chapter discusses opinions and views of a wide range of people and institutions about the morality or acceptability of polygamy versus monogamy, about the proper legal age for sex or marriage, and about the requirements for consent in marriage, I do not offer my own views or opinions about these matters.

My first conclusion is that, throughout its history, the world has experienced wide variations in marriage and family patterns across different societies. These have ranged from societies with extensive polygamy to societies based on monogamy, from societies with very young ages at marriage, even during very early childhood, to societies with mature marriage, and from societies with parents having complete say in the marriage decisions of their children to societies with marriage decisions resting primarily with the prospective bride and groom. Furthermore, the people in each society defined the prevalent marriage patterns in that society as both proper and desirable.

Second, although there are important differences in family patterns within northwest Europe and important variations outside northwest Europe, northwest Europe (and its North American diaspora) has for hundreds of years had quite unique marital patterns. These included monogamy rather than polygamy, mature marriages instead of the marriages of children, and marriages primarily arranged by the prospective bride and groom instead of by parents or other adults.

Third, the developmental model has defined northwest Europe (and its North American diaspora) to be at the height of a uniform trajectory of development that portrayed other societies along the same trajectory, but at lower levels of development. The societies portrayed at the height of the developmental hierarchy were frequently described as modern, developed, civilized, enlightened, and advanced, while societies perceived at lower levels of development were viewed as traditional, backward, less developed, and barbaric. Attributes of societies seen as highly developed, including their marriage and family structures, were also seen as desirable and to be achieved, while the attributes of societies viewed as backward, including their marriage and family structures, were seen as undesirable and to be avoided and changed.

Fourth, this developmental model of backwardness and modernity has for centuries motivated public policies and programs to transform marriage and family patterns in most areas of the non-Western world. These programs have been designed to change marriage and family patterns in these non-Western areas from what was seen as backward, including polygamy and young and arranged marriage, to what was considered modern, which included monogamy and mature marriages decided primarily by the prospective bride and groom.

Fifth, this developmental model of eliminating backwardness and bringing modernity was a key element of the confrontation of the American public
with Mormonism's adoption of polygamy in the nineteenth century. Polygamy
was defined by many in nineteenth-century America as a "relic of barbarism"
that needed elimination. It was this worldview that led the Supreme Court in
1890 to rule that polygamy was "a crime against the laws, and abhorrent to the
sentiments and feelings of the civilized world...(a) barbarous practice...a blot
on our civilization."[99]

Sixth, although the mainline LDS Church in Salt Lake City reversed course
on polygamy in the last part of the nineteenth century and the early twentieth
century, polygamy continued to be practiced by fundamentalist Mormon groups
no longer accepted and recognized by the Salt Lake Church. Governments continued to prosecute these polygamists well into the twentieth century, with this
prosecution upheld by federal courts using the same developmental arguments
of backwardness versus modernity that were used in the nineteenth century.

Seventh, the discourse of modernity versus backwardness, of the lifestyles
of Africa and Asia versus America, has continued to the present and has played
a role in the understanding of many members of the media concerning the
confrontation between the Texas CPS and the FLDS living in Texas. Although
the primary discourse has focused on such issues as underage sex, freedom of
choice, rape, abuse, religious persecution, and violation of human rights, the
discourse of modernity versus backwardness has been lurking persistently in
the background of media reports.

Eighth, although it is not possible to demonstrate the importance of the
developmental model and its values and beliefs for the officials in Texas, it
seems likely that this worldview—pervasive as it has been—would have played
a role in their belief systems, decisions, and actions. It is also likely that just
as this developmental model played a role in media interpretations of the confrontation in Texas, it has played a role in the public reactions to the raid and
its aftermath.

Ninth, the data from surveys of the American public in the last part of the
twentieth century and the early part of the twenty-first provide a description of
American opinion with little tolerance toward polygamy and adult men marrying girls (or young women)—and even less tolerance when the two occur
together. Americans generally see polygamy as morally wrong, and view older
men marrying girls (or young women) as child abuse; a substantial fraction
would like to see polygamists actively prosecuted, especially if such marriages
occur to women perceived as too young.

Finally, I close with some questions and a bit of speculation about the
future. It is likely that the battles over polygamy and youthful and arranged

marriages in the United States and elsewhere are far from over, although the direction of future battles is not clear.[100] It appears that the State of Texas will not limit its investigation and prosecution to underage marriage and underage sex, but will investigate and prosecute polygamy itself. And, if the State of Texas (or some other state) does prosecute people for polygamy itself, it is likely that the polygamists will appeal convictions to higher courts on the grounds that anti-polygamy laws are unconstitutional. This leads me to ask, if the polygamy laws are challenged, will the courts uphold precedent and rule that polygamy is a backward African or Asiatic institution that violates the standards of civilized society, or will they uphold or reject such laws on other grounds? And, will the polygamists challenge the appropriateness of applying developmental models as guidance for constitutional decisions?

I, of course, cannot predict the future of the actions of state agencies, polygamists, or judicial bodies, but, based on both the distant and recent pasts, it seems likely that the future will unfold with the developmental model and its picture of polygamy and young and arranged marriage as backward and threats to civilization playing a significant role. It is also likely that conceptions of backwardness, development, religious freedom, and the appropriate scope of individual freedom and the right of privacy will play a significant role in the direction of future public opinion and government action.

NOTES

Revision of paper presented at the annual meetings of the Mormon History Association, Springfield, Illinois, May 21–24, 2009. The author appreciates the input of several people and institutions into the preparation of this paper. The *Deseret News* and Dan Jones & Associates, Inc., kindly provided data from the April and June 2008 KSL Television *Deseret News* Polls conducted by Dan Jones & Associates. Rebecca Thornton provided information about international polygamy sources. Anne Wilde provided data about the number and diversity of fundamentalist Mormons associated with polygamy. Anne Wilde and Mary Batchelor assisted me with their background understanding of Mormon polygamy and the events in Texas. Linda Young-DeMarco assisted with the processing of data. Lee Ridley assisted with the location and procurement of bibliographical references. Judy Baughn and Brittany Chulis provided assistance with the preparation of the paper, including the references. Cardell Jacobson, Colter Mitchell, Linda Young-DeMarco, and anonymous reviewers gave useful feedback on earlier drafts of this chapter. The author appreciates the input of each of these individuals, but retains the usual responsibilities of authorship for errors of fact and interpretation in the work.

1. By polygamy I mean two or more women being married to one man at the same time. I use the term *polygamy* rather than the more technically correct term *polygyny* because polygamy is the term that has been used by most people in the

United States to refer to such relationships. This has been true for more than a century and continues to the present.

2. It is important to note that the Church of Jesus Christ of Latter-Day Saints headquartered in Salt Lake City, Utah, which I also refer to as the LDS Church, mainline LDS Church, or mainline Mormon Church, is an entirely different and fully distinct entity from the Fundamentalist Church of Jesus Christ of Latter Day Saints (FLDS) involved with the confrontation with the State of Texas.

3. *Big Bend Gazette* article by Marlys Hersey, dated July 1, 2008.

4. Bob Garfield, National Public Radio, May 4, 2008.

5. *Philadelphia Inquirer,* May 18, 2008. The author of the article is Martha Nussbaum, Ernst Freund Distinguished Service Professor of Law and Ethics at the University of Chicago.

6. May 15, 2008, article authored by Robert T. Garrett.

7. June 5, 2008, article authored by Jeff Warren.

8. Copied from the *Beehive Standard Weekly* web site on June 5, 2008.

9. April 24, 2008, article authored by David Van Drehle.

10. June 5, 2008, article authored by Alison Cook.

11. Article written by Kartik Sreepada and posted on June 4, 2008.

12. Article by Timothy Egan, April 23, 2008.

13. The article entitled "Polygamy Then and Now" was authored by Marlin K. Jensen and dated May 5, 2008. Jensen's article was reported in a May 6, 2008, *Deseret News* article written by Aaron Falk.

14. Letter written by Alberta Spence. Printed from *San Angelo Standard-Times* website on June 8, 2008.

15. See J. W. Burrow, *Evolution and Society* (Cambridge: Cambridge University Press, 1981); M. Harris, *The Rise of Anthropological Theory* (New York: Thomas Y. Crowell, 1968); M. Mandelbaum, *History, Man, and Reason: A Study in Nineteenth-Century Thought* (Baltimore: Johns Hopkins Press, 1971); R. A. Nisbet, *Social Change and History* (New York: Oxford University Press, [1969] 1975); S. K. Sanderson, *Social Evolutionism: A Critical History* (Oxford: Basil Blackwell, 1990); A. D. Smith, *The Concept of Social Change* (London: Routledge & Kegan Paul, 1973); G. W. Stocking, Jr., *Race, Culture, and Evolution* (New York: The Free Press, 1968); G. W. Stocking, Jr., *Victorian Anthropology* (New York: The Free Press, 1987).

16. A. Thornton, *Reading History Sideways: The Fallacy and Enduring Impact of the Developmental Paradigm on Family Life* (Chicago: University of Chicago Press, 2005).

17. J. M. Blaut, *The Colonizer's Model of the World: Geographical Diffusionism and Eurocentric History* (New York: The Guilford Press, 1993); R. A. Nisbet, *History of the Idea of Progress* (New York: Basic Books, 1980); B. W. Sheehan, *Savagism and Civility: Indians and Englishmen in Colonial Virginia* (Cambridge and New York: Cambridge University Press, 1980).

18. K. E. Bock, *The Acceptance of Histories: Toward a Perspective for Social Science* (Berkeley: University of California Press, 1956); R. L. Meek, *Social Science and the Ignoble Savage* (Cambridge: Cambridge University Press, 1976).

19. R. F. Berkhofer, *The White Man's Indian: Images of the American Indian from Columbus to the Present,* 1st ed. (New York: Knopf, distributed by Random House,

1978); D. Gordon, *Citizens without Sovereignty* (Princeton, NJ: Princeton University Press, 1994); Harris, op. cit.; Sanderson, op. cit.

20. A. Thornton, "The Developmental Paradigm, Reading Hstory Sideways, and Family Change," *Demography* 38, no. 4 (2001): 449–465; A. Thornton, *Reading History Sideways*.

21. W. Alexander, *The History of Women from the Earliest Antiquity to the Present Time* (Bristol: Thoemmes Press, [1779] 1995); H. K. Home, *Sketches of the History of Man in Two Volumes* (Edinburgh: printed for W. Creech, [1774] 1813); D. Hume, *Essays and Treatises* (Edinburgh: James Walker, [1742] 1825); T. R. Malthus, "An Essay on the Principle of Population," in E. A. Wrigley and D. Souden, eds., *The Works of Thomas Robert Malthus* (London: William Pickering, [1803] 1986); J. Millar, "The Origin of the Distinction of Ranks," in W. C. Lehmann, ed., *John Millar of Glasgow 1735–1801* (New York: Arno Press, [1771] 1979); M. d. Montaigne, *Essays* (New York: The Heritage Press, [1580] 1946); C.-L. d. S. Montesquieu, *The Spirit of the Laws* (Cambridge: Cambridge University Press, [1748] 1997); C.-L. d. S. Montesquieu, *Persian Letters*, ed. C. J. Betts. Harmondsworth, U.K.: Penguin Books Ltd., [1721] 1993); L. H. Morgan, *Ancient Society* (Tucson: The University of Arizona Press, [1877] 1985); W. Robertson, *The History of America by William Robertson* (Dublin: printed for Messrs. Price, Whitestone, W. Watson, Corcoran, R. Cross and 41 others in Dublin, [1777] 1780); A. Smith, *The Theory of Moral Sentiments* (Glasgow edition of the works and correspondence of Adam Smith; vol. 1 Oxford: Clarendon Press, [1759] 1976); W. G. Sumner and A. G. Keller, *The Science of Society*, Vol. III (New Haven: Yale University Press, 1929); E. A. Westermarck, *The History of Human Marriage* (London: Macmillan, [1891] 1894).

22. Alexander op. cit.; F. Engels, *The Origin of the Family, Private Property, and the State* (New York: International Publishers, [1884] 1971); G. W. F. Hegel, *Lectures on the Philosophy of History* (London: George Bell and Sons, [1837] 1878); F. Le Play,*Les Ouvriers europeens* (Paris: Imprimerie Imperiale, 1855), 9–12, 16–18, 286–287, 281–282, In C. Bodard Silver, ed., *Frederick Le Play on Family, Work and Social Change* (Chicago: The University of Chicago Press, [1855] 1982); H. S. Maine, *Ancient Law* (New York: Henry Holt and Company, [1861] 1888); Malthus, op. cit. ; Millar, op. cit.; Smith, op. cit.; A. Smith, *Lectures on Jurisprudence* (Oxford: Oxford University Press, [1762–1763] 1978); Sumner and Keller, op. cit.; M. Weber, *The Religion of India: The Sociology of Hinduism and Buddhism* (Glencoe, IL: The Free Press, 1958); Westermarck, op. cit.

23. See A. Thornton, *Reading History Sideways* (2005), for a more complete description of these ideas.

24. The idea that freedom and equality are fundamental human rights also comes from reading history sideways but in a somewhat different way which I cannot explicate here. For a discussion of this proposition about freedom and equality and its relationship to the developmental model, see Thornton (2005, especially pages 144–146).

25. In fact, the State of Texas is an example of changing laws on these matters. It has been widely reported that prior to the construction of the YFZ Ranch by the FLDS that Texas law allowed for the marriage of 14-year-olds, but after the FLDS moved to Texas a new law was passed raising legal age at marriage to age 16.

26. J. Comaroff and J. L. Comaroff, *Of Revelation and Revolution: Christianity, Colonialism, and Consciousness in South Africa* (Chicago: University of Chicago Press, 1991).

27. E. Dussel, *The Invention of the Americas* (New York: Continuum, [1992] 1995); E. LiPuma, *Encompassing Others: The Magic of Modernity in Melanesia* (Ann Arbor: The University of Michigan Press, 2000); C. Bernard and S. Gruzinski, "Children of the Apocalypse: The Family in Meso-America and the Andes," in A. Burguiére, C. Klapisch-Zuber, M. Segalen, and F. Zonabend, eds., *A History of the family*, Vol. II (Cambridge, MA: Harvard University Press, [1986] 1996), 161–215; D. C. Buxbaum, *Family Law and Customary law in Asia: A Contemporary Legal Perspective* (The Hague: Martinus Nijhoff, 1968); L. Harries, "Christian Marriage in African Society," in A. Phillips, ed., *Survey of African Marriage and Family Life* (London: published for the International African Institute by Oxford University Press, 1953), 329–462; T. Locoh, "Evolution of the Family in Africa," in E. van de Walle, P. O. Ohadike, and M. D. Sala-Diakanda, eds. *The State of African Demography*, (International Union for the Scientific Study of Population, 1988); A. Phillips, "An Introductory Survey," in A. Phillips, ed., *Survey of African Marriage and Family Life* (London: published for the International African Institute by Oxford University Press, 1953), ix–xli; D. W. T. Shropshire, *Primitive Marriage and European Law: A South African Investigation* (London: Frank Cass and Company, [1946]1970).

28. M. Cammack, L. A. Young, and T. Heaton, "Legislating Social Change in an Islamic society: Indonesia's Marriage Law," *The Ameican Journal of Comparative Law* XLIV, no. 1 (1996): 45–73; D. Chambers, "Civilizing the Natives: Customary Marriage in Post-apartheid South Africa," in R. Shweder, M. Minow, and H. R. Markus, eds. *Engaging Cultural Differences: The Multicultural Challenge in Liberal Democracies* (New York: Russell Sage Foundation, 2002), 81–98; P. Mody, "Love and the Law: Love-Marriage in Delhi," *Modern Asian Studies* 36, no. 1 (2002): 223–256; H. F. Morris, "Review of Developments in African Marriage Law since 1950," in A. Phillips and H. F. Morris, eds., *Marriage Laws in Africa* (London: published for the International African Institute by Oxford University Press, 1971), 35–61.

29. Current campaigns of the United Nations against such practices today sometimes refer to the practices as "harmful traditional practices." R. J. Cook and L. M. Kelly, *Polygyny and Canada's Obligations under International Human Rights Law: Family, Children and Youth Section Research Report* (Canada: Department of Justice, 2006). In a similar way, a UNICEF newspaper advertisement in Malawi in 2008 calls for a "stop to harmful cultural practices," and a 2007 UNICEF bumper sticker in Malawi says to "stop early marriages: give girls a chance to complete their education" (copies in author's possession). See also M. E. Latham, *Modernization as Ideology* (Chapel Hill: University of North Carolina Press, 2000); P. J. Donaldson, *Nature against Us: The United States and the World Population Crisis, 1965–1980* (Chapel Hill: University of North Carolina Press, 1990); P. J. Donaldson, "On the Origins of the United States Government's International Population Policy," *Population Studies* 44, no. 3 (1990): 385–399; R. Simmons, L. Baqee, M. A. Koenig, and J. F. Phillips, "Beyond Supply: The Importance of Female Family Planning Workers in Rural Bangladesh," *Studies In Family Planning* 19, no. 1 (1988): 29–38; S. Greenhalgh, "The

Social Construction of Population Science: An Intellectual, Institutional, and Political History of Twentieth-Century Demography," *Comparative Studies in Society and History* 38, no. 1 (1996): 26–66; S. P. Johnson, *World Population and the United Nations: Challenge and Response* (Cambridge: Cambridge University Press, 1987); S. P. Johnson, *World Population—Turning the Tide: Three Decades of Progress* (London: Graham & Trotman/Martinus Nijhoff, 1994).

    30. Beillevaire, P. "The Family: Instrument and Model of the Japanese Nation," in A. Burguière, C. Klapisch-Zuber, M. Segalen, and F. Zonabend, eds., *A History of the Family*, Vol. II (Cambridge, MA: Harvard University Press, [1986] 1996), 242–267); A. Macfarlane, *The Making of the Modern World: Visions from the West and East* (London: Palgrave, 2002).

    31. M. Cartier, "The Long March of the Chinese Family," in A. Burguière, C. Klapisch-Zuber, M. Segalen, and F. Zonabend, eds., *A History of the Family*, Vol. II (Harvard: Harvard University Press, [1986] 1996), 216–241; O. Lang, *Chinese Family and Society* (Anchor Books, 1968/1946); C. K. Yang, *The Chinese Family in the Communist Revolution* (Cambridge: The Technology Press, 1959).

    32. C. H. Bledsoe and B. Cohen, *Social Dynamics of Adolescent Fertility in Sub-Saharan Africa* (Washington, DC: National Academy Press, 1993); Buxbaum, op. cit.; O. Frank, "Family Welfare Policies in Sub-Saharan Africa: Views from Africa." Paper presented at the seminar organized by the IUSSP Committee on Policy and Population in Kenshasa, Zaire, February 27–March 2, 1989, Liege, Belgium: International Union for the Scientific Study of Population, 1989. Mody, op. cit.; Cartier, op. cit.; Lang, op. cit.; Yang, op. cit.; J. Banister, *China's Changing Population* (Stanford, CA: Stanford University Press, 1987); D. Davis and S. Harrell, *Chinese Families in the Post-Mao Era* (Berkeley: University of California Press, 1993); Bernard and Gruzinsky, op. cit.; Locoh, op. cit.; Dussel, op. cit.; Beillevaire, op. cit.; Macfarlane, op. cit.; J. Starr, "The Role of Turkish Secular Law in Changing the Lives of Rural Muslim Women, 1950–1970," *Law & Society Review* 23, no. 3 (1989): 497–523; R. McCaa, "Marriage Ways in Mexico and Spain, 1500–1900," *Continuity and Change* 9, no. 1 (1994): 11–43; R. McCaa, "The Nahua *Calli* of Ancient Mexico: Household, Family, and Gender," *Continuity and Change* 18, no. 1 (2003): 23–48; Chambers, op. cit. ; Shropshire, op. cit.; Harries, op. cit.; A. Phillips, "Marriage Laws in Africa," in A. Phillips, ed., *Survey of African Marriage and Family Life* (London: published for the International African Institute by Oxford University Press), 173–327.

    33. Harries, ibid., 340.

    34. Harries, ibid., 342.

    35. Phillips, ibid., xvi.

    36. Thornton, op. cit.

    37. Considerable efforts were also made in Canada to civilize the family patterns of aborigines in that country (S. Carter, *The Importance of Being Monogamous: Marriage and Nation Building in Western Canada to 1915*, Edmonton and Athabasca, Alberta: University of Alberta Press and Athabasca University Press, 2008). See also W. G. McLoughlin, *Cherokee Renascence in the New Republic* (Princeton: Princeton University Press, 1986); R. H. Pearce, *Savagism and Civilization* (Baltimore: The Johns Hopkins

Press, [1953] 1967); F. P. Prucha, ed., *Americanizing the American Indians* (Cambridge, MA: Harvard University Press, 1973); F. P. Prucha, *The Great Father* (Lincoln: University of Nebraska Press, 1984).

38. N. F. Cott, N. F. *Public Vows: A History of Marriage and the Nation* (Cambridge: Harvard University Press, 2000); E. Ewen, *Immigrant Women in the Land of Dollars: Life and Culture on the Lower East Side, 1890–1925* (New York: Monthly Review Press, 1985); S. A. Glenn, *Daughters of the Shtetl: Life and Labor in the Immigrant Generation* (Ithaca: Cornell University Press, 1990); P. Haag, *Consent: Sexual Rights and the Transformation of American Liberalism* (Ithaca: Cornell University Press, 1999); A. F. Khater, "Queen of the House?' Making Immigrant Lebanese Families in the Mahjar," in B. Doumani, ed., *Family History in the Middle East* (Albany: State University of New York Press, 2003); C. N. Robertson, *Oneida Community: The Breakup, 1876–1881* (Syracuse: Syracuse University Press, 1972); C. Weisbrod and P. Sheingorn, "Reynolds v. United States: Nineteenth-century Forms of Marriage and the Status of Women," *Connecticut Law Review* 10, no. 4 (1978): 828–858.

39. C. Hardy, *Doing the Works of Abraham: Mormon Polygamy, Its Origin, Practice, and Demise* (Norman, OK: Arthur H. Clark, 2007); O. Linford, "The Mormons and the Law: The Polygamy Cases," *Utah Law Review* 9, no. 1 (1964): 308–370; R. D. Poll, "The Mormon Question Enters National Politics, 1850–1856," *Utah Historical Quarterly* 25, no. 2 (1957): 117–131; G. D. Smith, *Nauvoo Polygamy: "But We Called It Celestial Marriage"* (Salt Lake City: Signature Books, 2008); R. S. Van Wagoner, *Mormon Polygamy: A History* (Salt Lake City: Signature Books, 1986).

40. Hardy, ibid.; Linford, ibid.; Poll, ibid.; D. M. Quinn, "LDS Church Authority and New Plural Marriages, 1890–1904," *Dialogue: A Journal of Mormon Thought* 18, no. 1 (1985): 9–105; G. D. Smith, "Nanvoo Roots of Mormon Polygamy: A Preliminary Demographic Report," *Dialogue: A Journal of Mormon Thought* 27, no. 1 (1994): 1–72; G. D. Smith, 2008, ibid.; Van Wagoner, ibid.

41. Hardy, ibid.; Quinn, ibid.; G. D. Smith, 1994, ibid.; G. D. Smith, 2008, ibid.

42. G. D. Smith, 2008, ibid.

43. Hardy, op. cit.; Linford, op. cit.; G. D. Smith, 2008, ibid.

44. Cott, op. cit.; K. Driggs, "The Prosecutions Begin: Defining Cohabitation in 1885," *Dialogue: A Journal of Mormon Thought* 21, no. 1 (1988): 109–125; E. B. Firmage and R. C. Mangrum, *Zion in the Courts: A Legal History of the Chuch of Jesus Christ of Latter-Day Saints, 1830–1900* (Urbana: University of Illinois Press, 1988); M. Grossberg, *Governing the Hearth: Law and the Family in Nineteenth Century America* (Chapel Hill: University of North Carolina Press, 1985); G. O. Larson, *The "Americanization" of Utah for Statehood* (San Marino, CA: The Huntington Library, 1971); Linford, ibid.; G. D. Smith, 2008, ibid.

45. Cott, ibid.; Hardy, op. cit.; Linford, ibid.; S. B. Gordon, "The Twin Relic of Barbarism": A Legal History of Anti-polygamy in Nineteenth-Century America." Dissertation, Princeton University, 1995; S. B. Gordon, *The Mormon Question: Polygamy and Constitutional Conflict in Nineteenth Century America* (Chapel Hill: University of North Carolina Press, 2002); Poll, op. cit.

46. Gordon, 1995, 2002, ibid.

47. Gordon, 2002, ibid.; Hardy, op. cit.; Poll, op. cit.; G. D. Smith, 2008, op. cit.

48. Gordon, 1995, op. cit.; Gordon, 2002, ibid.; Larson, 1971, op. cit.

49. Cott, op. cit.; K. M. Daynes, *More Wives Than One: Transformation of the Mormon Marriage System 1840–1910* (Urbana: University of Illinois Press, 2008); Driggs, op. cit.; Firmage and Mangrum, op. cit.; Gordon, 1995, 2002, ibid.; Hardy, op. cit.; Larson, op. cit.; Linford, op. cit.; C. Talbot, "Mormons, Polygamy, and the American Body Politic: Contesting Citizenship, 1852–1890." Dissertation, University of Michigan, 2006.

50. C. Hardy, *Solemn Covenant* (Urbana: University of Illinois Press, 1992); Hardy, 2007, ibid.; Quinn, 1985, op. cit.

51. B. C. Hales, *Modern Polygamy and Mormon Fundamentalism: The Generations after the Manifesto* (Salt Lake City: Greg Kofford Books, 2006); Hardy, 1992, 2007, ibid.; Quinn, 1985, ibid.; G. D. Smith, 2008, op. cit.

52. Hales, ibid.; Hardy, ibid.

53. D. M. Quinn, "Plural Marriage and Mormon Fundamentalism," *Dialogue: A Journal of Mormon Thought* 31, no. 2 (1998): 1–68; also see M. S. Bradley, *Kidnapped from That Land: The Government Raids on the Polygamists of Short Creek* (Salt Lake City: University of Utah Press, 1993).

54. These estimates were made by Anne Wilde and distributed informally as a packet of information about fundamentalist Mormons associated with polygamy. A copy is in the author's possession. Also, see A. Wilde, "Fundamentalist Mormonism: Its History, Diversity and Stereotypes, 1886–Present," in N. G. Bringhurst and J. C. Hamer, eds., *Scattering of the Saints: Schism within Mormonism* (Independence, MO: John Whitmer Books, 2007). Also the following web site: http://principlevoices.org/diversity-of-fundamentalist-mormons (April 25, 2009).

55. K. Driggs, "Twentieth-Century Polygamy and Fundamentalist Mormons in Southern Utah," *Dialogue: A Journal of Mormon Thought* 24, no. 4 (1991): 44–58; K. Driggs, "Imprisonment, Defiance, Division: A History of Mormon Fundamentalsm in the 1940s and 1950s," *Dialogue: A Journal of Mormon Thought* 38, no. 1 (2005): 65–95; Hales, op. cit.; Wilde, ibid.

56. Ken Driggs (Driggs, 1988, op. cit.) identified eighteen U. S. Supreme Court decisions, as well as numerous other appellate court cases, concerning the United States confrontation with Mormons over polygamy and related issues. See also Gordon, 2002, op. cit.; Daynes, op. cit.; Hardy, op. cit.; Talbot, op. cit.

57. Daynes, op. cit.; Firmage and Mangrum, op. cit.; Gordon, 1995, op. cit.

58. Gordon, 1995, ibid.; Gordon, 2002, op. cit.; Hardy, op. cit.; Talbot, op. cit.

59. F. Lieber, "The Mormons: Shall Utah Be Admitted into the Union?" *Putnam's Monthly*, V (1855): 225–236; *The Late Corporation of the Church of Jesus Christ of Latter-Day Saints v. United States*, 136 U.S. 1 (1890); *Reynolds v. United States*, 98 U.S. 145 (1879); also see Gordon, 2002, ibid.

60. Firmage and Mangrum, op. cit.; Gordon, 1995, op. cit.; Linford, op. cit.

61. Gordon, 1995, ibid.; Gordon, 2002, op. cit.; Talbot, op. cit.

62. Cott, op. cit.; Firmage and Mangrum, op. cit.; Gordon, 1995, 2002, ibid.; Grossberg, op. cit.; Hardy, op. cit.; Linford, ibid.; Weisbrod and Sheingorn, op. cit.

63. Gordon, 2002, ibid., 82.

64. Gordon, 2002, ibid.

65. Hardy, 2007, op. cit., 270.

66. Although this threat of decline was often expressed in terms of social or civilizational outcomes, Christine Talbot (Talbot, 2006, op. cit.) documents the belief among some anti-polygamists of a physiological decline associated with polygamy. Also see Hardy, op. cit.

67. Quoted in Hardy, ibid., 280.

68. Cott, op. cit.; Firmage and Mangrum, op. cit.; Gordon, 2002, op. cit.; Grossberg, op. cit.; Hardy, op. cit.; Linford, op. cit.; Weisbrod and Sheingorn, op. cit.

69. *Reynolds v. United States*, op. cit.

70. Lieber, 1855, op. cit., 234; italics in original.

71. Gordon, 2002, op. cit., 157.

72. Gordon, 2002, ibid., 157.

73. *The Late Corporation of the Church of Jesus Christ of Latter-Day Saints v. United States*, op. cit.

74. Cott, op. cit.; Gordon, 1995, 2002, op. cit.; Hardy, op. cit.; Talbot, op. cit.

75. Bradley, op. cit.; Driggs, 1991, 2005, op. cit.; Hales, op. cit.

76. *Cleveland v. United States*, 329 U.S. 14 (1946); also see Bradley, ibid.; M. A. Glendon, "Marriage and the State: The Withering Away of Marriage," *Virginia Law Review* 62, no. 4 (1976): 663–720.

77. Thornton, 2001; Thornton, 2005, op. cit.

78. G. Binstock and A. Thornton, "Knowledge and Use of Developmental Thinking about Societies and Families among Teenagers in Argentina," *Demografia* 50, no. 5 (2007): 75–104; A. Thornton, G. Binstock, and D. Ghimire, "International Dissemination of Ideas about Development and Family Change," in R. Jayakody, A. Thornton, and W. Axinn, eds., *International Family Change: Ideational Perspectives* (New York: Lawrence Erlbaum Associates, Taylor & Francis Group, 2008); A. Thornton and Y. Xie, "Knowledge, Values, and Beliefs Concerning Within and Between Country Inequality among People in Everyday Life in China and the United States," Paper presented at Conference on Social Inequality and Social Change, sponsored by Research Committee 28 on Social Stratification and Mobility of the International Sociological Association, Renmin University, Beijing, China, May 14–16, 2009; A. Thornton, G. Binstock, K. Yount, D. Ghimire, M. J. Abbasi-Shavazi, and Y. Xie, "International Fertility Change: Insights from the Developmental Idealism Framework," Paper presented at the Special Interdisciplinary Workshop on Fertility Declines in the Past, Present and Future: What We Don't Know and What We Need to Know, sponsored by the British Society for Population Studies and Cambridge Group for the History of Population and Social Structure, Cambridge, England, July 15–17, 2009.

79. Thornton and Xie, ibid.; Thornton, Binstock, Yount, Abbasi, Ghimire, and Xie, ibid.; also unpublished results.

80. I first learned of AAAP on March 13, 2009. The web site for AAAP states that the president is Buster D. Johnson, a Mohave County, Arizona, supervisor and that the executive director is K. Dee Ignatin, who was previously a reporter in Mohave County, Arizona, where she investigated the FLDS living there (http://tripleap.org/about_us). In an undated letter, Ignatin states that she "left Mohave County behind,

five months ago,.... with a passionate desire to protect Texas women and children from sharing the fate of their sisters in Utah and Arizona" (http://tripleap.org/ directors_page). Copied from web site on March 13, 2009. Mohave County, Arizona, is located on the border with Utah and contains Colorado City, which, with its sister city, Hildale, Utah, is populated largely by members of the FLDS.

81. Copied from the following web site on March 13, 2009: http://tripleap.org/ home.

82. Copied from the following web site on March 13, 2009: http://tripleap.org/ partners.

83. Copied from the following web site on March 13, 2009: http://tripleap.org/ yahoo_site_admin/assets/docs/kDeeGlobalEM_Oprah.66152542.pdf.

84. Statements transcribed by the author on July 24, 2008, from an interview contained in a YouTube recording entitled "Inside Look into FLDS Classroom, Life at YFZ." I could not locate a date for the interview itself.

85. Reported by Arland Thornton in *Reading History Sideways: The Fallacy and Enduring Impact of the Developmental Paradigm on Family Life*, 155.

86. Brooke Adams is a reporter for the *Salt Lake Tribune*, who is advertised on the *Tribune's* web site as the "nation's only polygamous beat writer." The interview was broadcast on National Public Radio on May 4, 2008.

87. Article written by Tony Woodlief in *World on the Web*, June 6, 2008.

88. Article written by Lisa Sandberg and Terri Langford, dated May 9, 2008.

89. The data were provided to the author through courtesy of the *Deseret News*. Articles reporting information from this survey were published April 9 and 10, 2008, by KSL and the *Deseret News*.

90. Texas Court of Appeals, Third District, at Austin. No. 03–08–00235-CV. In re Sara Steed, et al., May 22, 2008, 8.

91. Supreme Court of Texas. No. 08–0391. In re Texas Department of Family and Protective Services, Relator, May 29, 2008, 4.

92. The data were provided to the author through courtesy of the *Deseret News*. An article concerning data from this survey was written by Ben Winslow and published on June 25, 2008, in the *Deseret News*.

93. The introduction to the question was as follows: "As you may know, Texas state officials recently removed over 400 children from a polygamist ranch, but a Texas court ruled the children should be returned to their parents. Based on what you've heard or read about this case, which comes closer to your view?" The survey results reported here were obtained from searches of the iPOLL Databank and other resources provided by the Roper Center for Public Opinion Research, University of Connecticut.

94. The data in this paragraph were provided to the author through courtesy of the *Deseret News*.

95. The precise question was: "As you may know, polygamy is the practice of one man having multiple wives at the same time. Just your best guess, how do you think most Americans feel about polygamy? Do you think most Americans favor or oppose it?" The survey result reported here was obtained from searches of the iPOLL

Databank and other resources provided by the Roper Center for Public Opinion Research, University of Connecticut.

96. This was the decision of *Loving v. Virginia.*

97. The survey results reported here were obtained from searches of the iPOLL Databank and other resources provided by the Roper Center for Public Opinion Research, University of Connecticut.

98. Preceding this question was the statement, "There are some religious groups in this country that have a tradition of polygamy—where a man can have more than one wife at a time." The survey results reported here were obtained from searches of the iPOLL Databank and other resources provided by the Roper Center for Public Opinion Research, University of Connecticut.

99. *The Late Corporation of the Church of Jesus Christ of Latter-Day Saints v. United States,* op. cit.

100. Interestingly, in January 2009 the government of British Columbia, Canada, arrested, with the intention to prosecute, two fundamentalist Mormon men for the practice of polygamy.

PART III

Legal and Ethical Issues Surrounding the Seizure of the FLDS Children

Chapter 12

Child Protection Law and the FLDS Raid in Texas

Linda F. Smith

This chapter recounts the legal proceedings—what happened and why—and suggests what could or should have happened when the State of Texas acted to "protect" the FLDS children living on the Yearning for Zion Ranch.

A Child Abuse Report Is Made and Investigated

The Eldorado raid began March 29, 2008, with a series of telephone calls to a local family violence shelter. The caller claimed to be "Sarah Jessop," or "Sarah Barlow," a 16-year-old girl forced to be the seventh wife of a middle-aged man. She claimed that he forced her to have sex, impregnated her, beat her, and would not let her leave the Yearning for Zion (YFZ) Ranch with her baby. The family violence shelter forwarded this information to law enforcement officials and to the Department of Family and Protective Services (DFPS). Because the caller would have to have conceived her 8-month-old baby when she was, at most, 15 years old, law enforcement asserted that the felony of sexual assault of a child had occurred and sought a warrant.[1]

On April 3, 2008, the trial court issued a search and arrest warrant ordering the officers to seize various items of evidence (birth records, medical records, photographs, etc.) relating to the 16-year-old caller and to arrest Dale Barlow, the alleged perpetrator. Texas state troopers executing the search warrant and child welfare investigators spent many hours on April 4, 5, and 6 on the ranch investigating the facts and searching for "Sarah."[2] As noted in the prologue to this book, this particular individual has never been found and likely did not exist. Instead, "police have linked the calls...to Rozita Swinton, a 33-year-old Colorado Springs, Colorado, woman" who has a history of assuming different personalities and calling for help claiming abuse.[3]

Law and Critique

Even if "Sarah's" call was a hoax, that fact would not invalidate the investigation that DFPS conducted. Consistent with federal statutes, all states have laws that provide for the reporting and investigation of child abuse and neglect.[4] Texas's statute requires that any person "having cause to believe" that "a child's physical or mental health or welfare has been adversely affected by abuse or neglect by any person" is required to make a report.[5] Accordingly, the shelter that received the calls from "Sarah" was obligated to make the initial report to either a law enforcement agency or the DFPS.

Texas law requires DFPS to "make a prompt and thorough investigation" of reported child abuse or neglect "allegedly committed by a person responsible for a child's care, custody or welfare" and must involve law enforcement if the report alleges conduct that constitutes a crime that poses an immediate risk of physical or sexual abuse.[6] DFPS may defer to law enforcement and need not investigate alleged abuse by someone other than the child's parent or guardian. So, "Sarah's" alleged physical and sexual abuse by her "spiritual husband" was solely a case for law enforcement. What made it a child protection case was that "Sarah's" parents apparently induced her to accept this sexual relationship when she was only 15 and were not currently protecting her. Moreover, Sarah had claimed that her parents were about to send her younger sister to the YFZ Ranch, intending her to be spiritually united with an older man. This also made a claim of parental neglect or abuse.

Even though it now appears that "Sarah" did not exist, the DFPS workers were not wrong to look for her. Texas statute addresses anonymous reports and requires a preliminary investigation "to determine whether there is any evidence to corroborate the report."[7]

New "Victims" Are Identified

While DFPS workers did not find "Sarah," they reported they "observed a number of young teenage girls who appeared to be minors and appeared to be pregnant, as well as several teenage girls who already had given birth and had their own infants."[8] They identified six females who fit into this category and asserted that a dependable confidential informant had advised that "adult male FLDS church members.... engage in the practice of marrying multiple wives, at the initial time of marriage, the bride is often under the age of sixteen years."[9]

Law and Critique

While pregnant teenagers are not necessarily evidence of child abuse or child neglect, there are two reasons that DFPS was properly concerned about these girls—the criminal law and healthy psychological development.

Texas, like Utah,[10] criminalizes sex with minors based upon the age difference between the minor and the sexual perpetrator. Sexual intercourse is an illegal "sexual assault" if the victim is a child under age 17; but if the victim is 14 years old or older and the perpetrator is not more than three years older, there is no crime.[11] Accordingly, a 15-year-old pregnant by her 18-year-old boyfriend would not involve criminal conduct. But if a 16-year-old girl had a sexual relationship with a man 20 years old or older, the adult man would be guilty of a felony.[12] In sum, if these minor teenagers had become pregnant by middle-aged men (as was reportedly the practice in the community), they were victims of a crime. If their parents had promoted their relationships with these older men, they were victims of parental abuse or neglect as well.

The Texas statute requiring investigations of child abuse defines abuse broadly to include harm to a child's mental health:

"Abuse" includes
mental or emotional injury to a child that results in an observable and material impairment of the child's growth, development or psychological functioning;
...permitting the child to be in a situation in which the child sustains a mental or emotional injury...
sexual conduct harmful to a child's mental, emotional or physical welfare...
failure to take reasonable effort to prevent sexual conduct harmful to a child.[13]

Mental health professionals consider adolescence a time of identity formation when youth develop more abstract conceptions of who they really are and how they fit into their world.[14] While puberty is an important change in adolescence, the youth's developing cognitive abilities are also important to permit the youth to "establish autonomy and identity," the "normative developmental tasks of adolescence."[15] Accordingly, parents must walk the fine line between maintaining consistent boundaries and rules while permitting the adolescent to become more self-sufficient and independent.[16] Forcing 15-year-old girls into "spiritual unions" with older men is abusive in denying them the time and freedom to develop an autonomous identity.

Attorney Ann Haralambie and clinical psychologist Stacy Klapper warn that parents may inappropriately attempt to control the child's emerging sexuality. They raise the example of gay and lesbian youth being denied the right to develop their identity, noting that as a result "gay and lesbian youth are more likely to be abused and rejected" and many run away, attempt suicide and abuse substances.[17] The charge that the FLDS force their daughters into early sexual unions is, psychologically, the same sort of inappropriate and unhealthy attempt to control the adolescent's emerging self.

Taking Protective Custody of All the Children

Instead of filing protective cases regarding the girls who appeared to be pregnant teens or young teenage mothers, DFPS began "the largest child protection case documented in the history of the United States" by taking emergency custody of all the children on the Ranch without a court order.[18] First, 18 teenage girls were taken into custody; then 34 girls were taken to San Angelo to be interviewed.[19] Ultimately all the children—over 400—were removed over a three-day period. DFPS workers justified taking custody of all the children, explaining that the children were "unable or unwilling to provide information" such as their correct names, birth dates, and parents' names.[20] The director of the Children's Advocacy Center, which provides court advocates for the children, explained "When children live in a pretty secluded environment it is difficult to get them to open up....If you give them a little space you are more likely to get them to open up to you."[21]

Initially, the children's mothers were permitted to accompany them, first to interview sites in San Angelo and then to the Fort Concho historic site, where they would be temporarily housed.[22]

The Trial Court

As required by statute, DFPS filed "suits affecting the parent-child relationship" (SAPCR) of these 400+ children and sought emergency custody orders. On Sunday, April 6, Lynn McFadden, an investigative supervisor for DFPS, filed an affidavit supporting DFPS's petition to protect a child in an emergency and a hearing before the judge was scheduled for the following day, Monday

April 7.[23] The affidavit first recounted the call from "Sarah" in detail and then asserted that "further investigation" had "unearthed additional information concerning other minor residents of the YFZ Ranch."

> Investigators determined that there is a wide-spread pattern and practice among the residents of the YFZ Ranch in which young minor female residents are conditioned to expect and accept sexual activity with adult men at the ranch upon being spiritually married to them. Under the practice, once a minor female child is determine [sic] by the leaders of the YFZ Ranch to have reached child bearing age (approximately 13–14 years old) they are then "spiritually married" to an adult male member of the church and they are required to then engage in sexual activity with such male for the purpose of having children.... [T]here is a pervasive pattern and practice of indoctrinating and grooming minor female children to accept spiritual marriages to adult male members of the YFZ Ranch resulting in them being sexually abused. Similarly, minor boys residing on the YFZ Ranch, after they become adults, are spiritually married to minor female children and engage in sexual relationships with them resulting in them becoming sexual perpetrators. This pattern and practice places all of the children located at the YFZ Ranch, both male and female, to risks of emotional, physical and/or sexual abuse.[24]

Tracking the requisite statutory conclusions, the McFadden affidavit asserted that "an immediate danger exists to the physical health or safety of the children" who live at the YFZ Ranch and/or that the children "are the victims of neglect and/or sexual abuse." The affidavit referred to the YFZ Ranch as "the household" and stated that the children's continuing to reside on the YFZ Ranch would be contrary to their "welfare." It concluded that there was "no time" for an adversary hearing, that "all reasonable efforts" had been made to "prevent or eliminate the need for removal of the child" but that it was not "in the child's best interest to return the child to the parents' home at this time." Based on these allegations, trial court Judge Walther gave emergency custody of all 401 children to DFPS.[25]

Law and Critique

States generally permit social service workers to take children into custody in an emergency situation without a court order or permit courts to issue an order after an ex parte hearing attended only by DFPS.[26] In either case, within 1 to 3 days the parents should get an expedited "shelter" or "emergency" or "pre-liminary" hearing to address the removal and the danger to the child.[27] Texas statute requires a court hearing "no later than the first working day after the date the child is taken into possession."[28] However, under Texas statute, that "initial hearing" may be held with only the DFPS workers and the judge and the proof may be only the sworn petition and affidavit.[29] Such an ex parte hearing is permitted "if a full adversary hearing is not practicable."[30] It appears that no more than such an ex parte hearing was held on Monday April 7, confirming DFPS's custody and setting the full adversary hearing for April 17 and 18.

Many child protection cases do present themselves as emergencies—the single mother is arrested and the children are home alone, the child is living in a "meth" house and in immediate danger, the emergency room doctor concludes that the child's concussion was the result of parental abuse—and DFPS must take the child into care and then seek judicial authorization. However, it is unclear why this case was properly initiated with DFPS taking custody of all the children in an emergency. Perhaps there was an emergency for the underage girls who were being sexually assaulted by much older men. But it is more difficult to accept that there was an emergency for the younger children. Similarly, since the mothers were present and even accompanied their children to the first "shelter" at Fort Concho, it would have been "practicable" for them to participate in the emergency hearing (except for the fact that there were so many mothers). The fact that Texas statute and practice denied these parents any right to be heard within one to three days of the removal of their children may well have violated their constitutional rights. At a minimum it failed to follow standard national practice in protective cases.

Finally, it is not clear why DFPS took this comprehensive and emergency approach here, where only the teenage girls were at immediate risk of sexual abuse. Perhaps DFPS's standard operating procedure was to take custody in order to get the parent's attention and signal the seriousness of this case. Or perhaps DFPS sought to "encourage" the women and/or children to cooperate in the investigation by this approach.

Separating the Mothers from the Children

In the meantime, before the adversary hearing, DFPS began separating the children from the mothers who had accompanied them to Fort Concho. On Monday, April 14, mothers and children were bused to San Angelo Coliseum and separated according to the ages of the children. Fifty-seven mothers were forced to leave 100 children ages six and older in state custody while mothers of children age five and younger were permitted to stay with the 300 or so infants and toddlers.[31] The mothers of the older children were taken to a room to "get some information." At that point, police officers and child welfare workers surrounded these women and read a court order that the children would be taken from them and placed in foster care. The women were required to leave the building and invited to go to a domestic violence center or back to the ranch.[32]

At that point, DFPS began taking the children to foster and group homes throughout the state of Texas. DFPS spokesperson Marleigh Meisner explained:

> This was in the best interests of these children...It was also in the best interest of the investigation....We believe that children who are victims of abuse or neglect, and particularly victims at the hands of their parents, are certainly going to feel safer when they don't have a parent there coaching them.[33]

Law and Commentary

The unusual aspect here is that the mothers had been permitted to accompany their children who were taken into DFPS custody in the first place. Was this because the investigative interviews morphed into an emergency custody situation? Or were the mothers welcomed because taking custody of so many children would have been impossible without the mothers' assistance? Or did DFPS workers hope some mothers might assist by attesting to the abuse and victimization they suffered once they were away from the Ranch?

In any event, since Judge Walther had given DFPS legal custody of these children on April 7, DFPS had the legal right to decide where they would be placed. However, the surprise separation of half the families just days before the adversary hearing certainly raised questions. If the children were endangered by being with their mothers, why was it initially permitted? Since they had been together for 8 to 10 days with no incidents of harm being reported, why was it necessary to separate them? Perhaps DFPS decided to place the children before the adversary hearing so that situation would be the status quo once the parents got their day in court.

The Adversary Hearing

Throughout the nation, when a protective case is begun, the state must hold an adjudicatory (fact-finding) hearing as soon as practicable, often within 60 days.[34] Texas law provides that when a child is taken into possession by DFPS, it must give written notice to each parent and the "full adversary hearing" must be held in court within 14 days.[35] This is a very short time period to investigate and be prepared to try a case on the merits. If the hearing is not held in time, the trial court may be ordered to hold a hearing, but the case is not dismissed.[36] If the hearing needs to be delayed, the order for temporary removal of the children stays valid.[37] In this case, DFPS endeavored to go forward with the adversary hearing regarding all 400+ children on the scheduled hearing dates of April 17 and 18.

The statute is written to require that the child be returned to the parent at the conclusion of the adversary hearing unless the court finds sufficient evidence of three things:

> there is a danger to the physical health or safety of the child which was caused by an act or failure to act of the parent and for the child to remain in the home is contrary to the welfare of the child
>
> the urgent need for protection required the immediate removal of the child and reasonable efforts, consistent with the circumstances and providing for the safety of the child, were made to eliminate or prevent the child's removal; and
>
> reasonable efforts have been made to enable the child to return home, but there is substantial risk of a continuing danger if the child is returned home.[38]

It should be noted that while DFPS is charged with investigating cases involving emotional harm (see above), for DFPS to retain physical custody of a child requires proof of danger to the "physical health or safety" of the child.

The Testimony in the Trial Court Adversary Hearing

In this case, DFPS relied upon the testimony of the social workers who had been conducting the investigation for its proof and pursued the same legal theories that had been in the initial affidavits. The supervisory investigator Angie Voss testified that "there is a culture of young girls being pregnant by old men" and that she had found evidence that "more than 20 girls, some of whom are now adults, have conceived or given birth under the age of 16 or 17."[39] There was "a pattern of girls reporting that there was no age too young for girls to be 'spiritually married.'...[and] a pervasive belief that when 'Uncle Merrill' decided for them to be married, they would be married....No age was too young to marry, and they wanted to have as many babies as they could."[40] Several victims of sexual abuse were specifically identified: a 16-year-old girl who has a five-month-old baby, a 17-year-old girl with a year-old son, and entries in the Bishop Records of girls being pregnant at ages 15 and 16.[41]

Dr. Bruce Perry, a child psychiatrist, testified that the pregnancies of the YFZ children were the result of sexual abuse and that children aged 14, 15, and

16 were not emotionally mature enough to consensually enter into a healthy relationship of marriage. Dr. Perry testified that free choice was not really possible under the FLDS belief system that required obedience to the father and the prophet or eternal damnation would result.[42] He focused on the limited choices available to the FLDS children and characterized the environment to be "authoritarian."[43] The children were at risk "because their brain development could be impeded by an authoritarian atmosphere that discourages independent thinking."[44]

To support the argument that all the children were victims of abuse, DFPS investigator Voss testified that the residents of the YFZ Ranch "explained that they are one big family," all the mothers are called mothers to all the children, and all the children call each other brother and sister, and all have the same belief system. She concluded that all the children "are potential victims."[45] When asked why babies needed to be removed, Voss said, "what I have found is that they are living under an umbrella of belief that having children at a young age is a blessing and therefore any child in that environment would not be safe... when you find one child that's a victim in a home, you have concerns for all of them. And the ranch is considered one large home, one large community, I would have concerns for any children there."[46] Dr. Perry similarly testified that the pervasive belief system that underage marriage and sexual abuse of girls is okay creates a danger to all the children. It develops people who have a high potential of replicating sexual abuse of young children as part of their belief system.[47]

Lawyers for the parents argued that pregnancy by itself is not evidence of child abuse. They presented a "theological expert" on the FLDS, William John Walsh. He testified that the church did not have a doctrine advocating the marriage of underage girls to older men. While the church's prophets decide when a couple is ready to marry, there was no doctrine favoring underage marriage[48] but it was more a matter of matchmaking involving the parents as well as the girl.[49]

A second witness for the FLDS parents, Merylin Jeffs, age 29, testified that she was willing to move away from the ranch if necessary to protect her 7-year-old daughter from whom she had never been apart, and that she would not allow her daughter to marry before age 18.[50] Lori Jessop, age 25 and in a monogamous marriage to a 27-year-old man, said she had wed at age 18 and was concerned that girls became brides at age 15 or 16. Lucille Nielsen testified that she married at age 20 and pleaded to permit her 2-year-old son to stay with her. Linda Musser, age 56, volunteered to leave the ranch if necessary to regain custody of her 13-year-old son.[51]

Neither side presented detailed evidence about the individual children seized in the raid.[52] However, DFPS investigator Voss also testified that the Department's investigation had been thwarted by misinformation from the children and adults as to their identities, ages, and family relations.[53] Indeed, there were 20 or 30 young mothers DFPS believed to be minors who claimed to be adults.[54]

The Trial Court's Findings after the Adversary Hearing

At the conclusion of two days of testimony, Judge Barbara Walther entered findings that tracked DFPS's allegations—that all the children were in danger of abuse and needed to be immediately removed from their parents' care in order to protect them. She made the requisite finding that reasonable efforts had been made to eliminate the need for removal but that the danger remained. Judge Walther also ordered that all the children and parents undergo DNA testing, to definitively decide who were the parents of each child.[55]

Law, Procedure, and Critique of the Adversary Hearing

Prior to the adversary hearing, it was patently obvious that the choice to file protective cases on over 400 children opened "a Pandora's box of legal and logistical issues" including "enormous courtroom management problems."[56] University of Texas law professor Jack Sampson said "you won't just need a hundred lawyers to represent the children...You'll need dozens of judges if the state is going to try these cases....The mechanics of holding scores of trials in rural West Texas is virtually incomprehensible." As to the merits of the case, Professor Sampson commented: "Some of the parents, especially if they can be criminally charged, will lose their children....But the whole shooting match? Taking all the kids away? I just don't see it."[57]

Indeed, the idea that over 400 children with many sets of parents could have these issues decided in one massive case is very problematic. The statute deals with an individual child and that child's parent. It is not enough that there is a danger to a child's "physical health or safety." The state must show that the danger "was caused by an act or failure to act of the person entitled to the possession" of the child—in other words, by the child's parent.[58] Moreover, because the U.S. Constitution recognizes that a parent has a fundamental liberty interest in the care and custody of her child,[59] an individualized determination of each parent's rights to her child is also constitutionally mandated.

While there are limited circumstances in which a danger to one child can be inferred from the abuse suffered by another child, the statute limits such inferences by instructing the court to consider "whether the household to which the child would be returned includes a person who: (1) has abused or neglected another child in a manner that caused serious injury to or the death of the other child; or (2) has sexually abused another child."[60]

DFPS sought to prove its case by arguing that the entire YFZ Ranch was one "household" and by arguing that each parent had caused or failed to protect her child's safety by living in a community where the leaders promote sexual abuse (through spiritual unions) of minor girls. This is a difficult proposition to accept for parents who had NOT agreed to the underage marriage of their children. It is similarly difficult to make this finding regarding young mothers who had only pre-teen children and thus had never faced the issue of whether to encourage or oppose a child's sexual relationship / spiritual marriage. It is also difficult to reach the conclusion that there was a danger to the "physical health and safety" of young boys based upon DFPS's argument that they were being "groomed" to be adult sexual predators.

The statute required two additional findings that were also questionable regarding the preteen children and boys: that there was an "urgent need for protection" which "required the immediate removal" of the child and that "reasonable efforts" had been made to permit the child to stay or return home, but "there is a substantial risk of continuing danger" if the child is in the home.[61] While DFPS and the trial court concluded that it was impossible to address the pervasive cultural acceptance of under-age sexual unions while babies remained in the care of their mothers, it is not at all clear how that conclusion was justified.

The high proof that Texas law appears to require to justify removing the child from his parents is based on sound understanding of the child's psychological and emotional needs. Mental health professionals Donald Bross and Terri James-Banks explain:

> [A]ny attorney who has represented infants and very young children
> is aware that time can be of the essence in the secure attachment of
> children. In other words, it is not good for children to be moved from
> one caregiver, parent, or foster parent to another for more than a very
> limited time, generally measured in hours for infants and days for
> toddlers, without very important reasons of safety or, in some very
> limited circumstances, a clear diagnostic purpose. Every move must
> have an impact on the child and, unless carefully considered, may
> cause the child to experience a sense of loss and even depression.[62]

The decision by DFPS and by the trial judge to remove all the children from their parents put at risk the healthy development of the many babies, toddlers and young children.

The Service Plans and Review Hearings

After an adversary hearing that commits a child to the legal custody of DFPS, the law requires that a "service plan" be established for the child and a court hearing be held to review the situation.[63] The service plan must be filed with the court within 45 days of the custody order and set forth its goal (whether return of the child to the parent, termination of parental rights and placement for adoption, or other out-of-home care) as well as the steps necessary to return the child to a safe environment.[64] Within 60 days of the custody order, the court must hold a "status hearing" to review the child's status and the service plan developed for the child.[65]

Statute further provides that a "permanency plan" for the child be developed and a "permanency hearing" be held within 180 days of the initial custody order.[66] The court needs to have begun a "trial on the merits" within one year after temporary custody was removed from the parents and given to DFPS.[67]

By early May DFPS authorities had begun drafting service plans for the FLDS children and their families. Hearings on these plans began on May 19.[68] During those hearings, attorneys for the parents and children were critical about the lack of personalization and specifics in the plans.[69] The plans typically required educational testing of the children and of the parents and vocational assessments of the parents. Attorneys also complained that many of the plans had not been developed with any consultation with the parents. The plans permitted visitation, but failed to provide a feasible way for many parents to visit children scattered hundreds of miles throughout the state of Texas. Throughout the hearings Judge Walther reminded the attorneys that they were not there to re-litigate the findings that required the children be placed in foster care in the first instance.

The Mandamus to the Court of Appeals

Texas law does not provide for an appeal to challenge the findings of fact or the order of temporary custody that is made after the adversary hearing. The law provides the right to appeal only after the permanency hearing and a final order terminating parental rights (or otherwise giving permanent custody to someone else).[70]

Texas law does permit a party to file for the extraordinary "writ" of "mandamus" in the appellate court to challenge what happened in the adversary hearing. A writ of "mandamus" (in Latin, "we command") is a court order compelling a lower court or government official to do something. A "mandamus" case requires more than an argument that the trial judge made a mistake, it requires an argument that the trial court was behaving illegally. For example, parents have successfully filed for "mandamus" when the trial court did not hold the adversary hearing on time, and have obtained orders that the trial court promptly hold the hearing.[71] A mandamus order can be entered if the trial court had insufficient evidence that there was a danger to the child's health or safety and that it abused its discretion in giving custody to DFPS.[72]

The trial judge made her oral ruling on Friday, April 18, and by Wednesday, April 23, lawyers from Texas Rio Grande Legal Aid had filed a petition for a writ of mandamus and an emergency motion for a "stay" of the court's order. The motion asked the appellate court to prevent DFPS from separating the youngest children from their mothers, as that separation had not yet occurred. The appellate court did not "stay" (i.e., delay) the trial court's order, and DFPS began placing the youngest children in foster care. The appellate court did grant a hearing on the petition.

Texas Rio Grande Legal Aid represented 38 women; none of these women was the parent of any of the girls who had become pregnant as minors.[73] Their petition argued that there was no evidence that their children were in danger of sexual abuse, and therefore the trial judge had acted unlawfully in giving custody of their children to DFPS. They further argued that the state had failed to prove an "urgent need for protection" that required "immediate removal" and that the state had not made "reasonable efforts" to eliminate the need to remove the children. The petition argued in the alternative that even if DFPS was entitled to legal custody, the trial judge should have allowed the parents physical custody or visitation with their children.[74]

Legal Aid of North Texas filed a similar petition for mandaums on behalf of three other mothers (the "Bradshaw" case). This petition added the arguments that the mass hearing denied the mothers due process of law, given the lack of notice, of access to counsel, remote viewing, and inability to attend the hearing without surrendering custody of their infants to DFPS. This petition also argued that the only conceivable basis for the court's order was the unconstitutional goal to alter the religious education of the children.[75]

DFPS filed its briefs opposing both petitions. Amicus curiae (friend of the court) briefs were filed by Barbara J. Elias-Perciful, a lawyer involved in children's advocacy, supporting DFPS, and by Liberty Legal Institute, a legal advocacy group for religious freedom and parental rights. ("Friend of the court" briefs may be permitted by interested groups or experts who do not represent a party in the case, but seek to help the court.)[76]

The Texas Court of Appeals for the Third District at Austin heard this mandamus case brought by Texas Rio Grande Legal Aid and on May 22, 2008, issued its opinion. This three-judge Appellate Court unanimously agreed with these 38 mothers on all three primary points. The Court wrote:

> Removing children from their homes and parents on an emergency basis before fully litigating the issue of whether the parents should continue to have custody of the children is an extreme measure.... [I]t is a step that the legislature has provided may be taken only when the circumstances indicate a danger to the physical health and welfare of the children and the need for protection of the children is so urgent that immediate removal of the children from the home is necessary.[77]

The Appellate Court held that DFPS failed to "present any evidence of danger to the physical health or safety of any male children or any female children who had not reached puberty" and that the alleged "belief system" did not, by itself, put the children in "physical danger." Secondly, the Appellate Court held that DFPS failed to establish the need for protection was "urgent and required immediate removal." The Court noted that there were five minor girls who were pregnant, but they were not the children of the mothers bringing this mandamus. There was no evidence that these mothers had allowed or were going to allow their children to be victims of sexual abuse. "Evidence that children raised in this particular environment may someday have their physical health and safety threatened is not evidence that the danger is imminent enough to warrant invoking the extreme measure of immediate removal prior to full litigation of the issue...." The Court also concluded that the evidence did not justify treating the entire Ranch as one "household." Finally, the Appellate Court held that there was "no evidence" that DFPS "made reasonable efforts to eliminate or prevent the removal" of any of these women's children. The Court concluded that because the evidence of DFPS was "legally and factually insufficient" to support the findings required by the statute, the trial court had "abused its discretion." The Court of Appeals directed the trial court to vacate its order with respect to the children of these 38 women.

The Court issued a one-paragraph memorandum opinion in the companion Bradshaw case, indicating that the material facts were identical and the same relief would be ordered.[78] The court did not address the constitutional claims raised in either case.

Once these opinions were issued, these women, their lawyers, and many others in the FLDS community began to rejoice. However, their joy was cut short when DFPS decide to further appeal the case.

The Mandamus to the Texas Supreme Court

The very next day, May 23, 2008, DFPS filed a petition for writ of mandamus and motion for emergency relief in the Texas Supreme Court.[79] DFPS argued that the Court of Appeals had abused its discretion by inappropriately granting mandamus and judging the facts for itself. No further proceedings would take place in the trial court until the Texas Supreme Court resolved the matter.

Texas Rio Grande Legal Aid replied to DFPS, arguing that the Court of Appeals had been correct under Texas's statute and that DFPS's criticisms were without merit.[80] At this juncture, the ACLU of Texas weighed in with an amicus curiae (friend of the court) brief, urging the Texas Supreme Court to uphold the Court of Appeal's decision. The ACLU argued that parents' rights to custody of their children were fundamental constitutional rights and parents could be deprived of their children's custody only after "due process of law." The ACLU argued that due process required individual determinations for each child and that the mass hearings denied due process. It further argued that separating children from their parents solely on the parents' beliefs (rather than their acts) would violate the First Amendment.[81]

On May 29, 2008, the Supreme Court of Texas issued its Per Curiam ("for the court") opinion denying DFPS's petition, explaining: "Having carefully examined the testimony at the adversary hearing and the other evidence before us, we are not inclined to disturb the court of appeals' decision. On the record before us, removal of the children was not warranted."[82] The Supreme Court noted that the case involved only 38 mothers and their 126 children (117 of whom were under age 13) and addressed DFPS's claims that these children could not be protected if DFPS did not have custody of them. The Court referenced the statutes providing for investigations of child abuse and of "suits affecting the parent-child relationship" and noted:

> [T]he Family Code gives the district court broad authority to protect
> children short of separating them from their parents and placing them
> in foster care. The court may make and modify temporary orders for
> the safety and welfare of the child, including an order restraining a
> party from removing the child beyond a geographical area identified
> by the court. The court may also order the removal of an alleged
> perpetrator from the child's home and may issue orders to assist the
> Department in its investigation. The Code prohibits interference with
> an investigation, and a person who relocates a residence or conceals
> a child with the intent to interfere with an investigation commits an

offense. While the district court must vacate the current temporary custody orders as directed by the court of appeals, it need not do so without granting other appropriate relief to protect the children, as the mothers involved in this proceeding conceded.[83]

The Texas Supreme Court declined to address the constitutional issues, calling it "premature" to do so.

Three of nine Supreme Court justices filed an opinion concurring in part and dissenting in part.[84] They agreed that the trial court abused its discretion by removing boys and prepubescent girls from their mothers' custody, but they did not agree with respect to "the demonstrably endangered population of pubescent girls."

The Bottom Line: What These Decisions Meant

Although the Texas Rio Grande Legal Aid only represented 38 mothers (regarding their 124 children), any general rule set forth by the appellate courts would apply to all the parents and children in the case. Because the basis of the appellate cases was that DFPS had failed to present evidence that these mothers had ever consented to their children engaging in underage sexual unions (or "spiritual marriages"), any similarly situated mother should be entitled to regain custody of her children as well. However, the trial court could be justified in continuing DFPS custody of the five pregnant girls if the court received evidence that would meet the standard set out by the appellate courts. If DFPS had evidence that these girls were victims of sexual abuse and that their mothers refused to protect them from that abuse, DFPS could retain custody. Additionally, under Texas statute, their siblings could also be justifiably kept in DFPS custody.

It was incumbent upon the trial judge to undo the orders that were not justified and that separated children from parents who had not personally approved underage sexual unions. With respect to these mothers and children, the trial court would be justified in putting in place certain orders as outlined by the Texas Supreme Court.

Back at the Trial Court

Based on this opinion, the lawyers, DFPS workers, and parents anticipated that most of the children would be returned to their parents, but could not be certain until trial Judge Walther entered her order.[85] On Friday, May 30, the attorneys for the parents and the state arrived at the court with an agreement for the return of the children beginning Monday but a continuation of the investigation, including parenting classes and a requirement to remain in the state for at least 90 days. But Judge Walther "tweaked" that agreement, saying it would permit the return of all the children. She added conditions such as psychological testing and 24-hour access to the children. The lawyers who had won the mandamus (and other lawyers for the children) objected to such restrictions where there had been no evidence that their clients' children were abused or neglected. Judge Walther abruptly ended the conference, telling the attorneys to work on an agreement and get their 38 clients to sign it. Another weekend would pass with the children still in foster care and their futures unclear.[86]

Over the weekend, new agreements were drafted and Texas Rio Grande Legal Aid got their 38 mother-clients to sign the agreement, as directed by the judge.[87] On Monday, instead of taking up the plans prepared by the attorneys and signed by the 38 mothers, Judge Walther signed her own order releasing all the children except one 16-year-old whose attorney claimed she was a victim of sexual abuse. The court's order kept the children under the supervision of DFPS indefinitely, required parents to be photographed, fingerprinted and "ID'd" when they picked up their children, and required parents to attend standard parenting classes, not interfere with DFPS's ongoing investigation, and allow DFPS workers to visit, question, and examine the children, both medically and psychologically. Parents were prohibited from leaving Texas and required to give notice of any moves and certain travel. The lawyers who had won the mandamus decided to accept the order, and their clients began traveling to be reunited with their children.[88]

Thus, 61 days after the first children were removed, all but one of the children scattered throughout the state of Texas were being reunited with their parents.

The Law and a Critique

What was perhaps most surprising was that Judge Walther decided to lump all the children together and return custody of them all. The Court of Appeals case dealt only with 38 mothers and their children; they prevailed because none of these mothers was a parent of the minors who had become pregnant, and there was no evidence that these mothers would consent to their teenage daughters being sexually abused. The Texas Supreme Court refused to "disturb" the Court of Appeals order. Thus, neither appellate decision required that all the children be returned to the custody of their parents. The trial judge would have been justified in continuing custody of the minors who had given birth or who were pregnant and of their siblings if DFPS could show these mothers had consented to abusive relationships.

Just as the trial judge's initial order had been overbroad in sweeping up all the children, the final order was underprotective in sending all the children back—even minors who were pregnant or young mothers. Perhaps the initial order had sprung from a desire to protect everyone from a lifestyle thought to be harmful and the order on remand was the judge throwing up her hands regarding this secretive and recalcitrant community. Perhaps DFPS had no evidence of particular teens at risk because their mothers condoned underage unions. This suggests how weak the initial case was. Neither the judge nor DFPS attempted targeted protective intervention at the outset. Having been corrected by the appellate courts, DFPS and the judge again failed to target these few girls for protective intervention.

At the same time, the trial court entered further orders regarding the 38 mothers who had prevailed in the mandamus that were excessive and overly broad. DFPS no longer had custody, as it had lost the case for emergency protection. But DFPS had also filed a "SAPCR" case ("suit affecting parent-child relationship"), which was still pending. This is a garden-variety custody case that any parent or adult might bring under a different statute.[89] While this statute authorizes temporary orders "for the safety and welfare of the child," including restraining a party from removing a child from a geographical area,"[90] the trial court's temporary orders are much more intrusive, as if DFPS had been granted temporary legal custody. Similarly, while statute prohibits interfering with an investigation of abuse or neglect, and permits court orders if parents refuse to consent to certain inquiries,[91] there was no report of abuse regarding these preteen children to investigate. Moreover, had there been a report of abuse or neglect, DFPS's policies are to complete an investigation in 30 days (which could be extended to 60 days for good cause).[92] The investigation Judge Walther ordered had no time limit at all. The trial judge's orders were over-reaching, but probably not subject to appeal.[93]

The best spin that can be put on this stage of the case is that the judge would simply rely upon DFPS to do individualized inquiries into the families with teenage daughters at risk and bring back individual cases where abuse could be proven. The worst spin is that Texas has decided to seek retribution through the criminal law while continuing to treat all parents as suspects in an extended investigation.

Child Protection Investigations Go Forward

The tearful reunions of parents and children began as soon as Judge Walther signed her order. Some families returned to the Ranch; Zavenda Young (wife and mother of four children) returned with husband Edson Jessop, saying: "It's a beautiful place to raise children" and "I'm not afraid of them. I haven't done anything wrong."[94] By Thursday, June 5, 2008, all the children had been returned to their parents.[95] However, many of the families "settled into apartments and homes away from the ranch to await the results of a child welfare investigation."[96] Some parents reported their children were upset, and mental health professionals confirmed that the separation would have had a negative emotional effect. DFPS promised that it would examine what services would be offered; the county mental health center was offering services.[97]

Meanwhile, beginning on Monday, June 2, the FLDS leadership began to publicize a "statement on marriage" that included this pledge: "[T]he church commits that it will not preside over the marriage of any woman under the age of legal consent in the jurisdiction in which the marriage takes place."[98] (It is not exactly clear what is meant by "the age of legal consent." Although 16-year-olds can be lawfully married in Texas with parental consent, that would not decriminalize sexual unions between 16-year-olds and men over 20 outside the bounds of lawful marriages.) Willie Jessop claimed that the policy had been in place for 18 months but was being publicized in light of the scrutiny the FLDS were receiving.[99]

By July 4, a month after the return of the children, DFPS was beginning to arrange parenting classes for the FLDS parents. Thirty families had returned to the ranch, 33 were living in San Antonio, and others were in various Texas cities. Their attorneys stated that they wanted to complete the requirements the court had set and get on with their lives.[100] By late July, Judge Walther had ordered the massive child protection case broken up into various cases grouped by mothers, a move that was thought to be the first step in dismissing some of the cases.[101] By August 2008, DFPS had moved to dismiss the cases regarding 32 children where there was no evidence of underage marriages or their parents agreed to take appropriate steps to protect the children.[102]

One child—the 16-year-old daughter of Warren Jeffs—returned to her mother with certain conditions. Attorney ad litem Natalie Malonis told Judge Walther that she believed her client had been spiritually united with an older man and had a child by him. Judge Walther ordered that Warren Jeffs and FLDS spokesperson Willie Jessop not contact the girl.[103] The girl, for her part, denied that she had been a victim of sexual abuse and had petitioned the judge to assign her a new lawyer.[104] The girl's CASA (court-appointed special advocate) filed a report with the court opining that she was "at risk for continued sexual abuse" because, indeed, she had been "married" to a 34-year-old man the day after she turned 15. Attached to the report was the girl's own diary entry, dated December 27, 2006: "The Lord blessed me to go forward in marriage July 27, 2006, the day after I turned 15 years old."[105]

In early August 2008, DFPS filed a motion to return eight children to foster care because their parents had permitted illegal "marriages" of their older children and now refused to sign "safety plans" to protect their daughters from sexual abuse through underage "marriages."[106] However, by the anniversary of the raid, only one child remained under court supervision, a 14-year-old girl who was allegedly spiritually united with Warren Jeffs at age 12.[107] By July 2009 this case, too, was concluded with an agreement that this girl's aunt have permanent custody and her parent visit at the aunt's discretion.[108] In December 2008, DFPS issued a lengthy report regarding the "Eldorado Investigation,"[109] indicating that it had identified 12 girls who were victims of sexual abuse, their having been "spiritually married" between ages 12 and 15.[110] The report indicates that the costs to DFPS totaled over $12 million.[111] DFPS's web site asserts that the FLDS children "are safer today" due to its efforts, including having educated mothers and girls about sexual abuse.[112]

The Criminal Cases Begin

Whenever a child has been abused or neglected by a caretaker, the state may typically choose to litigate only a protective case, litigate only a criminal case, or litigate both protective and criminal cases. How (or if) these cases should be coordinated or prioritized is not set forth in statute or case law, but generally left to the discretion of the state actors.

On Tuesday June 3, 2008, the *Salt Lake Tribune* reported:

> Hours after signing an order releasing FLDS children from state custody, 51st District state judge Barbara Walther arrived at the Schleicher County Courthouse in Eldorado to swear in a grand jury that may be considering indictments related to the polygamous sect.[113]

In addition, DNA reports matching parents and children were being delivered to Judge Walther's court, based on her mid-April order for these tests for the protective case.[114] DFPS reported that after DFPS used them to determine family relations, it would explore whether this evidence could be used in the criminal investigation.[115] In late June the grand jury met; it was thought that women who conceived or gave birth before they were 17 would be subpoenaed to testify.[116] Several FLDS women, including Warren Jeffs' 16-year-old daughter, made brief appearances before the grand jury, as did the girl's attorney, Natalie Malonis.[117] On July 12, Texas authorities took a third genetic sample from a nineteen-year-old FLDS mother and her 2-year-old daughter, thought to be Jeffs' child.[118]

On July 22, 2008, the Texas grand jury met again and indicted Warren Jeffs and four other men for sexually assaulting girls under the age of 17.[119] The four other men—Raymond Jessop, 36, Merril Leroy Jessop, 33, Allan Keate, 56, and Michael Emack, 57—turned themselves in to authorities on July 28; all were charged with first degree felonies and faced five years to life in prison.[120] The sexual assaults of minors allegedly occurred in 2004 and 2006; the cases appear to be based on the births of four children who would have been conceived by underage girls and one additional sexual assault in 2006. Warren Jeffs' daughter is not among the victims, though her "husband" is a defendant charged for assaulting a different girl.[121] It is not clear whether any of the alleged victims are still minors. The grand jury charged a fifth man—Lloyd Barlow, the Ranch's doctor—for failing to report child abuse when he oversaw the births of children to minors on October 14, 2006, December 20, 2006 and May 20, 2007.[122] By March 2009, a dozen men faced Texas state-court indictments on charges ranging from sexual assault to bigamy to performing an illegal marriage, and a federal grand jury had begun to investigate FLDS church members.[123]

In May 2009, defense attorneys argued to Judge Walther that the evidence should be suppressed, because the search warrants were not based on probable cause, but on a hoax call that law enforcement used "as an excuse for staging a massively intrusive raid upon a disfavored religious group."[124] By March 2010 three of these defendants had been convicted relying upon records seized from the ranch. Merril Leroy Jessop, 38, was sentenced to 10 years in prison and Allan E. Keate, aged 57, to 33 years in prison because his offense occurred after Texas increased the penalty for sexual assault. Michael G. Emack pled guilty and received an agreed-upon 7-year sentence.[125] Merril Leroy Jessop, aged 35, was also convicted and sentenced to 75 years for the sexual assault of a 15-year-old girl.[126] None of these convictions have yet been tested on appeal.

It is unclear whether other prosecutions will be forthcoming. In particular, it is unknown whether any of the parents of these girls will be prosecuted for arranging such unions.

Similarly, it remains unclear how the criminal prosecutions will relate to the protective cases. Given that most (if not all) of the victims in the criminal case are likely now adults, there is no necessary relationship between these criminal prosecutions and the protective actions. However, given how insular and integrated the community is, any prosecution will likely have wide ramifications and effects. It is notable that the prosecutions have relied upon marriage and family records from the ranch and DNA results, and have not involved the testimony of the victims, the former child "brides."

Commentary

Various justifications exist for prosecuting crimes. Protecting the rest of society by removing the law breaker (specific deterrence) is probably the justification we think of first. Prosecution may also provide general deterrence by confirming that certain behavior is socially unacceptable and convincing the public to not commit the criminal act. Some crimes are more easily deterred than others—crimes that are planned (e.g., tax fraud) are thought to be more easily deterred than "crimes of passion" (e.g., assault).

In the case of the FLDS, Utah's successful 2007 prosecution of Warren Jeffs for promoting the "marriage" of 14-year-old Elissa Wall[127] may have already produced the desired general deterrent effect, given the "statement on marriage" recently released by the FLDS. Texas may be pursuing additional prosecutions to drive home this message.

Alternatively, Texas may be prosecuting the older men who have been "spiritually united" to underage girls to remove them from the ranch, prevent them from re-offending, and permit their victims to become independent of them. This approach may have some merit, as it would hold accountable the older adult men who decided to enter into relationships with minors. It might provide unprecedented freedom and autonomy to the now young adult women who were forced into underage marriages in the recent past.

However, it is not clear if any of the victims are willing participants in the prosecution, and prosecution against the wishes of the victim can be difficult. Indeed, some of them may oppose the criminal prosecutions, which may remove financial and emotional support from the community. If so, the FLDS girls and women would not be the only victims of sexual abuse or assault who would prefer that prosecution and prison not be the means of correcting the relationships. Finally, even if these prosecutions are successful, that will not ensure that the victims receive appropriate treatment and support.

Final Thoughts

While Texas claimed to be intervening to protect teen girls from sexual abuse, its extreme approach of removing all the children and its experts' explanations suggested a larger agenda—rescuing children from an authoritarian religion. Dr. Perry, testifying as to why the children, even pre-teen boys, should not be returned to their mothers, said:

> If they return...to that...environment, it reinforces this belief that
> they hold about the community and God and so forth. And so I think

that...the more their life before this happened is replicated, the more they'll believe like they did before the experience.....[128]

The major source of authority in the community are (sic) the men, the father of the household and the elder of the community. And when they are not around those individuals, then the formal presentation of those elements of the belief system are not as powerfully reinforced.[129]

Wherever these kids go, they can't be [in] traditional foster care. It needs to...have incredible training about the FLDS community, about issues of trauma maltreatment, about creating opportunities for these children to be exposed to similar but not destructive belief systems so they can begin to have an opportunity to create free choice about a variety of things.[130]

While mental health professionals attest that "authoritative" parenting is healthier than "authoritarian" parenting, this hardly justified removing custody from authoritarian parents or from parents who belong to authoritarian religious communities.

When Texas DFPS decided to remove all the children from the FLDS community, reportedly to end the practice of child sexual abuse, I wrote that their approach was too broad.[131] The state should have left the young children with the families who had never consented to underage sexual unions of their daughters. In that way there might have been some community support for the intervention to end what was clearly unhealthy for the teenage girls. It appears that Texas continued to cast too wide a net—demanding that protection plans be signed without findings of abuse—and may be pursuing criminal prosecutions without the support of the victims. A very aggressive approach to the criminal prosecutions could be as unsuccessful as the overly aggressive child protection case—uniting the community against the state, rather than providing support for the families who make appropriate choices for their teenage children and social support for all families to do likewise.

NOTES

I am very grateful for the helpful comments on earlier drafts from the editors and my fellow authors and for the College of Law Faculty Development Fund, which supported this research.

1. Leslie Brooks Long, "Affidavit for Search and Arrest Warrant" in State of Texas, County of Schleicher Court, No. M-08-001 S., April 2, 2008 (on file with author); Gretel C. Kovach, "Court Files Detail Claims of Sect's 'Pattern' of Abuse," *New York Times*, April 9, 2008 (retrieved May 30, 2008), http://www.nytimes.com/2008/04/09/us/09raid.html?fta=y&pagewant.

2. Leslie Brooks Long, "Affidavit for Search and Arrest Warrant" in State of Texas, County of Schleicher Court, No. M-08–002 S, April 6, 2008.

3. Lisa Rosetta, "Woman Linked to FLDS Calls Troubled," *Salt Lake Tribune,* June 1, 2008, A1.

4. Sue Badeau, Sara Gesiriech, Ann M. Haralambie, Amanda George Donnelly, and Donald N. Duquette, "A Child's Journey Through the Child Welfare System," in *Child Welfare Law and Practice,* eds. Marvin Ventrell and Donald N. Duquette (Denver: Bradford Publishing, 2005), 213–233.

5. Tex. Fam. Code § 261.101 (2008).

6. Tex. Fam. Code § 261.301 (2008).

7. Tex. Fam. Code § 261.304 (2008).

8. Lynn McFadden, "Affidavit in Support of Original Petition for Protection of a Child in An Emergency and For Conservatorship in Suit Affecting the Parent-Child Relationship" filed in the District Court of Schleicher County Texas, April 6, 2008.

9. Long, M-08–002 S. *supra* n. 2.

10. Utah Code Ann. §§ 76–5–401, 401.1, and 401.2 (2008).

11. Tex. Penal Code § 21.011 (2008).

12. Tex. Penal Code § 21.11 (2008).

13. Tex. Fam. Code § 261.001 (2008).

14. Laurence Steinberg and Amanda Sheffield Morris, "Adolescent Development," *Annual Review of Psychology* 52 (2001): 83–110, 91.

15. Laurence Steinberg and Jennifer S. Silk, "Parenting Adolescent," in *Handbook of Parenting,* 2nd ed., ed. Marc H. Bornstein (Mahwah, NJ: Lawrence Erlbaum Associates, 2002), 103–133.

16. Ann M. Haralambie and Stacy A. Klapper, "The Impact of Maltreatment on Child Development," in *Child Welfare Law and Practice,* eds. Marvin Ventrell and Donald N. Duquette (Denver: Bradford Publishing, 2005), 53–79, 69.

17. Haralambie, "The Impact of Maltreatment."

18. In re: Texas Department of Family and Protective Services (DFPS), 255S.W.3d613, 51 Tex. Sup. Ct. J. 967, 2008 WL 2212383 (Texas, May 29, 2008).

19. Ben Winslow, "52 Girls Removed from the FLDS Compound in Texas," *Deseret News,* April 4, 2008 (retrieved June 24, 2008), http://www.deseretnews.com/ article/contednt/mobile/1,5620,695267411,00.html?printView=true_

20. Brooke Adams, "FLDS Teen Whose Call Sparked Texas Raid Said She Feared for Her Life from Physically Abusive Husband," *Salt Lake Tribune,* April 8, 2008 (electronic, on file with author).

21. Brooke Adams, "401 FLDS Kids in Custody," *Salt Lake Tribune,* April 8, 2008, A1, A4.

22. Kovach, *The New York Times, supra* n. 1.

23. Adams, "401 FLDS Kids in Custody, *supra* n. 21."

24. McFadden, "Affidavit," *supra* n. 8.

25. Adams, "401 FLDS Kids in Custody." *supra* n. 21.

26. Badeau, "A Child's Journey." *supra* n. 4.

27. Ibid.; National Council of Juvenile and Family Court Judges, *Resource Guidelines: Improving Court Practice in Child Abuse and Neglect Cases* (Reno, NV: 1995), 26–30.

28. Tex. Fam. Code § 262.105 (2008).

29. Tex. Fam. Code § 262.106 (2008).

30. Ibid.

31. Brooke Adams and Kristen Moulton, "Our Children Need Us: FLDS Women Accuse State of Breaking Up Families," *Salt Lake Tribune,* April 15, 2008, A1, A4.

32. Nancy Perkins, "FLDS Mothers Say Texas Official Lied to Them," *Deseret News,* April 15, 2008 (retrieved June 24, 2008), http://www.deseretnews.com/article/content/mobile/1,5620,695270583,00.html?printView=true

33. Kristin Moulton, "Texas Defends Taking Children From Polygamous Compound," *Salt Lake Tribune,* April 15, 2008 (electronic, on file with author).

34. Badeau, "A Child's Journey," *supra* n. 4; National Council of Juvenile and Family Court Judges, *Resource Guidelines, supra* n. 27.

35. Tex. Fam. Code §§262.109, 262.201 (2008).

36. In re: B.T., 154 S.W.3d 200 (Tex. App. 2 Dist. 2004); In re: E.D.L., 105 S.W.3d 679, review denied (Tex. App. 2 Dist. 2003); In re J.M.C., 109 S.W.3d 591 (Tex. App. 2 Dist. 2003).

37. In re: Stellpflug 2001 WL 22804035 unreported (App. 4 Dist. 2003).

38. Tex. Fam. Code § 262.201 (2008).

39. Kirk Johnson and John Dougherty, "Sect's Children to Stay in State Custody for Now," *New York Times,* April 19, 2008 (retrieved May 30, 2008), http://nytimes.com/2008/04/19/us/19raid.html?_1 &ref=us&p

40. In re: Texas DFPS Petition for Writ of Mandamus, in the Supreme Court of Texas, No. 08–0391-CV-CV, (May 23, 2008), 3 (retrieved June 23, 2009), http://www.supreme.courts.state.tx.us/ebriefs/08/08039101.pdf and on file with author.

41. In re: Texas DFPS Petition, 3–4.

42. In re: Texas DFPS Petition, 5.

43. Brooke Adams and Kristen Moulton, "Judge Says FLDS Children Will Stay in Custody, Order DNA Tests," *Salt Lake Tribune,* April 19, 2008, A1, A4.

44. Adams, "Judge Says FLDS Children Will Stay in Custody."

45. In re: Texas DFPS Petition, 4. *supra* n. 40.

46. In re: Texas DFPS Petition, 4–5.

47. In re: Texas DFPS Petition, 6.

48. Johnson, "Sect's Children to Stay in State Custody for Now," *supra* n. 39.

49. Adams, "Judge Says FLDS Children Will Stay in Custody," *supra* n. 43.

50. Ibid.

51. Ibid.

52. Ibid.

53. In re: Texas DFPS Petition, 2, *supra* n. 40.

54. Adams, "Judge Says FLDS Children Will Stay in Custody." *supra* n. 43.

55. Ibid.

56. John MacCormack, "Next in the Polygamist Sect Raid, a Legal Marathon," *San Antonio Express-News in Houston Chronicle*, April 12, 2008 (retrieved May 2, 2008), http://www.chron.com/disp/story.mpl/metropolitan/5696448.html

57. MacCormack, "Next in the Polygamist Sect Raid."

58. Tex. Fam. Code §262.201(2008).

59. *Stanley v. Illinois*, 405 U.S. 645 (1972).

60. Tex. Fam. Code § 262.201 (2008).

61. Ibid.

62. Donald C. Bross and Terri James-Banks, "Family Dynamics in Child Maltreatment," in *Child Welfare Law and Practice*, eds. Marvin Ventrell and Donald N. Duquette (Denver: Bradford Publishing, 2005), 79–94, 93.

63. Tex. Fam. Code §§ 263.101, 263.002 (2008).

64. Tex. Fam. Code §§ 263.101, 263.102 (2008).

65. Tex. Fam. Code §§ 263.201, 253.202 (2008).

66. Tex. Fam. Code §§ 263.3025, 263.304 (2008).

67. Tex. Fam. Code §263.401 (2008).

68. Ben Winslow, "Texas Official Drafting Plans for FLDS children," *Deseret News*, May 8, 2008 (retrieved July 25, 2008), http://deseretnews.com/article/content/mobile/1,5620,695277366,00.html?printView=true

69. Amy Joi O'Donoghue, "Attorneys Agitated about FLDS Family Plans; Judge Questions Why," *Deseret News*, May 19, 2008 (retrieved July 25, 2005), http://findarticles.com/p/articles/mi_qn4188/is_20080519/ai_n25465014/print?tag=artBody;coll

70. Tex. Fam. Code § 263.405 (2008).

71. In re: B.T. 2004, supra n. 36.

72. In re Cochran, 151 S.W. 3d 275 (Tex. App. 6 Dist. 2004).

73. In re: Sara Steed, 2008 WL 2132014 (Tex. App.-Austin) not reported in S.W.3d.

74. In re: Sara Steed, Amended Petition for Writ of Mandamus (Tex. App.-Austin, April 30, 2008), on file with author.

75. In re: Bradshaw, Petition for Writ of Mandamus (Tex App.-Austin, May 9, 2008) with Appendix including excerpts from Trial Transcripts (on file with author).

76. *See* In re: Sara Steed, Brief of Amicus Curiae, 2008 WL 2412476 (Tex. App.-Austin, May 29, 2008) for Perciful brief and 2003 WL 25747590 for Brief of Liberty Legal Institute.

77. In re: Sara Steed, *supra* n. 73.

78. In re: Bradshaw, 2008 WL 2150524 (Tex. App-Austin, May 22, 2008).

79. In re: Texas DFPS Petition, supra n. 40 and Motion for Emergency Relief 2008 WL 2307376.

80. Response to Petition for Writ of Mandamus 2008 WL 2307380 (May 29, 2008).

81. In re: Texas DFPS Brief of Amicus ACLU, (Texas, May 29, 2008) (retrieved June 23, 2009), http://www.supreme.courts.state.tx.us/ebriefs/08/08039107.pdf and on file with author.

82. In re: Texas DFPS, 255 S.W. 3d 613, 615, 51 Tex. Sup.Ct. J. 967, 2008 WL 2212383 (Texas, May 29, 2008).

83. In re: Texas DFPS, 255 S.W. 3d 613, 615.

84. In re: Texas DFPS, 255 S.W. 3d 616–618.

85. Brooke Adams, and Julie Lyon, "State Supreme Court Says That District Judge's April 18 Order Must Be Vacated," *Salt Lake Tribune*, May 30, 2008, A1, A4.

86. Brooke Adams and Julie Lyon. "Meeting on Kids' Fate Gets Nowhere," *Salt Lake Tribune*, May 31, 2008, A1, A4.

87. Brooke Adams, "Return of FLDS Kids May Be Near," *Salt Lake Tribune*, June 2, 2008, A1, A4.

88. Brooke Adams, "Parents Rush to Pick Up Kids, Agree to Let the State Keep Tabs on FLDS Ranch," *Salt Lake Tribune*, June 3, 2008, A1, A4.

89. Tex. Fam. Code §§ 101.032, 102.003 (2008).

90. Tex. Fam. Code § 105.001 (2008).

91. Tex. Fam. Code § 261.303 (2008).

92. Texas Department of Family and Protective Services, *Child Protection Services Handbook* (2008) § 2223.4, 2223.7 available at: http://www.dfps.state.tx.us/Handbooks/CPS/default.asp

93. Tex. Fam. Code § 105.001 (2008).

94. Brooke Adams, "FLDS Family's Plight Ends Together at Ranch," *Salt Lake Tribune*, June 4, 2008, A5.

95. Brooke Adams, "All FLDS Children Reunited with Parents," *Salt Lake Tribune*, June 5, 2008, A8.

96. Julia Lyons and Brooke Adams, "Trauma of Raid May Linger for FLDS Kids: Parents Hope Love, Patience Will Heal Wounds," *Salt Lake Tribune*, June 6, 2008, B1, B2.

97. Ibid.

98. Adams, "Parents Rush to Pick Up Kids"; Brooke Adams, "Will FLDS Stick to Declaration?" *Salt Lake Tribune*, June 9, 2008, A1, A6.

99. Adams, "Will FLDS Stick to Declaration?"

100. Brooke Adams, "FLDS Parenting Classes Set," *Salt Lake Tribune*, July 4, 2008 (retrieved July 30, 2008), http://www.sltrib.com/portlet/article/html/fragments/print_article.jsp?articleId=9778881&siteId=297

101. Brooke Adams, "FLDS in Court: Texas Judge to Break Up Massive Child-Custody Case," *Salt Lake Tribune*, July 25, 2008 (retrieved July 30, 2008), http://www.sltrib.com/portlet/article/html/fragments/print_article.jsp?articleId-9997223&siteId=297

102. Brooke Adams, "Texas Wants 8 FLDS Kids Back in Foster Care," *Salt Lake Tribune*, August 6, 2008, A5; Ben Winslow, "Removal Is Sought of 8 FLDS Kids Again," *Deseret News*, August 6, 2008, A1, A5.

103. Brooke Adams, "Leave Girl Alone, Judge Tells FLDS Spokesman," *Salt Lake Tribune*, June 21, 2008, A1, A4.

104. Brooke Adams, "Teen to Lawyer: Leave Me Alone," *Salt Lake Tribune*, June 23, 2008, A1, A9.

105. Tribune Staff and Wire Services, "Records: Jeffs Conducted Teen Daughter's Wedding," *Salt Lake Tribune*, July 19, 2008, A8.

106. Adams, "Texas Wants 8 FLDS Kids Back in Foster Care," *supra* n. 102.

107. Ben Winslow, "Lawyers Want to Seal FLDS Case," *Deseret News*, March 25, 2008 (retrieved June 23, 2009), http://www.deseretnews.com/article/print/70529307/Lawyers-want-t…

108. Ben Winslow, "FLDS Custody Case Officially Ends," *Deseret News*, July 24, 2009, at A2.

109. Report: http://www.dfps.state.tx.us/documents/about/pdf/2008-12-22_Eldorado.pdf

110. Report: http://www.dfps.state.tx.us/documents/about/pdf/2008-12-22_Eldorado.pdf; see also Dan Frosch, "Texas Report Says 12 Girls at Sect Ranch Were Married," *New York Times*, December 23, 2008 (retrieved June 23, 2009), http://www.nytimes.com/2008/12/24/us/24abuse.html.

111. Report, *supra* n. 109.

112. http://www.dfps.state.tx.us/default.asp

113. Adams, "Parents Rush to Pick Up Kids," *supra* n. 88.

114. Brooke Adams, "DNA Results Arriving in Texas," *Salt Lake Tribune*, June 4, 2008, A1, A4.

115. Adams, "All FLDS Children Reunited with Parents," *supra* n. 95.

116. Brooke Adams, "Grand Jury to Convene; Indictments May Follow," *Salt Lake Tribune*, June 20, 2008, A1, A4.

117. Pat Reavy, "FLDS Grand Jury Ends for the Day," *Deseret News*, June 25, 2008 (retrieved June 22, 2009), http://www.deseretnews.com/article/1,5143700237823,00.html

118. Brooke Adams, "Texas Officials Gather More DNA Evidence for Criminal Case," *Salt Lake Tribune*, July 13, 2008, A1, A6.

119. Brooke Adams, "Grand Jury Indicts Jeffs, 5 Others," *Salt Lake Tribune*, July 23, 2008, A1, A4.

120. Emily Ramshaw, *The Dallas Morning Press*, "5 FLDS Men, Facing Charges, Turn Selves In," reprinted in *Salt Lake Tribune*, July 29, 2008, A9.

121. Adams, "FLDS in Court."

122. Ibid.

123. Ben Winslow, "Fight over FLDS Evidence Delayed until at Least May," *Deseret News*, March 9, 2009 (retrieved June 23, 2009), http://www.deseretnews.com/article/1,5143,705289715,00html

124. Ben Winslow, "Search Warrants Challenged," *Deseret News*, April 15, 2009 (retrieved June 23), http://www.deseretnews.com/article/print/7055297703/Search-warrant

125. Brooke Adams, "Trial for fourth FLDS man starts Monday" *Salt Lake Tribune*, March 8, 2010 retreived March 17, 2010, http://www.sltrib.com/portlet/article/html/fragments/print_article.jsp?articled=14524088&si

126. Brooke Adams, "Jury Sentences FLDS Man to 75 Years in Prison," *Salt Lake Tribune*, March 19, 2010. http://www.sltrib.com/polygamy/ci_14710442 (accessed 3/22/2010).

127. Ben Winslow and Nancy Perkins, "Warren Jeffs Sentenced to 2 Five to Life Terms for Child-bride Marriage," *Deseret Morning News*, November 20, 2007 (retrieved July 30, 2008), http://www.deseretnews.com/cgi-bin/cqcgi_plus. env?CQ_SESSION_KEY=VMNUBEWEMBAM.

128. In re: Bradshaw Petition, Appendix, Transcript of Hearing, Volume 5, p. 131, lines 1–7, *supra* n. 75.

129. In re: Bradshaw Petition, Appendix, Transcript of Hearing, Volume 5, p. 140, line 40–p. 141 line 3, *supra* n. 75.

130. In re: Bradshaw Petition, Appendix, Transcript of Hearing, Volume 5, p. 143, lines 18–24, *supra* n. 75.

131. Linda F. Smith, "Child Protection Law and the FLDS: There's a Better Way," *Salt Lake Tribune*, May 11, 2008, 06.

Chapter 13

The Intricacies and Ethics of Parental Genetic Testing

Deborah L. Cragun and Ryan T. Cragun

While the other chapters in this book have described various aspects of the Fundamentalist Church of Jesus Christ of Latter Day Saints (FLDS) and the April 2008 raid of the FLDS Yearning for Zion (YFZ) Ranch, this chapter focuses on only one aspect of the resulting legal struggle—the decision by the court to mandate genetic testing for parentage.[1] Parentage testing was requested by Child Protective Services (CPS) and granted by Judge Barbara Walther.[2] The media explained the justification of the DNA testing but also offered some criticism,

> The DNA samples will be matched against those taken from adults from the ranch run by the FLDS. The DNA testing of the adults from the ranch is voluntary. But the FLDS spokesman called it "unprecedented in our country on this scale." The parents have complied only because they want their children back, Parker said. "I think every American needs to be very fearful of what Child Protective Services is doing in Texas," he said. Some of the children's elusive or changing responses in interviews with child welfare workers have made murkier already ambiguous family relationships, including identifying the children's parents, child welfare officials say.[3]

As the quote above illustrates, the justification for parentage testing is based on several factors. Some FLDS parents and children were reportedly not completely forthright in volunteering their biological relationships. As a result, CPS indicated that it was having a very difficult time trying to discern which parents should be able to sue for custody of which children. Additionally, the relationships themselves are extremely complicated due to the practice of polygyny among the FLDS, and by the religiously directed reassignment of wives and children under Warren Jeffs.[4] Finally, CPS workers were also interested in trying to discern if any of the girls had been impregnated when they were underage, thereby providing evidence for criminal charges against male FLDS members. This last justification is illustrated in the following excerpt from the *Houston Chronicle:*

> What is not speculative, however, is the fact that almost 60 percent of the underage girls are pregnant or have given birth. Once complete, DNA test results could sort out familial relationships to determine whether children were fathered by adults whose age would put them firmly outside Texas laws on age of consent and statutory rape. Marrying young girls to much older adult males is widely reported to be common practice among FLDS members and part and parcel of their religious beliefs. So is grooming boys to view sex between older men and young girls as normal.[5]

The ACLU, FLDS members, and FLDS lawyers expressed concerns that the decision to perform parentage testing was made "without specific evidence that the parentage of all children was actually in dispute"[6] and that DNA testing is an invasion of privacy.[7] However, without complete records or full cooperation from the FLDS, DNA testing was portrayed as the only way to accurately determine who should have legal custody of the children. On the other hand, many of the FLDS parents denied being evasive, and the courts were later able to match many parents and children for custody hearings even before parentage test results became available.[8] In addition, the DNA tests became moot when the children were returned to their parents after the appeals court overruled Judge Walther's decision and the Texas Supreme Court agreed with the appeals court's decision.

Coerced parentage testing raises a number of practical and ethical concerns. In the discussion that follows, we describe what is involved in DNA parentage studies and explain what the results can and cannot reveal about the FLDS. This is followed by detailed information regarding genetic health risks among the FLDS that have been reported by the media. We then conclude by discussing a number of ethical implications related to topics reviewed in this chapter.

How Parentage Testing Is Performed

Genes[9] are subsections of DNA that contain the instructions for making specific proteins.[10] Proteins help determine the body's physical traits (such as eye color and height). Proteins also control the body's metabolism and serve as one of the basic materials used to build body structures. The pieces of DNA used for parentage testing are sometimes referred to as genes, even though they do not code for proteins and are not known to contribute to any physical traits.

The DNA of all humans is overwhelmingly similar, but certain DNA segments vary in size. One class of variable-length DNA regions is called short tandem repeats (STRs). Each STR is composed of repeated units that are 2–6 DNA base pairs in length. Parentage tests performed for legal purposes generally include 13–16 different STRs, 13 of which make up the standard STRs used for forensic testing in the United States.[11] These STRs were chosen mainly because they are relatively easy to use and interpret and they do not provide information about physical traits or whether a person has an increased risk to develop or pass on a genetic disease.[12] Each STR comes in many sizes; these are called alleles. The number of different alleles that exist for each STR in the human population is typically in the range of 15 to 90.[13] However, a single individual only has two alleles for each STR; one is inherited from the mother and the other from the father.

Maternity and paternity tests are performed using DNA from the child and the putative parents. DNA can be obtained from almost any cell in a person's body because each cell contains a copy of the same DNA. For parentage testing, a sample of cells is often taken by rubbing a small brush or cotton swab on the inside of a person's mouth. Once the DNA is extracted and isolated, millions of copies of each STR are made using a technique called polymerase chain reaction (PCR). The STRs are then separated by size using another technique called gel electrophoresis. After testing is completed, bands of DNA can be viewed on the gel without a microscope because each band contains millions of copies of a single STR. The pattern produced from multiple STRs is expected to be unique to each individual (except in cases of identical twins). This explains why this procedure is sometimes referred to as DNA fingerprinting.

Since half of a person's DNA is inherited from the mother and half from the father it is expected that for each STR, one allele will match up in size with one of the two alleles from a person's biological mother and the other allele will match one of the two alleles from the biological father. This is illustrated in figure 12.1, which shows a simplified illustration of a DNA profile of a child and her biological parents.

The final results of parentage testing are reported simply as a list of sizes, or number of repeats of the two alleles for each STR tested. When parents are related to each other through blood relatives, it is more likely that some of their alleles will be the same size. This will probably be found among the FLDS because many of the group's members share common ancestors. Although this may make it challenging to interpret the test results from the FLDS members,

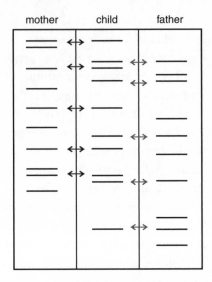

FIGURE 13.1. The above figure is a simplified illustration of three DNA fingerprints. The 10 DNA bands in each lane represent different sized alleles for each of the 5 STRs used in this example. Even though the STRs from each person form a unique pattern, the child's result shows clear similarities to the DNA fingerprint of her biological parents. Half of the child's alleles were inherited from her mother (as indicated by the black arrows) and the other alleles (indicated with gray arrows) were inherited from her father

there should still be enough variation to determine parentage. If necessary, however, the lab doing the parentage tests can include additional STRs in the DNA profile to clarify the relationships.

DNA Fingerprinting Has the Potential to Reveal Additional Information about the FLDS

Once the mother and father of a child are identified, their ages can be compared with the age of the child to determine whether the woman was a minor at the time she was impregnated by an adult male. Parentage studies could also discover information that FLDS members may not want to know, such as misattributed paternity. There is also the potential to glean additional information about family relationships or genetic risk factors from the results of parentage tests.

The greater the number of STRs that two individuals have in common, the more closely related they tend to be. There has been at least one case reported in the scientific literature in which DNA fingerprints from a mother, son, and the mother's brother were used to demonstrate probable incest.[14] However, relationships cannot always be confirmed from DNA fingerprints because people can have STRs that are the same length even if they are not related by blood. Although theoretically possible, sorting out biological relationships and creating a family pedigree using DNA fingerprints from the FLDS would be challenging, time consuming, and beyond the scope of parentage testing.[15]

Because 75–80 percent of individuals in the original polygamist group in Hilldale and Colorado City (from which the Texas group derives) are reportedly descendants of two of the original founders,[16] there are probably a significant number of individuals who are biological relatives. A couple's close biological relationship through a common ancestor is referred to as consanguinity, which is derived from the Latin: con, which means "shared," and sanguis, meaning blood. Although the terms "consanguinity" and "inbreeding" may be used interchangeably, "inbreeding" tends to hold a pejorative connotation in modern U.S. society, where the concept and practice are often stigmatized.[17] The most common form of consanguinity in the world today tends to be a relationship between first cousins.[18] Both first and second cousin relationships occur among the FLDS, according to former group members.[19]

Historically, consanguineous relationships have been quite common.[20] Famous historical figures, such as Albert Einstein and Charles Darwin, were married to their first cousins and consanguineous relationships were prevalent among the royal families in Europe. Consanguinity continues to be commonplace among a substantial percentage of the human population globally and is the preferred custom in parts of South Asia, the Middle East, and sub-Saharan Africa.[21]

However, because consanguinity in the United States is often discouraged or even illegal,[22] disclosure of consanguineous family relationships could exacerbate the stigma that is already associated with the religious and cultural practices of the FLDS. On the other hand, information obtained from DNA testing could theoretically be helpful in quantifying genetic risks that may exist within the FLDS community, though this is beyond the scope of parentage testing.

Genetic Risks Among the FLDS

Risks Associated with Consanguinity

To understand the possible genetic implications of consanguinity, it is necessary to review genetic inheritance patterns. Many genetic conditions exhibit an autosomal recessive pattern of inheritance. Autosomal refers to a gene that is not on the X or Y chromosomes; this means that both males and females are typically affected in equal numbers. Recessive means that both copies (alleles) of a particular gene must contain a disease-causing variant in order for a person to develop symptoms of the condition. This occurs when one gene variant is passed on to a child by each parent.

It is estimated that all people inherit at least a few recessive disease-causing variants in one of their two alleles,[23] but most do not have symptoms of autosomal recessive diseases because their second gene copy compensates for the disease-causing allele. However, anyone can have a child with an autosomal recessive condition if both she and her partner happen to be carriers of a disease-causing variant in the same gene. People related by blood have a higher chance of having a child with an autosomal recessive condition because they are more likely to both have inherited the same disease-causing variant from a common ancestor.

Family pedigrees and parentage studies can be used to estimate the average proportion of gene copies (alleles) shared by two individuals.[24] For instance, first cousins share an average of one-eighth of their alleles. This means that approximately 12.5 percent of their alleles are identical because they were inherited from a common ancestor. This information has the potential to help determine the chance that individuals are carriers for the same autosomal recessive disease. When both parents are carriers, there is a 1 in 4 (25%) chance with each pregnancy that they will have a baby affected with the condition, a 2 in 4 (50%) chance that the baby will be a carrier like the parents, and a 1 in 4 (25%) chance that the baby will not inherit a disease-causing variant from either parent.

Academic studies have consistently reported an increase in infant mortality in the offspring of consanguineous couples, even after controlling for important socio-demographic risk factors, such as income, education, and access to prenatal care.[25] Quantifying the increased mortality is difficult, and the magnitude of reported risk varies substantially from study to study.[26] However, based on combined data from multiple studies, offspring of first cousins probably have a 4–5 percent average increase in risk for pre-reproductive mortality above the population background risk.[27]

An increase in mortality rate among the offspring of consanguineous couples can largely be attributed to serious genetic conditions or birth defects. Although first cousins have an increased risk of having a child with a serious birth defect, the absolute risk remains relatively low.[28] Among the general population, the risk of having a child with a serious birth defect is typically in the range of 2–3 percent, while among first cousins the risk is approximately 4–6 percent, or twice the risk in the general population.[29]

Risks can be substantially higher if the parents are more closely related than first cousins. For example, among incestuous (i.e., father-daughter, or brother-sister) unions, risks of morbidity and mortality have been estimated to be anywhere from 6.8 percent to 31.4 percent; however, the small number of cases and inability to control for non-genetic variables must be taken into consideration when evaluating the upper limit of this range.[30]

The increase in morbidity and mortality among the offspring of consanguineous couples is largely due to an increase in the incidence of autosomal recessive conditions.[31] However, consanguinity does not increase risks for genetic conditions that follow other patterns of inheritance. One of these inheritance patterns is referred to as "X-linked recessive" because it occurs when the disease-causing variant is in a gene located on the X chromosome. Because there is no corresponding gene on the smaller Y chromosome, if the X chromosome a man inherits from his mother contains the disease-causing allele then he will develop symptoms. Women, on the other hand, inherit an X chromosome from both their father and their mother. This means that women do not typically develop symptoms of X-linked recessive conditions, since at least one of their two alleles is usually functional.

One well-known genetic condition that follows an X-linked recessive inheritance pattern is hemophilia, which results in a reduced blood-clotting ability. The spread of hemophilia in the royal European families during the eighteenth and nineteenth centuries is often erroneously attributed to consanguinity.[32] However, because hemophilia only requires one disease-causing allele for symptoms to appear in males, it was not the result of the consanguineous unions among the royal families. Another less well-known example is Alport syndrome, which is an X-linked condition that leads to kidney disease. The presence of this condition in members of a large Utah family has been misattributed to inbreeding among "polygamist ancestors" who were early members of the mainstream LDS church.[33]

X-linked recessive disorders, such as hemophilia and Alport syndrome discussed above, are not accurate examples of the detrimental effects of inbreeding. Similarly, consanguinity does not contribute to a higher incidence of autosomal dominant disorders in a population. In order for symptoms of an autosomal dominant condition to develop, a person only needs to inherit a single disease-causing gene variant from either parent. Whether or not parents are related does not influence the chance that a child will inherit a dominant disease-causing allele from an affected parent.

Chromosome abnormalities such as Down syndrome almost always occur sporadically. This means that the chance of having a child with a chromosome abnormality is not typically due to consanguinity or to a person's family medical history. However, because FLDS women typically have children until they are no longer able, there could be an increased prevalence of Down syndrome among FLDS infants because risks for chromosome abnormalities increase as a woman gets older. The prevalence of chromosome abnormalities could also be higher among the FLDS when compared to the general population because the FLDS do not tend to utilize prenatal testing or terminate affected pregnancies.

Other birth defects such as cleft lip, spina bifida, and congenital heart defects are influenced by a combination of genes and environmental factors. These so called "multifactorial traits" have been reported to occur at a higher frequency among consanguineous couples in a number of populations studied.[34] However, valid concerns about the methodology of some of these studies have been raised, and other studies fail to find a significantly increased risk for some of these types of birth defects.[35] Therefore, evidence that consanguinity increases the risk of multifactorial disorders is not conclusive.

The Case of Fumarase Deficiency

Among the FLDS group in Texas, it is likely that a number of individuals are carriers for an autosomal recessive condition called fumarase deficiency.[36] During the 1990s, fumarase deficiency had been reported in at least 20 children in Hilldale, Utah and Colorado City, Arizona, the FLDS towns from which the Texas group originated.[37] This condition occurs due to inadequate functioning of the enzyme fumarase, which is critical to the production of energy by mitochondria in the body's cells. Fumarase deficiency results in a combination of symptoms such as severe mental retardation, seizures, muscle problems, and brain malformations.[38] Many individuals who inherit this condition die in infancy or childhood, although survival into adulthood is possible. Those who do survive beyond infancy typically have IQs below 25 and their speech is limited, consisting of no more than a handful of words. Many are never able to walk or even sit without support.[39] Neurologic impairment is usually evident early in life due to poor feeding, low muscle tone, or slow developmental progress. However, if seizures are well controlled it is rare for a child with fumarase deficiency to lose developmental skills they have attained.[40] Individuals with fumarase deficiency require a tremendous amount of care; and they may benefit from a feeding tube, wheelchair, and/or physical, occupational and speech therapies. Unfortunately there is no cure for this condition.

Media coverage about fumarase deficiency amidst the reports on parentage testing and custody issues may have contributed to confusion about these topics. For instance, the title of a news story by NPR, "Gene Disorder Complicates

Sect Custody Fight," was misleading.[41] Although the content of the story was technically accurate, it failed to make an argument for how the presence of fumarase deficiency among the FLDS could complicate the custody battle. This story also failed to clearly explain that there are important differences between the DNA testing performed for parentage studies and genetic testing to determine if someone is a carrier for fumarase deficiency. The NPR report did not break new ground on this issue, but rather reexamined general information that had been exposed in the media a few years earlier about fumarase deficiency among the FLDS in Hilldale and Colorado City.

Discussing fumarase deficiency, especially in light of the DNA testing for custody purposes, should be done carefully and clearly, so as not to confuse the public. In reality, fumarase deficiency played no role in the custody battle. Furthermore, parentage testing cannot directly determine if someone is a carrier for this condition because it provides no information about protein coding genes. Parentage testing could, however, reveal that individuals are related to someone with fumarase deficiency. If this were to happen, then the chance that these individuals are carriers of fumarase deficiency could be calculated. Although testing to identify the gene variant causing fumarase deficiency among the FLDS is available, this type of DNA testing requires voluntary consent and would need to be performed at a specialized laboratory (only a few labs in the world perform DNA testing for fumarase deficiency).

Comparison of Genetic Risks in FLDS and Amish Populations

The FLDS share similarities to the Old Order Amish who emigrated from Europe to the United States in the mid-1700s, subsequently settling in Pennsylvania, Ohio, and Indiana, where they have remained isolated through religious and social mechanisms.[42] Both the FLDS and Amish founded settlements that began with a relatively small number of individuals, but grew substantially after generations of endogamy (the practice of mating within isolated populations). Despite this growth, genetic variation between individuals in Amish populations remains limited;[43] and compared to the general U.S. population, the Amish have a high prevalence of a number of rare autosomal recessive diseases.[44]

Given the potential impact that endogamy and consanguinity can have on the genetic makeup of a population, the question as to why more genetic disorders are not commonly found within the FLDS population has been raised.[45] This may seem puzzling at first, because the Amish have an increased risk for many rare genetic conditions, despite first and second cousin marriage being uncommon.[46] The answer may be due to the fact that Amish societies in the

United States were founded approximately two hundred years earlier than the FLDS and there has been more time for the degree of relatedness to increase between the Amish due to numerous generations of distant cousin marriages.[47] Based on the Amish experience, it is therefore quite possible that more genetic disorders will appear among the FLDS in subsequent generations (assuming cultural isolation continues and few if any new members from outside the population join). There may already be other recessive disorders among the FLDS that outsiders are not aware of yet.

Despite the increased risks for recessive disorders that are present among endogamous populations (such as the FLDS and Amish), the absolute risks remain quite low.[48] This means that autosomal recessive genetic conditions affect, at most, only a small percentage of children born into these communities.

Polygamy Is Not Responsible For Increasing Genetic Risks

Despite the many similarities between the Amish and the FLDS, there are also some important differences. Perhaps the most salient difference is the FLDS practice of polygyny (a specific type of polygamy in which men have more than one wife). This practice has been criticized by erroneously implicating polygyny as a major underlying cause of the relatively high rates of fumarase deficiency among the FLDS. This criticism is illustrated in the following quote from the *Phoenix New Times:*

> Polygamy leads to sexual predation, and that leads to genetic
> problems," says Rehabilitative Services' Tarby. "If you stop the sexual
> predation, you stop the genetic problem as well. But [FLDS members]
> don't think of it as sexual predation. That's the big problem."[49]

In reality, "polygamy" is not the "big problem" when it comes to genetic conditions. Polygyny can actually increase genetic variation in populations that are not endogamous or consanguineous.[50] Genetic evidence suggests that polygyny was practiced among humans until fairly recently in our evolutionary past.[51] The stigma of polygynous relationships is a relatively recent social invention based on the moral beliefs of late medieval Christianity.[52] From evolutionary, anthropological, and sociological perspectives, the criminalization of polygyny makes very little sense, though the regulation of such practice to consenting adults is an obvious criterion for legalization. At the very least, polygyny should not be blamed for the increased prevalence of fumarase deficiency among the FLDS. If there is any reason to be concerned about the FLDS, their lifestyle, and genetics, it should be with regard to underage marriages, consanguineous relationships, and lack of genetic flow into and out of the population, and not the actual practice of polygyny.

Ethical Implications

In this section we discuss a number of ethical issues related to genetic testing, but leave much of the discussion regarding FLDS culture and the raid itself to other chapters in this book. The goal of this section is to raise awareness of the many ethical conflicts and a few legal concerns related to genetic testing. We do not attempt to resolve all of these issues. Additionally, we refer the reader to chapter 12 in this volume for a comprehensive discussion of legal issues related to the FLDS.

The ethical framework used in this section relies heavily on the concepts of biomedical ethics as laid out by Veatch.[53] A discussion of ethics often includes an evaluation of costs and benefits using the "consequentialist" bioethical principles of beneficence and nonmaleficence. Essentially, this means that the ethical course of action is focused on the production of good consequences (beneficence) and the avoidance of bad consequences (nonmaleficence). However, actions based only on the likely consequences are not always ethical, since they often ignore the concept of respect for individual persons. Therefore, duty-based principles, such as autonomy (the idea that people should be able to make their own decisions free from the interference of others), fidelity (the concept that promises and contracts should be kept), veracity (duty to tell the truth), and justice should also be taken into account.[54] Additional considerations include legal aspects (i.e. criminal justice and privacy issues), the effects an action may have on third parties (including society at large), and practical realities (such as financial costs and the allocation of limited resources). These factors and bioethical principles often conflict with one another, making it difficult to determine the best course of action. In the following sections we discuss these conflicts.

Court Ordered Parentage Testing

Are the beneficent intentions of CPS to protect the FLDS children from abuse and/or the potential for abuse enough to supersede the responsibilities of society and the legal system to respect individual FLDS members' autonomy and privacy rights? This is a major question that should be asked when evaluating ethical and legal aspects of the raid and parentage testing.

According to the Uniform Parentage Act (160.502), court-ordered genetic testing to establish parentage is allowed in Texas.[55] However, if the parentage of all the FLDS children was not actually in question, then it could be argued that parentage testing for all of the children is not warranted because it violates individual privacy and autonomy. It can also be argued that FLDS parents felt coerced to submit presumably "voluntary" DNA samples, believing it was the only way they would be able to obtain custody of their children in a timely manner,[56] again violating autonomy.

Although fiscal matters should never be more important than the welfare of children, consideration of the financial costs raises additional questions regarding the reasonableness of parentage testing for all the FLDS children. Despite receiving a discounted rate, the State of Texas (i.e., Texas taxpayers) reportedly paid a total of $110,000 for expenses related to parentage testing.[57] This raises obvious questions of whether parentage testing was a wise use of limited resources and whether it is fair to burden taxpayers with the expense.[58] Even though this is a pittance compared to the millions of dollars spent on the raid itself,[59] many parent-child relationships had been sorted out before parentage tests were completed, and the results of all the tests were later considered to be moot because the courts ordered the children to be returned after concluding that the raid was not justified.[60] In hindsight, there were probably more prudent ways to determine parentage that would have been less of a burden on taxpayers and less disruptive to the lives of the FLDS members. Why Judge Walther ordered immediate DNA testing for all the children is not clear. However, CPS workers reportedly expressed their hope early on that the tests would prove helpful to the criminal investigation.[61]

Use of Parentage Testing in Criminal Investigations

Although unclear in the initial press coverage we reviewed, it was later reported that results from parentage testing will not be shared with individuals involved in the criminal investigation, and they cannot be used as evidence for criminal cases without a separate court order.[62] However, some of the articles expressed ambivalence regarding the use of these results in criminal investigations. To explore the ethics and legality of this issue, it will first be helpful to compare and contrast DNA tests performed for parentage studies with those used in criminal cases.

Parentage tests share a number of similarities to DNA tests used in criminal cases. Both types of tests are used for identification purposes. They are performed using the same lab techniques and most of the same genetic markers (STRs). Additionally, they do not examine DNA regions currently known to contribute to physical traits or health risks, distinguishing them from medical genetic tests.[63]

The DNA Identification Act of 1994 formalized the FBI's authority to establish a database containing DNA profiles for "law enforcement purposes."[64] The DNA identification act allows DNA to be obtained from certain convicts or parolees without a warrant, probable cause, or even individualized suspicion. The law also allowed for the creation of the Combined DNA Index System (CODIS), a software system maintained by the FBI that allows for state, local, and federal authorities to share and search DNA profiles. One section of this database contains the profiles of certain convicted criminals and parolees; separate indexes within CODIS contain profiles from missing persons, unidentified human remains, and relatives of missing persons who have voluntarily contributed a sample. Importantly, CODIS does not contain DNA profiles from parentage testing.

The American Civil Liberties Union has assisted in several legal challenges to "DNA fingerprinting laws," as "unreasonable search and seizure" forbidden by the Fourth Amendment to the U.S. Constitution.[65] The courts have agreed that obtaining a blood or DNA sample (for identification purposes) constitutes a search. However, the rulings have upheld that such testing can indeed be obtained without consent based on three main arguments: (1) criminals "have a diminished expectation of privacy"; (2) government and public interest to enforce the law outweighs individual privacy rights; or (3) the "special needs" clause in the Fourth Amendment.[66]

Considering the arguments above, using parentage studies as part of a criminal investigation of FLDS members is questionable from an ethical and legal standpoint. These adults were not reported to be convicts or parolees and would therefore not "have reduced expectations of privacy." Thus, without probable cause or at least individualized suspicion, using parentage tests to support a criminal case may be considered an "unreasonable" search under the Fourth Amendment. On the other hand, CPS workers and other government officials continue to argue that the need to protect minors (beneficence) outweighs individual autonomy protected by the Fourth Amendment.

Regardless of the legality, advocates of parentage testing for all the FLDS children are taking a "consequentialist" ethical perspective, arguing that the potential good in protecting minors from sexual abuse outweighs any potential for negative consequences caused by using the DNA test results obtained for parentage studies. In their minds, withholding the results of parentage testing out of concerns for privacy cannot be justified. However, failing to uphold the rights laid out in the Fourth Amendment ignores duty-based principles. The result is an ethical conflict between the principles of autonomy and fidelity and the principles of nonmaleficence (preventing future harm to children) and justice (i.e., the investigation and prosecution of suspected sex offenders).

Whether or not it is ethical or legal to use results from parentage studies in the criminal investigation may also be complicated by the "special needs" clause in the Fourth Amendment. The "special needs" exemption has been cited in court decisions to argue the Constitutionality of using evidence from administrative searches or seizures in criminal cases even though it was obtained without probable cause.[67] Courts have generally found that the "special needs" exemption applies only if the primary reason for the search is unrelated to law enforcement.[68] This raises the question of whether the "special needs" clause could justify using results from parentage tests in the criminal investigation based on the assumption that testing was ordered to determine custody rather than for law enforcement purposes.

Speculation that parentage studies will be used to determine if men fathered children with underage girls is not unfounded. Texas criminal investigators obtained a warrant in June 2008 to collect a DNA sample from Warren Jeffs as part of an investigation into allegations involving "spiritual marriages" with four underage girls at the YFZ ranch in Texas.[69] Although the officials indicated that the DNA testing was not related to the Texas custody cases,[70] performing DNA testing on the sample taken from Jeffs will only be useful in proving inappropriate sexual relationships if the results are compared with DNA test results obtained from FLDS children and putative victims. In this specific case, however, taking DNA from Jeffs was probably legal and ethical as he does have "reduced expectations of privacy" since he has already been convicted of being an accomplice to rape by performing the marriage of a 14-year-old girl to a 19-year-old male. Furthermore, the marriage records and pictures (which were confiscated during the raid of the YFZ ranch and cited in the warrant to obtain DNA from Jeffs) provide probable cause, or at least individualized suspicion.[71]

Situations that create conflicts are often resolved by balancing the ethical principles involved. Regarding parentage testing of the FLDS, the principles of autonomy (i.e., ability of the FLDS to live without interference from others) and fidelity (i.e., obligation to uphold rights laid out by the Fourth Amendment) can be weighed against the principles of beneficence, nonmaleficence, and criminal justice. These issues remain debatable, and different conclusions may be reached depending on the importance one assigns to each of the ethical principles involved. However, once the actual consequences of a decision are known, evaluating the situation may become easier and/or may lead to different conclusions than were reached before the decision was implemented. Considering the information we now have after the raid, taking DNA from all the parents and children was likely unwarranted. But, having done so, it may be ethical and legal to compare the DNA fingerprints that were created for establishing custody with the DNA sample that was obtained from Warren Jeffs after establishing probable cause and securing a warrant.

Disclosure of Genetic Information

A number of ethical and legal questions can arise regarding if, when, or to whom genetic information should be disclosed. For example, in cases where parentage testing reveals nonpaternity, which parties should have the right to know about the results? Even if infidelity is uncommon among the FLDS, a fair number of FLDS children have been reassigned to other "fathers" by Warren Jeffs.[72] This could complicate paternity issues; particularly if some FLDS members hold the alleged belief that when children are reassigned to a new father, their DNA changes according-ly.[73] Based on the ethical principle of veracity, the possibility of non-paternity should typically be discussed with putative parents as part of the informed consent process prior to performing parentage testing so that parties are aware of this possibility and can determine how this information should be handled.[74]

The potential that DNA fingerprints have to reveal information beyond parent-child relationships can result in ethical conflicts. For example, parentage tests could provide evidence that a couple is closely related by blood. Because Texas does not place legal restrictions on first cousin marriage, criminal pros-ecution for consanguinity is unlikely to be an issue. However, if the test results indicated that a couple could be more closely related than first cousins, should this information be revealed to law enforcement officials?

Other concerns stem from the knowledge that DNA encodes a great deal of personal information about disease predisposition and behavioral tenden-cies. These concerns should not be overstated because forensic and parentage tests examine fewer than 20 DNA regions, which do not encode proteins and are not known to be associated with any health, physical, or behavioral traits.[75] However, in the case of the FLDS, parentage testing could indirectly reveal an increased risk for a genetic condition if an individual is found to be related to a biological relative who is affected with that condition. Even though the principle of autonomy and the right to privacy make it clear that this information should not be revealed to the public, the question remains as to whether at-risk family members should be informed. For instance, if it were discovered that an FLDS member is closely related to someone who had a child with fumarase defi-ciency, what would be the proper course of action? Disclosing this information, so that the individual is aware of the potential risk to have an affected child, is supported based on the ethical principles of veracity and beneficence. On the other hand, privacy issues and autonomy (including the right a person has to not know) support the decision not to disclose such information. Although FLDS members with a family history of fumarase deficiency may experience this type of ethical conflict, it is unlikely that parentage testing will create such an issue as long as the DNA is used solely to determine parent-child relation-ships and family medical information is not obtained.

The chances that harm will occur as the result of DNA samples being used for additional testing are probably low, but this is often cited as a concern associated with DNA identification testing.[76] DNA is often stored by labs for varying periods of time and may be used for quality assurance purposes. Certified DNA labs generally have policies that require an individual's written consent in order to perform additional genetic testing beyond what is necessary for quality control;[77] and it is unlikely that any commercial lab would perform unrequested tests because it would incur additional expenses and cut into their profit. However, labs may allow DNA to be used for research purposes as long as all information that could directly identify the individual has been removed.[78] Although such testing may benefit society by contributing to scientific knowledge, it could infringe upon an individual's autonomy if the sample were re-identified.

There are two additional protections that may reduce worry about the above issue. The first is the requirement for research studies using human DNA to be approved by an institutional review board, which helps ensure that use of the samples is ethical and that individual rights are not violated. Furthermore, if privacy were invaded, two federal laws provide protection against disclosure of and discrimination based on genetic health information. The Health Insurance Portability and Accountability Act of 1996 provides certain restrictions concerning the release of personal health information[79] and offers limited protection against health insurance discrimination based on genetic test results. The Genetic Information Nondiscrimination Act of 2008 offers much greater protection against discrimination by both health insurers and employers once all provisions of this law took effect in 2009.

These laws are in agreement with the conclusion that an individual's autonomy to decide whether to share personal genetic information with others tends to trump arguments for disclosure that are based on other bioethical principles. Therefore it is generally unethical to disclose family relationships or other information obtained from genetic tests to the general public or other third parties. Respect for individual autonomy also dictates that the results of genetic tests and DNA samples should only be used for the intended purposes for which they were obtained.

Genetic Testing and Reproductive Freedom

DNA testing is available that has the potential to find the disease-causing gene variants in an individual with fumarase deficiency. If the disease-causing variant responsible for fumarase deficiency among the FLDS were identified, then a community-wide screening program could be initiated to determine whether healthy FLDS members are carriers and are therefore at risk to have an affected child. However, government officials involved in the Texas raid never mentioned or advocated testing for fumarase deficiency. Furthermore, FLDS members have reportedly shown no interest in finding out if they are carriers, according to the neurologist who diagnosed many of the affected children and spoke with a large group of FLDS members about the genetic nature of the condition.[80] While it has not always been part of scientific or health care practice to require the consent of individuals prior to performing genetic testing, it is now considered an essential part of medical and scientific practice to do so.[81] Despite the ethical responsibility of health professionals to do good for the patient (the principle of beneficence), the autonomy of the individual is typically the primary consideration, based on both legal precedent and codes laid out by various organizations of health care professionals.[82]

Even if FLDS members pursued carrier screening, it would only be effective in reducing the incidence of fumarase deficiency if reproductive decisions are altered based on the information. The professional position of genetic counselors is to allow individuals the autonomy to make their own reproductive decisions, based on accurate and complete information (National Society of Genetic Counselors Position Statements, accessible at www.nsgc.org). Nevertheless, arranging marriages in such a way that both members of each couple do not carry a disease-causing variant for the same autosomal recessive condition could be considered beneficent because it would reduce the number of individuals who are born with the condition. While this approach substantially reduced the birth prevalence of autosomal recessive conditions within Ashkenazi Jewish populations,[83] it is less likely that the leadership of the FLDS will be interested in genetic screening. Doing so is arguably not faith-promoting within a religion in which marriages are arranged by the group's leader based on alleged inspiration from God.[84] Unless a new theological principle is introduced into FLDS doctrine that justifies the use of genetic information in making these decisions, carrier screening will not likely be utilized among members of the FLDS population.[85]

Ethicists and the legal system of the United States typically support the idea that upholding reproductive autonomy is generally more important than other competing ethical principles or rights.[86] This freedom includes the ability to determine whether to have children, whether to perform genetic testing on embryos (a procedure known as preimplantation genetic diagnosis), whether to have genetic testing during pregnancy, and whether to terminate a fetus.[87]

Considering that restricting reproductive freedom is currently illegal in the United States and most modern Western societies,[88] this raises the possibility that the incidence of autosomal recessive diseases will continue to increase among the FLDS. Because birth control, prenatal testing, and abortion contradict the beliefs of the FLDS, they are unlikely to utilize these technologies. From the FLDS viewpoint, it is simply God's will for them to have one or more children with birth defects.[89] There is also a belief among the FLDS that these children are a special gift from God and that the resulting challenges parents experience in caring for them are part of God's plan to test parents and prove them worthy.[90]

The principle of autonomy would argue that parents should be able to have as many children as they want. However, the principles of beneficence, non-maleficence, and justice could be used to argue that it is unfair to knowingly bring a child into the world who will suffer severe medical complications and/or that it is unjust for others (i.e., taxpayers) to bear the financial burden associated with their care. The latter point may sound callous, but this issue has been raised in media reports about fumarase deficiency among the FLDS.[91] Though not believed to be the case at the FLDS ranch in Texas,[92] a number of FLDS members from the Hilldale–Colorado City area, including those who have children with fumarase deficiency, reportedly use governmental health programs such as Medicaid, MRDD services, and WIC.[93] These reports and the reality that caring for individuals with severe genetic conditions is expensive raise the following ethical and practical questions: Who should bear the financial responsibility for children with genetic conditions and special needs? Should this differ depending on whether the parents were aware of the risks or of the diagnosis prior to pregnancy or birth?

Ethical conflicts also arise when considering consanguineous relationships and reproductive freedom. A working group of medical and social science experts organized by the World Health Organization concluded that "consanguineous marriage is an integral part of cultural and social life in many areas [of the world] and that attempts to discourage it at the population level are inappropriate and undesirable, even though it is associated with an increased birth prevalence of children with recessive disorders."[94] This same paper essentially argues that the ethical principle of autonomy and the respect for cultural tradition outweigh the possible negative consequences of consanguineous marriage. Certainly the FLDS share a unique culture that limits their options when it comes to marrying someone in their faith, and it is unreasonable for us to expect that they would be willing to marry an outsider.

Additionally, there is a principle of egalitarian justice in play here: We do not try to stop non-consanguineous couples from reproducing after having a child with an autosomal recessive condition even though there is a 25 percent chance that their next child will also be affected. Why then should reproductive restrictions be placed on first cousins, especially when the risks for most biologically related couples to have a child with a serious genetic condition are substantially less than 25 percent? Thus, equality, autonomy, and culture are all complicating factors when it comes to the ethical discussions of consanguinity, genetic risks, and reproductive freedom.

Although freedom to make reproductive decisions should be respected, this should not be interpreted as a recommendation to health care professionals to refrain from informing all individuals (including those who are in consanguineous relationships or who belong to religious groups that reject genetic technology) of the possible outcomes, treatments, and reproductive options available to them. To the contrary, the ethical principles of veracity and autonomy dictate that all individuals should have access to accurate, scientific information when making their decisions.

The ability to provide such information to individuals can be complicated by religious worldviews and individual values or beliefs. Knowledge of genetic risks may lead to ethical conflicts and questions. For example, if individuals are at risk of having a child with a genetic disease but they do not believe the underlying cause is genetic, do they or the medical practitioner have a responsibility to inform family members who are at increased risk? Furthermore, the best way to approach groups of people, such as the FLDS, who may reject scientific information that does not easily fit into their particular worldview, values, and beliefs is not always clear.

Conclusions

In this chapter we have attempted to explain the intricacies of parentage testing. To do so we illustrated how parentage testing involves the comparison of DNA samples. Practically, such testing does not provide information about a person's genetic health risks. Therefore, parentage testing will not directly reveal whether FLDS couples are at risk to have a child with fumarase deficiency, an autosomal recessive genetic condition that causes health problems and mental retardation.

Although most FLDS children are healthy, fumarase deficiency occurs more frequently among the FLDS than any other population in the world. The relatively high prevalence of this condition has erroneously been attributed to the FLDS practice of polygyny. However, it is actually the result of reproductive isolation and consanguineous relationships within a population that arose from a small number of founding families.

Parentage tests have the power to reveal information about consanguinity, non-paternity, and biological relationships that could potentially be used to calculate genetic risks. The ethical course of action in such cases should be to inform the parties involved about these rare possibilities and to use the test results and DNA samples only for the intended purpose, which is to determine or confirm parent-child relationships. Privacy concerns and the principle of autonomy also dictate that results should not generally be shared with third parties, though maintaining confidentiality can lead to ethical conflicts under some circumstances.

The intersections between genetic testing, consanguinity, religion, and reproductive freedom can lead to a number of ethical conflicts, which were explored in this chapter. Although actions that respect individual autonomy generally prevail, breaching autonomy may occasionally be justified if arguments based on justice, beneficence, and nonmaleficence are determined to carry greater weight.

Reproductive freedom has and should probably continue to trump other competing issues, but concerns about the consequences of consanguinity and continued reproduction within the isolated FLDS community cannot be ignored. On the other hand, these concerns are not unique to the FLDS, and the absolute magnitude of genetic risks associated with these practices is relatively small.

NOTES

1. We use the more inclusive, gender-neutral term "parentage" over the masculine term "paternity," particularly since the maternity of at least some of the children also appeared to be in question.

2. CNN, "Sect Children Will Stay in State Custody, Judge Rules," CNN.com, April 18, 2008, http://www.cnn.com/2008/CRIME/04/18/polygamy.custody/index. html (accessed May 13, 2008).

3. Cheryl Getty, "Dozens of Sect Children Moved to Foster Care," CNN.com, April 22, 2008, http://www.cnn.com/2008/CRIME/04/22/polygamy.testing/index. html (accessed June 5, 2008).

4. When Warren Jeffs took over the FLDS, he excommunicated men who did not show sufficient allegiance, disagreed with him, or were not deemed worthy (Elissa Wall and Lisa, *Stolen Innocence: My Story of Growing Up in a Polygamous Sect, Becoming a Teenage Bride, and Breaking Free of Warren Jeffs*, New York: William Morrow, 2008). The wives and children of these men were reassigned to other men in the group.

5. *Houston Chronicle*, "In the Balance: Massive Abuse Case Forces Texas to Weigh Protecting Children against Individuals' Right to a Day in Court," *Houston Chronicle*, May 1, 2008.

6. ACLU, "ACLU Statement on the Government's Actions Regarding the Yearning For Zion Ranch in Eldorado, Texas." http://www.aclu.org/religion/ gen/35123res20080502.html (accessed May 27, 2008).

7. CNN, "ACLU Weighs in on Texas Polygamist Custody Case," CNN.com, April 20, 2008, http://www.cnn.com/2008/CRIME/04/20/polygamy.sect/index.html (accessed May 13, 2008).

8. Brooke Adams, "FLDS Update: Polygamous Sect's DNA Testing Results Arriving in Texas," *Salt Lake Tribune,* June 3, 2008, http://www.sltrib.com/polygamy/ci_9466525 (Accessed June 6, 2008).

9. This definition is highly simplified and is not inclusive of all known genes. For a thorough discussion of how the definition of a gene has evolved and continues to be disputed, see Mark B. Gerstein et al., "What Is a Gene, Post-ENCODE? History and Updated Definition," *Genome Research* 17 (2007): 669–681.

10. Ibid.

11. Christain M. Ruitberg, Dennis J. Reeder, and John M. Butler, "STRBase: A Short Tandem Repeat DNA Database for the Human Identity Testing community," *Nucl. Acids Res.* 29 (2001): 320–322.

12. John M. Butler, "Genetics and Genomics of Core Short Tandem Repeat Loci Used in Human Identity Testing," *Journal of Forensic Sciences* 51 (2006): 253–265; M. Dawn Herkenham, "Retention of Offender DNA Samples Necessary to Ensure and Monitor Quality of Forensic DNA Efforts: Appropriate Safeguards Exist to Protect the DNA Samples from Misuse," *The Journal of Law, Medicine & Ethics: A Journal of the American Society of Law, Medicine & Ethics* 34 (2006): 380–384.

13. Butler, "Genetics and Genomics of Core Short Tandem Repeat Loci," *Journal of Forensic Sciences.*

14. R. A. Wells, B. Wonke, and S. L. Thein, "Prediction of Consanguinity Using Human DNA Fingerprints." *Journal of Medical Genetics* 25 (1988): 660–662.

15. It is also extremely unlikely that any lab would complete such a family pedigree due to privacy restrictions.

16. Jason Szep, "Polygamist Community Faces Rare Genetic Disorder," *Reuters,* June 14, 2007, online edition http://www.reuters.com/article/idUSN0727298120070614 (accessed May 21, 2008).

17. Robin L. Bennett et al., "Genetic Counseling and Screening of Consanguineous Couples and Their Offspring: Recommendations of the National Society of Genetic Counselors," *Journal of Genetic Counseling* 11 (2002): 97–119.

18. Alan H. Bittles, "The Role and Significance of Consanguinity as a Demographic Variable," *Population & Development Review* 20 (1994): 561–584.

19. John Hollenhorst, "Birth Defect Is Plaguing Children in FLDS Towns," *Deseret News,* February 8, 2006, http://www.deseretnews.com/dn/view/0,1249,635182923,00.html (accessed May 21, 2008); Elissa Wall and Lisa Pulitzer, op cit.

20. Allen H. Bittles, "The Bases of Western Attitudes to Consanguineous Marriage," Developmental Medicine and Child Neurology 45 (2003): 135–138.

21. Alan H. Bittles, "Empirical Estimates of the Global Prevalence of Consanguineous Marriage In Contemporary Societies," Unpublished manuscript, 1998, www.stanford.edu/group/morrinst/pdf/MorrisonPN0074.pdf

22. States generally prohibit marriages between first- and second-degree relatives. A number of states, including Utah, also outlaw marriages between third-degree relatives (i.e., first cousins); however, a majority of states in the United States, including Texas, allow first-cousin marriage.

23. Amy R. McCune et al., "A Low Genomic Number of Recessive Lethals in Natural Populations of Bluefin Killifish and Zebrafish," *Science* 296 (2002): 2398–2401.

24. Methods used to estimate relatedness are rather complex and beyond the scope of this chapter.

25. Suzanne Joseph, "Kissing Cousins Consanguineous Marriage and Early Mortality in a Reproductive Isolate," *Current Anthropology* 48 (2007): 756–764.

26. L. B. Jorde, "Consanguinity and Prereproductive Mortality in the Utah Mormon Population." *Human Heredity* 52 (2001): 61–65.

27. Most of these studies were in countries with few medical resources and therefore may not reflect what is happening in the United States or other highly developed countries; Alan H. Bittles and James V. Neel, "The Costs of Human Inbreeding and Their Implications for Variations at the DNA Level," *Nat Genet* 8 (1991): 117–121.

28. Bennett, "Counseling and Screening of Consanguineous Couples."

29. Ibid.

30. Ibid.; Allen H. Bittles, "Genetic Aspects of Inbreeding and Incest," in *Inbreeding, Incest, and the Incest Taboo* (Stanford, CA: Stanford University Press, 2004), 38–60.

31. S. Bundey and H. Alam, "A Five-Year Prospective Study of the Health of Children in Different Ethnic Groups, With Particular Reference to the Effect of Inbreeding," *European Journal Of Human Genetics: EJHG* 1 (1993): 206–219.

32. Bennett, "Counseling and Screening of Consanguineous Couples."

33. Although not the focus of this book, as the mainstream LDS are distinct from the FLDS, it is worth noting here that genetic studies of the mainstream LDS population in Utah show little evidence of inbreeding (Jorde 1989, 2001). Studies also confirm that mainstream Mormons are genetically very similar to other Caucasians of European descent in the general U.S. population (McLellan, Jorde, and Skolnick 1984); L. B. Jorde, "Inbreeding in the Utah Mormons: An Evaluation of Estimates Based on Pedigrees, Isonymy, and Migration Matrices." *Annals Of Human Genetics* 53 (1989): 339–355; Jorde, "Consanguinity in the Utah Mormon Population," *Human Heredity;* T. L. B. McLellan, L. B. Jorde, and M. H. Skolnick, "Genetic Distances between the Utah Mormons and Related Populations." *American Journal of Human Genetics* 36 (1984): 836–857; Llinda Walker, Linda, "Fatal Inheritance: Mormon Eugenics," *Science as Culture,* January 17, 2004, http://human-nature.com/science-as-culture/walker.html (accessed May 22, 2008).

34. Abdulbari Bener, Rafat Hussain, and Ahmad S. Teebi, "Consanguineous Marriages and Their Effects on Common Adult Diseases: Studies from an Endogamous Population," *Medical Principles and Practice: International Journal of the Kuwait University, Health Science Centre* 16 (2007): 262–267; Mohammad El Mouzan, Abdullah Al Salloum, Abdullah Al Herbish, Mansour Qurachi, and Ahmad Al Omar, "Consanguinity and Major Genetic Disorders in Saudi Children: A Community-Based Cross-Sectional Study," *Annals of Saudi medicine* 28 (2008): 169–173; Mohammed Mehboob Elahi et al., "Epidemiology of Cleft Lip and Cleft Palate in Pakistan," *Plastic and Reconstructive Surgery* 113 (2004): 1548–1555; W. R. Murshid, "Spina Bifida in

Saudi Arabia: Is Consanguinity among the Parents a Risk Factor?" *Pediatric Neurosurgery* 32 (2000): 10–12; Fouzia Perveen and Subhana Tyyab, "Frequency and Pattern of Distribution of Congenital Anomalies in the Newborn and Associated Maternal Risk Factors," *Journal of the College of Physicians and Surgeons—Pakistan: JCPSP* 17 (2007): 340–343; A. Rajab, A. Vaishnav, N. V. Freeman, and M. A. Patton, "Neural Tube Defects and Congenital Hydrocephalus in the Sultanate of Oman," *Journal of Tropical Pediatrics* 44 (1998): 300–303; M. H. Rajabian and M. Sherkat, "An Epidemiologic Study of Oral Clefts in Iran: Analysis of 1,669 Cases," *The Cleft Palate-Craniofacial Journal: Official Publication of the American Cleft Palate-Craniofacial Association* 37 (2000): 191–196; Smitha Ramegowda and Nallur B. Ramachandra, "Parental Consanguinity Increases Congenital Heart Diseases in South India." *Annals of Human Biology* 33 (2006): 519–528; M. Rittler, R. Liascovich, J. López-Camelo, and E. E. Castilla, "Parental Consanguinity in Specific Types of Congenital Anomalies," *American Journal of Medical Genetics* 102 (2001): 36–43; Khalid Yunis, et al., "Consanguineous Marriage and Congenital Heart Defects: A Case-Control Study in the Neonatal Period." *American Journal of Medical Genetics. Part A* 140 (2006): 1524–1530.

35. S. A. al-Bustan et al., "Epidemiological and Genetic Study of 121 Cases of Oral Clefts in Kuwait," *Orthodontics & Craniofacial Research* 5 (2007): 154–160; Allen H. Bittles, "Congenital Heart Disease and Consanguineous Marriage in South India," *Annals of Human Biology* 34 (2007): 682–683; author reply, 683; C. Stoltenberg, P. Magnus, R. T. Lie, A. K. Daltveit, and L. M. Irgens, "Birth Defects and Parental Consanguinity in Norway," *American Journal of Epidemiology* 145 (1997): 439–448; M. K. Thong, J. J. Ho, and N. N. Khatijah, "A Population-Based Study of Birth Defects in Malaysia," *Annals of Human Biology* 32 (2005): 180–187.

36. Hilary Hylton, "Tracing the Polygamists' Family Tree," *Time*, April 20, 2008, online edition http://www.time.com/time/nation/article/0,8599,1732498,00. html?imw=Y (accessed May 21, 2008).

37. Hollenhorst, "Birth Defect."

38. For further information about fumarase deficiency, visit www.genetests.org

39. J. F. Kerrigan, K. A. Aleck, T. J. Tarby, C. R. Bird, and R. A. Heidenreich, "Fumaric Aciduria: Clinical and Imaging Features," *Annals of Neurology* 47 (2000): 583–588.

40. Ibid.

41. NPR, "Gene Disorder Complicates Sect Custody Fight," *NPR Weekend Edition*, April 27, 2008, radio broadcast http://www.npr.org/templates/story/story. php?storyId=89979940 (accessed May 22, 2008).

42. John A. Hostetler, *Amish Society*, 4th ed. (Baltimore: The Johns Hopkins University Press, 1993).

43. M. J. Khoury, B. H. Cohen, C. A. Newill, W. Bias, and V. A. McKusick, "Inbreeding and Prereproductive Mortality in the Old Order Amish. II. Genealogic Epidemiology of Prereproductive Mortality," *American Journal of Epidemiology* 125 (1987): 462–472; Luba M. Pardo, Ian MacKay, Ben Oostra, Cornelia M. van Duijn, and Yurii S. Aulchenko, "The Effect of Genetic Drift in a Young Genetically Isolated Population," *Annals of Human Genetics* 69 (2005): 288–295.

44. D. Holmes Morton, et al., "Pediatric Medicine and the Genetic Disorders of the Amish and Mennonite People of Pennsylvania." *American Journal of Medical Genetics. Part C, Seminars in Medical Genetics* 121C (2003): 5–17; Michael A. Patton, "Genetic Studies in the Amish Community," *Annals of Human Biology* 32 (2005): 163–167.

45. Dan Childs, "Polygamist Sects: How They Avoid Inbreeding Problems," *Huffington Post*, April 22, 2008, online http://www.huffingtonpost.com/2008/04/22/polygamist-sects-how-they_n_97975.html (accessed June 5, 2008).

46. Patton, "Studies in the Amish Community."

47. Khoury, "Old Order Amish."

48. Morton, "Amish and Mennonite People of Pennsylvania."

49. John Dougherty, "Forbidden Fruit: Inbreeding among Polygamists along the Arizona-Utah Border Is Producing a Caste of Severely Retarded and Deformed Children," *Phoenix New Times,* December 29, 2005, online. http://www.phoenixnewtimes.com/2005-12-29/news/forbidden-fruit/ (accessed May 22, 2008).

50. Melvin Ember, Carol R. Ember, and Bobbi S. Low, "Comparing Explanations of Polygyny," *Cross-Cultural Research* 41 (2007): 428–440.

51. Analyses of Y chromosomes and mitochondrial DNA from people around the world support the idea that modern-day humans arose from a smaller number of male ancestors than female ancestors; Isabelle Dupanloup et al., "A Recent Shift from Polygyny to Monogamy in Humans Is Suggested by the Analysis of Worldwide Y-Chromosome Diversity," *Journal of Molecular Evolution* 57 (2003): 85–97.

52. Stephanie Coontz, *The Way We Never Were: American Families and the Nostalgia Trap* (New York: Basic Books, 1992).

53. Robert M. Veatch, *Basics of Bioethics*, 2nd ed. (Upper Saddle River, NJ: Prentice Hall, 2002).

54. Duty-based principles are often represented by the use of "rights" language, particularly in reference to legal matters. Rights have a reciprocal relationship to duty-based principles, meaning that if an individual has a right, another party therefore has an ethical duty to that person (Veatch 2002).

55. "Family Code Chapter 10: Uniform Parentage Act," 2001, http://tlo2.tlc.state.tx.us/cgi-bin/cqcgi?CQ_SESSION_KEY=ASATEHRFZHCS&CQ_QUERY_HANDLE=126597&CQ_CUR_DOCUMENT=2&CQ_TLO_DOC_TEXT=YES (accessed June 17, 2008).

56. ACLU, "Government's Actions Regarding the Yearning for Zion Ranch." May 2, 2008.

57. John Mortiz, "FLDS Raid Costs Surpass $14M." *Deseret News,* June 14, 2008, http://www.deseretnews.com/article/1,5143,700234669,00.html?pg=1 (accessed June 18, 2008).

58. The government in Texas routinely pays for paternity tests as part of welfare reform so they may collect child support payments and thereby save money in the long run. However, if a man is determined to be the father, the state agency may legally seek reimbursement from him for the cost associated with the test (Uniform Parentage Act, 2001). Though some might argue that the same should happen in the

case of the FLDS, a strong counterargument could be made that it would be unjust to shift this financial burden to the FLDS unless the court order originally dictated that the FLDS would be held fiscally responsible and it was agreed upon prior to testing.

59. Moritz, "FLDS Raid Costs Surpass $14M."

60. Adams, "DNA Testing Results Arriving in Texas."

61. *Houston Chronicle*, "In the Balance."

62. Adams, "DNA Testing Results Arriving in Texas."

63. Herkenham, "Retention of Offender DNA Samples."

64. Ibid.

65. Tania Simoncelli, "Dangerous Excursions: The Case Against Expanding Forensic DNA Databases to Innocent Persons," *The Journal of Law, Medicine & Ethics: A Journal of the American Society of Law, Medicine & Ethics* 34 (2006): 390–397.

66. Simoncelli, "Dangerous Excursions."

67. Brian H. Bornstein, "Pregnancy, Drug Testing, and the Fourth Amendment: Legal and Behavioral Implications," *Journal of Family Psychology: JFP: Journal of the Division of Family Psychology of the American Psychological Association (Division 43)* 17 (2003): 220–228.

68. Bornstein, "Pregnancy, Drug Testing, and the Fourth Amendment."

69. Tracy Sabo and Gary Tuchman, "DNA Taken from Sect Leader in Inquiry," *CNN*, May 30, 2008, http://www.cnn.com/2008/CRIME/05/30/texas.polygamists/ (accessed June 26, 2008).

70. Ibid.

71. Ben Winslow, "Search Warrant Seeking Jeffs' DNA Accuses Him of More Child Bride Marriages," *Deseret News*, May 30, 2008, http://www.deseretnews.com/article/1,5143,700230371,00.html (accessed June 26, 2008).

72. Wall, *Growing Up in a Polygamist Sect*.

73. Ibid.

74. Whether or not this was discussed with the FLDS is not known.

75. Just because there are no known functions for DNA segments (such as STRs) that are used for identification purposes at present, it does not mean there never will be. The possibility remains that one or more of the STRs used for parentage testing could one day be found to be associated with health or physical traits.

76. Simoncelli, "Dangerous Excursions."

77. LabCorps, the company that reportedly performed the FLDS parentage testing, provides a copy of their privacy rights and restrictions at the following web site: http://www.labcorp.com/legal/priv_pol_NPP.pdf

78. LabCorp's policy regarding the use of samples and patient information for research purposes is found within the privacy rights document on their web site, http://www.labcorp.com/legal/priv_pol_NPP.pdf

79. Although HIPAA does not specifically designate a person's DNA as a personal identifier in and of itself, the information it contains is protected if linked to any additional identifying information as designated under the law.

80. Dougherty, "Forbidden Fruit," *Phoenix New Times;* Hollenhorst, "Birth Defect," *Deseret News*.

81. Veatch, *Basics of Bioethics*.

82. Ibid.

83. M. R. Natowicz and J. S. Alper, "Genetic Screening: Triumphs, Problems, and Controversies," *Journal of Public Health Policy* 12 (1991): 475–491.

84. Dougherty, "Forbidden Fruit," *Phoenix New Times;* Wall, *Growing Up in a Polygamist Sect*.

85. While it might seem strange to call for a new doctrinal approach to address the prevalence of a genetic condition, it is not unreasonable to believe that such an approach would actually be efficacious in dealing with this condition in this specific population. If the prophet were to consider fumarase deficiency a "marker from God" that should be used to arrange marriages, it is possible the membership of the religion would accept that assertion and follow that approach.

86. Veatch, *Basics of Bioethics*.

87. Of course, these freedoms are not the same as guaranteed rights because one must have the money for and access to pursue these reproductive options.

88. Veatch, *Basics of Bioethics*.

89. Szep, "Polygamist Community Faces Rare Disorder," *Reuters*.

90. Dougherty, "Forbidden Fruit," *Phoenix New Times;* Wall, *Growing Up in a Polygamist Sect*.

91. Dougherty, "Forbidden Fruit," *Phoenix New Times;* Hollenhorst, "Birth Defect," *Deseret News*.

92. Rick Casey, "For-Prophet Organization." *Houston Chronicle,* May 2, 2008, http://www.chron.com/disp/story.mpl/metropolitan/casey/5747910.html (accessed June 10, 2008).

93. Benjamin G. Bistline, *Colorado City Polygamists: An Inside Look for the Outsider,* 1st ed. (Agreka Books, 2004); Dougherty, "Forbidden Fruit," *Phoenix New Times;* Hollenhorst, "Birth Defect," *Deseret News*.

94. Bernadette Modell and Aamra Darr, "Science and Society: Genetic Counseling and Customary Consanguineous Marriage," *Nature Reviews. Genetics* 3, no. 3 (March 2002): 225–229.

Glossary

Apostle, Quorum of Twelve Apostles. Second-highest governing body of the Church of Jesus Christ of Latter-Day Saints. Most of the fundamentalist groups also have a Quorum of Twelve Apostles.

Apostolic United Brethren (AUB). A fundamentalist group that traces its history back to the main LDS Church.

Bishop. An ecclesiastical leader over a ward (local Latter-Day Saint congregation).

Book of Mormon. (*see* Scriptures)

Celestial marriage. A term synonymous with sealing for time and eternity, though nineteenth-century Mormons often used it to mean plural marriage.

Doctrine and Covenants (or D & C). (*see* Scriptures)

Endowment. A ritual during which Latter-Day Saints "receive the endowment" of knowledge they believe is necessary for them to be exalted. During the course of the endowment, members also make sacred promises to be faithful.

Exaltation. The highest status or reward possible in the hereafter. Both the LDS and polygamists believe that being married for eternity is one of the conditions necessary for exaltation.

First Presidency. Supreme governing body of the LDS Church, composed of the president of the church and two counselors.

FLDS. Abbreviated form of Fundamentalist Church of Jesus Christ of Latter Day Saints, one of the fundamentalist groups that traces its history back to the main LDS Church.

Garment, or priesthood garment. A cloth covering of the body that many believe provides a spiritual and sometimes a physical protection to the individual.

High Council. A body of twelve men who advise and assist the stake presidency in carrying out the administration of the stake organization.

They sometimes assist the stake presidency as the stake presidency sits as an ecclesiastical court.

Latter-Day Saints (LDS). Members of the Church of Jesus Christ of Latter-Day Saints.

Manifesto. A statement issued by the president of the LDS or Mormon church on September 25, 1890, stating his intention to abide by the federal laws prohibiting plural marriage and to advise all Latter-Day Saints to do likewise.

Pearl of Great Price. (*see* Scriptures)

Polygamy. The marriage of more than one spouse at the same time. Almost all polygamous marriages are composed of families with one man with more than one woman. Technically, the term for this type of marriage is "polygny," but authors tend to use the more general term "polygamy."

Plural wife. A woman who has been "sealed" or married to a man who has been married to a previous wife. Men are sometimes married to several women at the same time.

Priesthood. The LDS and polygamists believe that worthy priesthood holders, those having been properly ordained, can act for and on behalf of God in giving blessings and sealing ordinances.

Scriptures. Both the LDS Church and the fundamentalist groups use four books of Scriptures (in addition to the teachings of their prophets). The first is the King James version of the Bible. The second is the Book of Mormon, which Joseph Smith stated he translated from gold-like plates that he received. Third is a set of revelations given to the Church through prophets in modern times. Fourth is the Pearl of Great Price, a book reportedly translated from Egyptian papyri received by Joseph Smith.

Sealing. A Latter-Day Saint ritual for binding families together in marriage. Usually this is done for both "time and eternity." This is usually done in temples.

Seminary meetings. In the LDS and polygamous communities, instructional religious meetings conducted usually for teenagers. These are sometimes conducted adjacent to schools or, in the case of the fundamentalists, in their regular church buildings.

Stake. An ecclesiastical unit made up of several geographically adjacent wards, often compared to a Catholic diocese.

Stake president. The leader of a stake. A stake presidency consists of the stake president and his two counselors.

Temple. Building in which the most sacred Latter-Day Saint rituals (ordinances) are performed, including endowments and sealings.

Ward. The basic ecclesiastical church unit, the local geographically based congregation, often compared to a parish of the Catholic Church.

Index